GOODBYE, SARAJANE

A FOSTER CHILD WRITES LETTERS TO HER MOTHER

SEQUOYA GRIFFIN

GOODBYE, SARAJANE. Copyright © 2016 by Sequoya Griffin. Key Purpose Books LLC. All rights reserved. Printed in the United States of America. No part of this book may be used or reproduced in any matter whatsoever without written permission except in the case of brief quotations cited in critical articles and reviews. This is a work of non-fiction. Some names and identifying details have been changed to protect the privacy of certain individuals.

ISBN 978-0-9992325-0-7
ISBN 978-0-9993225-1-4

Library of Congress Control Number: 2017950589

Cover Design by eBookLaunch.com
Editor: Melanie Grunwald at Elegant Editing
Scriptures are taken from the King James Version

Music lyrics used by permission.
DREAMLOVER Hall, Dave/ Carey, Mariah (c) Warner/Chappell Music, Inc., Universal Music Publishing Group
JUST KICKIN' IT Mayfield, Curtis/ Dupri, Jermaine/ Seal, Manuel (c) Sony/ATV Music Publishing LLC
THAT'S THE WAY IT IS Michael Carlsson, Andreas/ Lundin, Kristian Carl Marcus/ Sandburg, Martin Carl (c) Kobalt Music Publishing Ltd., Universal Music Publishing Group
TROUBLES Augello-Cook, Alicia J/ Jr. Brothers/ Brothers, Kerry (c) Sony/ATV Music Publishing LLC
Copyright renewed. All rights reserved.

I give thanks to the Lord for using me to write this story.
At first I resented my life and what happened to me.
I understand now.

Jesus answered and said unto him, "What I do thou knowest not now; but thou shalt know hereafter."
John 13:7

This book is dedicated to every orphan, foster child,
and adopted child in the world. You are *chosen* by the Lord.

PROLOGUE

Karen told The Four to have a seat in the living room. Huh? We stepped into the living room and sat on the couch. I was surprised when Neal and Abram entered and took the opposite couch. Karen hovered around with an unreadable expression. She looked like she was anticipating something.

The doorbell rang. She opened the door and hugged a big man with a huge round belly as he stepped in looking very serious.

I instantly recognized him as Pastor Hall from our old church Abide in the Vine! We hadn't seen him in a while. But what was he doing here?

He greeted us and we said hello back.

Suddenly, Karen went from a normal expression, to launching into a crying fit, covering her face. She shook her body with her crying. It all looked absurd! We were so confused.

"You guys," she wailed. "I have brought Pastor Hall here for your support!"

What support? Were we having another counseling session?

"There is something very important I have to tell you guys. I have been withholding this information for a few weeks…because I didn't know how to tell you…"

What was she talking about?

She looked to Pastor Hall, who waited patiently.

Very dramatically, with a Broadway musical flair, she said, "I'm sorry you guys, but your birth mother has passed away."

As those words escaped from her mouth, I glanced up at her. She began her dramatic cry again. I didn't understand what she was saying…but in that split-second I subconsciously knew. As I broke down sobbing, she flew to my side, pushing Rae out the way who was seated next to me. Before her arms encamped around my face and neck, obscuring my vision, I caught a glimpse of Abram with his head down. He was smirking.

Dear Mama Katherine,

This is your daughter SaraJane.

I know you named me Sequoya at birth and I haven't seen you since I was ten-years-old. I want you to know that SaraJane is the name my adoptive mother gave me. I was going to look for you as soon as I had the opportunity, but you became an angel before then.

I heard you had been looking for me until the very end. I sure have a story to tell you! A lot has happened since I last saw you. I learned a lot about you. Guess what I found out?

Just let me begin...

PART ONE

Ye shall not afflict any widow, or fatherless child. If thou afflict them in any wise, and they cry at all unto me, I will surely hear their cry.

Exodus 22 verses 22-23

ONE

January 2000
Las Vegas, Nevada

Sandy and Ron Hue lived on the outskirts of Las Vegas in a large cozy ranch nestled along a beautiful trail of winding roads. A clan of horses trotted along the property. Visiting the area where the Hues lived felt much different than the nearby city we lived in.

The Hues were a humble couple who raised foster children. Their home had ten children of different ages and races. The older kids would tease me sometimes when I visited. After a while I had to avoid one of them. His teasing hinted at things that even he was too young for.

I didn't pay much attention to any of the children there, except one. He was now four-years-old. Sandy placed him in his high chair. I walked over and leaned beside him. Sandy had made a big cake. The dining room table was full of kids who had run in from the activity room or from outside riding the horses.

"Happy Birthday" echoed as my baby brother Elijah waited patiently for Sandy to cut the cake.

It was a regular noisy day at the Hues. I finished my cake, kissed Elijah, and wandered into the activity room. My brother Stanford was in the center of the room playing with a few action figures.

"What are you doing to Buzz Lightyear?" I laughed as my brother tried to discreetly stuff the famed action figure into his pants pocket. It was very funny because his pocket was too small to hide the toy.

"I'm not trying to do nothing!" Stanford protested.

"Yes, you are. You're trying to steal Buzz!" I was amused.

Stanford smirked as I joined him on the floor with all the toys. Whenever we spotted anything from Toy Story could possibly be game for our collection back home.

My baby sister Rae came running in to tell us that Kim, our caseworker, was here to pick us up. Reluctantly, we savored our last few minutes with Elijah as Kim talked with Sandy. I hugged and squeezed him tight. It wasn't very often we were able to see him.

An overwhelming sadness overcame me as I listened to the tires scrape over the trail of rocks that was leading us away from the ranch and to *our* own foster home. We lived all the way on the other side of Las Vegas. Kim chatted with us and asked us about Elijah's birthday party. She told us maybe one day we'd live with him again.

"When?" I asked. My heart pounded.

"Well, maybe is *not* definite," Kim answered. "But it's still a possibility."

I told myself not to get my hopes up, Mama. We hadn't lived with Elijah for a few years. We were already on foster home number three without him. We hadn't been with you either.

A few minutes went by before Kim spoke again.

"Where would you guys like to live someday?" she asked us.

More enthused, we named a few places. I shouted Miami even though I had never been outside of Nevada. It sounded cool when a girl from school said she was from there.

Kim asked us if we'd like to live in New York.

"New York?" I asked. "Isn't that far away?"

"Yes, but so is Miami," Kim laughed. "New York is a very nice place to live."

Without skipping a beat, she asked us what we thought about adoption. I knew where she was headed as soon as those words came out.

"No," I said firmly. "I don't want to be adopted."

We had been through this conversation back and forth so many times. Kim was always telling me there was no chance we'd ever live with you again. She informed us that your parental rights had been terminated. I didn't understand what she meant by that. I argued otherwise. I believed in my heart we'd be reunited with you no matter what!

Kim turned onto the freeway heading back into Las Vegas and you could feel the tension in the car. Stanford and Rae weren't as vocal towards Kim as I was. On this particular day, Kim decided to ignore my attitude. She pressed on. She continued talking about how much fun it would be to live in New York, to finally live with Elijah, and to be adopted instead of yet another foster home.

Then suddenly, she asked an unusual question.

"How would you feel being adopted by a white family?" A feigned compassionate expression replaced the smirk on her face as soon as I noticed. Startled, the three of us sat puzzled and confused. We responded in unison, "A white family!?!"

We weren't sure how to respond. We had been in foster homes and child haven centers with all races, but we never had white parents. Elijah's foster parents Ron and Sandy were white. Maybe they'd be nice. But how would it be with ten children, plus three more? And I didn't like all the dogs they had. Mama, I was terribly afraid of dogs. I refused to ride the horses or go anywhere near them as well. All I knew was that I was going back home with you!

"Are we going to the Hues with Elijah?" I asked Kim.

"Um…no. Not the Hues sweetie."

"Well, I don't want to be adopted by a white family," I said. "I'm going to wait for my Mama."

Kim ignored my statement. She looked at Stanford through her rear-view mirror.

"How come you don't want to be adopted by a white family?" she asked him. "How come?"

"I don't know," he said. "I just don't want to."

With that statement, we burst into nervous laughter. The tension disappeared as we thought about what Kim said. She told us not to feel upset and to be happy. She told us to appreciate that a family wanted to adopt us, no matter what color they were. She said we were lucky. We were chosen out of thousands of children waiting to be adopted. They would "age out" of the foster care system. A lot of kids who waited ended up reaching age eighteen, aging out of the foster care system with no parents.

Not me Mama! I wasn't going to age out of the system! Neither would I be adopted by this family in New York!
I wanted you to come get me! I was patiently waiting. Always. I pleaded with you in my head all the time. I prayed that God would pass the message onto you. As Kim headed to the Eastside, I tuned out her rambling, dismissing that nonsense of adoption.
My decision was made. I was determined that I was going to be with you no matter what anyone had to say! How could someone tell me I'm not allowed to live with my own mother? I didn't understand this concept. I built an inner army of resistance. I would rely on my inner army for what would become tough times ahead.

The following month in February, Kim told us we were meeting our new adoptive family.

What? I thought she wasn't serious! This joke had run its course. How come we couldn't have a say in who our new parents would be? How would we even know if we liked them?

"That's why you're meeting them!" Kim told us. "They will be your parents because they have chosen you. But in order for the adoption to be finalized they have to make a trip out here. If they don't, there will be no adoption."

"I hope they change their minds!" I said angrily.

"They agreed to fly from New York to Nevada. What more does it take to show you that a family cares about you?" Kim stared at me like I was missing out on heaven.

I put my head down as angry tears began to form. When I looked up, Kim was smiling with satisfaction. Why did she think my pain was so amusing?

That night I laid on the top bunk in the room I shared with Stanford and Rae. I felt hopeless. I silently cried. I wished with all my might that I wasn't going to be adopted. It had been two years since I last saw you.

It was a fateful Saturday morning in early February of 2000. Kim collected us from our foster mother's house. I was filled with anxiety as she drove with anticipation to McCarran International Airport. I didn't know what to expect. I couldn't wait for this meet and greet to be over. I would tell them, *'thanks, but no thanks! You can fly back home. No need to adopt us because we have a mother!'*

Walking through the airport was surreal. It seemed like we were moving in slow motion. We arrived at the gate where the Carlons were waiting for us. When I first saw them step forward to meet us, I was thinking *'Hell no they look creepy!'*

Rae nudged me. "Sequoya," she whispered. "They heard you say *ew!*"

I was unaware that I had even spoken.

The Carlons were directly in front of us now. They greeted Kim. The mother was drilling holes into each of us. The father and son looked extremely shy.

The mother jumped right in. "Hello, I'm Karen! But to you, I'm Mom!"

Yeah ok!

"This is my husband Neal, *dad*, and your brother Abram!"

Kim was looking quite proud of herself. We walked through the airport and out to the parking lot. I continued to feel Karen's eyes on me. I hadn't said one word besides a mumbled hello when Kim prompted us to be polite.

Karen smiled and said, "I like your hair."

I gave her a dirty look. Didn't she see that my hair hadn't been done today? My foster mother used a ton of gel to bun my hair up over a week ago.

Karen gave me another friendly smile. I turned my head away. We piled into a rented van that was provided thanks to Family Services. I kept an angry look on my face as everyone talked to each other. Stan and Rae were getting acquainted with this Abram character. He had fluffy dark blonde hair. He and Rae were the same age. They were both turning seven. They smiled shyly at each other.

Stan, Rae, Abram, Neal, and I were left in the car as Kim and Karen checked us into a shabby motel. Neal and I were silent as the others chatted shyly.

I studied Neal. He seemed very quiet. He looked as if he could be our older brother. How old was he really? Unlike Karen's blue eyes, his were brown, like Abram's. He had dark brown hair.

Mama, he just looked plain goofy!

Neal must have noticed me staring at him, because he looked over at me. He made his first attempt at getting to know me.

"How do you like Vegas?" he asked.

"It's nice," I said reluctantly.

"It sure is different from where we live in New York."

"Yeah, I know." *How did I really know? I didn't want to find out!*

"Just yesterday, it was snowing hard out in New York! So, it's funny that we hopped on a plane and less than a day later, we're now enjoying spring weather with you guys!"

I forced a laugh. I didn't know what to say.

Neal fell silent again. I wondered how long Kim and Karen would be in the motel office. I felt numb as I tried to piece the puzzles of how we ended up face to face with this strange white family.

TWO

Karen and our caseworker Kim had spent quite some time in the motel office. I finally saw them walking back to the van. Karen sheepishly looked at her husband.

"I spent all of your money," she laughed like it was a joke.

Neal didn't respond. There was an awkward silence in the van.

We arrived at a park. Kim was trying to pretend that everything was okay. But she already knew I wasn't happy. She had personally dealt with me for years. She and Karen were whispering a lot. Karen had studied me since she first laid eyes on me and I was letting her know where we stood. She seemed determined to get me to like her.

Kim instructed everyone to stand together as a group by the playground slide as she snapped pictures. It was so forced to me. I didn't like it at all.

It was still warm outside despite it being a little windy. Everyone wore a light jacket. We decided to have a contest to see who the fastest runner was. Stanford and I were both tied in first place. I was feeling warm now after running, so I took my jacket off.

Karen looked at me and told me to put my jacket back on. "It's a little chilly out," she stated.

"I'm not cold," I said. I gave her a crazy look.

Karen looked at Kim, and Kim looked at her as if to say, *'she's all yours.'*

Karen suddenly became hype. A little too over the top. She became very loud.

"Sequoya, put your jacket on. It's chilly!"

I refused.

"Sequoya! Put it on now!"

I could not believe this. This woman had her nerve. She was already trying to tell me what to do and we weren't even adopted yet. She was *not* my Mama, and never would be!

I shot her an angry look as I reluctantly put my jacket on. The others were observing the whole situation waiting to see the outcome. With a sassy twitch in my step, I calmly walked away and went to hide in the playground clubhouse.

I was so mad. Before long, Kim and Karen poked their heads in. I ignored them. The next thing I knew they had crawled their big selves all the way in! Kim was smirking again. They tried to get me to smile but I gave them the silent treatment. The others peered inside the entrance as well. They could see everything taking place.

Abram Carlon crawled in. He greeted me but I ignored him too.

Karen became upset after that. Kim told me that I was being stank. I didn't feel that I was. At the same time, I had no idea what the future held if you didn't worship Abram.

Kim gave Abram a hug and whispered in his ear while Karen tried to talk to me yet again. I ignored her. Suddenly, my head veers back as I receive a blow to the face.

Abram had punched me!

I lunged at him to knock him out, but Kim aggressively held me down so I couldn't move. She was dying with laughter.

"I told him to hit you because you're being stank!" she said proudly.

Tears of anger filled my eyes. I wanted to beat that stupid kid up so badly! I *knew* there was a reason I hated these people on first sight! I couldn't believe my own caseworker, Kim Folson, a black woman, had done this to me!

Drops of blood began to run from my nose.

That very moment was the foreshadowing of Abram being the one in charge over us, and the moment that Abram and I became enemies.

We left the park. Kim told us that we were going to visit Elijah next. The adults kept a close eye on everybody. Especially me. On the way to Ron and Sandy Hues ranch, I sank back into my thoughts.

I know if you were there Mama, that whole situation would have never in a million years gone down like that! A lot of stuff always seemed to go down. Kim didn't like you Mama. She took it out on us. We were only children.

After Kim let Abram punch me in the face while Neal and Karen looked on, I had been very angry. But somehow, I released it and just let it go. Or did I? Perhaps I was too traumatized, and so I shoved it into my unconscious. Maybe it would never happen again. My wishful, naïve thinking had always led me to give people the benefit of the doubt. In this situation, my passiveness would ultimately backfire and affect my younger siblings. I would be the oldest in this newly "constructed" family. If Abram had power over me, he gained power over everyone else as well. I needed to protect my siblings! I had absolutely no idea that something was being cemented.

We pulled into the driveway of the Hues. My attitude lightened at the thought of seeing Elijah. We went inside to greet everyone. I watched as Karen walked over to Elijah and said something to him. I couldn't hear his response. I walked closer and Karen was beaming with pride. She turned to Kim.

"It's meant to be!" she said dramatically. "When he first saw me, he looked at me and called me Mama! He doesn't even know who I am! This is meant to be!"

I rolled my eyes. Whatever. He was only four and any older female he saw was probably Mama to him.

Karen was all in Sandy and Ron's personal space. She thought she was the new person that Elijah would love as a parent. Eagerly she started asking ridiculous questions about Elijah's every day routine. Sandy and Ron answered with slight hesitation. Even though they were white, they too didn't want to see Elijah go to the Carlons.

Kim yet again instructed us to pose for another session of fake, forced pictures. I ended up sitting by myself on the couch afterwards. Kim and Karen tried to get me to smile for an individual picture. I refused. They snapped the photo anyway. That very picture I would see again. Uncertainty, anger, and depression was enveloped on my face as I crossed my right leg over my left leg, hands propped on my lap. After the brief visit, we said goodbye to Elijah and left the ranch.

Our next stop was a hair salon on the Westside. That's where our foster mother Benita worked! I couldn't wait. I knew she was curious to see these Carlons. The other cosmetologists in the salon wanted to see them too. I was praying that Benita would take one look at them, see they weren't right for us, and decide to adopt us herself.

The moment we stepped into the salon, the ladies stared at Karen, Neal, and Abram with questioning stares. I heard one of them mumble "What on earth do these people want with four black children?"

I loved how the unwanted spotlight made Karen and Neal grab Abram and huddle closer together. The Carlons were afraid to step further into the room. They acted like we were going to hurt them. I skipped over to Benita and gave her a hug. When I looked back at Karen, her eyes were on me. She hadn't seen me this happy since the whole visit began.

Benita and Kim broke the ice by inviting the Carlons to step closer. There was no need to be afraid of black women who worked at the salon! As the adults conversed, I wandered over to the window. The day was winding down. We were on Jackson Ave on the Westside of Las Vegas. This was the ghetto, but we lived with Benita in a nicer area on the Eastside. I laughed to myself over the fact that a white couple from New York was inside a Black hair salon trying to identify with Black children.

Before we left, it was decided that we'd stay the night with the Carlons in their motel so we could get familiar with them. I pleadingly glanced at Benita. I wanted to go back home with her. Kim said no.

"I'll see you all tomorrow," Benita told us. She laughed and gave me a look that said, *'Don't be clowning them!'* She already knew.

Once we arrived at the motel, Kim left us with the Carlons. We were stuffed into a small, cheap suite. There was the half living room/part kitchen, bedroom, and a bathroom. Karen said the bedroom would be for her and Neal. Rae and I would sleep on the small couch. Stan and Abram would take the floor with blankets. Once that was settled, Karen decided it was time we ate. I couldn't help looking at Neal, wondering if he ever spoke up. I could see that Karen was the overseer of everything.

Our motel was right next to a casino. Karen found a McDonalds and led us to a table. We watched the tourists walk by as we ate our food. I was angry the whole time. I rolled my eyes when Karen announced that it was late and we should head back, because it wasn't safe. She heard how dangerous Las Vegas could be at night.

"We can't risk anything!" she said.

We went back to the motel to watch the television. I should have cherished this brief television privilege. We had the first Carlon family argument that very night.

It started because Abram was taking too long in the bathroom. I had to use it bad. When he finally emerged, I ran in. I instantly ran back out and said he stank.

"I want to go back to Benita's!" I shouted.

An exchange of insults started between Abram and me. Karen was amped up now. Neal spoke up to defend his son. The Carlons jumped up as if they were defending themselves from an angry football squad. They were worried because Kim wasn't there. They were upset because they weren't in control of my attitude or my opinion of them. They knew by now that I wasn't easy.

They were very hyped for no reason, actually. I wasn't a threat. I was sitting down. I was talking back to them calmly, letting them see that they couldn't make me bow down. They stood above me and stared me down. They weren't hip to a young black girl from the West Coast who was full of anger. They were from a small, white, rural community in Upstate New York.

After everyone's adrenaline calmed down, we settled down for the night. I fell asleep hoping this nightmare would end. Maybe they had already changed their minds and didn't want us. That would be great for all parties involved!

I was the last person to wake up the next morning. When I saw that I was alone in the front room, I jumped up in fear. I didn't see anybody. Then I heard laughter. I walked into the bedroom to find everyone crowded onto the bed, laughing together, like one big happy family.

They looked at me. I even surprised myself when I accepted their offer to join them on the bed. Considering what happened the night before, I don't know what made me more sociable this morning. Maybe because Stan and Rae had opened up. If they were comfortable, I had to adjust as well, even though my heart felt another way.

Neal ended up taking Stan and Abram outside for a walk. Karen stayed back with Rae and me. She sat in the middle of the bed while we sat on opposite sides of her. She was staring at us with curiosity as we tried to undo the buns that were wrapped tightly on our heads. We were looking sad. It was a nappy mess! She offered to help us. She took a comb and attempted to comb my hair. She was shocked when the comb wouldn't budge. The gel had dried into our hair over the past couple of weeks and hardened our strands into a crisp texture.

Karen suggested we wet our hair in the bathroom sink. She splashed water on our hair. She tried unsuccessfully to comb through our hair again. I wasn't worried. I knew Benita would be doing our hair again soon. Karen looked puzzled. She didn't know how to care for our hair.

For that remaining Sunday, she talked to us about their desire to adopt us and for us all to be a family. We would move to New York. I didn't say anything. I held back my tears of frustration. They were determined to adopt us. At least Karen was. Neal just agreed to everything she said. He didn't share her enthusiasm and I didn't blame him.

Deep down, I told myself that we weren't going.

I would have to be carried on that plane kicking and screaming! Stan and Rae were excited and perked up. It made me mad. They didn't see they were being sold a lie. I was young but my instincts however, saw trouble ahead. I just couldn't put my finger on it. Something wasn't right.

Kim rejoined us that evening. She rounded us all in the van and drove across the city to Benita's house. I was so relieved. The Carlons joined us inside. I knew they were impressed by this nice, upscale neighborhood on the Eastside near the mountains. Their eyes scanned over the large two-story house, the balcony, and the fancy home furnishings that Benita proudly displayed. I saw their reaction once they walked in the front door.

The Carlons were also looking at Stan, Rae, and me as we comfortably pranced around, happy to be back home. I figured they might have lived the same way. Looking back at the situation now, I can see that Karen's plan was already being worked out in that head of hers. There were some changes she wanted to make. Our comfort, happiness, and feeling loved and accepted had to go. But for now, she plastered a fake smile on her face. Her eyes met mine and I saw something that I would see time and time again. I didn't understand it then. It made me uncomfortable, so I looked away from her. She and Neal sat down on one of the couches. Benita sat opposite from them with a glass of wine. She offered them a drink. Karen said no for both her and Neal. She gave Benita a look as if to say, *'So I guess you must be somebody huh?'*

Untouched, Benita took a sip of her wine and leaned back onto the couch. She began talking to them about their decision to adopt us.

Mama, my heart sank as she told them that it was all out of her hands. The courts wouldn't let her adopt us. I listened sadly. I didn't understand.

Kim saw me hovering around. She sent me outside to the backyard with the others. I tiptoed back to the patio door and eavesdropped. Benita was talking to the Carlons more seriously this time. She was explaining to them what kind of kids we were. She said good things. She also said we could be bad sometimes, but with the proper setting and love we needed, we'd be just fine. The Carlons were silently taking this information in.

Before Kim left with the Carlons, we crowded back into the living room to see them off. Karen turned into her "mom" mode. She tightly held Rae, who had been content in her lap all weekend. Poor little girl. Benita would later say, "Them people had Stan and Rae going for it but they didn't have you at all...you unveiled them inside and out!"

The Carlons gave each of us a bookmark as they got into the van. They said Abram's class back at school in New York had given each other bookmarks with their school pictures on them. I looked at my bookmark and saw Abram's picture on it. I was disgusted. Although I trashed that bookmark, I would soon discover that books would be there for me in times of deep solace.

That night, I told myself that I never wanted to see them again. I tried to talk to Stan and Rae about keeping the family promise. We had to remember that we'd be returning to our Mama someday. They were speaking happily about our new life in New York. The Carlons had promised them a lot and they were holding onto it.

I had a dream. In the dream, I saw the Carlons. The three of them were holding hands and standing at a distance from me. They extended a hand out to me. I refused to walk closer and join them. Before the dream ended, I only saw their backsides. They had turned away from me after my decline of their offer. That dream would be very prophetic. Neither party knew what they had signed up for.

Dear Mama Katherine,

I will tell you the Carlon story soon! Right now, I want you to just relax...

Before any of this happened, there was another story. It was yours. Yes, I told you I know a lot about you!

THREE

Katherine Kelly was born on November 3rd, 1960. She was brought up in the church. She had a very special spiritual gift of discernment that couldn't be denied. This was the main reason why Satan wanted to destroy her and her children. A humble evangelist, she chose not to be front and center. She preferred to be low-key and not take any leadership positions. She still gave her testimonies to the people close enough to get to her. These very same people she gave testimony to wouldn't believe her at first, but what God said to them through her would surprise them later.

Katherine wasn't perfect, but she was indeed a very special woman. She was outcast amongst her sisters. She was the favorite one amongst her brothers, as well as the rest of the family. She had strikingly good looks. A voluptuous figure, naïve pretty eyes, and the thickest crop of hair was styled beautifully on her head. She was very stunning; she was voted Most Likely to be a Model at her high school.

She and her siblings experienced a short stint with foster care. Her mother, Lillian Mae Kelly Hunter, had struggled with raising her ten children. But she pulled herself back together and was able to get her children back. At nearly seventeen, Katherine gave birth to her first child, Deniece Kelly. Her high school romance with the highly sought after Terry Ealy quickly crumbled. Katherine didn't miss a beat as she successfully finished high school. She started working as receptionist at the Reco Engineering plant and before long she had her own place.

By the early 1980s, she met Ben Slank, a gambler and handsome ladies' man who had followed his older brother to Las Vegas from Louisiana. Ben Slank was twelve years older than Katherine.

She and three-year-old Deniece moved into Dan's home. Katherine had her family believing that she was married to him. Ben was very secretive. It seemed like he was hiding something. Katherine wasn't even allowed to let her family know where they lived. Handsome Ben had also given her a $2500 ring. With a common determination like a lot of women, Katherine began to make sure that Ben was happy. You see, even though she was strong in the Lord, one of her biggest downfalls was always wanting acceptance... *especially* from a man.

Katherine spent a lot of time in the church, often staying hours after service was over. She would chat with members as she tried to make sense of her own life. She was a "good girl" who tried to faithfully maintain her position with God. Even though Ben was a very cruel man at first, her desire to have his acceptance drove her to make bad choices. His gambling and outbursts contrasted with the church-going Katherine. She told him that one day he would fulfill his destiny in the church, *'but you and I won't always be together.'* Ben thought she was crazy for saying that. He could never see himself at church.

Within six years, Katherine had given birth to a son named Daniel and a second daughter named Keyonna. Throughout her relationship with Ben she bent over backwards to make sure he was content. Because Deniece wasn't his daughter she was susceptible to unwarranted punishments. When it came to wrongfully punishing Deniece, Katherine went along with it because it was her goal to always keep Ben happy. Though it saddened Katherine, she simply allowed him to punish Deniece with cruelty. At times, she was forbidden to be around 'his' children. Deniece became a nervous wreck and began twiddling with her hair and yanking it out of her head. She experienced early childhood trauma that she didn't understand, and it came from an abusive stepfather who had easily manipulated her mother. Katherine and Deniece never had the opportunity to talk about this as she got older. They acted as if this period in their lives had never occurred.

By the end of the decade, Katherine and Ben were long since having problems. His gambling issues were getting too much out of hand. One day, he left. He just left. Katherine stayed in the house, continuing to attend church and go to work. By this time, she was a secretary at an elementary school and wanted to be a teacher.

In January of 1989, she spotted a man playing the organ at another church that she decided to visit. She was instantly mesmerized by him. He was serving time in a halfway house after completing a prison sentence of nearly three years. Katherine was introduced to Stanford Griffin.

Instantly blinded of his faults, Katherine developed an instant weakness for this man. She didn't hear what others had to say negatively about him.

Stanford Griffin was born on October 24th, 1956. He was raised in a family of nine children, who were Seventh Day Adventists. Both of his parents had high ranking positions at Nevada Test Plant. He was the favorite and most spoiled child, especially from their mother, Virginia. His stepfather Paul accepted him as his son, even though he was a love child from a different man. Paul still favored Stanford. It was claimed that Paul and Virginia favored his looks and talents before everyone else. They enrolled him in a private school where he honed his musical talent with the organ.

Stanford was equally favored amongst people outside of the family, especially women. He was of average height with creamy brown skin. His signature bushy eyebrows, dramatically long eyelashes, and brown piercing eyes accentuated his face. He was a basketball star in high school. Stanford was shy, but eventually overcame it once he realized he was one of the most desirable boys in school. He was seeing his sweetheart named Cora. They were both sixteen-years-old when they had a daughter named Erica. Their relationship significantly changed after the baby arrived. Stanford's newfound player ways ended up costing him Cora. After high school, Cora left Erica to be raised by her aunt and she took off to California with an older man.

Fresh on the scene after high school, preparing for college and basketball, Stanford was a little bitter. He became saddened when he found his biological father who already had a new family and didn't want to connect with him. Stanford allowed Satan to tamper with him during that summer following graduation. Now, drugs and other narcotics were certainly on the scene more than ever before. Once his parents found out what he was doing, they took away all the nice things they had given him. Sadly, his plans for college were out the window once the power of drugs dominated his life. He also discovered new ways of making money - hence hustling. Losing Cora added bitterness in the way he started treating women. He became the smoothest manipulator. Stanford was *turned out* now. Drugs had become his bitter pathway. One of his girlfriends at the time was a woman named Vicky Slank.

Uh oh. That sounds familiar, doesn't it? Vicky was the niece of Ben Slank! The father of Daniel and Keyonna. This was before Stanford met Katherine and discovered the connection. Stanford and Vicky did drugs together and traveled between the states of California and Nevada.

By 1986, Stanford faced prison time. Upon entering, he was tested and diagnosed with HIV. Devastated, he informed Vicky, because they both used drug needles together. She went to get tested. Her results were positive. Stanford took it hard when the doctors told him he would not live to see past the year 1990. They told him he would die within four years. Stanford's mother Virginia had a very strong faith in the Lord. She told him that all things were possible through the Lord. His body may have had a diagnosis, but not spiritually!

When Katherine met Stanford at Deliverance through Faith Church, they quickly became an item. There was quite a protest from the members, as many women wanted Stan, and men wanted a chance with Katherine. It was the usual hype that goes on when a couple starts dating. It caused a stir in the church. Stanford played the organ while Katherine sang in the choir. Katherine had a naturally gifted voice.

Stanford completed his stay at the halfway house. The new couple moved into a house at 2210 Packard Place in North Las Vegas. Members of the church insisted they get married. The pastor met privately with Katherine and told her that Stanford was not ready. Stanford was livid when he found out, and he accused the pastor of having a romantic interest in her.

Both Stanford and Katherine should have stayed in church no matter what. They attended other churches, but eventually stopped going altogether. Satan had crept back in. Stan allowed the temptation to continue his bad boy ways, manipulating and blinding Katherine. She was completely in love and didn't care what anyone said, even though Stanford hadn't even touched her yet! Sometimes, a woman will look for something exciting after being a certain way her whole life. Katherine's sister, Marlene, claimed that her older sister was the good girl who was bored and wanted excitement. That excitement happened to be Stanford Griffin.

She was so fully enthralled with Stanford. After four months of dating, Katherine became impatient. She felt he was hiding something.

"Are you gay?" she asked. "Do I look bad or something?"

He had recently been released from prison, so maybe it was a possibility. She threatened to ask one of her incarcerated brothers.

Stanford Griffin quickly reassured Katherine that he was not gay.

"Well, am I even desirable to you?" Katherine asked nervously. "You haven't even made a move on me."

Stanford finally explained to her that he had HIV, and that he contracted it with the use of drug needles. HIV had rapidly numbered in the 1980s, and needle users were catching the virus for sure. He explained that his illness was why he didn't touch her.

Katherine looked him right in the eyes and shocked him with the words that came out her mouth next.

"I don't care what you *got!* Aint nothing ever going to stop me from being with you!"

"What?" Stanford looked at her like she was crazy. Why did this woman love him so much? He had an illness!

After being dodged for a little bit, Katherine yet again approached him. Stan explained to her that he didn't want her to catch what he had and that she was a beautiful and special young woman.

"Listen," Katherine said. "I'm not going to get the virus."

"What?" This woman really must be crazy now.

"I know for a fact I'm not going to get it." She was looking at him confidently and just the way she was looking had him dumbfounded.

Stanford and Katherine became intimate.

By the end of that summer, Ben Slank, after months of being MIA, came looking for Katherine and found her in a new house with Stanford. He was infuriated. Stanford and Ben had verbal arguments over the phone. Ben despised Stan. More so, because Stan's ex-girlfriend, Vicky, was his niece. Vicky would later succumb to the HIV virus.

Ben tried to warn Katherine. He told her that he knew of Stan and his activities and that Stan was indeed bad news. She didn't care. She was naïve and she loved this man. One infamous phone call was a foreshadowing of what was to come. Stanford was at his mother's house when Ben called. Stanford answered the phone. His mother picked up the other handset in the house when she heard her son yelling. Katherine was on the line as well.

Ben informed Virginia Griffin that he would kill her son if he didn't stay away from Katherine. Virginia stated that everyone needed to act like the adults they were. They were too grown for all this mess. Then Katherine once again surprised everyone. She started screaming at Ben through the phone.

"I love Stanford! If I can't be with him, then I can't see myself living anymore!"

Everyone on the line was silent. Then she shocked them again.

"Besides, I'm pregnant!"

Stanford spoke up now.

"Why you didn't tell me?" he asked.

"You a fool...we been hunching so what did you think was going to happen?"

There was an instant click on the line, as Ben Slank hung up on his side.

On March 26th, 1990, Sequoya Griffin came into the world. She was a miracle child. Stanford had been frantic and paranoid that she would be born with the virus. She was tested and her results came out negative of the HIV antibody. Katherine's results were also negative of the virus.

"Didn't I tell you she was going to be okay? So, quit trippin!" Katherine said to Stanford. He beamed at her with amazement.

A year and a half later, Stanford Jr. followed, free of the HIV antibody as well. The enemy still toyed with such a promising family, becoming more determined for destruction now. Katherine and Stanford became completely addicted to drugs and alcohol. She was twenty-nine-years-old when she crossed over to the world of drugs, which her family could not believe at first. After all, it was the conservative good girl, Katherine! She stopped working with the school district at that time. She was so smart and had it all. Drugs distracted her ambition. With five children, a man in her life, and a drug addiction, the family took a severe downward spiral. The events that happened over the next five years would prove to be catastrophic.

Before Stanford Jr. was born, Ben Slank attempted to win Katherine back. He pleaded with her, saying he would marry her and accept Sequoya as his own.

"Let's forget everything that happened," he said. "We're going to start new."

Katherine didn't accept his offer, especially after Ben had slapped Katherine so hard when he finally saw the newborn Sequoya, nearly causing Katherine to drop the baby out her arms.

During another argument on the phone, Stanford said to Ben, "You know I got her now and she's not ever going back."

Deniece was getting older. At that time, Daniel and Keyonna remembered vivid events. Sequoya's earliest memories came when she was three. She didn't understand anything of course. Katherine and Stanford heightened their lifestyle by allowing a variety of people to be around, or live with them, on and off. They were involved with shoplifting and robberies. Screaming matches and physical violence were common. Katherine had gone from sweet and innocent to a wild woman. She had always been sweet on the inside, but the drugs gave her a different aura most times.

Deniece remembered the first time that she saw her mama looking disparaging. Her hair sweated out and wrapped in a scarf, Katherine had come home looking disheveled and was skipping circles in the front yard.

Deniece and one of her friends from school watched from an upstairs window. When Deniece questioned Katherine about this, Katherine slapped her and told her to mind her own business. She then knew something was not right. It was at that time that her friend revealed, "Your mama is on drugs."

Deniece was in denial. Her friendship with this classmate instantly soured over this revelation. There was much discussion about who initially introduced Katherine to drugs. Some adamantly claim it was one of her brothers, and that it intensified once she met Stanford, who occasionally ran with that brother of hers.

"Katherine always wanted to run behind me," her brother explained, reflectively. "I told her no, no, you can't be out here doing what I'm doing. You can only shield someone for so long before their mind is already made up. And there was plenty of times I had serious run-ins with Stan. But please get this one thing right...my sister was sharp."

Katherine and Stanford were destroying their family. They were too far gone. It was an intense passion, and it was also a love/hate relationship. Despite it all, everyone agreed that Katherine's weakness was Stanford Griffin, even when she was in danger. Katherine had begun her own autobiography. She had written that she nearly overdosed on drugs and became unconscious. She could hear the voices of Stanford and the others as they whispered anxiously. They thought she might be dead. They didn't know that Katherine could still hear what they were saying.

In their panic, she heard the chilling words, "Leave her in a ditch!"

Once Katherine became conscious, she should have never said another word to anyone ever again!

Both Stanford and Katherine fell out with their families. They had both been the favored ones, and now they had no sense to show for it! The house on Packard Place was becoming run down and full of roaches, with a young Sequoya feeling they were chasing her.

With the help of a local housing program, Katherine and Stanford moved into a much nicer neighborhood on the Eastside. This new house was located at 413 Carlin Avenue. When Sequoya was two, her paternal grandmother, Virginia Griffin, passed away. "Mama's boy" was instantly an outcast by his family. She left Stanford all her money. In her will however, she wrote if Stanford is on dope, he is to get nothing.

Katherine and Stanford planned to use his money to start a new life and to do better. This money would be a boost. At that time, there were six out of nine of Virginia's children who were still living. It was five siblings who went against Stanford one day, who was just one person. They despised him for being the favorite who would inherit their mother's insurance policy. Stanford and his siblings got into a brawl at the family home and they called the police on him. It was their word against his and he couldn't control his anger during the brawl. Stanford was escorted off the property. He and Katherine continued their bad lifestyle.

After Katherine became pregnant again, she and Stanford separated. Katherine's mother Lilian passed away when Sequoya was three. A week after her passing, Raeannah Griffin was born, uncannily resembling Lilian. Raeannah was free of the HIV antibody as well.

Stanford was ready to rekindle his relationship with Katherine. He came back to the house and stared at his newborn daughter who was asleep on the bed.

"That child ain't none of mine!" he screamed at Katherine.

Katherine told him he was just tripping over Raeannah's skin tone and that both she and the new baby had her mother Lilian's complexion, whom Raeannah resembled.

After things had calmed down a bit, the couple worked on their relationship. One day, Ben Slank came to their house claiming that Raeannah was his daughter. He and Stanford got into an altercation. Ben was knocked to the ground. Stanford had won, which was surprising because Ben was a very large man.

"And that's payback for putting your hands on my woman while she held my daughter in her arms!" Stanford shouted as he looked down at Ben while he was on the ground. "Furthermore, all three of these kids is mine!"

Stanford was facing robbery charges by the following year. He was sentenced to a twenty-two-year term, but he told Katherine he was going to get out way before then. By 1994 Sequoya began to have more vivid memories.

Her father was now in prison and any memories she had of him were very distant to none. Katherine continued to do drugs while Stanford was incarcerated. Her quest for love and acceptance surfaced again. She longed for Stanford, but unfortunately made a poor choice, becoming involved with a man named Ed Howard, who was among their acquaintances. It's stated that Ed wanted revenge on Stanford over another woman named Diana. If Katherine had been in her right mind and not drugged up, never in a million years would she have shared her house, bed, and man with other women.

"It was shocking," Marlene said about her sister. "Katherine? Oh no, not Katherine! We didn't even recognize her anymore."

Former classmates of Katherine's were buzzing as well.

"Katherine Kelly?" Debbie said. She went to school with Katherine for all elementary, middle school, and high school. "She was a great woman; very nerdy and studious in school. She had the most beautiful smile ever. She was always telling *us* to say no to the bad things! I heard she had met this man…and…and he changed her."

After Stanford went to prison, he said to Katherine, "Watch, I bet you'll get a baby by Ed!"

"No, I'm not Stan!" Katherine adamantly denied it.

Deniece was now in her late teens. She was trying to help Katherine get it together. She was a second mother to her younger siblings, always had been. She dropped out of high school to tend to them. Daniel would also leave the house and come back with food and money. He wasn't yet an adolescent, but he already knew the streets.

Sequoya studied him as he was leaving the house one day. He told Katherine that he was going to make sure all of them had something to eat. Sequoya shouted that she wanted to go as well. Katherine told her no. Sequoya plastered herself to the window and watched as Daniel strode out. He was bold and confident going out there knowing he had to do what he had to do.

Dear Mama Katherine,

So, what do you think? I told you I know a whole lot about you. I know even more, but it's all sealed in my heart. You see, I'm your daughter. And some of your undeniable traits are fused into my DNA. You aren't here anymore…but I believe one of my missions is to complete what you once started. I'm sorry to see that you became distracted. But little did you know, God had another plan. I'm going to tell you about my journey. Sit back, relax, and listen carefully as I recall the events I remember so vividly.

FOUR

It was right before my fourth birthday when I was taken away from my Mama. It was always chaotic in our home. I wasn't prepared for how chaotic things would become. We lost the nice house on Carlin Avenue and briefly moved into 1917 Carver Ave on the Westside. Deniece was sixteen-and-a-half. Daniel was nine and Keyonna was seven. Stanford was three and Raeannah was one.

Mama wasn't home on this night. Deniece thought if we were soundly sleeping, she could sneak out and come back in the morning. She had met someone who showed unconditional love to her. His home and family gave her some peace and sanctuary away from the traffic in our home. But as she was walking up to the house the next morning, she spotted Mama sitting on the curb sobbing. She had a sickening feeling that increased once she noticed the rest of us being put into a police car. We were being taken away!

The child protective workers spotted Deniece. But my sister was quick! She turned around and ran as they called out to her. One of them began chasing her. I don't know how she did it, but she outran him and was reported as a runaway.

We were sent to Child Haven in North Las Vegas. Child Haven was the place where children went immediately after being removed from their homes. After a few days, you went back home.

Or you didn't.

Child Haven was a handful of buildings that were scattered around a large courtyard. Each unit had rooms with bunk beds and spacious living rooms. Beanie bag cushions were sprawled on the floors for kids to sit opposite a big screen television. Each unit also had a large bathroom, kitchen, and dining room. I had three roommates in my room. They weren't always the same roommates, as some would leave and new ones would come. We were all waiting for the okay to return home.

Every day I was able to be with my siblings in the courtyard. But after a few days, half of them were gone. Stanford and Rae were eagerly waiting for me in the courtyard. Daniel and Keyonna weren't there. I panicked. I ran to the staff office.

"My brother and sister are gone!" I cried. "Daniel and Keke!"

"Hush now," the lady looked down at me as I clung to her desk. She ruffled through her papers. "I can tell you're such a paranoid little thing. Look at you."

"Are they coming outside?"

She looked amused as she set her papers down. "Your brother and sister are fine. Their daddy came and got them."

It took me a minute to digest what she said. Ben Slank had come to pick Daniel and Keyonna up. But not the rest of us.

Where were you Mama?

A couple of days later, I was also separated from Stan and Rae. I didn't understand what was going on.

This new place I went to was a huge house. The front doors had a sign that said *Volunteers of America.* I was rushed into the house by my transporter. The staff and transporter barely spoke. I heard the tires screeching away as I took a few steps forward into the front room. I was face to face with eleven young girls and three staff.

This house had six bedrooms, with each girl having one roommate. My roommate was this blonde girl who was very loud and obnoxious from the jump. Ridiculous. Everything had to be her way or the whole house would not rest. The staff was always upset with her. It didn't take me very long to realize that the other girls were always nice to me. I had relieved them from being the annoying girl's roommate. I was left to be her partner in every activity. She was always in trouble and at times I was blamed for being her partner in crime on the latest thing she did.

It was around this time that I developed my love for music. The staff at VOA always had loads of new toys and other things for us.

Where was all this stuff coming from? I received my first portable cassette tape player, along with a cassette that said *Mariah Carey: Music Box*. I hummed along to the cassette and memorized the song Dreamlover. I really connected with the lyrics. I wanted someone to come rescue me.

> *I need someone to hold on to*
> *The kind of love that won't fly away*
> *I just want someone to belong to*
> *Every day of my life*
> *Always*
> *So come and take me away*

Music became my best friend. The soothing voices of Whitney Houston, Toni Braxton, Mariah Carey, and Celine Dion helped me to drown out everything and everybody. I wanted to sing and write such beautiful stories that these singers were singing about.

I thought about you Mama. I thought about you and the others daily. I didn't understand why I wasn't home yet. I waited patiently. I didn't lose hope as I knew you would eventually take me back home with you.

The days turned into weeks.

The staff had a talk with me. They informed me that I needed what they called "counseling." This would be my first time going and they told me it would be fun. I would be in a group with other kids.

My eyes met with the other kids in the waiting room. I felt their irritation and curiosity through the empty stares. Duh. Why must everything be so serious with this "counseling" stuff? All we wanted was to be home again!

We followed our therapist into her colorful office. Drawings and pictures hung on the walls and the carpet floor was a rainbow. There were six of us in the office.

The next hour flew by. She asked us questions about how we felt. How did our week go? How was it at the places we lived? We had a snack of apple juice and graham crackers. We also played a few board games. My favorites were Candyland and Operation.

When it was time to go, I was told that I had to attend this session every week because I needed to form better relationships with others and I was angry often.

Of course, I was angry. I was waiting on my Mama and it was taking longer than I had expected.

The weeks rolled into months.

At VOA, I always had my Mama and my siblings in the back of my mind. I didn't know what was taking so long to go back home. But I lived as any four-year-old in my circumstance would. I simply settled into life.

The staff took us on field trips and had movie nights with us. We were always taken somewhere to "kill time" for the staff report log as I heard some of them say. The activities were fun.

They took us up to Lake Mead, driving the company van onto the shore. The person behind the wheel suddenly hit the accelerator and headed straight for the water. We screamed and screamed, our hearts jumping in our chest. Then she slammed on the brakes right before the water. We flew forward in our seats. After a moment of silence, everyone dissolved into laughter. The day was spent on the shore and splashing in the water.

We saw the ballet production of *The Nutcracker* and *Disney on Ice*. I wished that we sat near the front because we couldn't see the princesses up close. I wanted to scream out to them so badly! I wanted them to hear me as they glided on ice whenever they reached the edge of the stage.

Christmas time came around. I had never heard of Christmas before. Staff crowded the girls into the van. We drove around the city looking at all the beautiful lights on each house. The flashing lights lit up the city of Las Vegas. I felt hope. Somewhere, maybe Mama, Dee, Daniel, Keyonna, Stan, and Rae had found out about Christmas too. I gazed out the window in a trance.

We arrived at a gymnasium. We weren't the only kids there. It was a madhouse. Voices of staff shouting to their groups of kids echoed off the walls. I stood in one spot nervously.

A loud voice over an intercom shouts, "One...Two...Three....Go! Merry Christmas!"

I stood frozen as every kid broke into a stampede toward the opposite side of the gym. Huge stockings hung on the wall with a name on it. They scrambled in anticipation to find their own name. They happily tore down the stockings.

Why does everyone else always know what's going on? How come everyone knows what to do but not me? I felt left out on a big secret. I was tapped on the shoulder by my staff.

"Come on Sequoya..." she said. "Let's find your name. You don't want anyone taking yours."

Her smile was kind and made me feel much better. She held my hand and skipped with me through the crowd of loud voices and the piles of torn wrapping paper.

My wish was granted. I was informed that I was going home! But before I did, Mama had to come to the VOA house to visit me. She came at nighttime.

I jumped up and ran to her. We went to my room to be by ourselves. She inspected my hair. She looked satisfied.

"They got my baby's head fresh," she said. "Your hair is growing nice down the side of your head." She always said that.

An officer had pulled you and Daddy over one night. He wanted to arrest both of you. Then he saw me in the back seat with two long pigtails and big eyes. He said I was just too cute and that you and Daddy needed to take me home.

During our visit, she reassured me that everyone would be back home soon. She said she just had to take care of some things before we came back. She was talking about a lady named Kim.

Arriving home that day was one of my best memories of Mama. That was a special day. I was the first to be dropped off at her new apartment at Carey Arms. Mama and Dee were excitedly talking and embracing me as we awaited the others. When Rae and Stanford were dropped off, we screamed with excitement and grabbed them. Rae was one-and-a-half and already taking steps by now! She kept running back and forth with excitement, tiny legs were bowlegged as she danced which made it even funnier. She had the neighbors ooing and ahhing at her.

Dee grabbed Stanford and ran her fingers through his silky afro.

"Stanford Cordero Griffin," Dee said. "My Romeo is back!"

Our family was the center of attention that day as the neighbors visited with us. It was also bittersweet, because Keyonna and Daniel's father had decided to keep them. Ben said he would let Mama know when we could see them.

This was the start of the Golden Era for me. The period of time when I experienced my last couple of years with my Mama. I wasn't prepared for what the future had in store.

After a few months of being back home, weird things started to gradually happen again. I hadn't seen my father in a long time. At first, Mama was home every day. Dee was too. Then Mama started being gone again, coming back every couple of days.

Before long, we were taken again! I was separated from the others like the first time. I went to another girls' home located in Boulder City. There was a row of houses on the same street and they all housed girls.

When I first arrived at this place, I was taken to a doctor to be examined. I was placed on the examination table and the staff helped me remove my clothes and dressed me in a paper gown. They said everything was fine and that a doctor was going to help me get better. I thought I was fine, so I didn't know what they meant.

The doctor came in. Staff held my hand and leaned me down on the table. As he examined me I began to realize that I was kind of sore, but I didn't know why.

"She is very red and sore down there."

When he finished, I sat up and looked down at myself.

I panicked. Staff told me I would be fine. They asked me what happened at home. They asked me if anyone had been coming to our house and putting their mouth on me. Did I know my Grandma Lilian's brother? Why did he always want to be the one to change my diaper and close the door for a long time?

Everything was a blur to me. I didn't remember.

For the next year, I would do the best I could as any five-year-old would do. This period of time has a few memories, but it's mostly a blur.

I went to church for the first time. We went in the afternoons. Our group was the only one in attendance. The pastors greeted us with wide smiles. We took over the entire chapel and Sunday school room. We drew pictures relating to Scripture and always had a snack.

Right before my sixth birthday, I finally received news that I was returning home again! This time had taken even longer than the last. Mama came to visit me again.

When she walked in, I saw that she was holding a newborn baby. We went to my room and she placed the baby between us. I looked down at him as he wiggled about.

"This is Elijah," she said.

I smiled at him. I wasn't sure why, but I was afraid to touch him.

"What's wrong? Why do you look so mad Quoya? You coming home soon. Rae and Stan too."

"Mama...he's slobbering all over my bed!" I cried.

She laughed. Then she used Elijah's blanket to wipe his mouth as I glared at the whole scene.

"Sequoya, calm down. It's alright; he's not going to hurt you! Here, hold him."

I tensed up as she placed him in my lap. Then she scooted closer to me and put her arms around me. I relaxed after a few minutes. Elijah's breathing was a steady rhythm after wiggling so much.

She ran her hands through my hair. "See, long and pretty! Growing nice down the side of your head!"

I can't help smiling. I always felt so special when she said that.

"I bought you something for your birthday next month," she said. "It's a princess couch. Big too…it has all the princesses on it. The seat of the couch opens into a dresser."

We talked a little more. Now I was more comfortable with Elijah and holding him like he was my own baby.

FIVE

It was spring of 1996 and everything seemed so good. It felt so good to be home! We were living in the Carey Arms Apartments. Apartment C I remember so well. Deniece moved back in with us after staying with her friends. Keyonna and Daniel remained with their dad.

This is the time that I have always cherished. This was my Golden Era. The good times. I became closer to Dee who was nineteen now. She was so pretty with such a bright smile and green eyes. People in the neighborhood always flocked around her and her boyfriend Rich.

I always annoyed Dee and Rich when they were in her room by themselves. They laughed as I nonchalantly looked around the room. There were pictures of them together all over the walls and Dee's dresser. They were the happiest couple I had ever seen together.

"Sequoya, what you doing? Get out!" they'd always say, smirking.

I continued to roam the room touching and looking at random things. Out the corner of my eye I studied them. They were kissing each other's forehead. Dee kissed his, then Richard kissed hers, then Dee kissed his...and he kissed hers back. Over and over.

Rich's brother knocked on the front door one day. He asked me where Dee and Rich were. I knew they had been in Dee's room for a long time.

A few minutes later, Dee came out the room laughing.

"Sequoya, why you tell him we was hunching?"

When I wasn't trying to be grown I joined the other neighborhood kids outside with Raeannah and Stanford. We got into all sorts of adventures. There were two gas stations across the street from each other just a little way outside Carey Arms. We weren't supposed to leave the complex by ourselves.

The gas station on the right we always called "Mama's Store" and the one on the left we called "Dee's Store." Stanford and I were bored and we wanted to get a snack. We were hungry after playing outside all day.

"Let's go to Mama's store and get some of those donuts," I said to Stanford.

"There's six in the bag," he said. "I'll take three and you get the other three."

We took the journey to "Mama's store." When we got there, I stood near the door as Stanford slyly walked over to the donuts and stuffed them in his pants pocket. Then we left.

As we sprinted back we kind of panicked because we saw Mama talking to the neighbors! We didn't know she was home. She saw us coming and she was still talking as we slowed our pace.

She called out to us to walk faster since we got to the store fast enough. Then she took us upstairs. Even though we were scared the funniest thing ever happened. She told Stanford to take the donuts out his pocket. Then she started to whoop us both with the donuts! Of course, it hurt a little because she used the force of her hand but it was still funny.

"You know not to leave this area!" she yelled. "And you know not to walk in somewhere and take something!"

Later that night she came in and hugged us and we laughed together, talking about the incident. She handed me and Stanford the crushed bag of donuts. Even though she was stern at times she always made us feel better in any situation.

I awakened in the middle of the night to find her in our room. She was sitting on the floor by the window looking out into the night. She didn't know I was awake.

I watched as she was on her knees crying, just crying really hard. She started talking to her God and asking Him to help her. To help her have the things that she needed for herself and for all of us. She cried and begged to Him, and she was also thanking Him. She was in pain and needed His help.

As a little girl, I was told that I knew too much for being so young. I didn't think about certain things; they just came to mind. But If I knew so much...then how come I didn't know about everything that was going on with you?

Dee and Rich had been together for years. They were trying to have a baby. Dee came out the bathroom crying one day. Rich comforted her. Dee was crying about her period coming.

"Don't even trip," Rich told her. "We're going to have our baby."

I'm not sure why, but my little body walked over to comfort them.

"Why are you guys crying?" I asked them. "Dee, Rich can't have any kids."

They both looked at me very confused.

"What?" Dee said through her tears. "Mama, what did Quoya just say?"

"That was God talking through my baby," Mama answered.

I awakened early one morning, which was becoming a habit. Rae was sound asleep beside me and I could hear Stanford on the top bunk in a deep sleep.

As I rubbed my eyes and face I felt a moist substance. I threw the sheets off me and jumped up. I saw blood on my hands. I ran my fingers over my face again and felt my face covered in blotchy scratches. What was wrong with my face?

"Mama! Mama help me!" I started crying. I ran to her room in a flash. She was wide awake on her bed and didn't look surprised when I ran to her.

"My face Mama!"

She pulled me on the bed with her and examined my face.

"It's alright baby," she reassured me. She went to the kitchen and came back with a wet cloth. She wiped my face thoroughly and the splotches and dried blood came off. I laid down beside her.

"Mama, why was my face covered with blood?" I asked.

As the days turned into summer I felt that nagging feeling again. The nagging feeling that I had buried deep in the back of my mind when we first returned home. The feeling that we would have to leave again.

We still hadn't seen Daniel and Keyonna. Their dad always said he was bringing them over to visit, but they would never come. One day Dee swore up and down this time that Ben said they were coming. Stanford, Rae, and I were happy. We waited the whole day.

The day turned into night and the street lights popped on. I still believed they were on their way. Stanford and Rae were already inside. I finally retired. Dee was just putting them to bed.

"I'm not taking my outfit off yet!" I was mad. We each had a new outfit for the visit and mine was my favorite color, lavender. My sandals were new and fancy. My hair was specially done for the occasion.

"Then you sleeping in it...no problem with me," Dee laughed.

"Are they still coming?" I sounded hopeful.

"Not today Sequoya," Dee shook her head and sighed.

"But they never come! We never get to see them!" I stripped my outfit off. I flopped on the bottom bunk next to Rae and burst into tears.

Dee was silent while she finished tucking Stanford in. I could tell that when she looked over at me she felt sorry for us because we really thought we were seeing Keke and Daniel.

"I know you wanted to see them," she said. "For whatever reason, it couldn't happen today. It's messed up but you should know by now their dad won't let y'all visit with them."

Besides the family division, the nagging feeling lingered that we'd have to leave again. After a while we were going to the food pantry they had at the Carey Arms whenever we didn't have anything to eat. Mama wasn't around again.

43

I was unaware that Ben Slank had married an elementary school principal and had two stepdaughters who didn't like Keyonna. The girls and their mother beat Keyonna up badly just because she said she wanted to visit her siblings.

The day of July 13th, 1996 was a normal stifling, hot summer day in Las Vegas. On this day, neither Mama nor Dee was home with us.

The house was beyond messy. Toys, dirty clothes, trash, these sharp needle things were all over. We had adapted to navigating our way around the mess. Stanford and Rae were beside me on one section of the living room. Baby Elijah was lying on his back on the floor. Most of the time I laid him on the floor like this. I was only six.

I noticed that his diaper had dissolved into a crumbled down piece of white tissue over the past few days. It was falling off and was accompanied with pee and feces. It had traveled down his legs.

Elijah was wiggling his arms and legs about. He seemed to know something was wrong with him.

"He needs his diaper changed," Stanford informed me.

"I know," I said.

I stood up and walked over towards a pile of mess. I found a diaper and crouched back down next to Elijah. He felt my presence and started to squirm even more.

Stanford and I grabbed tissue from the bathroom. I removed the soiled diaper and we began wiping Elijah down. We cleaned him the best way we could, using the tissue to get everything off his legs and body. Rae watched us. She wasn't potty-trained and she wandered around without a diaper. We had adapted to the incredible stench in our house.

After Elijah was clean I slipped the new diaper on and fastened the two sticky parts that held the diaper together as best as I could. Elijah seemed more relaxed now. I felt accomplished as I pushed the dirty diaper to the side.

The day turned into the early night and I didn't know this was the day our lives were going to drastically change again. It was going to change for the good, and at the same time it was going to change for the bad. I knew deep down the change was going to come once again. I already accepted that my Golden Era had run its course.

Our front door opened. We looked towards the door with excitement. It didn't take us long to realize that it wasn't Mama *or* Dee! It was a tall man who stood in the doorway staring us over. He surveyed the apartment.

For some reason, we weren't afraid. He didn't scare us. In fact, he was a gentle giant. We finally had someone here with us. He stepped in and closed the door.

"Who are you?" I asked him.

He stared into my eyes. I stared back into his…a staring contest. Then his expression clouded over and he seemed to be sad.

"You don't need to worry about that," he answered. He roamed the apartment. As he kicked through the mess he shook his head. When he opened the refrigerator, he abruptly shut it closed again. We were quiet as he walked over to the front window and looked through the blinds anxiously. Then he sucked in his teeth and turned back around to face us.

"Can't believe this," he was saying.

The details of the rest of that day are still unclear to me. I do recall that he cleared off one of the couches so we could sleep on it. I vowed to myself to not fall asleep at all. Not that I was afraid. I was just on guard for what would happen next. I never mentioned Mama or Dee to him, and he didn't mention anything either. He sat by the kitchen entrance in a chair and just folded his arms.

"Can you make me some more cereal?" I asked him. That's all we had in the house at the time. He had fixed us some earlier.

Without a word, he poured what had to be my third bowl. I instantly sucked the milk from the bowl, without eating the plain cheerios.

"See," he said. "Soon there won't be any more milk left because you won't eat the cereal."

"More," I demanded.

He shook his head and poured the milk. I sucked all the milk from it. He gladly poured the last of the milk. I repeated the same thing and he took the bowl of soggy cheerios from me.

"All gone; what a surprise!" he exclaimed.

I hid my smile as I relaxed back on the couch. The others had drifted off to sleep. The man slouched down into the chair and crossed his arms. We had another staring contest. I was struggling to stay awake and he was just waiting until I passed out. We both knew he was going to win but I still fought it.

I jumped out of my sleep screaming. He sprang up from the chair and looked at me like I was a ghost.

"You okay?" he was asking.

I nodded my head. I was mad that I had fallen asleep and I didn't know for how long. I went to the bathroom. I was really terrified by the roaches crawling all over. They had multiplied. They were covered all over the toilet, sink, and mirror. Crawling endlessly. I ran out the bathroom crying. I hopped back on the couch and curled into a ball.

"You okay?" he asked again.

"Yeah," I cried. "It's just the roaches!"

"I know," he said. "I didn't want to bother you while you were sleeping, but they were crawling all over you on that couch. That's probably why you woke up."

I leaped off the couch again, bawling. He comforted me. I refused to sit back on the couch until he checked it. He checked through the cushions. Then he lifted the couch. I ran again after seeing a fort of roaches underneath. I ended up sitting on his lap as he sat in the chair at the kitchen entrance.

"The roaches. The roaches kept crawling on you. They crawled all over you while you were sleep...the roaches kept crawling on you." As I was passing out I kept hearing his voice reminding me of the roaches. I didn't understand why he kept chanting this revelation.

When morning came, he was pacing the apartment. He told me about the roaches again. There weren't any on me when I woke up so I wasn't afraid anymore.

"Get your shoes on," he told us.

"Where are we going?" we asked.

"You don't need to worry about it," he simply said. "Just get your shoes on."

We perked up a bit. It took us a while to find our shoes but we found them and got them on. After being in the house for what seemed like ages, we were finally going somewhere. It was very hot in the apartment.

We waited. After some time had passed I began to think he asked us to put our shoes on for no reason at all. We leaned back into the couch and waited some more. Then he opened the front door and looked out. My heart thumped when I heard sets of feet on the staircase leading to our apartment. They were fast and loud thumps accompanied with loud voices. It wasn't Mama or Dee.

Two officers walked in and greeted the man. He kept looking over at us on the couch, shaking his head like he had done the night before. He calmly spoke to them. One of the officers was a female. She picked Elijah up as if he was her son.

We were led out the apartment and down the stairs. We squinted our eyes as the hot sun's glare was beating down on us. Everything happened so fast. We were placed into the back of the police car. We crouched next to each other silently. We were leaving home again. We were leaving Mama all over again and this time she wasn't here. My Golden Era was gone and there was nothing I could do about it.

As we drove away I glanced out the window and saw the man who had taken care of us. I wondered who he was.

Something tells me you knew him Mama. Anyway, at least he saw to it that we got out of that apartment. I wonder what you and Dee did after you came back to see us gone...

Four years before I ever heard of a place called New York and that a family named the Carlons even existed, we were removed from our mother for the last time.

I awoke the next morning at Child Haven yet again. The memories of the previous day brought back the image of the man who had stayed with us. He called Child Protective Services and reported us alone in the house. Now we were back at square one. When would this end?

My roommate was named Cynthia. We heard the morning buzz of kids getting their day started. Cynthia used the bar on the top bunk to swing herself down to the floor like a jungle animal.

Most of the girls were dressed for the day and were eating breakfast at two long cafeteria tables. I noticed that our unit was much larger than the other one I'd stayed in last time. This living room was very spacious with a wrap-around couch. I had never seen a couch extended that long. There was a big screen television.

I was the last girl to get ready, so I scowled at the small table that was placed in the living room. There were only a few folded outfits left. You had to wear the clothes they gave you. Every morning they set out the clothes table in the living room. I surveyed the other girls eating breakfast. One of them wore a lavender overall outfit that I was immediately jealous to see on her. Another had on a cute green top with matching Capri bottoms. It was first come first serve. I would have to be up early every morning to get a nice outfit. Staff handed me a bin with my name on it. It contained a toothbrush and toothpaste, a brush, comb, and other hygiene products.

When everyone was dismissed from breakfast I went to a staff member.

"Yes?" she asked, looking down at me.

"I need to see my brothers and sister," I demanded.

She looked surprised.

"I came here with them yesterday," I explained. "I think they're in another building. Can I see them?"

"Well, you can't just *see* them," she said, like I had committed a crime by asking. "I need to look at your chart first and see what's going on. You *just* came in."

I followed her into the office. Through the doorway, I noticed Cynthia was on the living room couch with other residents. She saw me and waved me over. I listened intently as staff was on the phone.

"All of you just came in and a caseworker will see ya'll soon. Stanford and Raeannah are in a building together, and the baby Elijah is in the building with the infants."

I was relieved. I was also sad. I didn't want to be separated like before.

"I can tell with you being the oldest, you want to look out for them," she concluded.

I wasn't the oldest in my family, but I didn't know at that time how prophetic her words would be. I stood up and went to the living room where Cynthia made room for me on the couch. Names and greetings were a blur and I didn't say too much back. Before I knew it, the girls decided to do something else and I was left alone on the couch.

I don't know how long I sat there. I was thinking about seeing my siblings soon and meeting my caseworker. This was all just a nightmare. Everything would be normal again soon.

I became a nervous wreck. My nerves didn't want to calm down. I began twiddling with my hair. I would divide it in sections, and feel it. It felt nice…but I felt it had to be removed and I couldn't understand why. I would take a section into my hand, feel it, and then start twiddling. Then I would twist it in knots and pull hard, yanking it out. It didn't hurt. It felt good. I left my hair lying around.

After a few days, I was talking to the other kids more. I tagged along with Cynthia to the recreation center. We sneaked from building to building, peeking into the windows. Cynthia made it her mission to help me see my siblings. I didn't see Elijah's building but I saw Stanford and Rae one afternoon.

I was called to the office to meet my caseworker. Looking up at her through my six-year-old eyes, she seemed very tall to me at the time. She had short dreads. Her smile was fake. She looked amused. One day I'd tower over *her* and look down at *her* amused.

We'll get there soon Mama...but for now I was just meeting her.

She flashed her big purple gums and white teeth. "So, this is Sequoya!" her voice boomed loud and very dominating. Her name was Kim Folson. She told me to call her Kim.

"Am I going to see the others?" I asked as we walked across the courtyard.

"Yes," she reassured me.

We stood at the entrance building for infants. Stanford and Rae were already waiting at the door. I was so relieved. Kim led us inside to the sounds of babies cooing and crying.

We were seated. Kim was studying the three of us with the same amused look.

Elijah was carried out to us. When I asked Kim if I could hold him, she hesitated.

"Maybe you can hold him for just a minute," she finally said. "But you have to stay seated where you are. He is just a baby."

"I know!" I snapped. They would never understand that I actually took care of my brother! I changed his diaper and I was only six-years-old. Did they know that? I sat up straight and held my arms out as she placed Elijah on my lap.

Before Kim left for the day, she informed us that we weren't returning home. I felt sick inside after hearing those words. Each time I asked her when we'd be able to live with Mama she said it wasn't possible at this time. I didn't believe her. We were going back to our Mama!

Kim swung by the next afternoon. I sat twiddling my hair feverishly. She plopped down on the couch beside me.

"So," she said. She wiggled, doing a celebration dance. "I have some good news."

"We're going home!" I perked up.

"No, not home," she answered. Her lips turned into a small pout before smiling again. "A very nice lady wants to take you guys! She's elderly. She has other children in the house too but there's enough room."

I was silent. Kim noticed the change in my attitude.

"Sequoya, she is very nice and you'll be with your siblings this time. You can't see your mother right now. Would you rather stay here?"

"No," I sulked.

"Well, why don't you just try this out? Can you do that for me?"

I nodded. I perked up again. Going to this new place was one step closer to returning to our Mama.

"Be prepared to leave any day now," Kim added.

She left and I soaked this new information in. Maybe it wouldn't be so bad.

Staff came in the living room smirking. Then she gave me a scolding look. She was looking at the floor.

"Yeah, it's her hair again," she called to another staff.

I looked down at the floor as they picked up strands of hair. I could not help messing with my hair! I went to the courtyard. Life seemed more promising now. Some kids were coloring the pavement with different colors of chalk while others played jump rope. I walked around in my own little world. Some of our group leader staff were young.

They turned the stereo up loud and the music blared across the courtyard.

Kick off your shoes and relax your feet
Party on down to the Xscape beat
Just kick it, Just kick

They laughed and smiled hard while dancing. "My *song!*" one of them said.

I smiled a little as I hummed to this tune. I felt carefree. I felt hopeful.

Our unit was told that it was movie night and we'd be watching Jurassic Park. Before the movie, everyone had to be dressed and ready for bed. I went to the clothes table to pick out a freshly washed nightgown. I noticed a silky pink material underneath the last item, at the very bottom. I pulled it out. It was extra-long and had fluffy frills on the collar and the bottom. It reminded me of a princess. I instantly grabbed it.

The bathroom was crowded. A group leader saw me holding the gown. She smiled knowingly. She helped me bathe. She took some special time doing my hair in the mirror, being careful of the sides and back of my head where the hair was disappearing. She brushed it down, using most of the hair on top to cover the missing spots. Then she pulled the gown over my head. It flowed past my feet to the floor. I felt very special!

"You are a beautiful princess!" she told me. "Did you know that?"

I smiled hard and stared into the mirror. Was I really? I hadn't felt this special in a long time!

"Now go out there and show everyone what a princess you are!"

I skipped to the living room. Upon seeing me in the gown, some of the girls glared at me. Cynthia called me over.

"That's the best nightgown here," she said.

Cynthia didn't seem angry like the others. She had been there for a while and knew everything.

"Jurassic Park is a scary movie," she said. "I saw it. I don't get scared."

"I don't think I will," I said.

The lights were dimmed. Staff informed us that if we became scared then we had to go to bed.

Right before the movie started, Cynthia leaned into me and whispered that I'd probably never see her again. I didn't understand what she meant.

Within the first few scenes of the movie, I was terrified but tried not to show it. Girls were sent to their rooms. The dinosaurs were so huge and their footsteps seemed like they would bust through the television. I almost screamed when Staff leaned down beside me.

"Sequoya, you need to go to bed. The movie is scaring you."

I felt like I was floating on a cloud as I went to my room, tripping over my gown. I didn't feel like a princess at all anymore. I left the door cracked and peeked into the living room at the screen and still watched it. After a few minutes, Staff shut my door in my face and I was left to go to bed.

My eyes opened suddenly. I sat in the darkness in fear. It was the middle of the night. I had quickly fallen asleep after being sent to bed. The room was looking real spooky. It was thundering and lightning outside. From my position on the bottom bunk, I looked towards the window at the storm that lit up our ceiling and walls. Then my heart really jumped because Cynthia was by our window and she had it open as she was climbing out of it!

"Cynthia!" I started screaming.

I ran to the window. I tried grabbing a hold of Cynthia's legs but she kicked at me with frustration and held onto the window seal.

"Get off me!" she said through clenched teeth. She kicked at me.

"Why are you running away? Why are you leaving me?" Cynthia hadn't told me of her plans to run away.

"I'm not running away," she hissed angrily. She didn't sound like herself. I tugged at her legs as she kicked at me again. The wind of the storm was cold on my face as I shook my head.

"I'm not running away," she panted again, almost out of breath. "My daddy is coming to take me home! It's time for me to finally go home."

"You never told me you were going home yet."

"I told you that everyone here has to go home soon, right?"

"Yes."

"I'm going home." Cynthia's whole attitude had darkened. Her face was very angry and her voice very cruel. From our open window, the lightning kept flashing, lighting the sky, along with our faces. It was scary. I ignored the steady rain coming down into the room.

I decided I was stronger than Cynthia as I grabbed a hold of her legs again, confident she'd fall from the window sill.

She no longer kicked back; she began smiling. I didn't understand why she wasn't falling down; she wasn't even kicking anymore.

I begin screaming and pleading with her again when I realize she wasn't falling because her dad was now holding her arms for her! He was lifting her out the window away from me! She was now in her dad's arms. The rain quickly soaked them.

She smiled again. "Everyone has to leave someday. You're leaving too!"

I leaned my head out the window. Then I screamed at her dad, who said nothing.

Cynthia told me goodbye as he slammed our window shut in my face. They sprinted off in the storm. I couldn't believe this! For some reason, I didn't believe that man was her dad! He had ignored me!

SIX

By morning I was very angry. Staff believed me when they saw for themselves that Cynthia had left. I was upset they didn't take it as seriously as I did. Whenever I tried to talk about it, they listened but would stop me as I went further into detail. They told me that Cynthia was not kidnapped. They said that Cynthia's guardian had come to get her through the main door, not our bedroom window. I felt they were just telling me that because I was a kid who had witnessed something bad.

What they told me did not seem accurate to me. What child leaves in the middle of the night? I knew what I saw. Now I knew why Cynthia told me that I might not see her again before we started watching Jurassic Park.

With my roommate now gone, I was also informed that I was leaving as well! There wasn't time for me to mope or try to put the puzzle together. Kim Folson came to sign me out. She took my small duffel bag and led me off the campus. Stanford and Raeannah were waiting in the car.

Kim was all smiles and told us we'd all be together. Except for Elijah. When she said this I didn't cause a scene. I was still in a daze. She explained to us that Elijah had already left. He would live with a very nice lady and her husband by the mountains. She said we could have visits with him.

On July 24th, 1996, a week and a half after we arrived at Child Haven, we departed from it. It would be our last time there. As Kim drove us to our new setting, I realized that I had developed a new attitude. I would go along with everything that came our way. But I would wait it out until we were back with you! I had no other choice.

We arrived in a busy neighborhood on a street called Freeman Ave that ended in a circle. Almost every house had kids playing outside in the yard. Some were in the street. Kim stopped in front of a white house with green shutters.

We followed Kim inside the house. It took a minute adjusting to the darker light. The first person I noticed was the elderly lady. She wore a long flowing dress and a hat to match it. She smiled though her creamy colored, wrinkly skin and reached out to hug each of us.

I welcomed her embrace. I didn't know what to think or say. I stood there quiet and awkward as Kim talked. I looked around at the living room and noticed the walls were decorated with photographs of people I didn't know.

The couches and chairs were covered in plastic. My eyes wandered to an area on the far left of the living room that led to another room. The room didn't have a door. It was blocked off with a make shift curtain of assorted colored beads. It must be fun to run back and forth between them. On my right was a hallway that I couldn't imagine what was back there. The unknown was very frightful.

Then my eyes looked straight ahead past the living room to the dining and kitchen area. A teenage girl sat in one of the chairs. She was a little heavy. Her skin was very light and she had long, black curly hair. I knew she wasn't black. Her eyes seemed genuine behind a set of nerdy glasses. She was smiling.

Stan and Rae were already beside her. They looked at her shyly as she leaned down to talk to them. Then, from out the mysterious hallway emerged an older boy who looked a little younger than her. He walked out as if he was all tough. A devilish smirk played across his chocolate face. He quickly walked over to the girl and spoke to her in a quiet voice, as if we weren't allowed to hear what he was saying.

"These are the new kids Jimmy," the girl said proudly.

Jimmy looked at each of us before dramatically disappearing into the hallway. He was really trying to show off.

Kim's voice was existent to me again as she introduced the elderly lady as our new foster mother, Mary Williamson.

"She has three other children here," she said.

Mary smiled at each of us. She told us to call her Mama Mary.

So now I had you, Mama Katherine, and now Mama Mary...

Kim left. Next, we were led down the hallway to our rooms. The first room was the boys room. Mary placed Stanford's things on his bed. Jimmy was on the other bed. As we exited the room I saw he was still trying to look cool. Next, we went to Mary's room. Then we passed the bathroom and directly across from her room was the girls room.

The girls room was a lot more spacious. I listened as Mary explained that she'd renovated the house, extending our room into part of the backyard. We had two large closets and four beds. There were dressers, including a large one with a mirror. Tamera, the teenager, had her pictures and makeup and hair accessories on top. It reminded me of Dee's dresser back at Carey Arms. An aching filled my gut. I wandered over to my bed near the back window where Mary had placed my things. I sat down and listened to her and Tamera talking.

I followed them back to the living room. We toured the den with the beaded curtain at the entrance. There was a television that stood on the floor, and a sofa. The walls had pictures and the cabinets held sports trophies.

Proudly, they led us back to the living room. I wasn't very talkative. Everything and everyone had come so rapidly. I recall Mary Williamson, or Mama Mary, being absent for the rest of the day. Tamera and Jimmy babysat us. Later in the evening, another girl returned. Her name was Diedra but she told us to call her "DJ" like Tamera and Jimmy called her. I liked her right away and we were the same age.

Tamera told us she was the oldest. She was going on sixteen. Jimmy was twelve. I broke out of my shyness when I saw a bowl of fruit on the table.

"Can I have one?" I looked at Tamera nervously.

"Yeah," she said, laughing.

I took the dark purple fruit and stared at it.

"It's called a plum," Tamera said.
I half smiled, biting into the juicy fruit.

On my first night at Mama Mary's I rearranged my meager belongings from my small duffel bag. Tamera took the few outfits that I had. I watched as she neatly folded each item. She concentrated very hard, making sure the corners folded perfectly together.

I took out the rest of what I had. My only item was a box of baseball cards that I received at Child Haven after a local baseball game. I didn't know anything about the sport. I just knew that the cards meant something to people who got them. It was something that belonged to me that couldn't be taken away from me. I took each card out, about fifteen of them. I studied each man's face. Whoever they were, they were very important. I lined the cards on my nightstand. I did a head count as I placed them back in the box. I did this a couple more times before the night was over.

The next morning, I did the regular head count of the cards before making my bed and getting dressed. I grabbed the cards and went to the front room. Mama Mary and Tamera were in there.

Mama Mary looked me up and down. "Girl, if you don't put those lousy cards back in your room…" she began laughing. "And tie your shoe. You can't be walking around here like that. Tamera, just look at those shoes!"

Tamera tried to hide her laughter. A sudden feeling of sadness welled inside of me. I put my head down, staring at my green shoes with beads glued on them. They were donated from Child Haven. I bent down to tie my shoe.

"Sequoya, Mama is just playing!" Tamera exclaimed. "You look like you about to cry…Mama jokes around a lot!"

I looked up to see them looking with dear regret. Mama Mary eyed me with a concerned look. She told me to stop crying, tie my shoe, and put the cards away. Then she told me something that shocked me.

"We're going to get you some new shoes to wear," she said.

It took me a second to process what she said. I didn't say anything, but smiled hard with wonder.

Mama Mary and Tamera stifled another bout of laughs.

"Her mood changed fast!" Tamera giggled.

"Girl, go on and do what I told you," Mama Mary was really amused. I turned back towards my room.

DJ and I were excited to be in the same class.

"Can't get away from each other now. You have to sit in each other face all day!" Mama Mary said.

DJ and I weren't fazed one bit. We had spent the last summer weeks trying to imagine what being in the same class would be like. Should we tell the whole class we were sisters? Would they know we were foster sisters? Or would the teacher already know? Maybe we'd be seated next to each other.

I tried to ignore a familiar nagging feeling. This would be a new school, not the school that Dee walked me to every morning by the Carey Arms. I missed Dee. I told myself to stick through and not cry every day like I had the first week at Mama Mary's. One day our family would be together again. At least Stan and Rae were with me.

Since I was pulling my hair out, Mama Mary and Tamera bribed me with gifts to get me to stop. Mama Mary took me to get my hair done. Little did I know at the time, one of the ladies who worked there would have a surprising link to our family. But that was in the unseen future. The few times Mama Mary sent us to get our hair done, this mysterious lady wasn't the one doing our hair. Her booth was further in the back. We were kids and didn't know her…but she surely knew who we were.

The hair stylist took some braiding hair and used it to make box braids. She styled it in a way so that it fell down and covered the baldness.

We knew the area well after playing outside all summer. This was the Westside of Las Vegas. I was unaware at the time that one of my dad's siblings lived in their deceased mother Virginia's house only a few blocks away!

Mama Mary warned us about the consequences of not returning home on time.

"That switch is waiting if necessary," she always said that, almost in a growl.

Jimmy and Tamera attended other schools. I liked hearing her get up earlier than us. It was still dark. She dressed as the house was quiet. She carefully did her huge curly hair then she applied her makeup. Then she put her glasses on last. Her school was far away so she had to walk to a bus stop.

When she was ready, I faithfully walked her to the door. She'd tell me to get in bed to catch my last few minutes of sleep before I had to be up. When she left, I'd walk into the boys room since their window was the closest to the front yard. Watching Tamera walk in the dark seemed scary to me. I watched until I couldn't see her anymore, and it hurt to tilt my head as I pressed it against the hard window. Small traces of the sun's light would appear in the sky by that time.

DJ and I walked to Matt Kelly Elementary on our first day. Our teacher wasn't in sight. The room was rowdy as our fellow classmates were laughing and running around. The back of the room had a circular table with a group of girls huddled underneath.

Another girl sat to the side by herself. I sat down next to the lone girl and we both smiled shyly.

"What's your name?" she asked, fiddling with her long silky black hair.

"Sequoya. What's your name?"

"Nisha MacDonald."

Then an idea came to me. "Let's be best friends!" I exclaimed.

Nisha didn't miss a beat. Her eyes lit up. "Yes, we are best friends!"

This was the most exciting idea because DJ was my only friend but she was also my foster sister. Nisha was not my foster sister. So, she would be my best friend.

I told Nisha that I lived in a foster home of six kids. I pointed over at DJ. Nisha nodded, surprisingly not asking me any questions about it. Nisha lived right across the street within the notorious gray apartment complex with her mother, younger brother, and sister.

Chatter in the classroom turned loud. Soon we were running and jumping around. The girls underneath the table had abandoned their meeting. The room became chaotic. At one point, Nisha and I chased each other on our hands and knees, crawling across the floor shouting with laughter.

I guess we were the last ones to notice anything, because suddenly the whole room was quiet. A foot stomped down hard in front of Nisha and me. We jumped back.

"*Enough!*" the woman's voice boomed. "We are *not* starting the year off like this, and most importantly, we are *not* animals like they want us to be!"

I timidly looked up. She had long, woven dread locks and a serious face. She stared down at us sternly. Our classmates looked relieved they weren't the ones being scrutinized underneath her glare.

"Everybody form a circle on the center rug now," she demanded, stepping away from Nisha and me. We followed the rest of the class to the giant rug.

DJ sat next to us and whispered something about needing to start our own club. Just like the girls who had been underneath the table.

"Now we have our own club. Me, you, and Nisha," I said. I felt I was becoming part of something special.

Our teacher sat in a chair beside her new students seated on the rug. She smiled and looked at each of us. "My name is Mrs. Dowdell," she said. "It's pronounced Dow-will-dell!" She had us chant her name.

She explained that she was excited for this new school year, but she would not tolerate horseplay. She told us that we'd learn many things, especially about African-American history and the country of Africa. Our class was a variety. My new best friend Nisha wasn't black but I never asked her what she was. None of that mattered. I was so happy to have a new friend.

"I want to know every one of you. So, in our circle one by one, I want you to state your name, and what you want to be when you grow up."

What did I want to be? I wasn't sure. My wish was going back home to my Mama. I wasn't sure what the title to that was.

"DJ," I whispered nervously. "I don't know what I wanna be!"

"Me neither," she answered quietly.

I'm not sure what made me think of what I said next, but I thought I had the best answer.

"And what do you want to be when you grow up?" Mrs. Dowdell smiled at me eagerly.

"A hoochie mama," I said very seriously.

"A what?" she asked me in disbelief.

Being a hoochie mama, from my little understanding, meant you were grown and cute. I heard the term a lot. But Mrs. Dowdell's smile disappeared and her eyes widened. By the end of her rant, I knew a hoochie mama was very bad, and something I should never consider being or mentioning again.

Mama Mary was a very sweet lady but she was also stern when it came to following rules. It was instilled within her to bring up children the right way. I rarely got into trouble with her. It took one situation for me to realize how real it could be.

As DJ and I got into our school routine, we formed a club with Nisha and a few other girls. One of the girls told me that DJ and I would be expelled from the club because we didn't attend meetings. What meetings? We met at school so I was confused.

She said that DJ and I never stayed after school with them or went to their houses. I knew that Nisha lived right in the apartments across the street from the school.

"Okay, we'll meet everyone after school at Nisha's house!" I said, up to the challenge. How dare anyone try to kick me and DJ out of a club for no reason!

After school, DJ and I were only focused on the club. We seemed to have forgotten that we were to walk straight home from school. We didn't even walk by the pre-school area to pick up Stanford. He came to the afternoon classes.

The club crossed the street and walked over to the apartment complex. Nisha proudly led us to her front door and knocked. An older version of Nisha opened the door.

"Mom..." she started before her mom could say anything. "These are my best friends from school."

Nisha's mother just smiled and motioned for us to come in. We met her younger brother and sister. Then Nisha's mother left us to ourselves. We painted each other's nails and played with each other's hair. We played with Nisha's dolls. We ate dinner. A lot of time passed by!

The other girls left before DJ and I did. They said we were still in the club. DJ and I stayed and talked to Nisha and played with the baby. We only left when her mom said that Nisha had had enough fun and she needed to unwind.

We were on an adventurous high. We felt on top of the world because we rarely did things without the other kids in Mama Mary's house. We were walking around the corner almost to our house when we stumbled upon another adventure. An elderly couple sitting on lawn chairs in their front yard.

"How are you two young ladies doing today?" the old man asked.

"Good!" we said. We stood there for I don't know how long, chit chatting. They were very nice. We told them about school and going to our friend's house for the first time. We were only a two minute walk from home and it was beginning to get dark.

I saw a motion out the corner of my eye so I turned to my left. There was Mama Mary's car rounding the corner and coming toward us! DJ saw her at the same time I did. Mama Mary screeched her car to a halt in front of us. She ordered us in the car. Then she looked at the lady and thanked her for letting her know where to find DJ and me. No wonder the couple kept asking us so many questions and kept talking to us!

Mama Mary informed us we were in trouble. She said anything could have happened to us, especially since we lived on the Westside.

"Both of you will receive a whooping tonight," she said calmly.

My stomach tightened into knots. Everyone looked sorry for us when we arrived home. Stanford told us he knew his way back home and he had come home on time. Jimmy was whistling and shaking his head. "Wow," he kept muttering. He kept saying it so much.

I looked at Tamera for support. She told me that if Mama Mary said she was giving out a whooping, then she was giving out a whooping. I thought we were in the clear at first because Mama Mary got on the house phone and had a hearty conversation with someone. She was laughing hard and throwing her head back. The rest of us had gotten ready for bed and were in the den. I was anxious. Then it was bedtime.

"Sequoya and DJ, y'all go in the room first," Mama Mary said. She was calm. We hung our heads and slowly walked to the girls' room.

Mama Mary came in and shut the door. She walked toward us. She had one arm behind her back.

"What are you supposed to do after school?" she asked us.

"Come right home!" we both said. We had all the right answers to her questions. I added that we were to walk home with Stanford as well. She knew all about us going to Nisha's house too.

Mama Mary told us we were being disciplined with the hope that we'd never break those rules again. Then she withdrew her arm that she had behind her back. She held a belt. DJ and I began hollering as she lunged for us. We kept trying to use each other as a shield, but Mama Mary was skillful in striking both of us. The whooping wasn't that long, but it was long enough!

Afterwards, we got into our beds still crying. I was sad and exhausted. But I sure had learned a lesson!

Our first year at Mama Mary's found us in the house with more foster kids besides Tamera, Jimmy, DJ, Stan, Rae, and me. The house became populated.

Mama Mary came home with a newborn baby one day. Where had *he* come from? We hovered over the new baby. I listened as Mama Mary and Tamera talked about Baby Ronald. He needed a home. Baby Ronald was her great grandbaby. Mama Mary had a grandson who couldn't care for the baby, and neither could the mother.

Tamera took to the new baby as if he was hers. Whenever we wanted to hold or see Baby Ronald we had to ask Tamera, who could be real bossy at times.

Tamera invited her high school friends over. They reminded us that they were older than us. Most days to avoid any conflict, we went outside to play in the Freeman Ave Circle. Our next-door neighbors were a group of rowdy kids whose parents were never home. A fence separated their yard from ours. It reminded me of The Lion King, where Simba's side of the land was flowing with beautiful sunshine, scenery, and fresh air. Scar's side of the land was permanently dark and gloomy. Our yard was Simba's while theirs was overflowed with trash, a horrible stench, and uneven grass that needed to be mowed. Even though our yards were different that didn't matter. We jumped the fence to their yard, or they jumped the fence to ours. We spent all day outside until the sun went down.

One day Mama Mary informed us that two new foster kids were coming. Two new girls. How would everyone fit into our small house? The boys were happy they still had their room to themselves. It was just Stanford and Jimmy. Baby Ronald rotated a lot in the house. Each room took turns having him, including Mama Mary.

Adding the two new girls would now make six girls. Mama Mary said we'd make it work. We arranged our beds in the room a little closer to each other. Mama Mary brought in two more small beds.

The new girls were Roshonna and Jill. Roshonna spoke up fast.

"It's Roshonna, but my name is Russia. Call me Russia."

Both girls were the same age, three years older than DJ and me. They had come from another foster home together. They said they were sisters, but it was obvious they weren't.

Russia, with her caramel skin and searching eyes, was calm and quiet. She reminded me of myself. Jill was very energetic and loud. She wasn't even there for five minutes before she broke into a run in the house. She began screaming and laughing, her bouncy blonde hair in a tangled mess.

Tamera and Mama Mary were listening to the new girls' caseworker while staring directly at Jill. The look on their faces only told one thing: Jill *must* go!

That's exactly what happened. Jill only stayed with us for a few days. When her caseworker came back to get her, I noticed that she and Russia said goodbye to each other very hurriedly. So much for being sisters!

What we weren't prepared for was DJ leaving us! Her biological family was able to take her back after some time. We were sad to see her go. Especially me.

I noticed another kid in my class walking the same route. I hadn't noticed he lived near me. After a couple of days of observing him I determined he must get dropped off in the mornings but walked home in the afternoons. He never spoke to me in class. And when we walked home from school, if I happened to look in his direction, he would suddenly look away as if I wasn't there.

"Someone brings you to school every morning?" I asked him one day on the route home.

"Yeah, my mom. I walk home. I always see you and DJ. She left, right?"

"Yes."

"When are you going to leave?"

He was looking at me with earnest.

"I don't know how long it's gonna take but one day I'm going to go back with my Mama."

"But if you don't...I'll be right here for you."

I looked at the handsome Joshua in alarm. Honestly, I was shocked. I mean, Joshua?

"I will!" he said again. Then he took my hand!

"You want to walk home from school every day?" I asked.

"Yes, but will you be my girl?"

"Why?" I wanted to know why he liked me.

"Because you cute Sequoya. Let's be boyfriend and girlfriend." He was squeezing my hand.

"Okay," I agreed.

After that, Joshua seemed to light up. He insisted that we also sit together during lunch as well. I was still wondering why he liked me. But I decided to go along with it.

We were near Freeman Ave when he suddenly stepped behind me and then I was ahead of him. Before I could turn around, I felt my bottom being pushed on. Both of my cheeks were pushed on! Joshua had taken both of his hands and pushed, as if he was doing push-ups.

"What are you doing?" I looked at him as he stepped beside me again and he was grinning wide.

"You my girl now and I was making it official."

"By pushing on my booty?"

"Yeah! You ask too many questions."

I was laughing to myself because he was so serious as he pushed on my bottom. Every day after that, Joshua greeted me after school with a push on my bottom with both hands. He did it on the playground at recess too.

But after a few days, I grew annoyed and tired of him and the booty game. After school as he walked toward me and was prepping his hands to touch me, I stepped back and told him to not do it anymore.

"What do you mean not do it anymore. I can't touch my girlfriend's booty?"

"I don't want to be girlfriend and boyfriend anymore."

Joshua looked at me in disbelief. "Why?" he asked.

"I just don't," was all I could say in the nicest way possible.

Joshua began to cry. Tears began to flow down his face.

"You don't wanna be my girlfriend anymore..." he wailed. I watched as he turned and ran from the school.

"Wait!" I called after him. "Wait and walk with me!"

Joshua was running like a track star and screaming at the top of his lungs. He didn't wait and walk home with me after that ever again and he didn't acknowledge me at school.

Yet another summer came and went, pushing itself off the calendar. Nisha and I were in the same class again. I still saw Mrs. Dowdell in the hallways. She always gave me that *look*. A look that meant she was watching me, and that I was responsible for becoming a respectable black woman someday. I would never forget her.

After DJ left, Russia was the one with whom I spent more time. She reminded me of myself but at the same time I couldn't possibly measure up to her. She was very smart. I mean, *extremely* smart! Her teachers were always sending her home with appreciative notes along with an A plus on every assignment she did. I admit that I use to watch with envy as she excitedly jumped in the air after each report card she received. She was not only intelligent, but she was talented as well. She could jump up and do a split in the air at the same time.

Mama Mary allowed Russia to be a basketball cheerleader for a little league during the basketball season. I wanted to be just like her. I begged Mama Mary to be in cheerleading but she said I was too young. I would have to wait the few months until football season.

In the meantime, I tagged along to every practice and game she had. I dreamed about being a cheerleader. I paid attention to every cheer they did. They were very creative. They focused more on their chants and dancing than extreme stunts.

Finally, by 1997, Mama Mary gave me the okay to be in the cheerleading football league! Russia and I were on the same team. Mama Mary took us to sign up and I watched as she paid for it. She was kind of grumbling about it. Rae wanted to be in it too. Mama Mary told her that she was only four and that she had to wait.

Our team was called the Jaguars. The boys practiced on the field while the cheerleaders practiced nearby. I really felt that I belonged now. I had never been involved in something so fun and creative. I was coming out of my shell, and this was a brief period in my youth where I was not shy, but extremely confident. I felt very beautiful and on top of the world.

Within no time, I learned all the chants, and as a young girl I knew how to free style. A typical cheer would include the girls divided in a few rows acting very grown. Each girl had her own chance to be put on the spot, which we loved! When it was my turn, I was prepared!

The girls began chanting.

"*D-o-w-n* and that's the way she get down! *D-o-w-n* and *that's* the way she get *down!* Hey Sequoya?"

"What?"

"*Let* us see you get *down!*"

"*Too shy!*"

"*Let* us see you get *down!*"

"I'll try!" Then I pretended to be shy and danced. "*D-o-w-n* and this the way I get down."

"*D-o-w-n* and that's the way she get down!" They copied my dance move. Unsatisfied, they prodded me again.

"Hey Sequoya?"

"Yeah?"

"*Let* us see you get *down!*"

"No way!"

"*Let* us see you get *down!*"

"Okay!" I really broke it down now. "*D-o-w-n* and this the way I get *down!*"

They go, "She *said* a *D-o-w-n* and *this* the way she *get down!*" They copied my dance move. Every girl had her own turn.

Another favorite was called "Razzle Dazzle."

"Razzle Dazzle!" Clap- Clap- Clap! "Razzle Dazzle!" Clap- Clap- Clap!

"My name Sequoya I'm *number one* my reputation has just begun! So, if you see me just step aside, cuz Sequoya baby don't take no jive!"

Then the girls would scowl and chant, "Oooh she *think* she bad!"

"Correction baby I *know* I'm bad!"

"Oooh sheee think she fine!"

"I'm fine enough to blow yo mind."

Cheerleading was too fun! I had never experienced anything like it. I couldn't do all the extreme flips and stunts that some of the older girls knew how to do, but I was still very happy. A confidence was coming to me as I paraded around in my cute uniform at the games. We received a lot of attention at these weekly games that we traveled to each weekend.

Team pictures were very special. Mama Mary made sure our hair was done. There was a hairstyle called "tie knots." Hair extensions that already came pre-braided. Your hair was braided in cornrows. Then, the stylist takes a crotchet needle, loops the braided extension, and sews it onto the cornrow. This was repeated until your whole head was full of these famous tie knots. You could wear them long or short. Mama Mary made sure that mine were very long.

For individual pictures, I put my right foot on a football helmet that was placed upright in the grass. I pointed my right pom pom in the air, and placed my left pom pom on my hips. My tie knots cascaded to my waist. I proudly smiled as my picture was snapped.

By the end of the season, the Jaguar cheerleaders had our routine down for the yearly dance competition. The weekly games had been completed. Now it was time for the girls to compete. The boys who played in the league attended the dance competition as well. We danced our behinds off! When we popped and dropped, we did it so hard. We shook our pom poms and we flung our hair.

And we won first place in our division! We screamed as we jumped up and down! Russia of course did her jump and split in the air. We ran to receive our team trophy. Besides the main trophy, we were each given a tiny one for ourselves. I held mine tightly as pandemonium was all around me in the gym.

The next day, our team had a party at the roller rink to celebrate. The celebration continued that night, as all girls were invited to our cheer coach's house. It was a big house in the suburbs just outside the city.

Dear Mama,

We took over her house! It was funny because we drove her crazy. She left overnight, leaving some of the older girls in charge of everyone. We had so much fun. After the day's events, we finally went to sleep. Some of us woke up early after we heard someone turn the TV on. They were trying to be quiet but kept laughing. Then we heard some crazy stuff. So now we all got up to look at the screen. That was the first time I ever saw Jerry Springer. They said it was a bad show and we weren't supposed to watch it. Since Coach was gone, we were sneaking to watch it. But once we heard her car door slam, we plopped back to our sleeping spots. Someone rushed to flick the TV off just in time!

SEVEN

On a late fall afternoon, I stood on the blacktop watching my classmates during recess. A community park separated our school from an enrichment center. A track wrapped around the park. Locals were jogging or riding bikes. I never focused on them because I was engulfed in recess. But one day something happened.

As I stood on the blacktop, I heard my name being called. It was low at first. "Sequoya," the voice said.

I was too timid to look over, and I didn't want to get into any trouble with Mama Mary.

"Sequoya," the voice was louder now. It was now very familiar...but it seemed too good to be true. How could it be?

I gave in and glanced in the person's direction. She was on a bike but also leaning against the fence. One hand was holding the fence and the other was holding the bike handle. One leg was on a pedal, the other on the ground. She wore a shorts overall set and tennis shoes. Her legs glimmered in the sunshine.

I was getting ready to shout her name in excitement but she held her hand to her mouth, telling me to be quiet. I realized this was supposed to be a secret. I glanced at my classmates, saw they were still playing, and calmly walked over to the fence.

"Dee!" I finally said. No one on the playground could hear me.

"Hey Quoya," she said. Her green eyes were filled with such happiness and victory. We couldn't hug each other because of the fence so we just touched hands through the holes.

"How did you find me?" I asked.

"It wasn't hard," she said. "We're still allowed to know where you're at. I knew you guys would be placed in this school."

She told me that she rode her bike all the way over here. She said she even saw me on other days before today, but she didn't approach me. She only watched.

"Are you and Mama coming to get us?"

She didn't really answer. She just told me that one day we'd all be together again.

"Why aren't we allowed to see Mama?"

"Because they don't want our family together," she simply said. "I'm not even supposed to be sneaking over here to see you. They keep saying that me, Daniel, and Keke have to go through Family Services to see you guys. We in the process of that now. They stalling on us."

"Is that why it's taking so long?"

She nodded.

"Are you going to come see me every day?" I looked at her with hope.

"I will try; can't promise. I've been trying to catch Stan on his recess too…but he's too caught up on the playground." We both laughed.

"For now, this is only between us," she said.

I nodded.

"Gimme kiss."

I leaned my face against the fence, and she kissed my cheek. She quickly looked around.

"I have to go now," she said. She smiled at me.

"Bye Dee," I said, feeling deep sadness.

"Bye Quoya."

I watched as she balanced herself on the bike and pedaled away. When I no longer saw her, I turned back toward the playground. No one had been watching me. Thank God.

Dear Mama,

Starting the next day, I looked forward to recess. I positioned myself near the fence and pretended to play with my classmates. At the same time, I watched for Dee. But she didn't come back. Every day I watched. I was sad for the first couple of weeks. I hoped she hadn't been seen or gotten in trouble.

As more weeks passed, I was no longer standing near the fence. I returned to the blacktop. I still glanced at the park but eventually I stopped. I was still happy to have seen her...even if briefly.

One day our caseworker Kim came to pick us up and told us we were going to Family Services. My heart thumped.

"We get to see Mama and them?" I asked.

"Not yet," she said, looking at me.

"When do we get to see them?"

"Sequoya, stop asking so many questions. Let grown folk handle grown folk things please."

I was angry but I held my tongue. When we arrived at Family Services, I was very surprised to see a young boy in the waiting room. A Caucasian couple was with him. The lady lovingly held the boy's hand.

"Elijah!" I screamed. We ran to embrace our baby brother.

He was going on three and we hadn't seen him since we departed from Child Haven two years before. He was walking now! He had a big mischievous smile. He instantly took to us as if he remembered everything.

"The four of you are just so cute...look at this," the lady said. She introduced herself and her husband as Ron and Sandy Hue. Elijah had been in their care since he was an infant. They lived near the mountains on a huge ranch with nine other foster children.

I looked around in the waiting room to see the other kids who had come along. They were watching this whole exchange. One of them was a bit older and his stare zeroed in on me. Even when I looked away and looked back, he still stared.

"This isn't half the crew!" Ron Hue joked.

"It would be nice if you guys could come to our home," Sandy continued. "We have horses too! Have you ever gone horseback riding?"

We shyly shook our heads. I already knew I wasn't getting on a horse.

"We'll see about setting up a visit soon," Kim said. "For now, it's picture time!"

Picture time? I looked at Kim and the Hues. They looked happy, but Kim was even more so.

"Come on," she motioned for us to follow her as she held Elijah's hand. Ron stayed back with the other children.

We were led to an office. A man with a camera was setting lights up. A grayish-white backdrop was behind a round table.

"Hey there, sweetie pies!" the cameraman's voice boomed with excitement.

We stared at him.

"You guys get your pictures taken today. Look at you all spruced up!"

I looked down at my clothes. I wasn't really spruced up. I wore an oversized blue t-shirt with a teddy bear on it, and jeans. Rae wore a red long-sleeved shirt and corduroy patterned overall dress. My hair was in tie knots and hers was in box braids, both of our hair with the top half up and the back down. Stan wore a red t-shirt and jeans. Sandy dressed Elijah in a nice white buttoned-down shirt, and light blue denim overalls.

"Who's first?"

"Let's get Elijah out of the way first," Sandy suggested.

Elijah was placed in a chair at the table. He smiled a goofy smile that made us laugh. The cameraman made these funny sounds that made it even funnier.

The rest of us were next. After that, he told us to seal the deal we'd be taking a group picture.

"Yay!" Kim exclaimed. She was really over the top on this day.

The four of us crowded the table. Kim and Sandy fussed over us. They placed Elijah back in the chair. They had Rae stand on his right side, and me on his left. Stan was placed behind Elijah. The adults studied us for a minute. At the last second, they told me to kneel down.

Then Elijah began to fuss. Sandy had a panicked look. She reached into her purse and unwrapped a lollipop.

"I didn't think he would get impatient but I knew it was coming!" Sandy said apologetically. "Is it okay?"

"Sure!" cameraman said.

Elijah clutched the lollipop with his right fist and smiled again. He was content. Then cameraman suggested I take my left arm and place it on Elijah's shoulder.

"*There* we go! Now I want you all to smile. And you are extremely happy for this one, *extremely!*"

He quickly flashed a few pictures.

"Nice!" Kim looked very satisfied.

"These kids are charmers," he concluded. He looked at his camera, flipping through the pictures. "Very precious indeed."

After our visit with Elijah, Sandy and Ron promised to have us at their ranch soon. We perked up. I was happy because to me it meant we were getting closer and closer to being reunited with our Mama!

Dear Mama,

It was the beginning of the next year when I finally heard something. We got notice that we were finally allowed to see Dee, Daniel, and Keyonna! It had been a long time. I was elated! I was also told that you wouldn't be there, which I didn't understand at all. But at least we could see the others.

Kim drove us to Family Services. Stan, Rae, and I played with the other children in the waiting room. I inspected some of the toys as my heart beat. I watched as children visited with their parents. Whatever the case of their separation, everyone was ecstatic.

Finally, Dee and the others walked in! They checked themselves in at the front while at the same time grinning at us very wide. They seemed so grown up to me. Dee was twenty-one, Daniel was fourteen, and Keyonna was twelve.

"There's your brother and sisters," Kim prodded us. She sat in her chair with amusement.

As if her mention was our cue, we jumped up and ambushed our older siblings! The six of us were a sight to see as we embraced.

The other families smiled at us and they could tell it had been a long time for our family.

We found a comfortable couch and crowded together on it. Kim remained in her chair across the room. I saw Dee look at her kind of angry. They hadn't said hello to Kim.

None of us spoke about the last time we had been home. Dee didn't bring up her seeing me at school, and I didn't either. We just talked about how much we missed each other. They told us that Mama was getting better. I asked them what happened. They said nothing bad happened but that Mama just needed some time.

Daniel and Keyonna lived with their father Ben Slank. He wouldn't let them see Mama either. This was an occasion where he just gave in and let them come with Dee to finally see us. Dee was the only one who had contact with our Mama. She had her own apartment.

"I'm going to prove to the courts that I can get y'all," she told us. "I have my own place now *and* a job."

"Does Rich live with you?" I asked.

"Yeah," Dee smiled. "He keeps asking about y'all. He's waiting too."

"I can't wait to come back home," I said.

We told them about Mama Mary and the other kids. They weren't really interested about what family we were with. They just told us our family would be reunited.

Dee had a Polaroid camera. We took pictures and chatted the visit away. The time flew by too fast for us and before we knew it, Kim rose from her chair and said it was time to get ready to wrap it up. She said she needed to get us back to Mama Mary's.

We held each other as a group and we cried. Dee and I were the last to break away from each other. I sat on her lap as she held me extra tight. A giant tear slid out of her eye...down her cheek...and splashed down on my arm. I can still see it so vividly.

Kim told us we'd see them again in two weeks. That made us feel better.

She kept her promise. Two weeks later we were back at Family Services to visit them. But this time my Mama had a surprise for us!

I was watching by the front doors of the building and saw the three of them walking up. A van pulled up beside them. For a moment, they talked to whoever was in the passenger seat. Then they looked toward the building anxiously.

What was going on? Why didn't they come in right away? Kim was in her chair.

Then Keyonna came in. Daniel and Dee were still outside.

"Hey!" Keyonna said to us, before checking in. We crowded around her.

"Are they coming in too?" I asked her. I noticed she had a look on her face.

She looked over at Kim. Then she lowered her voice. "Don't be all loud, but if you want to give Mama a hug *real* quick, she's outside. She's not allowed to come in. You gotta do it quick."

My eyes widened. But it was too late, because Rae screamed *"Mama!"* and she bust through the double doors and ran towards the van. I saw Mama jump out the van when she saw her youngest daughter running. She scooped her up and held her tight.

Kim had already heard and seen the commotion. She said a few words to alert staff, and then ran towards us.

"You stay *right here!*" she hissed at me and Stan. She glared at Keyonna, who glared at her right back.

I was mad too. I followed Kim outside and Stan followed me. Keyonna stood near the doors looking pleased.

"Didn't I tell you to stay inside?" Kim turned around. "Get inside!"

"I wanna see my Mama!" I shouted defiantly.

She couldn't stop us. Stan and I ran towards Mama and she welcomed us into her embrace.

I heard Kim talking crap to our Mama.

"Katherine, you know you aren't to just pop up like this."

Mama ignored her.

"Okay, you got to hug them. Nice. You are good now. Now it's time for them to go back inside."

Mama continued to ignore her as she held us.

"Katherine. The staff is already alerted."

Only then did Mama finally look at her. They both looked at each other with such anger...that's when I knew there was more to this whole thing, but I didn't know just what.

"Come on," Daniel spoke. "Let's go back inside now. Love you Mama..."

"I love you too!" she said. Her eyes looked sad but still defiant just like the rest of our attitudes. I hugged her again.

"I love you guys," she repeated. "Okay, go back in now...they might call the police on me...but I don't care I got to see you! I have every right to be on this property. So just go inside and watch me from the door."

"Right," Dee agreed with sass.

Then Mama looked at Kim very smugly, who was still looking at her mad. At that moment, that's when I first saw Kim in a different way. I didn't like her anymore.

Why was she so mad at you?

We went back inside and took our place to watch Mama by the doors.

The staff was anxiously crowding the door, acting like my Mama was America's Most Wanted. It made me so mad! She was only a mother who wanted to see her kids! She wasn't harming anyone.

The police didn't come. Mama eventually got back in the van and the driver remained put there.

What made me even more mad was that Kim and the staff decided our visit would not be in the main center room. Instead, they took us behind the office area that no one ever went past. They escorted us into a cubicle. So, all six of us were crowded in there, and Kim stood guard near it. What for? Mama was outside and not coming in! They were going overboard.

"Why can't we see her?" I asked.

"Because you can't," Kim snapped.

Dee, Daniel, and Keke glared at Kim. They tried to control themselves.

"We gonna be together again someday," Dee reminded me. "I'm going to get you guys...I have a place and an income."

Kim chuckled. I was now seeing her mean side for sure. She thought because I was a kid I didn't see it. But I sure did.

"I wanna go back out to see Mama!" I said. I was getting ready to throw a fit.

"You're not stepping past my chair," Kim said.

"Calm down Quoya," Daniel told me. "Come here." He reached for me and held me tight. "We gonna do this the right way. They want us to act out. Don't do it."

Kim was looking at us amused. She decided to keep on talking. "You can't see your mother because she can't even maintain a case plan! That's why you can't go back home."

"But you don't have to talk to them like that...they're young. And don't say *nothin'* bout my mom you feel me?" Daniel said to her.

Kim's eyes looked evil. She was about to say something else, but stopped. Dee was about to say something too. She stopped when Kim stopped.

Kim didn't say anything else to us for the rest of the visit. She sat there with that same amused look. And like the first visit, we cried again when it was time to leave. I didn't know that we wouldn't see the three of them for a while. I also didn't know that Kim, along with Family Services of Nevada, was already hatching a plan.

In February of 1999, a month before my ninth birthday, Mama Mary told us we were moving to a much bigger home with more space.

We were very excited. She already had the house picked out. We went up to the new house and called shots on which rooms we'd have. This house wasn't on the Westside either. It was in North Las Vegas in a very nice neighborhood. Neat and quiet and tucked away.

Yes, this house was indeed much better! The carpets were a light fuzzy brown and the spotless white walls were eager to be filled with decoration. Every time we went to visit the new house, Mama Mary allowed us to bring one item to place in our rooms.

However, it was right after Valentine's Day when our caseworker called Mama Mary to tell us we'd be moving to a new foster home. I happened to be holding an unopened box of Valentine's sweet heart candy when she called to say she was on her way for a first visit.

Mama Mary looked calm. Tamera, Jimmy, and Russia looked calm too.

"We're leaving?" I looked at Mama Mary with disbelief and uncertainty.

"That's what Kim told me," she answered. She explained that Kim told her there was a nice couple on the Eastside who lived in a very nice house and they wanted to take us in.

I tried to understand what was happening. After all this time at Mama Mary's and being comfortable again, we had to leave to another foster home. So abruptly!

I had thought after we left Mama Mary's that you would be ready for us again. Maybe we just had to go to one more house. How many houses would it be?

"But what about the new house?" Images of bringing our items to the new house flashed through my mind.

Mama Mary looked kind of reluctant before speaking.

"Sequoya, Stan, Rae...I love all three of y'all so much. But I'm an old lady. I'm in my seventies. I already have Tamera and them who won't be able to return home. Your caseworker is working on getting you back home eventually."

I let this news sink in. Mama Mary was taking Tamera, Jimmy, Russia, and Baby Ronald with her to the new house. The rest of us were moving into another foster home.

There wasn't much time to elaborate on it. Kim arrived. I clutched my box of Valentine's sweet heart candy. Kim drove us five minutes away to the Vons Supermarket parking lot.

"I thought they lived on the Eastside," I pointed out.

"They do Sequoya. They're on this side right now. We figured it wouldn't hurt for you to meet them first."

She parked the car. A few minutes later, a nice SUV pulled up and parked a few cars down from us.

"That's Jerry and Tiwanda Banks. Very nice churchgoing people!"

We stepped out the car and walked towards them. Jerry and Tiwanda looked to be in their mid-thirties. Jerry was a little shorter than Tiwanda. They had larger than life smiles. I did notice that while Jerry continued to smile, Tiwanda's smile only lasted for about two seconds. She looked at the three of us next to Kim, sizing us up. Her expression looked impatient...and distant. As if she'd rather not be here.

"Say hi to the Banks!" Kim told us.

"Hi," we mumbled. I don't know about anybody else, but suddenly I felt the atmosphere change.

"Mary Williamson is of old age and she isn't able to handle seven children in her new home," she told the Banks as they nodded.

"We have three," Jerry informed us all, smiling at each of us. "Our oldest, Shontae, is twelve. She is ours. The other two children are Calen and Janice. A brother and sister around your ages."

As more information continued to come in from Jerry, I looked at his mean-looking wife.

Yes, that's what it was Mama. She was a mean lady and she wasn't hiding it either.

That was then, at that very moment, I felt I needed to do whatever I could to please Tiwanda Banks and be accepted by her. I didn't have a say on whether I went to her house or not. I didn't even want to go. But if I pleased her and she liked me, maybe she wouldn't be mean.

"This is a gift for you," I said shyly. I held out my box of candy to her. "It's unopened from yesterday."

Tiwanda looked at the box of candy. Then she looked at me.

"I don't eat candy," she said, very short and curt. She turned her head back toward her husband and Kim.

I looked down at the box of candy. I felt like I wanted to sink away somewhere. I looked at Rae and Stan, feeling that maybe if I looked at them, I wouldn't look so stupid in front of these strangers. I was praying that somehow Mama Mary would be allowed to take us with her. I didn't want to go with the Banks!

Dear Mama,

After this short impromptu meeting with the Banks at Vons Supermarket, I tried my best to enjoy our last few days with Mama Mary and the others! They were getting ready to move to a brand new house and they kept telling us to be happy because we were also moving to a nicer neighborhood as well. I didn't care what they said to encourage us. I didn't want to go. I didn't like Tiwanda and I already knew she didn't like us.

Days went by. I went to school. I didn't tell anyone I was leaving yet. I figured we had more time. Kim kept telling us she didn't know what day we were leaving; we just had to be prepared. Mama Mary and Tamera packed our belongings.

One day on the playground at recess, I sat on a bench with my best friend, Nisha Macdonald. The sun was shining brightly and I watched as the breeze blew her long silky black hair. As we laughed and carried on, an assistant from the office came out to the playground and called me over and told me I needed to come to the office.

"You in trouble?" Nisha asked.

"I don't know," I said, not revealing anything. I was surprised it was during the middle of the school day. Of all times!

"When you get back, let's play a game before recess is up," she said.

"Okay."

I didn't hug her goodbye. I didn't tell her I was leaving. I had an idea why I was being called into the office, but I thought I'd still get to finish the rest of this school day at Matt Kelly Elementary. Once in route to the Banks home, I didn't know that the next three months would feel like one hundred years.

"Don't call me Tiwanda. Call me Mom."

I looked up at the menacing lady as I nervously held my belongings. I had attempted to ask her, "Tiwanda, where do I put my stuff?" and before I could finish, her eyes had darkened even more.

"S-s-sorry," I stammered. "Mom, where do I put my stuff?"

She looked at Stan, Rae, and me as we stood with our few bags in the front room. She scowled and smirked at the same time. Kim had just left a few moments before and Tiwanda had smiled cheerfully as she watched her go. Now the smile was completely gone.

"This way," she ordered.

We hurriedly followed her past the elegant front room. As we turned right to climb the carpeted stairs, I surveyed the kitchen and living room. There was a big glass table. The chairs were glass as well. Another table, a plastic "playhouse" was off to the side by the glass patio doors that led to the groomed backyard. Two children sat there quietly eating a snack. Calen and Janice. They watched as we climbed the stairs.

Tiwanda made a left at the top where there were two small bedrooms and a bathroom.

"Kids' hallway," she said.

She entered the first room and told Stanford to start placing his items in the drawer. He would share this room with Calen. In the next room, Rae and I put our items away. Both rooms had bunk beds.

"Janice is on the bottom and you two are at the top."

I was irritated. I was already in an uncomfortable home. Now I would have to share the top bunk with Rae, and we sometimes bickered over little things.

"Come back downstairs when you done," Tiwanda instructed.

It didn't take us long to put away our stuff. The three of us timidly walked downstairs together. I looked to my right at the other side of the hallway. Straight across the girls' room to the opposite end was a master bedroom. Another small bedroom was to its right. I figured it was their daughter Shontae's room. Opposite that room was another bathroom.

We were instructed to sit at the playhouse table with Calen and Janice. They were now finished with a snack of juice boxes and pretzels, which Tiwanda also gave us. She didn't introduce us to them so the five of us just smiled at each other. There was already an instantaneous and uncomfortable feeling in this house and everyone knew it.

"Finish your homework in the garage," she told Calen and Janice, who threw their napkins and juice boxes in the trash. The dining room connected to the living room, which led to the garage door. We watched them step into the garage.

We have to do our homework in the garage?

Tiwanda watched as we finished our snack and threw our trash away. She instructed us to follow her to the garage. Once inside, I was a bit surprised. I thought it would have a car in it that took up space.

There were no cars in the garage, and carpeting had been installed. The walls were painted different colors. An assortment of toys filled several bins. Calen and Janice sat at another playhouse table doing their homework.

"Every morning you get ready, you wait in here," Tiwanda said. "Come down here to wait before you walk to school. After school, you walk home, place your backpack in here, and go to the dining room for your snack. Then come back in here and do your homework. After homework is done you find something to do in here. There's a lot of stuff in here. I'll take you to school and pick you up on your first couple of days so you know the way. It's not far."

We nodded.

"Your school is called Stanford Elementary," she continued. This time, a very brief smile was on her face. She looked at Stanford, who smiled too. We were going to a school that was also named Stanford. Interesting!

Tiwanda told us she would call us when it was time to eat dinner and she left us in the garage, which the door would always be open. We looked over at the light complexioned boy with very nice curly hair and the deep mocha brown skinned girl with short pigtails. You could still tell they were brother and sister. They seemed to come alive now that we weren't in front of Tiwanda.

We introduced ourselves. Calen told us he was five. Janice was six, which Rae would be soon. I was eight, but turning nine the following month. Stanford was seven. Shontae would be the oldest in the house at twelve.

We met Shontae at dinner. As soon as I saw her, I knew she wasn't Jerry and Tiwanda's biological daughter like they claimed she was. They had pictures of her all over the house as an infant. She was Oriental with olive skin. She had long jet black hair and slanted eyes. She was dressed very nicely and the colors of her hair accessories, clothes, and shoes always matched. When she spoke, she sounded "black." Her dialect was stronger than ours. I knew she wasn't their real daughter but I pretended she was. Shontae pretended as well. It was all she ever knew.

Shontae sat with Jerry and Tiwanda at the glass table while the rest of us sat at the playhouse table. Jerry had arrived home from work and smiled his signature wild smile when he saw us. Then he had gone upstairs. This was his routine. We wouldn't see him a lot, but when we did, it was a relief! He was always much nicer than his wife. If he was around, we knew we were saved for the time being.

Mama, I wish Tiwanda was the one who went to work every day and I wish Jerry was the one who stayed home.

EIGHT

We had left the happiness of Mama Mary's on the humble Westside. Now we were with a very mean lady on the fancy Eastside who I wanted to impress so badly. Everyone did. Even Shontae.

As the weeks went by, I felt like I was in a living nightmare. Every day felt like one long year. We were shown our new school, which would be our only haven during the day. I didn't make any friends. My grades were bad. After school Stan and I met outside and solemnly walked home in silence, not looking forward to arriving at the Banks. Sometimes we lollygagged. Then we got in trouble for arriving later than usual. Rae went to the same pre-school that Calen and Janice went to. Tiwanda dropped them off and picked them up every day.

She would get angry over the smallest things. One day, Shontae stood in front of her looking very scared. I happened to be walking downstairs to head to the garage. I stopped at the foot when I saw Tiwanda looking at Shontae, who was trying not to cry. Her slanted eyes were now almost to the size of little slits.

"So, you really thought you were slick huh?" Tiwanda spat at her. "Huh? What? You really thought you were slick?"

Shontae shook her head no.

"Tell me you thought you were slick! Open your stupid mouth and tell me!"

"No...I didn't think I was slick," Shontae pleaded.

As soon as Shontae had spoken as instructed to, Tiwanda lunged her right fist and punched Shontae square in her face. Blood spurted from her nose. She covered her nose and mouth and began to whimper muffled cries. I could tell she was really trying not to cry despite the pain she was in.

"Now you got blood on my carpet?" Tiwanda shouted. "*Clean this mess up!*" She shouted obscenities as Shontae rushed to the bathroom.

I tried to duck off into the garage real fast...but not fast enough.

"Sequoya," Tiwanda said.

Fear raced my heartbeat. My ears became hot. I should've never stood there to watch. I should've just walked straight to the garage.

"With your oversize head...eaves-dropping self. Come here."

I hung my head and walked over to her. She led me away from the blood stain.

"Stand right here. Don't move." Then she headed upstairs.

I stood there. I was shaking nervously. I was preparing myself for a blow to the face like Shontae had gotten. I watched as Shontae came back with a bucket and sponge. She had washed her face while she was in the bathroom. Now she kneeled on the carpet and began scrubbing. She didn't look in my direction.

I saw Tiwanda's fluffy house slippers coming down the stairs calmly. When she made it to the bottom she looked at Shontae for a minute. Satisfied, she walked over to me. My eyes were glued to her as she smiled a sinister smile. She was holding a white plastic cup.

What was in the cup? Was she going to poison me? Was she going to kill me?

"I have a special surprise for you," Tiwanda said with a very serious expression.

I didn't respond. Tears were already forming.

"You don't like surprises?" she scoffed.

I didn't say anything.

"What? Huh? You don't like surprises?"

I began to cry.

Tiwanda grabbed me by my shirt. Her eyes were on fire. She looked so evil. I began to lose my footing. Shontae continued to scrub the carpet as if we weren't there.

My body gave under me and I fell. Tiwanda sat the cup down for a second. Then she had the nerve to get on top me and pin me down! I couldn't move now. I cried louder.

She slapped me. Then she covered my mouth with her hand to stifle my screams. She allowed me to roll over on my side as she reached for the cup.

"Shut up!" she hissed. "Look at your surprise. I want you to drink it."

I didn't want to die Mama. I was about to die in that lady's house without ever seeing you again.

Tiwanda released her hand from my mouth and slapped me again to warn me not to scream. The sting from the second slap burned even more. I sat upright and controlled my stifled screams as she sat in front of me holding the cup and smiling.

"Well, you can't drink it," she laughed wickedly. "It's not liquid. It has to be eaten."

By now I could feel myself about to pee my pants.

She held the cup in front of my face. "Look!" she exclaimed, as if she was happy to give me a special surprise.

I looked down into the cup. I saw a spider with skinny wiry legs. It sat at the bottom of the cup. It wasn't moving. It was very still.

"No!" I screamed. "Tiwanda please! I'm sorry! I'm sorry!"

"Eat this spider!" she hissed, eyes rapidly flaming over.

She held me back down. I prayed Jerry would walk in the door at any moment to stop his wife. Shontae scrubbed away at the carpet. The others had crept from the garage and poked their heads from behind the living room wall.

"Please! Why?"

"Eat up," Tiwanda laughed again.

"I don't want to die!"

"Eat it!"

I screamed again. Tiwanda used one hand to hold me down and the other to steady the cup. We thrashed around. I couldn't understand why she was doing this to me! She enjoyed it too. She shouted obscenities as I screamed and cried.

Shontae grabbed the bucket and walked away. Tiwanda turned to glance at the wet spot. Satisfied, she didn't call after Shontae. Then she started laughing hysterically.

Her shoulders shook from laughing. She threw her head back and just laughed. We were very confused. The other kids bolted back to the garage.

"I'm going to save this spider for the next time you get on my nerves," Tiwanda said as she got up. "Now take yourself to the garage!"

I walked to the garage as I wiped my tears that had soaked my entire face and neck. I would do my absolute best to not make Tiwanda mad. I never wanted to see that spider. The fact that she saved it in a cup in her room made its presence known in the house. It was in the same house!

I prayed for God to please get us out.

I dealt with life as it went on. My ninth birthday came and went. I told Tiwanda ahead of time. I didn't tell her in hopes of getting a present. Or having her take it easy on me around the house. I only told her to strike up conversation one day on the way home from church.

"My birthday is March 26th," I said.

"That's cool," she stated. She kept her eyes on the road.

I continued my attempt to converse with her.

"Hey Mom..."

"What?"

"Did you know that your name kind of rhymes with one of my big sister's? Her name is Keyonna...and yours is Tiwanda. Keyonna and Tiwanda!"

"Cool."

I looked down at my hands as her cold distant tone reminded me that she wasn't my foster mom because she loved me. She was my foster mom on a business level only. I didn't understand that then. And she was so serious about us calling her "mom" instead of her first name. She was on a real power trip.

Tiwanda made sure we were fed and dressed nice. We were dressed our best with her. Our hair was done in different styles and hair accessories. Sometimes the hair accessory on my head would be so tight I would get a headache and try not to cry. The insides of my head were pounding. Shontae studied me one day as I put my hands to my head and moaned. She walked over to me and calmly loosened the hair scrunchie that was wound a few times. She loosened it just enough so that it stopped the aching, but was still secure in my head. Once she did that, it felt like a miracle! The tight feeling went away. I thought, *Now I know what to do in case someone does my hair too tight!*

We attended church every Sunday with the Banks. They smiled their usual broad smiles. Tiwanda chatted with every member of the congregation. The rest of us were silent and behaved. I knew it was all a facade Tiwanda put on. Back in the car on the way home her mean side returned.

We were always in trouble and couldn't understand why. Whenever she felt we did something bad, she would order us to "The Wall."

As soon as she said wall time, we scurried to the wall in the living room right before the stairs. Then we plastered our faces to the wall. If we turned around, she added more time.

"Fly," she would say.

We raised both arms in airplane position. We had to leave our arms in the air! As the minutes, and sometimes hours passed by, our arms ached. Terribly. We cried. We shook. But if we dare lowered them for a second, we were smacked and told to keep our arms up.

"Down," she would say, when she felt like giving our arms a rest.

We'd plop our arms down in relief! Sometimes she would laugh and say "fly" right after she said "down." The feeling of raising our arms right back up would make us want to die. She liked to play back and forth with the fly and down routine.

Sometimes she left us standing there as she went about her business in the house. That's when we timed it so we could lift our arms before she came back in the room. We were caught a few times, because she would creep back into the room without making noise.

After that, she assigned Shontae, Calen, or Janice to do a regular walk through on us. They reported to her if they caught our arms down.

"*Oooh* your arms are down!" one of the little ones would say.

"I'm telling my mom that you keep putting your arms down," Shontae would inform us.

Tiwanda would come in the room after hearing reports and smack or punch us. She would ask us if we liked being hit, or was wall time better? She made it sound like she was doing us a favor by putting us on wall time instead of beating us. She still did both, so what was the difference?

One time Stanford was subjected to stand at the wall for nearly twelve hours. He had dried crusted tears on his face. His ankles were bruised and had blisters on them. They split open.

"You got blood on my carpet?!" Tiwanda screamed.

How come Shontae and the others never got wall time?

Although there were times that she did in fact discipline the others, they never got it as bad as us, and they didn't get wall time. I figured since Shontae was their daughter she was special. I was trying to figure out what made Calen and Janice special as well. They weren't her children. Eventually, I caught a glimpse of why she may have treated them better.

She would exclaim how much she loved Calen and Janice.

"I just love y'all!" could be heard whenever she knew we could hear. As far as I was concerned, her voice didn't sound genuine to me. Her eyes would stare satanic holes into the rest of us, while smiling at Calen and Janice.

One day as we stood in the upstairs bathroom taking turns getting washed up, Tiwanda walked over and started her rant. Rae and Janice were sharing the bathroom mirror and sink. I watched as Tiwanda looked at the situation. She smirked.

"You're so pretty Janice!" she exclaimed.

Janice lit up as she finished brushing her teeth. Rae was silent and just continued at the sink.

"Pretty Janice! Go Janice...Go Janice Go Janice...Go Go...Go Janice!" Tiwanda was now clapping her hands and dancing to her own beat.

Janice grinned wide. As she finished up and walked out the bathroom, Tiwanda reached out and touched her gently on the shoulder. A touch that someone gave to someone when they really liked them. Then she looked back at Rae and me and smirked again.

"Janice is prettier than Raeannah," she said.

We didn't say anything. Tiwanda did this all the time. A grown adult was pitting two six-year-olds against each other. Such a shame.

Mama, we all knew that your baby girl Rae was the pretty one. Tiwanda was just very spiteful.

Tiwanda constantly glared at us. If she wasn't glaring, she pretended to pity us.

"Aw. Janice and Calen has a real mother who loves them and she's waiting for them to come back. I don't know about yours...that's too bad."

As usual we wouldn't say anything. There were times I was going to. Instead I would just say mean stuff back to her in my head. It sure felt good!

One night she took me along with her to drop Calen and Janice off somewhere. She dressed them both very nicely. Janice had on a cute striped dress and a bow in her hair. Calen had on slacks, a nice dress shirt, and a tie. Tiwanda combed his hair and sprayed it. His curls were very shiny. She also packed a duffel bag.

"You get to eat at Applebee's tonight!" she told them.

They smiled excitedly. I wasn't dressed or made up nice so I wondered why I was even coming with them.

On the way, she continued to tell Calen and Janice how special they were. I accidently glanced into her driver's mirror at one point. She was staring dead at me as she worshipped them. I looked away and studied the scenery out the window. I controlled myself from crying.

She pulled into the Applebee's parking lot. "Stay in the car," she told me.

The three of them stepped out and stood near the entrance. A few minutes later, a woman dressed in a tight black dress and heels walked toward them. Her hair was in a nice flat-ironed bob. She was an older version of Calen and Janice.

Calen jumped into her arms like he was spider man. His legs wrapped around her waist as she squeezed him so tightly. Janice hugged her mother's legs, waiting for her turn.

Tiwanda stood beside them. She was smiling widely as she handed the duffel bag to their mother. From inside the car I strained to hear what was being said. I understood that Calen and Janice were having a special dinner visit with their mother. They were spending the night with her as well. This visit would be a transition that would allow them to return home.

It angered me to see Tiwanda acting so happy for them. You could see her gums as she smiled too. Usually her happiness was fake but there was something underneath it this time that made it real. Something I hadn't noticed before until now.

As Tiwanda drove back home, we didn't say a word to each other. The silence always reminded me that she thought of me just as business. She made that well known. When I saw her talking and laughing with Calen and Janice's mother, I noticed that she was trying to impress. Yes, she was trying to impress their mother. Everything she did to make them look their best that night...the things she told them daily in front of us. She was trying to impress them too...not just the mother. I noticed that she respected them.

Respect. Yes, Mama, that's the word. Tiwanda respected their mother for some reason. She never hurt that lady's kids. It made sense now. But if only she met you. If she met you, she would have been very sorry she ever put hands on us!

Calen and Janice were quickly returned to their mother. We came home from school one afternoon to see they had left without a goodbye. Just like I left Mama Mary's without saying goodbye to Nisha.

With them now gone, Tiwanda didn't have to be nice to anyone! Shontae kept staying after school for academic activities. On the weekends, she jumped at every opportunity to go with Jerry to wherever he might be going. He invited us a few times, but Tiwanda quickly shut that down. Jerry didn't argue. He was glad to leave the house. I was envious of Shontae getting to escape. But Jerry was her father and he wasn't ours. He didn't have to fight for us.

We were headed to the garage one morning to wait until it was time to leave for school. Tiwanda had become very irate at something that Rae must have done. Something about grabbing the wrong shirt set out for her.

She was shouting obscenities with her hand wrapped around the back of Rae's neck! She kept shouting about how dumb and stupid my sister was. Rae was trying not to cry. I became angrier.

"With your over-sized head!" she shouted.

Tiwanda loved to call Rae and me that. We'd be eating at the playhouse table in dead silence. Tiwanda would stare at us with pure hatred.

When we looked at her, she would sneer and say, "Has anyone ever told you that you have a huge…gigantic…over-sized head?"

We didn't speak. We just sat there in silence.

On this particular day as I watched her berate my sister, I wanted to run up on her and start punching her over and over and over!

"Now take your big over-sized head and wait in the garage!" she screamed. She released her grip from Rae's neck. Then she grabbed her by the head and shoved her forward with all her strength, sending Rae tumbling and trying to regain her balance. There was no need for Rae to walk into the garage. Tiwanda had thrown her in there. She looked at the scene. Satisfied, she walked back upstairs.

The rest of us tried not to cry. We hated Tiwanda with a passion! She physically and mentally tormented us. She pushed us down the stairs when she saw us at the top. She was constantly calling us names. She was also speaking about a punisher called "Hank." We hadn't met Hank yet. Every day we feared this Hank, whoever he was. She told us we'd meet him very soon.

Rae got up from the floor. We stood around in the garage waiting to head to school. Thoughts of anger filled my whole being. I hated living at the Banks! How long would we be here? How many days had we already been here? It felt like years.

In front of the others and so Tiwanda couldn't hear me, I became bold. We rarely talked to each other about Tiwanda's cruelty. We just took it in silence. There were even times we feared talking to each other. We had to survive on our own and do our best not to get on her bad side.

"I hate Tiwanda," I said, calmly and boldly. The others perked up at my words. They stared at me.

"She's evil. Mean. A witch! But when Jerry comes home she pretends to be nice. Jerry probably doesn't like her either. I can't even see how he's with her!" My third-grade self was on a rant. I was talking grown folk talk, and at the same time releasing this built-up pain. I kept my voice low.

Eventually they talked too. We stood there venting. Each saying what we truly wanted to say about Tiwanda from our heart. Our faces were angry! We were hurt. This temporary venting helped us.

"She's a witch!" we kept saying. It felt so good to just say it out loud.

Right before it was time to leave for school, I told Stan and Rae that this was all between us. They nodded. We all knew that if this ever got back to Tiwanda, who knew if we'd even be alive.

My stomach lurched as Tiwanda came back into the garage to get us. She looked at us but she couldn't detect what had just taken place. I felt very satisfied. Like I got away with something. It made me feel great!

Rae got in the car to be driven to her school while Stan and I headed up the street. For some reason, I became scared again. Tiwanda was probably looking at the back of us. She could probably see that my walk was a little nervous. Could she tell that we just got done talking about her and calling her names like she did to us every day? Would she run us over with her SUV?

I tried to steady my walk. I couldn't wait to round the corner to be out of her sight! Stan looked a little nervous too. Tiwanda just had that fear implanted in us.

I wiped my sweaty palms on my pants as we rounded the corner.

"Stan…" I said.

He looked at me nervously.

"Remember…don't ever tell Tiwanda what we talked about okay?"

He nodded. We could see in each other's eyes that we now regretted it. Tiwanda's fearful aura had settled all over us. It was very creepy.

I relaxed during the school day. By the time Stanford and I were walking home I had forgotten about the morning rant.

We arrived at the Banks and ate our afternoon snack and then headed straight to the garage to do our homework. Rae was in there playing with the toys. Everything seemed cool at the moment. Tiwanda wasn't really paying attention to us.

Not too long after, we heard a loud booming voice in the house. At first I thought Jerry must have been very excited about something that happened during work. But the voice we heard was more dramatic. Not exciting like Jerry's. It was obnoxious. And terrorizing!

Loud footsteps thundered to the entrance of the garage. Our heads snapped to look at a tall menacing man. He had the same evil sneer as Tiwanda, but he was a male version. He was all muscle and wore a white muscle shirt with blue jeans and sneakers. He growled at us.

Wait…was that a growl? Yes, indeed. We were scared. Perhaps if we just stared at him with our frightful expressions, maybe he wouldn't hurt us.

This man didn't care that he was frightening us. He stomped all over the garage. Big stomps that froze us in our seats. He kept sneering. This man was probably Hank. Tiwanda kept talking about a punisher named Hank.

"So y'all think y'all can just come up in my sister's house and run it?" he shouted. "Huh?"

"No!" we all said at the same time.

"You *don't* run nothing!"

Tiwanda came into the garage and smiled her evil smile as he ranted. "Especially that one right there," she pointed at me.

The man looked at me and laughed.

"Are you gon' bust a grape?" he asked me.

I was confused. I didn't know what he meant. So, I feverishly shook my head no. They both laughed again.

"This is my brother," Tiwanda said smugly. "He just got out of prison. Do you know what that means?"

We didn't say anything.

"It means he will kill you."

We started to cry. I felt the room spinning.

"Did you really think you could just talk crap about me in my own house? While living here? Huh?"

How did she find out? Wow! I looked at Stan and Rae, but they had the same looks on their faces. They were wondering the same thing. There was no time to figure this out. We had to survive.

"So, I'm a witch Sequoya?" Tiwanda asked.

I shook my head no.

"So, let me get this straight. I was a witch this morning...but now I'm not?"

I looked at her and her brother pleadingly.

"Speak!"

"I'm sorry Tiwanda! Hank, I'm sorry!"

They both roared with laughter. "You still doing Hank?" he asked her.

"Yes."

They had a verbal communication with their eyes. Then they looked back at us. Her brother was very excited to speak now.

"I'm not Hank. I'm Donovan. Hank is a belt. He has been used on other children before you came here. He has killed many children...because Hank isn't a regular belt. He's huge. He's got marks from previous killings."

We sobbed even harder. Other children had been killed. And now we were next.

"Don't cry now!" Tiwanda spat. "I'm a witch remember?"

"You're not a witch!" we pleaded.

"Come on," she ordered. "Right now!"

We followed her out the garage and through the living room and up the stairs. Donovan was close behind us. I was so sick in my gut to feel him walking behind me. But I was about to be killed by Hank anyway. It was over for me.

Tiwanda stopped at the hall closet right above the foot of the stairs. We had to stand in a line. We watched with groping eyes as Donovan assisted Tiwanda with pulling down a very large belt. They had to remove a few items from on top of it because it had been hidden.

This belt was very large. It didn't look like a regular belt, just like Donovan had said. It was wide in both height and width. They both held one end of it. Maybe it was a belt for a huge animal. It was a tan color and had holes in it.

When they turned it over, we saw little sharp spikes on the inner side of it!

"These spikes are what killed the other kids," she informed us. "What you do is you pull your pants down and we strike you on the behind just a few lashes."

"And blood just spurts everywhere!" Donovan said. He raised his arms in the air.

"Yes," Tiwanda nodded. "Hank will splatter your blood all over these walls. We've had to repaint the walls because of the other kids' blood. And we'll have to paint them again after yours."

We whimpered as they described stories of Hank. I desperately wanted to ask them what happened to the parents of the kids when they found out their children had died.

Oh, my God, Mama! We had to stay alive for you!

We cried and kept saying sorry as Tiwanda and Donovan laughed.

"Shut up!" she shouted. "You ain't dying today! You will see Hank this weekend."

I didn't know what was going on. They placed Hank back at the top of the closet. We were ordered back to the garage. Donovan stomped around in there to intimidate us even more. I was relieved briefly when he left.

Dinner started. We sat at the play table. I nibbled on whatever I could because I had absolutely no appetite.

Shontae sat with her parents. I could tell that Tiwanda already turned the story around in her favor. Jerry had glared at us after he came in the dining room. He had always been the nicer one but he was never around. Occasionally he would intervene to calm her down when she bombarded him with ridiculous lies about how we behaved. This time, I knew he wasn't going to stick up for us.

Tiwanda got up and pulled out a big knife from one of the counter drawers. She looked at Jerry expectantly. He didn't say anything. Then Tiwanda walked over to our table proudly holding the knife.

"So, you guys been mistreating my wife?" Jerry's unusually mean voice asked us.

We didn't say anything.

"I'm really getting tired of coming home hearing her unhappy because of you!"

"I just can't take it anymore!" Tiwanda cried. "All I do is take care of them and they never listen to me!"

I looked at this crazy lady. Was she serious? Jerry couldn't see through this? We listened to everything Tiwanda told us. All we did was stay in the garage, on the wall, or at school!

"How about I just let her slice your throats!"

We could not believe this was Jerry saying this to us. We put our heads down and cried. Tiwanda walked over to us and held the knife in front of our faces. She told us to lift our heads up.

Stanford had a problem with his eyesight that we weren't aware of just yet. He always squinted a lot. He would lean his head forward and squint at whoever was talking to him. But every time he did this, Tiwanda always claimed that he was "crossing his eyes" at her.

"I told you about crossing your eyes at me boy!" she said. It only made him more nervous. He tried to be successful with looking at her, but he squinted because he couldn't help it.

Tiwanda used her free hand to backhand him as hard as she could. He fell off the bench and tumbled to the floor. Then she held the knife very close to Rae's neck as Stanford hurriedly picked himself back up.

"Give me a good reason why I shouldn't just slice your big over-sized head right off," Tiwanda addressed Rae.

Rae just sobbed. I looked at Jerry, who quickly looked away to avoid us. He was just going to let her do whatever.

"Can I slice her Jerry?" she asked her husband.

Jerry didn't respond. Tiwanda continued to wave the knife in each of our faces. I was looking at the sharp silver object...knowing any moment that she could just slice my life away.

Minutes passed with Tiwanda hovering over us. Her face had surely turned mad. Her eyes were bugged. Her clenched teeth were in a permanent taut expression.

"Come eat," Jerry finally instructed her.

It was cold and windy on the following evening when Tiwanda instructed Stan, Rae, and me to get in the SUV. Jerry and Shontae went on an outing. I knew this was the night that Tiwanda and her brother were going to kill us.

Tiwanda didn't speak to us as she breezed the car through the Eastside. If I thought her house was fancy, well these houses certainly showed out. You could see the view of the whole city from the hills. The lights of Las Vegas were beautiful. I was thinking about how the lights surrounded these houses that had loving families inside of them. Parents were most likely hugging their children and reading them a story this late. Or staying up to watch a movie and laughing. My fate was much different.

Tiwanda parked the car. The porch light turned on as an older lady opened the front door. I recognized her as Vera, who was Tiwanda's mother. We saw Vera at church a few times. But she never came to the house and we certainly had never been to hers. She was very snobbish.

"Go inside and don't say a word," Tiwanda instructed us.

We were too scared to greet Vera. She didn't mind that we didn't say hello because all she said was for us to take our shoes off at the door and to not sit on her furniture at all.

"*Hi* Mom!" Tiwanda said.

Vera gave an equally obnoxious greeting. Like mother like daughter. She closed the door and they looked at us briefly.

"Sit on the floor," Vera said. "Take your coats off and set them by your shoes."

She headed out the front room. Tiwanda followed her.

I anxiously looked around at her home décor but couldn't really focus because I heard a man's voice. Donovan was laughing from somewhere inside the house! Well here it was; we were finally in the place where we were going to die. I wished that Jerry had come with us to intervene.

The voices in the house were getting louder. It wasn't just Tiwanda and her mother and brother. It was very noisy back there. We sat on the living room floor in silence and glanced at each other. What else could we do now? Maybe we could run, and bolt down the hill. But they would probably hear the front door.

So, we just sat there for what seemed like ages. I was praying that Tiwanda and Donovan would forget about the whole thing. The adults were having a good time laughing and catching up. It was getting late and maybe Tiwanda would be tired.

Or so I thought. Donovan and Tiwanda came in the front room and he grinned his sinister smile.

"*Hank* sure has been waiting to see you!" he said.

"Get up and come to the room," Tiwanda said, and we stood up to follow them down the hall.

Cigarette smoke emanated from Vera's master bedroom. We stepped in the foggy room and the first thing I saw was a man on the bed holding a camera. It was pointed directly at us. There were about four adults. One of them was a woman. They were very comfortable on Vera's bed. Several of the adults were holding a clear pipe that they put to their mouths.

Then Vera came out the bathroom laughing. She walked out to the hallway. She made a grand exit as she waltzed in her fluffy bathrobe and slippers.

Donovan shut the door to the room and lined us up against the wall.

"Who Hank gonna kill first?" one of the men asked. The woman laughed as she smoked her cigarette.

"This one right here!" Tiwanda pointed at me.

I held my stomach and began crying, which made Stan and Rae cry too. The adults seemed to really think this was funny.

"You the main one huh?" the man asked me. His eyes were looking me up and down like he was trying to figure me out. They kept darting to my face and to my legs and to my feet and back to my face.

"I don't wanna die. Please!" I cried.

He opened his mouth and laughed so hard the bed shook. He threw his head back and almost pushed one of the other men off the bed. After he settled down, he then studied Stan and Rae.

"Get Hank," Tiwanda instructed Donovan, and he walked in the bathroom. Tiwanda must have transported Hank to Vera's while we were at school.

She ordered us to pull our pants down.

"Why?" I asked.

"You always got questions and something to say. Pull your pants down for Hank!"

We started screaming and crying when Donovan carried the huge tan colored belt out. He stood there cradling it, with the spikes part pointed towards us. The guy holding the camera angled the camera on Hank, then back to us again as we cried.

"*Pull* your pants down!"

We still hadn't pulled our pants down. We fearfully listened to everything Tiwanda told us, but this was just so frightening and unbelievable. No matter how scared we were, we just couldn't bring ourselves to strip in front of these adults. Hank with the spikes was just going to have to kill us how we were.

Donovan hovered around us with Hank for the longest time as we cried and held our pant buckles with all our might as Tiwanda tried to tug on them.

It was battle time and we fought to the exhaustion. The adults on the bed were laughing louder and louder. They really enjoyed this. These people were real sick to be laughing at children about to be murdered!

We squirmed…screamed…kicked…rolled around on the floor. We pleaded for our lives. The adults in the room laughed so hard and loud. The sound became very deafening. The smoke in the room choked me.

I just focused on trying to live. Why did Tiwanda hate us so much? What did we ever do to her? If she didn't want us, why did she become our foster parent? Just to kill us?

It was a miracle when someone pounded on the bedroom door.

Without missing a beat, Donovan walked to the bathroom with Hank. The guy holding the camera lowered it and sat up straight.

"Get off the floor!" Tiwanda hissed at us. "Stand up and stop crying! You are disturbing my mother!"

We bolted up. Tiwanda walked us in the bathroom, where Donovan was walking out after he placed Hank in the sink underneath the cabinet.

"Use the bathroom and wash your faces. Shut up!"

Tiwanda stood outside the bathroom door but left it cracked.

As I sat on the toilet I wasn't surprised to discover that I had already peed my pants. My heart was still pounding and my ears still ringing. But somehow, I knew we had escaped Hank for the time being.

After we cleaned ourselves up, we saw the adults had opened the screen door in the bedroom. They were outside on the patio to continue their cigarette smoking. No one was laughing anymore and the cold air from outside was clearing the smoke out.

Tiwanda told us to go back in the living room and put our shoes and coats on because it was late and we had to get home to get to bed.

"I'm going to let you guys slide this time," she whispered to us as we walked down the hallway. "We aren't going to kill you. Hank will stay over here. You better be grateful! I'm giving you a second chance."

We nodded. There was nothing to say. But somewhere deep in her voice, I could detect a little bit of worry. Was she sorry? Or was she scared?

Dear Mama,

In the end, they never beat us with Hank. Tiwanda was a little nicer to us for a few days after that. We still didn't trust her. And sure enough, she went right back to being who she was. She was always so nasty when Jerry and Shontae weren't there. But when Jerry was around, she put on her usual fake act and cried about us mistreating her.

She was just so evil and spiteful! She picked the pettiest fights with us about things we didn't understand. We were kids. Not grownups! One time she left and got her hair done in a braided updo style. It looked very nice. When she walked in the door she didn't say anything to us and we didn't say anything back. By this time, we didn't speak until we were spoken to. And there were many days of getting ready for school, going to school, coming home to do homework in the garage, eating dinner, and going to bed. She mumbled mean things to us for no reason. So, we tried to be nonexistent and avoid her. But on this day, she looked very angry as she watched us eat our snack at the table.

Needing to vent on us as usual, she decided to use Rae.

"What you say?" she asked Rae.

Rae snapped her head up in fear, but also with disgust in her eyes that only a tired little girl would have at a despicable human being. Even at her young age she was already forming a disdainful look she would give at her oppressors, or anyone who pissed her off.

"What you say? Huh?"

"Nothing," Rae said. "I'm eating my snack."

"*What you say?*"

By now we were really confused.

"I don't know," Rae said. "I'm just eating."

Tiwanda crossed her arms and glared at Rae.

"Stupid bum. Do you see my hair? I got my hair done today you bum. What do you say?"

"Oh…your hair looks nice Mom…" Rae said, looking puzzled.

Tiwanda clacked her teeth together and continued to glare at her. "I know *that's* right!" she shouted. Then she turned away from us and stomped upstairs.

Mama, what in the world was the matter with this lady? She was upset because she got her hair done and we didn't tell her she looked nice? First of all, she was so cruel and abusive so of course we didn't speak to her! Anything we said or did was grounds for punishment. Every time I tried to be nice to her she responded very shortly and rude. Something was indeed wrong with her if she felt she needed validation from children.

One day I sat in our room on the bottom bunk waiting for her to call us for dinner. From the upstairs window, I could see Tiwanda's backyard and over the fence into another person's yard. Beyond that I could see the mountains on the Eastside. The sun was still out but would be setting soon. It looked peaceful and beautiful out there. Whoever was out there was free! I wasn't. I was locked into Tiwanda's cruelty. Though it had only been a few short months, I felt many years had gone by.

As I looked out the window I stared crying. Tears rolled down my cheeks as I realized Tiwanda was going to make her threat come true. She knew what our worst fear was. Without us even telling her, she already knew. She always boasted about it.

"You guys are going to be here until the day you graduate!" she would sneer. "How do you like that? That means you're here forever!"

We had a long way to go Mama. But as I looked out the window to what freedom looked like, I decided to pray. I prayed to God for a release from the Banks home. I cried and prayed as the tears flowed. I prayed to be free someday. It seemed impossible. Like a far off dream.

I would soon discover that God has the utmost place in His heart for His children.

NINE

I was called into the front office at school. My class was studying these packets to prepare for a test. We were spending Monday through Thursday reading the big packets, and then Friday was our test. It was only Tuesday.

"Sequoya," my teacher said as she set the phone down. "The principal would like to see you. Don't worry honey, you're not in trouble."

I walked to the office where the principal invited me into her cubicle. I took a seat. Stanford was seated there too.

"Tiwanda and Jerry Banks are your foster parents I see," she thumbed through a file she was holding.

"Yes," I said. I wondered what was going on now. I already knew my grades were beyond bad. Stanford's grades were bad too.

"I have some news for you. You'll be moving into a new foster home tomorrow."

"What?" I asked. I looked at her like she was lying. This had to be a joke.

"Both of you…and your sister Raeannah…you are to leave tomorrow afternoon according to your caseworker, Kim Folson."

"What foster home are we going to?"

"Um…I'm not sure honey. From what I'm looking at…it doesn't seem to be too far away. But you'll be switching schools. The other school is called Mountain View Elementary."

I soaked all this information in. Wow! We were leaving! God heard my prayers and He answered me!

"So be prepared to leave class tomorrow afternoon."

Stanford and I walked home from school with such happiness. We were the happiest kids alive in this moment as we smiled at each other and looked at the sky and thanked God. But we made sure to look and act normal as we rounded the corner. Obviously, Tiwanda must know we were leaving but we still wanted to keep calm and not show how happy we were.

We walked in the door and set our backpacks in the garage then headed to the dining room with Rae to eat our snack. Tiwanda was still upstairs.

"We're leaving to a new foster home tomorrow," I whispered to Rae.

"I know. I heard Tiwanda talking on the phone."

We shut our mouths when we heard Tiwanda walking down the stairs. She looked at us with her usual sneer.

"You *bums* are finally getting outta my house tomorrow. How exciting! To *another* foster home...not with your mother. Hmmm, I wonder why? You will bounce from home to home. How sad!"

She went to the kitchen to prepare dinner. She seemed angrier on this day. I didn't care one bit. All I knew was that we were leaving!

The next day, I floated into the school with a new confidence. But I still wouldn't be fully relaxed until we were officially moved out of the house. We still had to get our things when we left the school in the afternoon.

Still, we were leaving. There was hope on the horizon!

I waited all day. I impatiently sat through lunch and recess. I daydreamed at my desk as the afternoon passed. My teacher didn't give me a study packet to work on like everyone else. I got to read a book instead. I was so happy I didn't have to take that test on Friday!

Finally, the phone in the classroom rang! My teacher glanced at me as she walked over and picked the receiver up. When she sat it back down, I stood up.

"Sequoya, today is not your last day. I'm told that you'll be leaving Friday instead."

What? The horror on my face clearly showed. I slumped down in my seat as she plopped a study packet on my desk. I didn't open it. I just stared down at it. I realized that I had to face Tiwanda for two more days. But if I made it this far, I certainly could do it!

We walked on eggshells back at the Banks house those last couple of days. Tiwanda wasn't physical with us. That was a miracle. She was still very menacing with her sneers and words.

On Friday at school, I decided to be patient and relax. Just in case I was told bad news again. I participated in class activities and talked a lot with my classmates, whom I hadn't interacted with since being the new girl a few months before. I was in *every* conversation, even if I didn't know what anyone was talking about.

By late afternoon when the phone in the classroom rang, I didn't budge. I kept my head down and studied the packet. We had ten minutes left before our teacher took the packets away and handed us our test.

She walked over to my desk. I didn't look up until she spoke.

"Sequoya," she said softly. "Your caseworker just called the school. You're leaving today. She'll be here shortly. Get your things."

I stood up and walked into her embrace as she held her arms out. I never spoke to my teacher about anything, but I always felt she knew something was going on at the Banks. A lot of times I caught her looking at me with sadness. Then she would look away. She was always very nice to me. She never scolded me for my bad grades or for getting answers wrong when I was called to the marker board.

Everyone muttered their goodbyes as I quickly cleaned out my desk. Before I walked out the door, I turned back around. My teacher smiled.

I walked through the hall anxiously. The principal said her goodbye to us and informed us that Kim was picking us up at the Banks instead, so to go ahead and walk back.

"Good luck!" she said.

We didn't run like we wanted to. We walked all the way back to Tiwanda's with major legwork going on! We were so happy we were leaving. We were also in disbelief.

As we approached the house, the sight of Kim's car was confirmation of this reality! The front door was wide open.

"They here," Tiwanda's voice called from inside. It was fake and high pitched. More fake than usual...because she didn't want to reveal her true nature in front of Kim.

We walked in to see Kim talking to Tiwanda. Raeannah was trying to cram as much of her stuff inside her bag as she could. Jerry and Shontae weren't there.

"Come on! Hurry," Kim greeted us. I was happy she was with us on our last day at the Banks. Who knew if Tiwanda would have tried to kill us?

We didn't have to think twice about gathering our bags. Tiwanda was roaming around acting as if everything had always been fine. But her eyes told something different.

Upstairs, she mumbled things under her breath.

"You should be happy. I sure am!" she was saying. Kim was downstairs so she didn't hear anything.

We had very little time with Kim rushing us. The excitement and anticipation was too much for us to grab everything. Kim told us we'd return later to get everything. I really wanted my miniature laptop that I received while at Mama Mary's. It was built to only play games on it but I felt grown up as I liked to pretend it was a real laptop.

Tiwanda waved her hand in the air with one last show of fakeness as we got in Kim's car. We waved back. I drew in my breath as Kim's car did the U-turn away from the Banks home. We didn't turn around to look. Whew! We were gone!

I looked in Rae's bag to see if she had my miniature laptop. I had whispered to her to get it from the garage. I saw that she hadn't.

"Rae, I thought you grabbed it!" I groaned.

"I couldn't! Tiwanda wouldn't let me get all our stuff!"

"I left my Woody doll," Stan added. I knew he was a little irritated about that because the Woody doll was life sized, just as big as us. He got that at Mama Mary's as well.

Kim told us that grabbing everything wasn't a necessity.

"But if it's that important, I will take you guys back to get everything later like I said," she reassured us.

We were approaching an area closer to the mountains. I could see the copper and brown structures in the distance. A firm blue sky was the backdrop. So beautiful.

The houses were getting bigger. The lawns more spacious. The neighborhoods more lavish. I was full of anticipation...but still thinking about the Banks. Was it really over? Had it only been three months? How would it be when we returned to get the rest of our stuff? Most of all, what would be next for us?

We turned on a side street and passed a church before making a right onto Brynehurst Drive. Kim stopped at the fourth house. I looked at our surroundings. Big houses neatly lined behind full sidewalks, accompanied by tall trees. The mountains stood a little far off. It looked like we were so close that maybe it was just a walk away. I wasn't too sure.

We were getting out the car when the front door to the house opened. For some reason, I had prepared myself for another Tiwanda. I was surprised when a lady stepped out with her arms outstretched. The image of Tiwanda quickly vanished. This was not a Tiwanda, but I couldn't quite name it. I wasn't scared either.

"*Hey y'all!*" she exclaimed. Her smile showed neat white teeth. Her face was done in flawless makeup and her hair styled down her shoulders. She wore a fancy outfit and heels. Her nails were long and the colors glistened when the sun hit them.

We just stared at this beautiful lady in awe. Kim motioned for us to walk, so we took faithful steps forward.

"Come on in y'all!" she said.

We smiled shyly as she embraced each of us.

"Oh, my goodness little girl, you look *just* like Ben!" she said, looking at Rae.

This confused us, but we didn't have the understanding nor the time to figure what she meant. Once inside, we were in awe again.

We had noticed from the outside that this was the biggest house we had yet to live in, but we didn't expect the inside to be so nice. Much nicer than the Banks. The ceiling in the front living room was very high. The carpet was smooth. The walls neatly decorated with odd objects, mirrors, and accompanied with family pictures. The large lamp in the corner had about a hundred tiny bulbs that illuminated the front room areas. There was a vase tree in another corner. On its branches hung several stuffed animals. A jungle scene. One of them was a monkey with long arms.

"Go on and look!" the lady said. "This is Mama Benita's house. I'm y'all Mama Benita!"

Kim was smiling. So were we. We dropped our bags and skipped past the wall-sized mirrors leading to the kitchen and dining room area. Delicious canopies of fruit were on the counter. Shiny black seating stools lined the counter. The eating table in the dining room was stone. A fireplace was in the back of the dining room.

The dining room led us to the backyard patio where Benita proudly showed us the Jacuzzi. It needed to be cleaned out. It was full of cobwebs and spiders.

"Don't worry; we'll get it up and running!" she said.

The thing we have always loved about Benita's was her backyard. The left side yard didn't have any grass. The ground's surface was paved with rocks. Hence, we nicknamed it the "Rock Yard." In the middle of this yard sat an old convertible that no one used anymore. Benita told us it belonged to one of her sons. It would serve as a favorite past time. We made believe we were driving all over the world.

Benita and Kim led us back inside.

"Y'all have to see y'all room and the upstairs!"

We thundered up the stairs. Our room was in the middle of the hallway. It was small but it was so nice! Benita told us it used to be an upstairs sitting room. We had our own television and walk-in closet. There was a bunk bed. Rae and I would share the bottom.

Stan would have the top. We checked out our bathroom and then Benita led us down the hall.

"Now this is the guest room!" she said, beaming with pride. "Occasionally y'all can take turns staying in here...only if you're behaved!"

This was the first king-sized bed I'd ever seen. The headboard had carved designs in it. A large screen television stood on a plaque that matched the headboard's design. The wall decorations were different from the downstairs. The colors were darker and more drastic, same for the curtains and bedspread. The décor was just so special. There were tiny statues and paintings of African people. Everything in the room was African. Hence the nickname for this room would be the "African Room."

Benita's room was another story alone. It was the largest bedroom. She had a vanity station outside her spacious bathroom. The headboard to her bed had shelves and mirrors. Her television stood on a towering case. Dozens of her high heels and organized outfits were well stocked in her closet. Her room led out to a balcony that served as a favorite spot. We could look down over the other houses and feel like we were on top of the world. In the distance we could see the top of the Stratosphere Tower on the Las Vegas Strip. At night, the lights of this city sparkled with promises.

When Kim left us on our first day at Benita's, we were already comfortable. We were talking and laughing with Benita. We didn't say it aloud, but our pain that we had endured at the Banks was over. We just felt it. It was a miracle to us.

Benita was kind of like Mama Mary! We instantly felt safe.

She didn't mind telling us her age. She proudly put one hand on her hip and used her other hand to flip her hair, claiming she was "only about fifty-six." She certainly didn't look like it. She looked much younger!

She pointed to her pictures on the wall. It was a grand timeline of her journey. We saw her at various stages in her life. She was very well traveled! She had taken many exotic trips and cruises and attended many shows. In each picture, her outfits and hair were extravagant. At times, dramatic. She stole the show everywhere she went. She was a natural trendsetter. She posed with a confidence I wanted to have.

Dear Mama,
So that's how we met Benita Burkes, who would be our third and last foster parent. She's the one in the beginning of this story who was with us when we met the Carlons from New York. Little did we know, you and Benita already knew of each other. Our first day at this house set the tone for the kind of relationship we had with Benita. It was May of 1999, and for the time being we enjoyed our comfort. We had no clue what would take place a year later.

There was a problem enrolling us in school during the last couple of weeks. Benita seemed irritated at the school system. Our new school suggested we wait until August since the school year was basically ending.

"And I don't think y'all wanna go back to Stanford," Benita chuckled to us. "I'm not gonna have y'all near that area again. I'll handle it."

Whatever she did worked, because she told us it was now summertime for us. We'd go back to school in August.

Benita was a hairstylist and she commuted to the Westside every day to work in a salon. Mama, remember I told you that we went to get our hair done at a salon while we lived with Mama Mary? Well guess what? One of the ladies who worked there happened to be Benita!

You see, Benita confided in us about something.
Ben Slank!
I guess Benita and Ben Slank dated each other way back in the day...before he met you. Benita also told us that she knew you and that you knew her.

Mama, I don't know about all of that...I was just a child. But I instantly saw the advantage in this situation. I asked Benita if she could take us to see you since she knew you! And if she could call Ben and have him bring Daniel and Keyonna over! It had been a long time since we saw them.

"We'll see," Benita had laughed. "We'll see. Your brother and sister's dad don't even know I have you guys as my foster kids."
"Why?"
"Because I haven't told him yet."
"Oh...well when are you going to?"
"You ask too many questions than you actually should Miss Sequoya! You look like your mother too."
I didn't say anything. But I missed my Mama so much!

Shortly after arriving, Kim took us back to Tiwanda and Jerry's to grab the rest of our stuff. We weren't scared at all. We knew we were safe. To our surprise, we saw two new foster children there! They were two boys who were a little older than us. Yet they still had to sit at the play table. They were quiet and looked at us with curiosity. I felt sorry for them. I said a quick prayer in my head that God would set them free as he did for us.

Tiwanda offered us cake for a snack. We stood near the counter eating the cake after we had retrieved our things. Kim stepped outside to take a call. Tiwanda looked at us with hatred when she knew Kim couldn't see. That same sneering look.

"Raeannah," she said, and Rae looked at her.
"Yes Tiwanda?"
Tiwanda smirked a minute before speaking.
"Never mind...it's just you gobbling that cake like you ain't never ate before...with your big over-sized head!" She looked and sounded so happy just to say this to Rae again.

We didn't say anything. We didn't flinch. We were free and she couldn't harm us! She knew it too, because after taunting us again she didn't say another word. She was just a bitter, jealous woman. She was ill.

Benita's children were all grown up. Her two daughters were the ones we met. Nene was a beautiful woman just like her mother. She had honey golden skin and a voluptuous figure. Her bottom stuck out and her smile was both pretty and calculating. Some would call it devious. Men stopped in their tracks to stare at her. She wore it proudly.

She watched us a few days out the week while Benita worked. She had two daughters named Monie and Tiara, who were a little older than me. They looked nothing like their mother. They were irritated in public whenever someone asked, "Is she really your mom?"

If Nene wasn't watching us, she was out exploring life, or flying back and forth from Texas and Nevada. Whenever she came around and took us out with her, I admit I felt special to be in her presence. The way men tripped over her was funny and exciting for a nine-year-old girl like me who had yet to understand men.

It wasn't just the men because I wasn't focused on that. It was also Nene's immense confidence. And the way she talked to me like I was an adult, not a child. Her voice was sultry and she fascinated me with tales of men who chased her, even all the way back in her youth.

"Sequoya," she said one time as she took us to the park. Instead of playing with the other kids I sat next to her at adjoining swings. "You see that man over there looking at me?"

I looked at a man who was looking in our direction. When he caught us looking, he looked down in a respectful manner. Then he lifted his head back up to look into Nene's eyes again. He was on her!

"Yes," I said.

"He wants me *so* bad Sequoya! Just look at him! He's been looking ever since we got here. He's not gonna stop till he gets my number."

I looked back and forth from the man to Nene. They had some serious eye language going on.

"When a man wants you...he will do the most at times," she continued. "When I was little...I really liked this one boy a lot...he really liked me too...he loved me Sequoya."

Nene's eyes began to have a faraway look to them as she glanced away from the man invading her with his deep stares. Her voice was also turning into her signature sultry tone. It made her sound like both a young girl and a woman at the same time. Whenever she talked like this I would study her.

"This one boy at my old school really liked me a lot too," I chimed in, thinking of the little kid whose heart I broke back at Matt Kelly Elementary.

"But this boy Sequoya was *in love* with me!" Nene shook her head. "He chased me Sequoya..."

I was quiet as I listened. She was now using her finger to twirl at a strand of her shoulder length freshly flat-ironed hair. Everything she did was so fascinating.

"After school, he followed me and said he liked me. I played like I didn't like him back. It's a tactic you have to learn at times...to protect yourself in the end...but it doesn't always work like that."

"What did he do when you acted like you didn't like him?"

"Girl! He couldn't believe it. He chased me because I started to run!"

"Why were you running?"

"Sometimes you have to do stuff like that Sequoya...you will see when you get older. But let me tell you...he chased me all the way from the school and down a hill and we ended up at a park kind of like this one."

"What happened next?"

"Nothing. I never told him that I liked him back. I broke his heart."

"Why didn't you tell him?"

"I don't know," Nene shrugged. "Sometimes when you're young...you're afraid to go for what's in your heart. But when you look back on it, you have a sense of peace because it was meant to teach you something."

I didn't exactly understand everything she was saying.

"Excuse me ma'am." The man who had been staring at Nene approached us at the swings.

I pretended to look at something interesting in the grass. I really tried to go unnoticed whenever a man was talking to Nene, because I liked to be around to witness these exchanges.

"Hi," Nene answered.

She smiled her beautiful and calculating smile at him.

Occasionally Benita dropped us off with her other daughter named Michelle. She lived in a rundown apartment complex on the Northside. Michelle had pre-teens who were already out exploring the world so we rarely saw them.

We called her Shelle instead of Michelle. Unlike Nene, who was thick with a big bottom, Shelle was thin and leggy, with dark skin. She wore her hair in long braids. She was older than Nene. I never saw them both in one place at the same time, but Nene always mentioned her older sister. It wasn't always positive.

"Sequoya," Nene said one time. "Look." She had raced in Benita's house out of breath.

Nene held a Polaroid picture out to me. I saw both Shelle and Nene in the same picture. Other people were in the picture too. A group pose. The women were squatting on the ground in sexy poses and the men were throwing up hand signs.

"You and Shelle look pretty!" I said.

"I just ran into her when I passed through the neighborhood," Nene said. "Someone wanted to take a picture of all of us…"

"I like it," I said.

Nene looked at the picture again with sadness.

"What's wrong Nene?"

"Look at the picture Sequoya…"

I looked.

"You don't see it?"

"See what?"

"Look at Shelle," she insisted.

I studied the picture again. Shelle didn't come out as clear as the others in the picture, but I figured it was the glare of the sun or something.

"She is fading away," Nene said.

"Fading away?" I was confused.

"Sequoya," she said, sighing. "Shelle is on drugs. That's why she's so skinny. And when the guy took the picture...when it first printed out...I swear to *everything* I love, Shelle was in the picture for *just* a minute. Then she vanished!"

"Why?" I was becoming paranoid again. My young mind was always on standby.

"Because it symbolizes her drug use. The drugs are taking her away."

I didn't understand anything but I listened.

"She's fading from the picture quickly...she's dying."

As Nene ambled on about her sister's drug use, I was quiet. I didn't understand anything at all.

Later when I was getting ready for bed, I went into Benita's room and told her about Shelle. I was worried.

Benita grunted.

"Shelle is gonna be okay," she said. "Nene has no place to talk. They're both doing the same things."

Again, I didn't understand anything, so I was silent.

Even though Nene lived in a better place than Shelle, I got bored at Nene's because she only talked to us for a second then she would leave us with her daughters Monie and Tiara. They bossed us around. Monie liked to talk about her mother's looks compared to hers.

"I didn't use to be fat," she said. We were in Nene's living room. Monie had carried a photo album from the basement and was thumbing through it.

She showed me her baby and toddler pictures. She was tiny with a huge smile. I noticed that her smile wasn't happy like that anymore. To me, it was now fake and mean with her bossiness. She had changed in just a few short years. I didn't ask her why she was so big now.

"Tiara is lighter than me...because her dad is light skinned," she pointed out.

"You and Shelle came out like Benita," I said.

"My dad and I are the same color that's why," she explained.

I had seen her father before. He was tall with an average build. He wore baggy coats and jeans with timberlands. He always seemed quiet when I saw him.

I couldn't help feeling sorry for Monie as I watched her look at her old pictures. I wished she could go back and look the same as well because she was so depressed about it. But I didn't know what to say.

Later, we were playing outside in the driveway when Nene arrived back home. She hopped out of her jeep with a huge smile on her face. She was wearing a tiny white tank top and very small denim shorts that looked like underwear because they were so tight. Where on earth was she coming from?

"Guess what y'all!" she exclaimed. She grabbed Monie in a hug.

I perked up. Any news that Nene brought with her was always so exciting.

"I'm going to be in a music video!"

We jumped up and down with Nene to celebrate her excitement. I spent a lot of time watching music videos from the big screen television in the African Room. Nene sure looked like she would fit perfectly in them.

"Is it going to be on BET?" I asked.

"Yes!"

I was in such awe of Nene.

Benita sent us to a day camp for the remaining five weeks of summer before school started. This was easier for her than deciding which of her daughters' houses we were going to. There were times we arrived at Shelle's and she wasn't there so Benita took us to the salon with her. We played in the backyard of the salon on the

Westside of town, which wasn't as pleasant as our side of town. But every time I was on the Westside, I knew we were only a few blocks from Matt Kelly Elementary, and Mama Mary's old house. I knew she had moved into a better neighborhood with Tamera, Jimmy, Russia, and Baby Ronald. I also wondered if Nisha Macdonald ever thought of me...how suddenly I left school during recess and never came back.

Summer camp was a highlight for us! Every morning we dressed and ran downstairs to eat breakfast while Benita was still getting ready. She already had a yummy lunch packed for each of us. Then she drove us over to a community center. Once there, we checked in and reported to the gymnasium with many other kids. We were divided into groups for most of the day but everyone knew someone from another group. Stan, Rae, and I quickly made new friends.

There were competitions being held. Which group could write and act out the best commercial? Which group could perform the best song for talent day? It was so funny how every girl knew lyrics to catchy tunes such as "Bills Bills Bills" by Destiny's Child and "Where My Girls At?" by 702.

Thursday afternoons were movie time. A sea of children crowded the stage and laid on mats to watch the latest movie on VHS while we snacked on the flaming Hot Mama Pickles.

Every Friday, everyone was ecstatic because that meant a field trip to Wet & Wild Las Vegas, the infamous waterpark located on the Strip. That waterpark was everything! Each Friday was just as exciting as the last and we never tired of it. Wet & Wild was a place that brought so much joy to Las Vegas residents and its tourists for many decades before being sold and torn down for yet another casino.

I was in the fourth grade now. Benita told us that two kids from down the street would walk with us. She left to start her commute to work and we stood in the driveway and saw two kids walking from one of the houses that was kiddy corner to us. I hadn't seen any kids at that house all summer so I was surprised.

The girl was around Rae's age and the boy was around me and Stan's age. The girl was walking a sassy confident walk. She seemed a little more advanced than Rae and I. Her hair was in long braided plats with colorful barrettes that matched her outfit. The boy was confident too but seemed a little bit dorky to me. He was dressed nicely as well.

"Hi!" she said. "We're walking to school with you guys since we all go to the same school."

She studied each of us carefully and glanced at our house.

"That lady is your foster mom?"

"Yes," I confirmed.

"What's your names?"

"Sequoya."

"Sequoya?" she said, shocked. "That's my name too!"

"We have the same name!" I was in awe. I never met anyone else who had my name before.

"Except I don't have an S sound. I have a Shhha sound! It's spelled S-h-a-q-u-o-i-a. Shaquoia."

"Shaquoia. Well mine is S-e-q-u-o-y-a."

"This my brother Tyree."

After introductions were made, Shaquoia looked us over again.

"Y'all look nice. That means you match. You know how to dress."

"Thanks," I said, noticing the look of approval on her face.

She looked very serious. Even though I was older, for some reason I felt like the younger one. This first meeting would start an everyday ritual where Shaquoia would check to see if we were matching, even on the weekends. If she happened to catch us on a day that our attire wasn't fitting in her eyes, she would let us know. It was very important to her.

"How long y'all been here?" Tyree asked.

"Before the summer started," I answered.

"Oh, you came just when we went to our dad's."

"Yeah, every summer we go to our dad's," Shaquoia explained. "He lives in California."

Mountain View Elementary was a very nice school on the Eastside. The walkways and fields were neatly groomed and not a trace of garbage litter was on the ground. This was the most beautiful school we attended. Very colorful. The teachers walked around very happy. They enjoyed their job.

My teacher was named Ms. Shagloff. She was the youngest teacher at Mountain View while the other teachers were much older. She seemed nervous and jittery at first, because she told us this was her first teaching job she had landed. She became more animated and comfortable during story time when she read *Harry Potter and the Goblet of Fire* out loud to us. I felt I was right there in the story as she read it with such character in her voice. The whole room was stone silent and listening as she read.

Stanford's teacher wasn't as memorable. Rae's teacher was Mrs. Applebee. We giggled and thought about the restaurant and she laughed saying she got that a lot.

Every day after school we stopped at Mrs. Applebee's classroom to pick Rae up since her class was closer to the front of the school. Mrs. Applebee's desk had blocks with big letters that spelled her name, along with a radio. She always had the same song on repeat. The words to that song would resonate within my soul and give me such hope.

> *When you want it the most there's no easy way out*
> *When you're ready to go and your heart's left in doubt*
> *Don't give up on your faith*
> *Love comes to those who believe it*
> *And that's the way it is*

For me, that song meant to never give up on my dreams and what I desired out of life. And I desired more than anything to be with my Mama.

One day we arrived home from school to see a Caucasian teenager at the dining room table looking very moody.

Her straight black hair was pulled into a bun at the nape of her neck. This girl was rail thin but still dressed in tight clothes that accentuated her emaciated body. She looked at us as we walked in the dining room. Her huge eyes surveyed us with slight interest, then looked bored, as she was listening to Benita speak.

"This is Crystal," Benita told us. "Now, she's older than you all. She's fifteen. She goes to El Dorado High School. She needs her space so don't disturb her. She's going to be staying in the African Room."

"Hi," we said to her, and she quietly said it back.

"I already told her about y'all. Okay I have to get back to the salon. I put your food in the oven. Just pull it out and heat it up in the microwave later."

Benita grabbed her keys and headed out the door.

"Crystal," she called again before leaving, "The house phone is good just be mindful of long distance calling like I told you."

"Okay," Crystal answered with a clipped response.

After Benita left there was an awkward silence. We looked at Crystal with curiosity. She looked at us the same. We told her our names and she smiled politely.

Then she walked in the living room and grabbed the house phone. Before heading up the stairs, she said, "I'm going to be in my room." We heard the door to the African Room close.

We looked at each other. Benita told us not to disturb her so we didn't. We went outside to play with Tyree and Shaquoia. We told them about Crystal.

"Weird," Shaquoia shrugged her shoulders. "Does your foster mom get all colors of kids?"

"Yeah," I answered. "She told us one time she had two Mexican sisters named Aerin and Aerika around Rae's age and they always asked Benita can they have a 'dink.' That was their way of saying can they have a drink. Benita and Nene always say 'dink' when they say drink now."

"We were probably living with our dad then," Shaquoia said. She couldn't recall seeing Aerin and Aerika before.

Benita had told us about a lot of foster kids she had. She reminded me of Ron and Sandy, the ones who had Elijah.

"Yo," Tyree said in a nonchalant voice. "Don't look up, but that girl is looking at us from the African Room window."

Of course, the rest of us looked up. Crystal was staring down at us as we stood in the street.

She ducked out of view.

Benita dropped Crystal off at school on her first couple of days so she would know the route. Crystal insisted she would walk home.

A couple of nights later, Benita had to speak with her about coming home later than usual after school. Crystal stood with her arms crossed and a defiant look on her face.

"Get here when you're supposed to," Benita warned her.

"Okay," Crystal said, which was her favorite word. She responded to everything with "okay." Then she still did what she wanted to do.

Benita had to restrict the house phone because Crystal was calling somebody long distance.

"Why is she doing that?" I asked Benita in her room one night with the door closed.

"Because she thinks she's grown. I don't know who she thinks she's calling...she's from Las Vegas. All her real family lives here. She has cousins that go to school with her."

"Why is she in foster care?"

"That's her business. You can ask her if you want and it's up to her if she wants to tell you."

The next day after school, I waited until Crystal got home way later than us. Benita was still at work.

We were in our room with our door open and we saw Crystal pass by as she walked to the African Room. She shut the door. A few minutes later, giggling, we crept to her door. She had the television on the music video channel as I always did.

"Shh!" I said to Stan who started to sing the current song playing. He busted into laughter.

There was silence as the TV muted. We dashed back to our room laughing. A few minutes later, we were at her door again. This time I started singing the next song that was playing.

The TV muted again and we started running. But Crystal flung the door open and caught us before we made it to our room.

"What are you guys doing?" she said in mock annoyance. "If you want to come in, all you have to do is ask."

We were surprised. She looked at us like a bossy teenager in charge.

"I want to watch music videos," I said. "Can I come in?"

"Sure," her eyes were the kindest they had been so far since she had arrived.

Stan and Rae asked to come in as well. The four of us crowded on the bed to watch the TV. Crystal sat Indian style on one side of the bed holding the remote.

"I know every song that comes on," I said proudly.

"I can see that."

"What songs do you know?"

"I know a lot of them...not all though."

After more videos had played, Crystal sighed with annoyance and said, "Ugh, I wish Benita would turn the long distance back on. She restricted it."

I was about to say something, but didn't. Crystal was looking at each of us like she was expecting more information to come out of us regarding the phone.

"How come you're in foster care?" I asked her.

She blinked for a second before speaking.

"I really don't have to be," she said in an uppity matter.

"Then why are you here?"

"It's just temporary," she said, not really explaining much information like I had hoped.

"Oh. You have cousins at El Dorado?"

She nodded.

"Are you going to live with them?"

Her eyes had a painful look about them after I asked her this. Then they hardened over again and she shrugged her shoulders.

"I don't know yet," was her answer.
"We're going back to live with our Mama someday," I said.
She smiled.
"We have more brothers and sisters too. Seven of us in all."
"Wow."
"How many of you are there?"
"Just me."
"Oh."

A couple of minutes later, Crystal said, "Well I'm going to take a nap. You can watch more videos tomorrow."
"Okay," we said. We got up to leave the African Room.
"Do you want the door closed?"
"Yes," she said in her short clipped voice again.

Crystal was late coming home on time a few nights later. Benita was home early.
"This has *got* to stop!" Benita said, agitated. "She doesn't listen at all."
"What is she doing after school?" I asked.
"Hanging behind people who could care less about her...and who knows what else."
"She lets us watch music videos with her in the African Room."
"And that room is about to be cleared out."
"Why?"
"She doesn't want to be here. And she doesn't want to be with a black family."
"She said that?"
"No, but her actions say so. When I dropped her off at school, she begged me to not pull up in front of the school. She wanted me to let her out on the corner. She looked around to see if anyone was watching before she got out the car."
"Why? You have a nice car!"
"It doesn't matter to her if my car is nice or not. It matters that I'm black, and not white. But it's okay. She's going to get her wish. I'm going to call her caseworker for her."
"She's going to leave soon?"

"Sure is. We don't need that type of bad energy around us."

Crystal left a few days later and Benita had the African Room cleaned. Even though she wasn't there very long, I still wondered why she was in foster care. I didn't ask Benita again though. Benita had the long-distance feature on her house phone put back on.

Having a foster mother who did hair professionally was an advantage. Benita made sure our hair was on point. We never had to worry if she was slacking on our hair when she was busy with her daily customers because she made up for it. Stanford's was always cut short with his Romeo waves and his hairline edged up nicely. Rae and I had a variety. Benita helped our hair grow back after the damage of hair relaxers. At our tender ages, Tiwanda Banks had put a relaxer in our hair, rather than having the patience to press or flat iron.

Benita had corrected the damage. During the year we stayed with her she kept our hair steadily conditioned and styled as it grew. Most times when she picked us up after school and brought us to the salon, we plopped right in the chair to get our hair done.

One afternoon Benita told me she was going to style my hair with her brand new pressing comb. She inspected my hair and informed me that my hair had grown and I would love the results after she used the pressing comb. I hadn't pulled my hair out in a long time either.

I hopped in her styling chair and she went to work. She washed my hair, conditioned it thoroughly, and blow dried it. At first, the pressing comb scared me. She reassured me that if I just sat still and not fidget then I wouldn't be burned. She wrapped toilet paper around one hand while her other hand carefully guided the pressing comb through my hair.

When she was done, she smiled and spun my chair around so I could look at myself in the mirror. I grinned so hard as I saw myself. My hair was slick and smooth, and shoulder length. She also flipped the ends in loose curls, combing it out. With each movement I made, my hair bounced like the girls in the commercials who flossed their hair for the camera.

Benita closed the shop for the day. I was in the passenger seat still marveling over my hair in the car mirror when I saw two boys passing the car as they were on the sidewalk.

I instantly felt shy. I did something I still do to this day if I'm being stared at. I didn't bother to look their way. Not out of snobbishness, but because I was terribly shy, even when people stared out of admiration.

As they walked by, one of the boys almost stopped in his tracks as he looked at me through my open window. Then he continued walking with his friend. I heard him exclaiming to his friend in excitement.

"Yo man! *Look* at that girl's hair!" he said with such excitement, and I smiled hard. From my peripheral vision I could see in the rearview mirror that he turned around again to get another look.

Benita looked over at me as she started the car. She was laughing but at the same time very proud.

When Christmas time came around, Benita told us she'd be taking us to the airport so we could go to the North Pole. Of course, we were very excited. But also confused because what did she mean the North Pole? She said other foster children were going too. She told me I ask too many questions. I needed to just go with the flow.

I thought about the surprise when I lived in VOA, the girls' orphanage. They placed children's names on stockings hung on the wall. I figured it would be something just like it.

She drove us to McCarran International Airport one night. The parking lot was filled with cars. Once we got inside I could see that Benita was right! The airport was filled with foster kids.

The crowd was guided through the airport and to our terminal gate. We strapped on our seatbelts and ate yummy snacks from the flight attendants. They spoke over the intercom about how happy they were to take us to the North Pole.

It was nighttime and as the plane flew over Las Vegas, I glanced out the window at the city lights. This was a magnificent view! I noticed we seemed to be flying in a circle...because I kept seeing the Stratosphere on the strip over and over. I was going to say maybe we were lost and hadn't left yet, but I decided to go with the flow Mama.

When we finally landed, we were led through the jetway...and back into McCarran International Airport!

"Hey, we didn't go to the North P..." I was getting ready to say, but stopped.

My mouth dropped open when I saw the whole airport had been transformed into a magical place. There was fake snow, poles, presents, Santa and his reindeer, elves, candy, stockings, everything possible!

Everyone was loud and shrieking as we were led to our gifts and a chance to see and talk to Santa. I realized that's why our plane kept going into circles. To give them time to set up this surprise. It was awesome because it really looked like the North Pole.

When Christmas finally came, Benita gave us more gifts, which we weren't expecting because we were already content. We walked down on Christmas morning to see the whole den and the whole dining room filled with gifts. Among some of our favorites was every single doll and action figure from the Toy Story franchise. We loved those movies. She often took us to Toys R Us so we could find whatever toys we liked and play with them all day before leaving.

Benita bought each of us magma speed bikes. Mine was a deep purple. It was my absolute favorite. That morning, the three of us got on our bikes in the driveway. Shaquoia and Tyree came outside and told us about the gifts they received too. They hopped on their own bikes to ride with us to the mountains. We wanted to see if we were close enough and how long it would take because the mountains seemed so close. We detoured after a while to head back home. We had gotten tired and riding our bikes up the ever-slanting mountain slope was tough!

Mama, life felt good at the moment.

On New Year's Eve, we were in the African Room watching cartoons when Nene stopped by. Monie was with her. They came upstairs and we ran in the hallway and followed them to Benita's room.

Benita turned on the radio and opened her patio door that led to her balcony.

"You know what this year is?" Nene asked us.

I was looking at her skin hugging outfit with high heels and beautiful makeup and glitter on her face and hair. She held a drink in her hand.

"It's a new year!" we said excitedly.

"But it's not just any new year," she explained, taking a sip of her drink. "It's the year 2000!"

"The year 2000," I repeated.

"Yes, Quoya! It's a *new* millennium!"

I smiled and leaned on the railing of the balcony. Nene was so happy and excited for the year 2000, and she was dancing along to the music from the radio.

"She's going out tonight," Monie said to me. "I'm spending the night here."

"Where's Tiara?"

"At her dad's."

"Oh."

Benita gave the rest of us sparkling grape juice. We danced on the balcony without a care in the world. It was now the year 2000, and a new millennium like Nene said. I didn't know what that meant. I also didn't know that the year 2000 would mark a major life changing experience in my destiny.

TEN

*D*ear Mama,

In the beginning of 2000, our caseworker Kim told us we were being adopted by a white family from New York. I was adamantly resistant, as I have told in the beginning of this story. When Karen, Neal, and Abram Carlon flew to Nevada to meet us on that heartbreaking Saturday in February and they let Abram punch me in the face, I was even more resistant. But Kim kept on talking to us about adoption with this family. Mama, I was nauseous when Kim explained that we'd never be able to return to you. Why? I became a very angry child. As Kim explained the facts about our new life setting that I was in denial of, my sense on it differed from Stan and Rae's. I was older and I remembered you more. And I could detect that something wasn't right with how our adoption was going down. That's why I was so standoffish when they came to visit us. And they showed me who they really were by letting Abram punch me in the face and not doing a thing about it!

As a young girl, I may not have understood everything that went on, but I seemed to have a very keen sense when something was wrong. One morning I awoke and stayed in bed before getting up. Stan and Rae were in the African Room. Monie had spent the night on the bottom bunk in our room. She had gotten up before me. I heard her and Benita moving around in her room from across the hall.

The phone rang. As soon as it did, I immediately knew someone had died. I wasn't sure how I knew. It was just the strong feeling I felt when I heard the ring. An eerie one.

"Hello," I heard Benita ask as she picked up the phone.

Then I heard her gasp. I already knew who had died.

"Monie!" she screamed. "Earl is dead!"

My heart started beating so bad. How did I know? How could I have possibly known?

I couldn't hear or see Monie's reaction from our room. The image of her quiet father with his jeans and timberlands and his jeep flooded into my mind. My heart broke for Monie and Nene.

Over the next week, Nene and Monie stayed at Benita's and occupied the African Room. The rest of us were there to comfort them and make sure the house was nice and clean. Monie listened to her mother as she told her stories about her father.

Nene took us along as she ran errands and got the funeral arrangements in order. We were sitting in the parking lot outside the funeral home and Monie began crying because her mother got to see her father at his wake and she hadn't. The rest of us were content with staying in the car.

"You know what Monie!" Nene yelled. "This is too painful for me. Both of us. You aren't the only one hurting!" She was standing outside the driver's door. She got back in and slammed it shut very loud. Monie continued to cry.

An acquaintance of Nene's had walked her back to the car after they both had seen Earl in his casket.

"Hey Monie," he peered at her and the rest of us in the backseat.

She cried louder.

"Geno, I can't deal with this today. Can you please take her in there so she can see her daddy?"

"Of course," he obliged. "Come on Monie."

He opened the car door and held his hand out to her. I watched as he led her inside the funeral home. Nene leaned her head against the steering wheel and wept silently.

A couple of weeks after the funeral I was in the African Room with Nene listening to her tell me about Earl. She was crying and sitting cross legged on the bed. Her eyes were swollen.

She would always cherish Monie's father. Whatever the circumstances of their relationship, he had meant a lot to her.

"Sequoya, I knew the last time I saw him would be the last time," she said. She shook her head as if to say she should have seen it coming.

I listened. I didn't let on that I somehow knew Earl was dead before Benita had answered the phone.

"He was taking the truck somewhere but it was really late. We had just talked about what we were doing with ourselves. I just knew his mind was already made up."

I wanted to ask her what she meant but I didn't. The tears ran down her face and I stared up at her wishing this could all go away. Could it have been prevented?

"I saw it Sequoya."

"Saw what?"

"The look in his eyes."

I listened, getting anxious and filled with sadness.

Nene got up and walked to the window and stared out in a trancelike state.

"His eyes were dead. He had death written all over them. When I last looked in his eyes, I knew. Then he left. They found him and the truck flipped over."

She plopped back on the bed and racking breaths and flowing tears just made me so very sad.

"I miss my husband Sequoya!" she cried. She clutched the pillow that was now moist with all her tears. "I miss him very much."

Nene and Monie took a trip back to Texas for a while. The rest of us continued to go to school and Benita worked a lot of hours at the hair salon.

Sometimes we walked home and stayed by ourselves until she came home. Or we played outside with the neighborhood kids. A couple days out the week, she left work to pick us up and take us back to the salon on Jackson Avenue on the Westside. On those days, we played in the backyard of the salon because we grew bored watching people get their hair done.

One late afternoon, I was in the side yard. I was so bored. I wished I was at home in the African Room.

There was a gate that separated the side yard from the front of the salon and the street. I walked back and forth periodically. Then I walked toward the back of the building. From where I was standing, I could still see Jackson Avenue.

After a minute, I noticed the most beautiful woman walking down the street. She wasn't walking on the sidewalk; she was literally in the street. Right in the middle.

She was so beautiful. Her hair was up and styled so beautifully at the top of her head. She wore a cute top and a shorts/skirt assemble with pedal pushers. She was the epitome of what they called "A 90s Girl" back then. The sun gave her skin a bronze look. Her legs were divine. Even from a distance, I could see that her eyes were very pretty. They looked in my direction.

She had stopped when she saw me in the side yard. She suddenly walked toward the side, as if she didn't want anyone in the salon windows to see her. She remained in the street, but closer to the sidewalk on the other side.

For some reason Mama, I knew that beautiful lady was you. I hadn't seen you in a while. And the times I remembered being around you, you didn't look and dress that nice. I had always remembered you sad and the rest of us fighting to stay with you. Back at the Carey Arms Apartments, I always heard Dee exclaiming how you changed outfits two or three times a day before all the bad stuff started to happen. You loved to dress.

One time a lady tried to kill you over a fancy jacket you owned. You went to retrieve it after you left it at a party she had thrown at her house. She was a very materialistic lady who was known for throwing lavish parties in her beautiful home. She invited you to the party. But you left your jacket there when you went home. So, you called her to let her know the next day.

"Yes, I have your jacket," she told you. "I kept it safe for you don't worry! Come right on over. I'll be in the back but the front door is unlocked."

You put a young Dee in the passenger seat of the car, and then you headed to the lady's house. But something felt very strange to you. A strange feeling that intensified when you parked by her house. You told Dee you would be right back and she watched as you took careful steps up the pristine driveway. The door to the house was cracked.

You didn't ring or knock at the door. You didn't want to go inside. Instead, you slowly turned back around and your gaze met Dee's. Your expression was calm. Then you simply walked away from the house and you got back in the car. Dee asked how come you didn't get your jacket.

You were far away from the lady's house when you explained why.

"I knew I wasn't supposed to go to that lady's house. I wasn't even supposed to go to the party she held. The Holy Spirit warned me. As I was going to walk in her house again…I saw a vision. The lady was on the other side of that door already…holding a gun directly toward me. The Spirit gave me the privilege to see through the other side of the door as if it wasn't there."

After that day, you didn't call the lady, and she didn't call you either to ask why you didn't show up to get your jacket. You never heard from her again. When you asked someone about her sometime later, they informed you that the bougie lady who threw lavish parties had moved away.

I always listened carefully to the stories Dee told me about you. So, I recalled her stories about how you loved to dress. I just personally had never seen you looking so nice. You also looked younger.

I knew this beautiful woman standing there in the middle of the street on Jackson Avenue was my Mama. But at the same time, I was so full of doubt. I was confused…because she didn't speak to me. She just stood there. I waited for her to call out to me.

She didn't even smile. Just studied me. I began to wonder if it was really her. Maybe I was wrong, and she was just someone who resembled her. Or, was she waiting for me? Maybe I should run to her, I thought.

But I became scared. What if I ran to her and it wasn't her? What would the woman say to me? She still hadn't said anything. Why was she standing there looking at me then? She didn't even motion for me to come over.

After a minute, she walked away. I wanted this beautiful lady to stay. I walked in the salon and went to Benita's booth.

"I just saw my Mama," I told her.

"What?" she asked, staring at me.

"I just saw her," I repeated. I was now processing the fact that I had seen her. I know for a fact what I had seen, and it was her.

Benita stopped working on her client's hair. She walked out the door and looked up and down Jackson Avenue and came back in. She didn't ask me any questions.

"That was my Mama," I repeated.

"No, it wasn't," Benita said.

"Yes, it was," I persisted.

"Sequoya," she eyed me sharply. "I don't want to hear it. No more. You did not see her." She continued her client's hair. She seemed annoyed.

I sulked and walked out to the backyard to tell Stan and Rae I had seen our Mama.

Tyree and Shaquoia were the neighborhood kids we spent the most time with. Tyree's father had sent him a go cart for his birthday. It was the most elaborate gift in our neighborhood. It was shiny red. We watched as he zipped through the street and the girls took turns sitting in the passenger seat. Tyree was a good driver. He never crashed once, no matter how fast he was driving.

In March, my birthday approached. I awoke that morning to Benita wishing me a happy tenth birthday and to come downstairs to see what she had bought.

On the dining room table was a CD player with headphones. Next to it was a CD with a girl on the cover in a childlike pose, smiling innocently up at the camera. The CD said *Britney Spears: Baby One More Time.*

I grinned hard and tore open my gifts.

"There you go," Benita smiled. "All them music videos you watch in the African Room all the dang time."

She helped me put the batteries in and I placed the CD in the port and put the headphones on.

"Okay, ya'll go play outside for a while," she told us.

We went outside on that Sunday morning to join Tyree and Shaquoia. I had my headphones in the whole time as I learned all the lyrics to the songs. I walked around and watched the others play.

A little while later I glanced up to see Rae and Stan running back toward the house in excitement. Benita was in the doorway smiling.

Tyree motioned for me to pull my headphones off.

"Your foster mom said to go inside," he said.

"Oh," I said. I obviously hadn't heard her since my headphones were loud.

I walked upstairs to Benita's room to see Stan and Rae already grinning.

"Here," Benita instructed me. She held out the phone.

I set the CD player down on her bed and grabbed the phone.

"Hello," I said into the receiver.

"You know who this is?" the voice said with extreme happiness. "Happy Birthday!"

"*Keyonna!*" I screamed.

"What's up sis?" she asked, laughing a merry laugh.

I glanced up at Benita, who smiled.

Keyonna and I talked very excitedly. I told her what I got for my birthday and how good I was doing in school. The last time we had seen each other, I was eight, and that was the day our Mama had sneaked to see all of us at Family Services and they threatened to call the police. Now I was ten, so it had been two years.

Mama, my heart beat so fast as Keyonna told us that it was a possibility that we were going to see you!

Keyonna spoke to Stan and Rae too. Then she spoke to Benita again. After a minute, I could tell that Benita was talking to someone different. I knew it was Keyonna and Daniel's father, Ben Slank.

A few minutes later we got in the car in route to see them. We were all so happy. Anxious too. I could not stop thinking about Mama. Benita told us that we might or might not get to see her that day.

She pulled into the parking lot of a church in North Las Vegas. We eagerly walked to the front doors. My legs couldn't get in front of me fast enough. I could hear the choir singing.

Then, before we went inside, I heard that voice.

"Look at my Sequoya. With your hair growing nice down the side of your head!"

"*Mama!*" we all screamed and ran to her. She started crying as she embraced each of us. I merged myself into her warmth, processing the fact that she was really here.

She and Benita greeted each other. I was too young to realize that Mama and Benita had been with Ben Slank at different times, but they both understood the past and Mama didn't have a problem with her being our foster mother. She wanted to bring us to our Mama so she could see us. How awesome.

I just kept looking at her. I noticed she wasn't dressed up like the time I thought I saw her at the salon. This time she had a bun on her head, a casual dress, a housecoat over the dress, with pumps on her feet. Her face was ever more beautiful. We clung to her and Benita led us through the double doors of the church.

Upon entering, we saw the choir in the front standing up and singing. Guess who was in the choir?

Daniel and Keyonna! They had on their robes and they blended with the other members of the choir. Once they looked to see who had entered, grins broke across their faces mid-song. The corners around their eyes and mouths crinkled with excitement. We grinned back. Keyonna was now fourteen and Daniel was sixteen.

Ben Slank was seated near the front row. He got up and walked over to us. He was dressed in a very nice suit and his demeanor was that of a serious, changed man, just like Mama had predicted when

Daniel and Keyonna were just babies. He had thought my Mama was crazy when she told him his destiny would be in the church.

Ben hugged and kissed Benita on the cheek, then he hugged Mama dearly as well. We were seated in the second row, except Benita. She whispered something to Mama and Ben, and then she told us she'd pick us up later. She smiled at all of us contently, like she had done a great deed. Yes, she had! She left and we crowded around Mama on the bench as she put both arms around the three of us.

We watched Daniel and Keyonna in the choir. During the sermon, a green eyed young woman with hair in a long sleek ponytail, oversize t-shirt, jeans and sneakers, plopped down on our bench with a grand smile.

Dee! She was now twenty-three.

Our bench was the commotion of church! We tried to contain our excitement throughout the sermon. It all seemed so surreal. The only one missing was baby Elijah, who was with Ron and Sandy Hue on their ranch.

Before service concluded, the pastor, who was Ben Slank's brother, focused his attention on our bench. He told the congregation that our family was reunited but that we needed prayer.

Mama was already crying. She and Dee held our hands as we all got up to stand in front, facing the congregation, who stared at us intently with love.

"Aw," could be heard among the members as they studied our family. Daniel and Keyonna were instructed to join us.

We held each other's hands in prayer. The pastor prayed over us with fervent determination. This was a family that his brother was a part of. This was a family that had been broken up and shattered. This was a family who God had a special purpose for; even though we didn't seem to understand why things were happening that really hurt us.

As he prayed, I suddenly felt Mama's hand squeeze mine tighter. I looked up at her when she started shouting a bunch of words that I didn't understand. It was like a different language! She shouted them with her eyes closed and head down, with tears escaping from her closed eyelids.

When service was over we remained up front and the pastor took a photo of us. He told us all to make a goofy face, and I opened my mouth very wide in a shocked expression. But as soon as he snapped the photo, everyone began laughing at me.

"Gotcha!" Daniel grabbed me into a hug. "You're the only one who made a crazy face. Wait until we see this one. Miss Birthday Girl!"

I grinned and clung to my big brother. We walked outside and Dee went to get her car.

"We're gonna meet you at Dee's," Keyonna said to Mama, looking very serious. I saw that Mama suddenly had a serious expression too. She nodded.

"I'm going to see you guys in just a minute," Mama told us. "You ride with Keke and them." She kissed each of us with a loud smack, which caused us to giggle.

Then she clutched her housecoat around her tightly, and began walking away from the church. I almost panicked because she was leaving. But then Keyonna said in a conspiring voice that she couldn't be seen with us.

Why? We were her children! I just didn't understand.

Dee pulled up front in her car.

"Come on," she said anxiously. Daniel and Keyonna had the same demeanor. The three of them seemed like they were the lead characters in a secret mission movie, and the rest of us were being hustled around because we weren't supposed to be seen. Naturally, I became paranoid as well. Whatever was going on...I wanted to do my part in making sure things went smoothly.

"We're going to Dee's house!" Keyonna said happily. We were all scrunched in the car as Dee drove smoothly.

Daniel kept saying things that made us laugh. Six-year-old Rae was the cutest with her remarks.

"Daniel," she said. "You think you all that and a bag of chips!"

The three older ones burst into laughter.

"Dang, she still says that," Dee said with wonder. "She never forgot."

"I am all that *and* some!" he said as he hugged Rae close.

"I live right there," Dee said a few minutes later. The door was already ajar.

Once inside...I saw Mama! My beautiful Mama. She was seated in the dining room area in a chair. One of Dee's homegirls was cooking something in the kitchen that smelled good! My stomach growled.

I ran over to Mama and she grabbed me on her lap. I felt so loved and peaceful. A special love that only a mother can give to her daughter who she loved very much. I was in my own world as I watched Dee and her friend cook.

Our family snapped some more pictures together. In one of them, Stan, Rae, and I sat on the couch. Stan looked straight at the camera while Rae and I looked to our right at something interesting.

Suddenly and uninvitingly, the Carlons came flooding back into my mind, as I realized we had been introduced to them just last month. I opened my mouth and broke the news about the Carlons and the horrendous visit that took place. I told them that Kim said we were getting adopted by them whether we liked it or not. I told them about their son punching me in the face.

"See!" Daniel said angrily. "It's already starting...it's already starting!"

Everyone watched as I angrily described it all. My narration made everyone angry. Eyes flared. Jaws and fists clenched. We all sat staring at each other, very heartbroken at this news. Mama was quiet as she stared at me.

"They're going to make you slaves," Daniel said angrily.

"Yeah, that's why they want y'all," Dee said. Her face was twisted with anger and disgust. "What do they want with four black kids? I just don't get it."

"I don't want to go," I said sadly, hoping my words would solidify me being able to stay in Nevada. I didn't understand how deep all of this ran.

"Kim is so messed up for this!" Dee said. "She is willingly taking four black kids and shipping them off to them white folks!"

"Don't they get a lot of money for taking a lot of kids?" Daniel wondered, in a sarcastic manner.

"What I don't understand is…why does it have to be far away to New York?" Keyonna said. "Why can't you be adopted somewhere closer? It's not that serious. This is really messed up."

None of us could believe we were going to New York. As the go-to person who knew more than Stan and Rae, the older ones asked me when were we going, but I didn't know. We were shocked. We all had the same adamant attitude. There was no way we were going to the Carlons! What for?

Throughout the conversation, Mama kept a silent demeanor. She looked kind of bittersweet. At moments, she was looking at her six oldest children with a reminiscent expression on her face. She looked like she was thinking hard about something. She was looking in each of our eyes.

After a while, we shrugged off the Carlon ordeal and continued to enjoy our time together. We weren't going to let the thought of them rain on our parade. This was our day!

Daniel turned on the television. *My Cousin Skeeter* came on. We sang the theme song together. I enjoyed seeing Daniel and Stanford being brothers and laughing at each other's jokes. Daniel was being the big brother to Stanford that he always needed.

Within a few minutes, all of us were rowdy. We were jumping around and laughing loudly on Dee's black wrap-around couch. I was screaming along with them. We thought Daniel was so cool how he effortlessly jumped over the couch, back and forth. The rest of us couldn't get over the couch, we kept crashing into it.

We went outside in the courtyard and the neighbors wanted to see who Dee had at her house. The neighborhood was buzzing on this beautiful Sunday late afternoon, my birthday.

Stanford ended up being threatened by a bunch of neighborhood kids for no reason. Once Daniel heard the commotion going on, he marched over to them and gave those kids a shrill warning.

They scattered with the quickness as they realized our big brother Daniel was very serious.

That moment was something very special between Daniel and Stanford. A big brother protecting his younger brother no matter what.

At one point Daniel came and stood between Rae and me. He wrapped both arms around each of us and asked how we were doing in school. We excitedly told him about Mountain View Elementary.

"Do you like any boys?" he asked us.

I grinned hard, and he caught my expression. He raised his eyebrows.

"Well, there's a cute boy in my class," I piped up. "But every day after school he and a group of kids go into this cave that's a little way from the school. They say it's a hideout."

"It's a dark scary cave," Rae added. "I'm too scared to go in it."

Daniel frowned briefly.

"I don't care how much you like a boy!" he said with authority. "Don't go in any caves! For no boy. Period! And just because you're ten-years-old now doesn't mean you're grown Sequoya."

I nodded and giggled as I clutched my mini purse that Dee gave me. It felt comforting to have a big brother lecturing Rae and me about what not to do.

Before the food was ready, Dee came out and headed to her car, saying, "I'm going to pick up someone you would like to see! Who wants to go?"

"Me!" Rae screamed.

"Come on Rae Boo!" she said and she grabbed Rae's hand.

I wandered back inside and found Mama on the couch sitting quietly. She embraced me as I wrapped my arms around her. We sat there for a few minutes. Then she stood up, grabbing my hand.

"I want to show you something," she said.

She led me down the hallway to one of the rooms. She switched on the light. Against the wall next to the closet looked to be a treasure chest or something like that. She cleared the clothes and other things that were on top of it. Once the surface was clear, I saw the white chest and my heart started beating.

"My princess couch!" I exclaimed as she smiled.

When you came to visit me at the VOA house, you shared with me that you got me a princess couch with all the princesses on it. That was for my sixth birthday.

I ran my hands over it. I lifted the seat, saw a bunch of miscellaneous things piled inside, then lowered it. I sat down on it.

"I've had it all this time," Mama said proudly. "I will save it for you no matter what." She sat with me on the seat and we embraced for a while, in our own world again.

We heard Deniece and Rae arriving back to the house. I recognized a male voice. We walked to the front and there was Richard, Dee's longtime boyfriend!

"Yo!" he exclaimed.

We gave him a hug and he was grinning wide. He had a fresh outfit on with a durag over his thick, silky hair. He always reminded me of one of the high yellow men from the group Bone Thugs N' Harmony. Richard stared into Dee's eyes with such happiness and love for her on this day.

Dee's friend said it was time to eat.

"Did you wash your hands?" Mama asked me. I nodded timidly. She looked toward the kitchen area like she didn't care that I had just fibbed.

Geesh Mama, how did you know that I kind of lied? Actually, why did I even lie in the first place? It wasn't that serious. But I guess I was being a typical child who was eager to eat and didn't want to wait. I felt my hands were clean enough at the moment. I did happen to feel a little guilty for lying to you. As we ate, my conscious wore on me and I wanted to tell you I had lied about washing my hands. I have always had a confessing nature about myself. But I was already enjoying the chicken and hot sauce and mashed potatoes and gravy and string beans and corn and cake and frosting and juice and...

After dinner, Dee turned on her music center speakers. There was a microphone attached to it. She spoke into the microphone, announcing it was my birthday and all.

"Let's hear a little something," Rich said, as he sat on the couch smiling.

Dee happily switched her hips and gave him a *that's right* flirty look. She pressed a button and a familiar voice blared into the room.

"Aaliyah!" I shouted. Even at ten I already recognized people's music off top.

We listened as Dee sang along to "One in a Million." When the second verse started, she handed the mic to me and I giggled and ran to the bathroom and closed the door, singing where they couldn't see me. The cord led a trail to the bathroom. When the next song came on, Dee opened the bathroom door and we laughed and passed the mic to others.

It was getting dark now. None of us spoke about what that meant. We knew that eventually Benita would come to pick us up. I wanted to stay here so badly. I was with my family, and my *soul* was soothed and happy. I hoped Benita would let us come here often.

The polaroid pictures had come out perfectly. Daniel wrote on the white subject part of each picture. He wrote *3/26/2000 Sequoya's Birthday* along with a phone number we could reach them at. He wrote the same thing on each picture.

"I want you all to memorize this phone number," he said seriously, looking at us. We looked at him and nodded our heads in a serious manner as well.

"Memorize it," he said again. "No matter what. If anything happens and you need to call, we will always be here. Memorize it and don't you *ever* forget it."

The way he was saying this sent a chill down my spine. I didn't know what it was, but I knew we had better memorize that number. He handed the pictures to me, giving me the responsibility of keeping them safe. I felt so grown up as I tucked them into my purse and I reassured him that we'd indeed memorize the number.

He looked at me with such approval on his face, and he also had faith in me. This was very important.

Raeannah began coughing and wheezing. Her chest began to heave.

Oh no.

She was having an asthma attack! She and Elijah suffered from asthma.

"Did you bring your inhaler?" I asked, and she shook her head, her eyes beginning to roll.

We became worried. Mama and Dee started crying. Mama grabbed Rae in her arms trying to soothe her. She claimed she was taking her to the hospital.

"We gotta do something!" Keyonna said anxiously. "But Mama, what if we get in trouble?"

I looked at all of them as they exchanged worried looks among each other. That's when I understood everything more clearly. Mama wasn't supposed to be around us and if she took Rae to the hospital, she would have to reveal her name. If Kim or anyone at Family Services found out we were with our family, it would be a problem.

"Just say you're Benita Burkes," Dee said, her voice quivering. "This is crazy. They probably won't even check to make sure."

A little debate went on about what should be said or done. First it was calling the ambulance and having Dee go to the hospital. But Mama insisted she was going with her baby girl. Then Dee said we shouldn't call an ambulance, we should just go in her car. There wasn't a need to bring unnecessary attention to the complex. That would put us at even more risk. I found out from anxiously listening to the conversation that Benita was at a special event. She was at an extravagant show at one of the showrooms in a Casino on the Las Vegas Strip. None of us wanted to disturb her.

"Mama, just get in the car and take her!" Daniel said in exasperation.

Finally, Mama carried Rae outside with the determination of a mother. She didn't care if she would be in trouble or not, she was only concerned about her daughter's health. Dee and Keyonna went with her. I didn't want to go. Part of me was scared, and part of me was also mad that out of all days, Rae was having an asthma attack. On a day where we could be caught. It added to everyone's fear and anxiousness. But it wasn't her fault. Benita had surprised us with this visit, so none of us had grabbed anything before we met Mama and them at Ben Slank's church.

After they headed to the hospital, Daniel sat with Stanford and me on the couch and talked with us for what seemed like the longest. He was only sixteen, but he had so much passion for the Lord and he quoted Scriptures to us. He encouraged us and prayed with us.

"Memorize that number," he kept telling us. "Repeat it over and over until it's in your memory."

It made me clutch my purse tighter, where the pictures were safely secured. We sat and watched the television. We were happy in each other's presence. It was dark outside by now.

The others returned a couple of hours later. We bolted up to open the door and Rae was walking and smiling again. Mama walked in so happy. Everyone sat down on the couch and we talked. No one seemed worried anymore about the asthma attack or being questioned at the hospital. Everything had gone smoothly.

Then, not too long after, we heard a knock at the door. We all started crying again as we opened the door, knowing it was time to leave.

"Hey y'all!" Benita exclaimed. She had on heavy makeup and glitter and a turquoise outfit with matching heels. She had obviously gone home to change for the show after dropping us off at the church. At first, she looked all merry to see us, but I noticed she tried to hide a frown when she saw all of us looking sad, like we didn't want her to interrupt our fun.

"Hey," some of us mumbled.

"How was the show?" Dee asked neutrally.

"It was alright," Benita answered. "It was very nice. How was church?"

"Really nice."

She watched as we embraced each other again, with tears.

If I wasn't mistaken, Benita looked sort of agitated. I didn't understand that, because she was the one who offered to let us see our family. She had a history with Daniel and Keyonna's father before he met you. So, what was the problem now?

In a hushed, calm voice, Keyonna explained to Benita about the hospital visit.

"But she's all fine now," she reassured her.

Benita looked even more agitated. She pursed her lips together and looked at Rae who suddenly looked guilty for not carrying her inhaler with her. There was uncomfortable tension after this, but no one brought up any details of how Rae was checked in with the hospital concierge.

We hugged and kissed and declared we'd see each other again. Mama and Daniel and Keyonna and Dee walked us out to Benita's car and buckled us in.

Mama told us she loved us and we said it back. Daniel once again reminded us to memorize the phone number. Benita waved as she pulled out the parking lot.

I turned back to watch, and I vowed to myself I would see my family again. There was just no way I was going to those Carlons!

Once my family was out of sight and Benita pedaled it back toward the Eastside, I turned back around in my seat and started bawling my eyes out. I just let it *all* out. It had been two years since I saw them, and each visit affected me in such a way that I couldn't do nothing but cry. I had no idea why all of this was happening to our family. All I knew was that since I was very little, I had been sad and craving for our family to be back together. Every time we were happy when we use to live back home, in the back of my mind my young subconscious would nag at me and say something was going to happen. Usually it was us being taken away again.

I cried so hard. Benita didn't say anything. She focused on the road.

It was nearly ten-o-clock at night when we arrived back on Brynehurst Drive. I was surprised to see Tyree and Shaquoia run from their house to ours. A few more neighborhood kids came running too.

"I told them when we got back they could enjoy some birthday cake," Benita explained. She escorted everyone into the dining room and began cutting slices of cake and serving them.

"Dang," Tyree said. "You guys were gone all day! You never came back after church."

Stan and Rae were sociable with everyone but I was still crying. I wasn't hungry. I had already enjoyed dinner and cake with my family and had just been snatched away again.

Benita hovered around with the same look on her face and I knew she was angry about something, but I didn't care. Maybe she was regretting letting us see our family. Would she be in trouble if Family Services found out about the hospital visit? Maybe she wasn't prepared to see how loving we acted toward each other. Or maybe it had something to do with Ben Slank and Mama. Who knows? But she began glaring at me.

"Sequoya, it's your birthday. Quit crying and eat some cake," she said to me. "Tyree and them are here at ten-o-clock on a school night to wish you a happy birthday and this is how you're acting?"

The room was silent as she scolded me.

"I just don't feel hungry," I cried, more tears streaming down my face.

Everyone else was gobbling the cake. I felt sick. I wanted to be with my family. Why was Benita demanding I eat cake when I didn't want to? I could easily eat some of it tomorrow after school.

The neighborhood kids were looking at me like I was anti-social. First of all, I had just seen my family after a long time and that's how I always was after seeing them. They didn't understand! They hadn't been yanked from their families and told they had to be shipped away!

I sat there at the dining room table crying and clutching my purse in my hands. I still waited patiently while everyone finished eating. Then they went home. Stan, Rae, and I went upstairs and got ready for bed. Once in bed, I continued crying.

Never in my wildest dreams would I have imagined what would take place the very next day.

The Monday morning of March 27th started like any other day. I was still sad but had a deep good sleep. I was a little slow at getting ready for school but we left the house on time. Before Benita left for work, she placed a large canopy of fruit on the dining room table.

I still didn't have an appetite but I admired it. It was tall and looked almost like a miniature fountain. There were strawberries, grapes and berries, orange slices, and many other fruits I didn't recognize. There was this custard looking dressing that was all around it like icing on a cake. The fruit canopy was covered with plastic. I figured Benita must have gotten it at the event she had attended while we were with our family.

Benita left to work in a hurry and we walked to school with Tyree and Shaquoia. Besides my backpack, I had my new purse that Dee had given me. I reached in it to feel our family pictures. We'd start memorizing the phone number Daniel gave us once we arrived back home.

I began to feel better throughout the day. I was able to eat lunch. By the time the end of the day rolled around I was in better spirits as a large group of us began to walk home when the last bell rang. We lived in different directions so the group would get smaller and smaller and less noisy.

By the time we were closer to Brynehurst Drive, it was mostly just us three and Tyree and Shaquoia, sometimes a couple others who lived nearby. There were more of us on this day.

Some of them were still talking about the birthday cake from last night. The cake sounded like a good idea, just as I had predicted last night. I was hungry now.

We invited everyone into Benita's house. We brought the cake out the refrigerator and set it on the dining room table. We cut the slices ourselves and used clean plates from the dishwasher. We ate away, laughing and goofing off.

"That fruit looks good!" one kid said.

We all agreed.

"Benita set it out this morning," I said.

"Yeah, I think that's why she put it here because the cake needed to fit in the refrigerator," Rae said proudly.

"I want to try it," the kid said. "It just looks so good!"

We agreed.

The kid leaned over it and slowly lifted the plastic wrap and picked a grape that had the dressing sauce on it. He put it in his mouth and chewed.

"Mmm!" he exclaimed, closing his eyes for a minute. "Where did your mom get this?"

"I don't know," I said. "I think she got it somewhere last night."

"I just want one more," he promised, and this time he chose an orange slice.

We watched as he ate it. He said he was only going to eat one more, but that turned into several more. He ate that fruit like he had never ate something that tasted like that before.

Well now that made us want to try it too!

Once I ate a grape, I wanted more as well. The frosting was something I had never tasted before, and the way it was added to the fruit made it even more tasty. It was very delicious! I hoped Benita would bring more home.

Soon all of us were gobbling this fruit canopy. Hands reached forward and grabbed, and mouths opened.

A few minutes later we heard Benita's car in the driveway. For some reason, I was really scared. I hadn't been scared while eating, but the sound of the car and the way everyone else stopped eating added a flair of spookiness in the air. We looked at each other. Then we looked at the fruit canopy, which had diminished into a limp pile with melted custard pooling around it.

"I have to head home," the kid who had started eating first said. "See you tomorrow." He licked his lips and he and his friend flew out the front door. I knew they would pass Benita in the driveway on the way out.

I listened but didn't hear anything. I nervously began clearing the dishes and I put the rest of the cake back in the fridge. The whole time my heart was pounding. Rae and Stan looked scared too. Tyree and Shaquoia looked calm. They knew they wouldn't be in trouble. They didn't run out like the other kids. I think they stayed to be nosy.

We heard Benita walk through the front door and living room and approach the dining room.

"Who the heck y'all got running out my house like...."

She saw the five of us at the table. Then her eyes went to the fruit. She squinted at the fruit, studying it like there was no way it could be gone. She looked confused. Then suddenly her eyes hardened and her face was full of fury.

"*I'm sick of y'all!*" her voice boomed very loudly, and it made all of us jump.

This was her loudest we had ever heard her, and the angriest. She had been mad last night. Now she was fully unleashing it with eyes blazing and face contorting.

"Did I say you could eat that?" she screamed.

"No!" I said as we shook our heads timidly. "You didn't say we could or couldn't."

That made Benita even madder. She began calling us names and screaming very mean and vulgar obscenities. We looked at her in surprise. This was a new deep anger she was showing us. Is this how she really felt about us this whole time?

"Sorry Miss Burkes," Tyree said quickly, and he and Shaquoia got up and quickly walked out.

Benita ignored them as they left. The three of us were left to face her wrath, and the helpers who helped us eat were all free to go home. We should have never let them in the house. I regretted it.

"I do something nice for y'all and risk *my* foster care license?" she was saying, eyes glaring. "No one else would have let you see your family *but me!*"

We looked at her with fear and realization. Was Benita in trouble or something? I hoped not.

"And then you got the nerve to cry and complain?" she directed this one at me.

She stomped over to the fruit canopy and threw the rest in the trash. She placed the dish in the dishwasher. She opened the fridge and dumped the rest of the cake in the trash even though there was still enough left.

We began apologizing to her, but Benita didn't want to hear none of it. She told us to shut up in very vulgar terms. She was so extremely angry and her aura sent shock waves down my spine.

"Can't do nothing nice for y'all," she continued. "I really can't stand y'all. I do everything for y'all. These kids in this neighborhood actually hate y'all because of me!"

Hate us? They had better lives than us! They were with their real families, and that's all I ever wanted. How could someone hate a child who had to jump from foster home to foster home? No home was permanent, everything was temporary. How would they like to live at the Banks? How would they like to go to the Carlons? Benita was defending them so bad, starting last night when we had arrived home, saying I was rude for being anti-social.

"Y'all are just pitiful."

Just pitiful. Words like these, along with the vulgar terms, were beginning to remind me of life at the Banks house. For a moment it felt like we were there again.

Rae began coughing and wheezing again.

"And you can't even remember a stupid inhaler!" Benita directed this low blow at her. "If you would have remembered, you wouldn't have had to go to the hospital! I should beat the living crap out of you right now!"

"You not my Mama *or* my Daddy!" Rae suddenly screamed, her little body jerking angrily at Benita. She had heard enough of this grown adult.

Uh oh, here we go. The resistant side of my baby sister was making an appearance.

Benita looked incredulously at Rae.

"Little girl, I will beat the living crap out of you!"

"I'll call the police on you!"

"Oh, is that right?" Benita screamed. "Call them! In fact, I will get the phone for you...yes you can call them alright and before they get here I will beat the crap out you!"

Benita walked over and grabbed the house phone then she stomped back over to us. She held the phone out to Rae, who reached for it.

Benita changed her mind and slammed the phone on the dining room table. She got in Rae's face and screamed with spit coming out her mouth, *"If you even dare call police and put my whole life in jeopardy I got something for you!"*

The three of us glared at Benita as she glared at us. After seeing our faces, she lit into our behinds like she had never whooped any kids before. We all ran scrambling, but she patiently found each of us.

We got beat up and down and in and out in that house that day!

"Get out my face!" she screamed at us after she had released her physical aggression on us. "Go to your room and don't say nothing to me anymore!"

We walked upstairs to our room crying and breathing heavily. We sat in silence, processing what just happened. We heard Benita slam her own bedroom door shut and the walls shook.

After a few minutes, we began whispering to each other.

"Why is she so mad?"

"She never said don't eat it."

"I think she's really mad at something to do with Daniel and Keyonna's dad."

"She wants him?"

"What if she went to the show with him last night and something happened?"

"Can't she get another fruit thingy? She has money."

"That's messed up how everyone else just ran. I'm not talking to them no more."

"Is she in trouble with Family Services?"

We halted our conversation when we heard her bedroom door open. Benita's footsteps stomped to our door and she flung it open.

She glared at us, but we knew she hadn't heard what we were whispering about.

"Sequoya," Benita addressed me, looking at my purse.

I looked at her.

"Give me them pictures y'all took yesterday."

"Why?" I held my purse close. I was confused.

"Give them to me," she said firmly. Her eyes were cold. "I need them."

"Why?" Tears began to form in my eyes again. "These are from my family for my birthday!"

"I said give me the pictures. You don't have a choice." Her face was sinister now. "If I have to pry them from you, and if I have to destroy this whole house and *burn* it down, I will get those pictures from you."

"Okay, okay. But why do you need them?"

She didn't answer. She reached for my purse, and snatched it as I screamed.

She fished through it, got the pictures out, and stuffed them in her back jeans pocket with a look of victory on her cold evil face. She threw my purse on the floor.

"What are you going to do with them?" I panicked. I felt very sick again.

She didn't answer. She walked out the room. Then she stopped and walked back to the entrance.

"You, come with me," she pointed at Rae. "Get up."

Rae got up to follow her. Benita told Stan and me to stay in our room and if we came out, there would be consequences to pay.

"Can I go?" I asked.

"No."

"If you plan to kill my sister, I'm going to call the…"

"Child please, don't nobody want to touch her. **Stay in your room if you want to eat.** I'll be right back."

They walked out the front door. Stan and I thundered downstairs and watched from the window as she pulled out the driveway. We could see Rae in the backseat with very scared wide eyes as Benita took off with a determined look on her face.

Stan and I wondered out loud what was going on. Why did she only want Rae to go? My head was spinning. How could something like missing my family and eating some fruit cause Benita to be this angry?

Less than an hour later, the car pulled back in the driveway. Stan and I thundered up the stairs and in our room to make it seem like we had been there the whole time.

When Rae reached the top of the stairs and hurried into our room, she was crying. Benita walked up the stairs and slammed her bedroom door shut again.

"Did she beat you?" we asked her.

"No," Rae wailed.

"Why are you crying?"

Rae couldn't speak at first.

"Rae!" I yelled, holding her. "What happened?"

She kept crying. Her face was all scrunched up.

"What did she do to you?"

She looked at me with reluctant eyes. Tears poured down from them.

"The pictures..." she gasped.

My heart almost stopped.

"What do you mean? Where are the pictures? Does she have them?"

My heart sank into a black cloud as Rae told us that Benita went to a house and picked an acquaintance up. She and Benita talked a bunch of crap about us, including our real family. They said vulgar things in front of Rae. Then they rolled the car windows down. Benita handed her friend our family pictures, and her friend proudly ripped them to shreds. Then she tossed the shreds out the window. The wind scattered them into the air. Benita dropped her friend back off, then drove back home with Rae in silence.

I curled up on the floor, crying with such deep pain that I had never truly felt before.

Those were our family pictures! I hadn't seen my family in a long time. Seeing them on my birthday had meant so much to me.

I could not believe Benita had done this to us! I didn't even know she was capable of that. What was worse, she wanted Rae to see it. Benita knew better than to have me watch that! I would have done something crazy.

Well, the pictures were gone. Also, the phone number Daniel told us to…

Oh no! The phone number, Mama! We were going to remember it after we got home from school!

I cried so hard. Our connection to our Mama was now gone.

ELEVEN

For almost two weeks, Benita did not speak to us. We woke ourselves up for school and she came home from the salon later than usual.

She left everything out for us like she always did, the things we needed for food, bathroom, and laundry stuff. She left us alone and it was strange that we didn't run into her at all. After a couple of days, we started to contemplate if this would be a new way of life with her.

There were certain times we were in the house at the same time, but we weren't in the same room to see her face and she couldn't see us. But we heard each other.

Tyree and Shaquoia never brought up the fruit canopy...and they only asked us one question. They asked if we had received a whooping. We said yes. They were quiet after that. We didn't hang out with them after school during this time. We went to our room without being told to. We stayed alert to what might happen.

One day, we braced ourselves when we heard Benita's footsteps approaching our room door. She opened it and looked at us with an unreadable expression.

"Today you guys have a doctor's appointment. You need physicals. Your appointment is at four-o-clock," she said in a businesslike manner.

It was past three-o-clock, so we walked down to the car and got in the backseat. Tyree and Shaquoia were in their yard playing. When they saw us, they were surprised and looked at each other, talking about something.

In the doctor's office, Benita still wasn't talking to us. Only when she had to. In front of the doctors she smiled like everything was fine.

The three of us had a physical and were told we were healthy. We had to get our blood drawn too.

Benita drove home in silence.

After everything had died down a few days later, we were playing in the house. We tested Benita by walking out our bedroom and playing in the hallway when she was in her room. She didn't say anything. So, we went in the African Room to play. We were a little nervous. She still didn't say anything. Finally, we played right in the hallway outside her bedroom door.

We had put together a little skit to show our neighborhood friends and everyone at school. We did this often, and I loved writing the skits and songs.

After a few minutes, Benita opened her bedroom door and told us she wanted to see it. She motioned for us to come in to perform. We had finally made a breakthrough with her. We walked in her room and lined up in front of her to begin our skit.

She was watching us with a big smile on her face, which made us try our hardest with this skit too.

Benita melted over. Her eyes were watery. She had always been proud of us.

"Y'all are so talented!" she exclaimed, clapping. She opened her arms and we walked into her embrace.

"You know what?" she added. "We all have to forgive each other. God loves for His people to forgive. And you are God's children. Man, I can't stay mad at y'all for long. I just can't."

Relief washed over our faces. Benita wasn't mad at us anymore! She didn't hate us. Things settled back to normal.

Or so we thought.

Benita had forgiven us. The month of April whisked on by. We had put the incident behind us. We were back to riding in her car with her and staying after school at the salon again. One afternoon after picking us up, she said she had the day off. She headed in a direction I wasn't familiar with.

We were nearing an area that had many office buildings. The grounds and courtyards had grass that boasted a firm shiny appearance. Adults wore nice business outfits. I could see some of them in the courtyards talking with each other and walking on the sidewalks with a spruce in their step.

"Today y'all will be talking to a very nice lady named Michelle Graven," Benita said neutrally.

"For what?" I asked apprehensively.

"She wants to talk to you and help you," Benita explained. I noticed that she didn't get on my case about asking questions. She seemed very soft with us lately. Was it because of what happened? Or was it because of something else?

"She's a counselor?" I asked.

"They call her a clinical psychologist."

"What's that?"

"Basically, they all do the same thing. I have to take you to her a couple of times."

"Why?" What did a couple of times mean?

Benita didn't answer. She found a parking spot and we walked the sidewalk along the tall building. There were many windows on each floor of the building but they were dark, you couldn't see through.

The lobby had marble floors. Women in heels clicked by in earnest. Men's shoes clacked. People gave a lingering stare in our direction as they passed us. I knew they most likely felt sorry for us. How many children came here?

We took the elevator up a few floors and Benita spoke to an attendant. Then she sat down with us in the waiting area and told us that Michelle Graven would be out in a minute.

"I'm going to wait out here until you guys are done," Benita said. "All of you are going in with her."

A few minutes later, a woman opened the door adjacent to the attendant's desk and walked toward us, smiling brightly.

"Hi!" she said.

Benita stood up to shake her hand.

"I'm Benita. Their foster mother."

"I'm Dr. Michelle Graven!"

Then Benita tilted her head toward us.

"This is Sequoya, Stanford, and Raeannah," she told her.

The woman focused her attention on each of us and shook our hands.

"Sequoya…Stanford…and Raeannah," she smiled brightly again. "You three get to come with me!" She said it like it was a fun place we were going.

"I'll be right out here," Benita told us again.

Dr. Michelle Graven motioned for us to follow her through the door and down the hallway. When we entered her office the first thing I noticed was a glass door that led out to a balcony at the far end of the room. The sprinklers were showering the trees and flower beds in the back courtyard.

Then my eyes focused on the inside. I saw a television, nice plush couches, and a center table with a candy dish. Another table held arts and crafts. A section of the room had all the toys. Dr. Michelle Graven's desk was full of files and family pictures.

"Take a seat anywhere you want," she said. "I think I'm going to sit here today." She sat on the couch nearest the television.

The three of us timidly sat on the couch opposite her. She smiled at us again. She had shoulder length brown hair. She wore dress pants, a blouse, and a blazer jacket with heels. Her blouse looked a bit oversized on her, but she didn't seem to mind.

"Look at you guys," she smiled again, her eyes crinkling at the sides.

We smiled back timidly.

"This office is yours right now," she said. Her arm made a sweeping motion over the room. "You can do anything you want. Watch TV…go on the balcony…arts and crafts…anything you'd like."

We were eying the candy dish.

"Go right ahead," she said. "It's refilled every day."

After we selected candy we relaxed back into the couch.

"I want to watch cartoons," Stan said.

"Sure! It's after school so I know there's something on." She grabbed the remote and switched the TV on. Then she handed the remote to Stan.

We chewed on our candy. I vaguely watched the cartoon. This counseling session was a little different from what I remembered at the VOA house. I had been with a group of kids and we had a schedule. Now I was only with my brother and sister. Dr. Michelle Graven didn't start talking about our situation right away. She talked to us normally.

A few minutes into the cartoon she stood up and went over to her desk and looked through her files of papers. She glanced at us a couple of times.

"You guys have a little brother named Elijah," she said, smiling again.

"Yes...he's four," I looked at her.

"My son is five," she said.

"You have a son?" She looked young to me. But maybe because she was a clinical psychologist she was older, but just looked young.

"Yes, I do," she beamed. "He's at home. I will see him at dinnertime. Might be a late one tonight. Hopefully my husband already has it prepared...if I'm lucky." Then she laughed.

"Benita cooks us dinner," Rae spoke up.

"I bet she cooks good food!"

Rae nodded and smiled.

"What do you like to eat Sequoya?"

"I don't know."

"I bet I can guess."

I smiled.

"Hot Cheetos?"

"How did you know I like Hot Cheetos?"

Dr. Michelle Graven laughed.

"It's the red kind...not the regular kind," I made sure to say.

"I know. But there must be something else that you like too."

"I like spicy food."

"She does," Rae said. "She puts hot sauce on everything."

"Sometimes she drinks it straight from the bottle," Stanford put in.

"No I don't!" I lied. I was mad.

"She got in trouble with Benita because of it," Stanford continued.

Dr. Michelle Graven's face had turned red from laughing. She grabbed a tissue from the tissue box on her desk and dabbed at her eyes. I noticed she rubbed her belly a little before picking up her files again.

"What do you like to eat Dr. Michelle Graven?" I asked to change the subject away from me. I also felt proud of myself for saying *Dr.*

"Call me Michelle," she slightly frowned before smiling again. "I like to eat tasty dishes like lasagna...and spaghetti...and anything else with pasta..." She named more dishes as we listened.

For the next few minutes we talked about food, school, and living at Benita's. She spoke to us like we were normal. I had felt that with everything happening in my family, maybe none of us were normal. I was reminded that there were many foster children in the world. But why were we in foster care?

"How come we're in foster care?" I suddenly asked Michelle.

She looked at me surprised. She opened her mouth to speak, abruptly shut it, and then pursed her lips together.

"Well," she thought carefully before speaking. "Some parents aren't able to care for their...um...their children who they love very much...so there are other parents who step in to help."

"Like Benita?"

"Yes."

"Benita is helping my Mama?"

"Yes," she nodded. I noticed she began writing something on a piece of paper.

"Before we came to Benita's...we were at an evil lady's house named Tiwanda."

"Yeah, she's a witch," Stan said.

"I can't stand her," Rae added with vengeance.

"Why?" Michelle asked.

We took turns telling Michelle what happened at Jerry and Tiwanda Banks house. Michelle's rosy face was turning whiter the more details we gave her. Her eyes looked very concerned.

"Have you ever told anyone these things?"

"No."

"Why?"

"Tiwanda said no one will ever believe us."

Michelle scribbled feverishly on her notepad.

"Are you writing down everything we're saying? Please write down what Tiwanda did to us," I said.

"Yes, I'm writing it down, so I can make sure I don't forget or miss anything that is important in your lives," she explained. "Jerry and Tiwanda Banks are rotten!"

I felt satisfied that Michelle was on our side. I also felt very relieved. Stan and Rae looked relived too. We were getting it all out. We still had so much anger towards Tiwanda even though it had been a year since we left her house. I felt I had enough anger to last a very long time!

"She has more kids there too...we saw them the last time we were there to get the rest of our stuff." I said.

"They have no business having foster children!" Michelle said angrily, still writing on her notepad. "I'll make sure they're investigated. How does that sound?"

"Good!" the three of us looked at Michelle in wonder and nodded our heads.

After we talked about the Banks, we told her about the two-and-a-half years we spent with Mama Mary, Tamera, DJ, Jimmy, and Russia.

"Sequoya, you have quite the memory," she smiled at me.

"And before that we were at Child Haven a couple of times...I was also at VOA House...when I was there, Stan and Rae were..."

"We were with this weird family," Stan said.

"What made them weird?"

"I don't know. There were other kids there too."

"Were they nice to you guys?"

"Yeah...but one of the girls who was older kept trying to fight me."

"Did you fight back?"

"No, she's a girl."

"She was nice to me," Rae said.

I was quiet as they described this one, because this was the first I was hearing of it myself. I had been at the VOA House during this time.

"One day she pushed me, and I fell down on the grass," Stan explained. Then he lifted his hands up so the insides of his palms showed. "That's how I got Psoriasis. See?"

Michelle studied his hands.

"I also have it on my knees and elbows."

"Hmm.... I see. I heard from your caseworker Kim that it's been clearing up."

"Yeah, it's not as bad as it used to be."

"Our sister Keyonna used to have it," I said.

"Oh?"

"Yes. It's all gone now. We saw her on my birthday and she looked at Stanford's hands and said she used to have the same thing. Hers is all gone now. She used cream."

"You saw her on your birthday?"

"Yes."

Then the memory of what happened after that came back. It was an illegal visit and Benita had gone to great lengths to cover it up. The whole ordeal was still a knife in my heart.

"How was your birthday?"

"I don't want to talk about it."

"Okay. Did something bad happen on your birthday?"

"I don't want to be adopted by a white family!" I said angrily. "I know that's why we're here!"

Michelle didn't flinch at my sudden outburst. She looked at me. It was a look that said she felt sorry for us.

"I want to stay here and go back with my Mama! I don't want to go to New York!"

Michelle looked down at her desk for a minute before looking back up.

"Can I give you a hug Sequoya?" she asked.

I didn't answer. Stan and Rae were on the couch beside me observing this. Subconsciously, this was the tone being set without us even realizing. I was the one to voice and act out our anger. For now, I was the rebel warrior. They looked on, secretly happy.

Michelle got up from her desk and walked over to the couch and sat beside me on the edge where there wasn't much room. She wrapped her arms around me.

I began to cry.

She held me close with a rocking movement. A few minutes passed. My face was tear-soaked and thoughts of this unfair decision were burning fury inside my entire existence.

I felt powerless. I didn't have a say. All I wanted was to be with you, Mama. Why couldn't I at least be somewhere near you? New York was far away from what Dee and them told us. It just didn't make since. I was only ten, but there was something terribly wrong that I couldn't put my finger on. It made me very sick.

"The Carlon family wants to take all of you. Even Elijah. They have opted to adopt all four of you so you can grow up together. That doesn't happen very often. Elijah was adopted by a lady in Utah not too long ago. But after a few months, she decided to give him back to Ron and Sandy. It didn't work out for her. And once she heard that the Carlons were taking you, that helped her make the decision as well. She wanted Elijah to be with you."

I looked up at Michelle, taking in this news. This made me even sicker. Why was she talking about the Carlons like it was actually happening?

Oh no!

"No!" I screamed. "I don't want to go to New York!"

Benita was faithfully in the waiting room when we finished our session. Michelle walked us out and hugged us, saying she would see us in two weeks. Then she grabbed Benita off to the side to talk to her for a few minutes.

The rest of the session had been spent talking about the pros and cons of going to New York with the Carlons. Mostly, Michelle was trying to be neutral, but I could tell she was also trying to prove a point about the whole "growing up together in a nice family" scenario. I knew Michelle was just doing her job but deep down I knew she could never relate to the feeling of being snatched away from your family. I don't know what she meant by a nice family. Their son had punched me in the face and got away with it!

I thought about Crystal, the fifteen-year-old Caucasian foster child Benita had the previous year. She didn't want to be with another race family. So, Benita called her caseworker and made the proper arrangements for her. Crystal had a say in where she wanted to be. We weren't allotted that same privilege at all.

The thought of the Carlons made me so sick. There was something especially eerie about Neal, who looked much younger than Karen.

Karen had cold eyes.

Nene and Monie returned home from Texas a few days later. They seemed to be in better spirits. They still talked about Monie's father a lot. We told them about the Carlons. They shared our same reaction. Why in the world were we being sent all the way to New York with these white folks?

"Mom, why are you letting them go to New York?" Nene asked Benita, with an alarmed look on her face.

"I don't have a say in this," Benita answered, on edge.

"You should adopt them Mom! This ain't right."

"They won't let me."

Conversations like this were taking place nearly every day, as Benita's friends and acquaintances heard of the news. Stan, Rae, and I received many sympathetic looks. At the same time, I wanted to lash out at Benita. What did she mean they weren't going to let her adopt us? I didn't even know it was an option.

Or was it really? I felt Benita was saying that as an excuse. Between her and everyone she knew there wasn't one person who stepped up and said they would take us. We were being treated like a charity case, and the spectators were of no help.

My ten-year-old self was in a race against time and I didn't have a fair start at this war.

One day when we got home from school, Benita was in the living room on the couch holding a photo album. She had a pained look on her face. She had just got off the phone too, as I heard her saying goodbye and she set the phone down.

She didn't usually sit in the living room.

"Them white folks sent you something," she said reluctantly.

"Sent us what?" I asked. We walked over to her.

Before handing it to me, she said, "I just called Kim to cuss her out because they're sending you guys to a shack on a farm!"

"A farm?" I twisted my face in horror. I heard about farms in school. All I knew was that it was for animals, like far away in the country.

I snatched the photo album from Benita.

On the cover it read:

To: Sequoya, Stanford, Raeannah, and Elijah
This is a photo album of our house and the yard and our town of Candor, New York. Here are pictures of the inside of the house and the boys room and girls room. We hope you like your rooms! We had them painted for you. Included in the album are pictures of our dogs Sampson and Crackers. And our cat Ernie. We hope you like the pictures. We love you and look forward to adding you to our family!
From,
Mom, Dad, Abram

With a sick twisting horror, I opened the album with Stan and Rae crowding around me. We saw a medium-sized, two-story pale blue house with a dark blue station wagon in a dirt filled driveway. I could see other houses in the distance, but within space of each other. There were trees and fields in the background and they stretched as far as I could see.

The inside of the house showed wooden décor. The living room was modest, with mismatched furniture. A wooden staircase led up to the second floor.

The boys room was blue and filled with posters of action figures and other random stuff. There was a bunk bed set in it. The girls room was pink, and the borders of the walls were lined with a different colored pattern that I was too sick to pay attention to. We had a white bunk bed set in our room. Our closet had a curtain made from this cotton cloth material. I guess that was the door to our closet?

There were pictures of the dogs and cat. There were pictures of the outer perimeter of the house from all sides. From the back of the house, I could see a large cornfield off to the left. There was a big sized barn that I could see, but not up close. Beyond that were more trees stretching off into a big hill that was full of even more trees. It looked like a mountain that was covered in trees.

Oh no!

"I thought we were going to New York?" I gasped. "This is a farm. Look Benita! Look right here! That's a barn!"

"I saw it. That's called Upstate New York. It's not like the city."

"I thought it was a city."

"Me too."

"What did Kim say?"

"She didn't really say anything. I just got done telling her that something has to be done. There must be another family that can adopt you."

"Kim didn't care that it's a farm?"

Benita shrugged her shoulders.

Anger seethed into my veins. Kim was just going to let this happen to us.

"Can I call her?"

"Sequoya, she's not going to listen to you."

"She never has!"

"And you're just now figuring this out?"

"I hate her!" I screamed, sending the photo album flying and hitting the wall.

Surprisingly, Benita didn't yell at me for throwing an object. She looked to see if I had hit or knocked anything off the wall but I hadn't. I left the album on the floor and thundered up the stairs.

Dear Mama,

Now I knew why Dee and them hated Kim! I had seen it in your face too Mama! Kim was working with Family Services to send us far away so our family couldn't be together! It was all an evil plan like they said! Kim was supposed to be on our side! She was a traitor and she found it all amusing. I should have known after she let that devil punch me in the face and she had laughed at me. I hate her and she got dry crusty dreads that will never grow with her ugly purple gums! I hate the Carlons and their ugly run down gutter shack farm house!

I cried for days and I was also in denial. Everything was happening so fast. I just could not grasp it. It was a nightmare that I was praying was a big joke. At any moment, a huge bright light would shine and say, "Just Playing!" "The Carlons are imaginary." Or, "The Carlons have changed their minds!"

But the Carlons, especially Karen, were determined. She called Benita's house a few times, but we told Benita we didn't want to speak. Karen wanted to know if we had received the photo album. Benita told her yes, and then got off the phone, making an excuse about having to start dinner or something. Each time Karen called, I heard her eager and determined voice chattering away like she was going to reach through the phone and come looking for us. Benita rolled her eyes as she listened to her.

This whole New York/adoption to a farm scenario was making my tolerance level crumble to new heights. I had been angry and sad most of my early childhood life, but now it was transforming to something even deeper. Without realizing it, I was already developing an inner army of defense. I was bucking and preparing myself.

Tyree and Shaquoia laughed at the photo album and made their own jokes.

"You better take all your clothes there," Shaquoia said. "I don't think these people will know how to dress y'all. Or do your hair."

Our hair! Oh no!

I told Shaquoia about the visit in February, when they came out and Karen had poured water on our hair in the motel bathroom.

"Wow," Shaquoia covered her mouth with her hand. "Yeah, you guys are in some serious trouble. I wish my Mama could take y'all."

I wished with all my being that we could be sisters and brothers with Tyree and Shaquoia!

One day after a long day's play on Brynehurst Drive, we were exhausted. It was getting dark. Tyree and Shaquoia were back in their house and Stan and Rae had gone inside to take their baths. Only Nene, Monie, and I remained outside.

We were leaning our weight on the hood of Nene's car. The sun was setting very beautifully. The three of us looked at the fading colors as they burned in the sky.

"This air feels so nice right now!" Nene said. "Look at the sunset."

I breathed in the fresh cool breeze as I watched Nene put her arm around Monie. I thought she was going to put her other arm around me because she was between us, but she didn't. Monie wrapped her arm around her mother's waist. They began their own conversation. I kind of tuned myself out.

A few minutes later, still holding onto each other, they eased themselves off the hood of the car. They slowly began to walk out the driveway and down the sidewalk. I thought they might be going for a walk, but they stopped suddenly. Their backs were to me. They held each other even tighter and looked at the sunset together.

This was a special and private mother daughter moment. Nene had been though a lot. She had lost her husband and Monie had lost her father. It would be rude if I followed them to interrupt.

Observing them, I felt guilty for having felt a pang of envy when they embraced happily and walked down the sidewalk together. I wanted my mother too, just like Monie had hers.

I looked toward the sunset and said a prayer for my Mama.

"Lord, please let me be with my Mama again…please!"

On our second visit with Michelle, she asked us if we wanted to join her at the arts and crafts table. She was assembling multi-colored construction paper, scissors, colored pencils, crayons, and glue. Today she wore a red top, slacks, and heels again. Her blouse wasn't as big this time.

We joined her at the table.

"I want to do a project with you," she said. "Would you like to draw a picture of your ideal family?"

"Yes," we agreed.

"As you can see, I've already started mine."

I got to work drawing Mama, Dee, Daniel, Keyonna, Stanford, Rae, Elijah, Richard, and me.

A few minutes had passed when Michelle suddenly asked, "Have you heard from the Carlons?"

My mood went dark again as we nodded our heads. Michelle waited a couple more minutes before continuing.

"They seem very excited from what I hear."

"That lady needs to calm down," I snapped.

"Why do you say that?"

"She keeps calling Benita's house."

"That means she's excited."

I shrugged my shoulders, annoyed.

"Who are you drawing?"

"My *real* family!" I said with a sassy smile.

Michelle smiled then looked at Stan's and Rae's drawings.

We continued and a few minutes later Michelle held her drawing up.

"I'm all done! Want to see?"

She had drawn three people at a park sitting on a blanket in the grass. A picnic basket was next to them.

"This is me, my husband, and my son Eric at our favorite park. We're about to eat our sandwiches. My son likes to eat his bologna sandwiches with chips and pickles on them."

"But you're missing somebody," I suddenly said.

"I am?" she asked, surprised.

"Yes."

"Who am I missing?"

"The new baby."

Michelle's eyes grew wide as I pointed at her stomach, which her red blouse couldn't conceal all the way.

"You're pregnant," I informed her.

"Um...yes...I..." Michelle attempted to get her words together. "Yes, I'm pregnant." She was looking at me very surprised.

I had guessed, and I was right! I had even surprised myself. Her stomach wasn't that big but to me if was protruding enough for me to understand.

"How come you didn't draw the baby?"

"Well...it's still so soon and I didn't want to confuse you."

"Is it a boy or a girl?"

"It's too soon for me to know."

"Oh."

Michelle was still looking at me curiously.

"Can I see your drawing?"

"Yes." I held it out to her and told her the names of my family members. Then she asked to see Stan and Rae's.

After arts and crafts, she invited us out on the balcony to look at the scenery. She didn't talk anymore about the Carlons. She talked about neutral things.

I was thinking about the picture she drew and her having another baby. I don't know why, but I felt a little deceived that she had kept that from us. She had looked at me surprised when I confirmed it, like we weren't supposed to know. She had drawn the perfect happy family at a nice picnic. She had nothing to worry about, because she had a happy life. I felt a little envious.

When the session ended and we met Benita in the lobby, I didn't know that was our second and last session with Michelle. It was the end of May 2000, and an unfathomable fate had closed in on us. I had no idea we were out of time.

Dear Mama,

My voice was not heard. No matter how much I screamed and cried. No one would listen. No one would let me speak! We were going to the Carlons gutter shack farm house in New York. Very far away. As each day passed by I was in denial. Kim was in happy spirits. Of course she was. She was sending us away. She hated you and our family. She had been my caseworker for as long as I could remember. For someone who was my caseworker for that long, that shows she had a personal vendetta.

I also didn't know that she had visited my Daddy Stan in prison and showed our picture to him. When he asked if his people could take us, she said no. So, he asked her, "Then why did you come to this prison to dangle my children in front of me?" Kim didn't really have anything to say. She ended up saying something like, "I want you to see how grown up they're getting." Yeah right! She was using and abusing her social worker rights to torment our family! It was all part of the plan.

The month of May had been filled with school, appointments, Family Services phone calls, and spectators commenting on our adoption.

Then one day, Benita came home from work early, looking sad.

"What's wrong?" we asked her.

"You guys are leaving the day after tomorrow."

"No!" I cried. I sank to the floor in tears, unbelieving of this.

Benita looked sad. "I'm so hurt. I love y'all and I'm going to always be Mama Benita. You hear me? *Always!*"

I was the most inconsolable. How could they just announce us leaving so soon? I thought we still had a lot more time! That was way too fast.

For the next two days, we recited Benita's phone number to her over and over. We had it memorized for sure! She said we could always call her anytime.

"I have something for you Sequoya," she said to me, and she took me in her room and went through her dresser.

She pulled out a picture of herself. She was younger, more stunning, and wore a beautiful dress. She sat in a princess like pose. People were in the background. She was in a tropical looking place.

"You look so pretty Mama Benita."

"This picture is yours. Hold onto it. See how happy I am? Look where I'm at. I'm somebody important. And everyone knows who I am and they're looking at *me!*"

I nodded.

"This is also you," she handed it to me.

"Me?" I asked.

"Yes. You are going to be happy and successful...no matter what anyone tries to do to you. They will not be able to dim your beautiful self! You will shine. You hear me! Look at me and tell me that."

I held the picture and cried, looking up at Benita. She wiped the tears on my cheek as I repeated what she told me.

The faculty and staff at Mountain View Elementary hugged and spoke to Stan, Rae, and me. The students in the school seemed to be in awe about New York...but they knew I didn't want to go.

"I'm going to come back to Nevada someday," I told everyone. "Just watch!"

"I sure hope so!" my teacher Ms. Shagloff said. "I'm going to miss you."

At the end of the day we went to Rae's classroom.

"Can you play the believe song?" I asked Mrs. Applebee.

"Believe?"

"Yes. It goes like this...Don't give up on your faith, love comes to those who believe it...and that's..."

"The way it is!" she beamed, finishing the line for me. "Of course, I'll play it!"

Mrs. Applebee told me it was Celine Dion and the song was called "That's the Way it Is." She placed the CD in her disc player. I told her I would always love and remember her playing it.

"It's a very beautiful song," she said.

Tyree and Shaquoia walked home with us in our doleful state. Tyree was walking beside me, holding the end of my backpack string like he often did. I often held his as we walked too, but only because he held mine.

"He has to tell you something," Shaquoia said, smirking at Tyree.

"No I don't!" he protested.

"Just tell her Tyree," she sounded older than him, even though she was his little sister.

"Shut up Shaquoia."

"I'm going to tell her."

"I'm dead serious Shaquoia, shut up!"

"He likes you!" she said, laughing.

Tyree kicked Shaquoia. She screamed angrily and kicked him back. He let go of my backpack string. He changed the subject and the rest of the walk home was spent talking about our moving away.

When we reached Brynehurst Drive we saw Benita already in her car in the driveway.

"Come on," she called out to us. "We have a few things to do before tomorrow."

"Are we going to see you guys before you leave?" Tyree asked, looking at me.

"Yeah," I answered.

Benita ran a few errands. The four of us were sad and she was crying right along with us. She stopped by the salon so we could say goodbye to everyone who worked with her.

Then she stopped at this fancy doll looking place. The outside looked like a huge doll house!

My mouth fell open at all the fancy and beautiful rows of dolls lined on the walls and in the isles. There were small ones, medium sized ones, and large ones. The large ones were nearly life sized. At least for my ten-year-old self. When I stood next to one, it was only a few inches shorter.

What really got me were the ones that were made to resemble little black girls like Rae and me! These dolls were so beautiful! Their dresses and shoes were so nice. Their hair was big, bouncy, and curly. Huge and beautiful chocolate eyes stared back into mine.

"Pick which ones you want," Benita told Rae and me. "Pick a big doll."

We didn't have to be told twice! We both selected life-sized dolls. As soon as we grabbed them, we were alarmed at the heaviness. They weren't as light as regular dolls. This added to the realness of them.

"Those dolls are one hundred-and-fifty dollars each," the lady behind the counter said, looking at Benita skeptically.

"Oh!" I exclaimed, beginning to put mine back.

"No, that's yours!" Benita scolded me. "That's your doll and I brought you here for it."

Benita gave the lady behind the counter a shady look as she calmly reached in her purse and pulled out the money for both dolls.

The lady took the bills without saying anything. She rang the dolls up and handed Benita her receipt and change.

"I want to hold mine," Rae said.

"Me too," I added.

We reached for our dolls and held them close as we left the store.

"Why was she acting like that?" I asked Benita.

"They always do that because they think we don't have money."

"Why?"

"It's a big mess Sequoya. But always keep calm when this happens."

"You looked at her mad. It made me mad too!"

"Right, but you still have to stay calm."

"Okay."

Benita went to another store and bought Stan a little video game system. We arrived back home and she assisted us in packing everything. I packed slowly. I was still in denial. Maybe at the last minute tomorrow, Kim would call us and say the move to New York was canceled. Oh, how I wish!

My wish had not been granted.
The next day, Benita took us out to eat a very nice brunch and by the time we got back there were voicemails left on the answering machine from Kim. She would be at the airport with Elijah. She was already in route to retrieve him from Ron and Sandy Hue.
For the first time in a long time, I genuinely smiled inside. Elijah was coming with us! He was a baby when we were taken from our Mama the last time and placed at Child Haven. We hadn't lived with him since. He was now four.
Nene, Monie, and Tiara dropped in to say goodbye. After they left, we put our belongings in the car. Tyree and Shaquoia played with us in the street. Tyree took Rae and me on a ride up and down Brynehurst Drive in his go-cart. He gave me a huge squeeze of a hug afterwards. He and his sister stood in the driveway with us.
A while later, Benita ran out the house.
"We have to go!" she said urgently, eyes wide. "Kim confused the flight time!"
"Now?" I asked, appalled.
"Yes, get the rest of your stuff and come on."
"Aw!" Tyree and Shaquoia were saying. They hugged us again, and helped us get situated. I was so mad. The evil forces of this situation were doing everything in their power to make this adoption serious.
I ran through Benita's whole house, backyard, and the Rock Yard one last time, telling myself that I would see it again after the Carlons changed their mind once I got to New York. I would let them know where they stood with me. I blew a kiss at the African Room and did a tribute dance in the entrance of it. I was alone and no one saw me.
Benita locked the front door and we got in the car.

"Bye!" Shaquoia and Tyree waved to us fervently. We waved back.

We looked back at them as the car pulled out of Brynehurt Drive and turned the corner. They stood in the street together, brother and sister saying goodbye to their friends who were leaving off to New York.

Once out of sight, all of us began sobbing. Benita too. She had tears running down her face and her eyes were in a squinty expression.

"When you guys call me, I'm going to call them over to the house so you can speak with them," she said through racking sobs.

Benita got on the freeway to join the packed cars.

"I'm going to always be Mama Benita," she kept saying through her tears.

We recited her phone number to her in unison. We had made a song out of it. She smiled as we sang her phone number to her. When we neared the airport, she became a little frustrated because there was a specific turn that we had to make to get to the terminal Kim wanted us at. The turn was tricky if you didn't pay attention.

"I can't find Paradise!" she kept saying, circling in traffic a few times. "We are going to be late!" Cars were honking.

I prayed we would miss the flight!

Benita turned back around and started over again and a few minutes later I looked up and saw the street sign that read Paradise.

Deep down, I'm a good person no matter what life throws at me.

I said, "There's Paradise right there," I pointed to it.

Benita screeched her tires. She looked at it, and then looked at me with surprise through her tear-soaked face. She turned on Paradise and we were on our way to the terminal our flight would depart from.

We cried harder when we arrived and our stuff was unloaded. Benita came with us inside, parking her car right there because we didn't see Kim or Elijah. The attendant looked at all our crying faces and reassured Benita that her car would not be tampered with as she escorted us to our gate.

We cried as we were checked in and told where we needed to go. McCarran International Airport was full of people rushing about. Everyone was acting urgent, like they were all going to miss their flight. This airport was huge and it was now nighttime. But it was alive as ever. We were led up to these glass elevators where we could still see everything and everyone as it carried us up to the level we were headed to. I looked down at the bodies that began to look like tiny ants running around. My tears began to blur the image. How high were we going up?

When we stopped at our level, we walked out and Benita walked us to our terminal. Kim sprang up from her seat in the waiting area…and I knew it was real. We were leaving.

"I'm going to *always* be Mama Benita!" Benita said again, crying.

Kim studied us. She had no tears at all. She looked happy and she smiled her big toothed smile, purple gums showing and all.

My baby brother Elijah turned in our direction as he was still seated. He looked at us apprehensively. I could tell he recognized us, and we had just seen him at his fourth birthday party in January. He didn't smile or say anything though. He looked like he didn't know where he was or what was happening. Of course he didn't! Kim had whisked him away from Ron and Sandy earlier and brought him to this weird looking place with loud intercoms!

"Elijah!" I cried through my tears. I ran to him and hugged him, and he hugged back quietly.

Benita embraced us tightly as our gate was already getting called onto the plane. She had snot running from her nose by now. Kim stood by patiently.

"Call me as soon as you get there!" Benita said.

We told her we would. I told myself that once we landed, I'd call her and she'd have the arrangements made to send us back.

It was time to board the plane and we still held onto Mama Benita.

"We have to get on," Kim prodded us. People were looking at us with us curiosity.

After one last big squeeze, Benita let go of us and said her last goodbye in a quivering voice. Then she walked away slowly, a very slow and painful walk. If I wasn't mistaken, it looked like she was walking away like she knew she had just done something that wasn't right. I saw it and felt it. She didn't turn to look back.

Kim escorted us onto the plane. Everything was a blur. The flight attendant greeting and seating us, the other passengers finding their seats, the whole thing was seen through a blur of my tears.

Stan, Rae, and I were seated together. They were still crying just as much as I was. I had the window seat. Kim was seated behind us with Elijah.

Dear Mama,

We cried even when the plane ascended. It was nighttime and the city lights of Las Vegas below made my hopes and dreams seem impossible, because I was now leaving those lights. My dreams felt shattered. I was leaving the only place I had ever known. I was leaving Dee and Daniel and Keyonna. I was leaving Benita. And I was leaving you, Mama.

But it's not over, I was telling myself. Trust me, it's not over.

I repeated this through my tears and even as I drifted off into a tumultuous sleep, in route to a new, unknown and frightful life in Upstate New York.

PART TWO

And if a house be divided against itself, that house cannot stand.

Mark 3 verse 25

TWELVE

I awakened to the sun shining in my face.

Wow, so bright. I shut my eyes against the brightness, and a second later I realized I was still on the plane. Someone had opened the blinds to my window seat. Probably Kim's evil self.

Sure enough, I heard her annoying laugh. It was torture to my ears. Ugh.

The flight attendant was speaking on the intercom about our descent into Detroit, Michigan. Once my eyes felt strong enough to open again, I saw Stan and Rae were up too. They were looking just as wide eyed and groggy as I felt. Suddenly I remembered we had fallen asleep crying with our snacks on our seat trays in front of us. I stretched as best as I could and turned around to face Kim.

"Turn around," she said. "We're about to land."

"What happened to our snacks?" I asked.

"They gone," Kim laughed as if I asked a stupid question. "Once you fell asleep they threw it away."

I scowled as we prepared for landing.

Going through the Detroit airport was a daze as well. We were still in an emotional trance. There was one more flight to catch.

Something happened that gave us a momentary spout of laughter. We were going down the escalator when Elijah stepped onto the first step and fell. But he sprang back up in a second, like a bungie cord. He was only four. He brushed himself off, which would be symbolic. He hadn't hurt himself. My baby brother was so cute!

Our second flight was on a very small plane. Only a few other passengers were on. Everyone acted very serious and businesslike.

Our seats were much bigger and more comfortable. The flight stewardess sat next to me. She told me that my siblings and I were very cute and she kept smiling at us.

"Are you excited about going to New York?" she asked me.

"No."

"Aw. Why not?"

"Because I want to be with my real family."

She didn't say anything.

"I'm going to return to them someday."

A few minutes passed.

"How long does this flight take?" I asked her.

"One hour and twelve minutes," she said with clear diction. I could tell she liked to fly a lot.

"It looks so different out here."

"I can imagine."

"Do we have to fly over any water?"

"Only briefly. But we'll be fine. Don't worry." Her smile was full of compassion.

I still remember the scenery as we descended. We were only familiar with the mountains and deserts of Nevada. Looking out the window and down at New York, we saw country green trees and hills. The vast fields were like a Prairie. From up in the air, the spotted white clouds above the green trees reminded me of broccoli and ranch dressing.

I was appalled when we landed at a very small, desolate airport. I just couldn't comprehend it. The contents of my stomach almost came up when I saw Karen Carlon.

No!

I had prayed that I would never see this lady again.

I didn't see Neal. Only Karen and Abram and someone else I can't recall.

Kim's footsteps slammed on the pavement merrily as she smiled bright and walked towards the Carlons. It was a happy dance. She did this so loudly, and Rae looked up at her very annoyed. It was too early for this nonsense!

"Hey Karen!" she said with grandeur. "Here they are. All in one piece!"

Karen smiled. "Hi!" she said to us, her blue eyes being calm and polite.

Abram stood beside the other person, already with a dominant stance about himself. He gave a half-wave at us.

Kim and Karen exchanged words about our trip. Then Kim looked around at the vast and empty country surrounding us. She looked very amused, and at the same time very happy. She also looked like she couldn't wait to get the heck out of here and back to real civilization.

"Well," she said after we got our bags out of luggage. "I just spent so many hours on two flights with barely enough sleep. And guess what? I have to do it *all* over again right now!"

"Hope it goes comfortable for you," Karen said. "Thank you very much for flying with them and making sure everything was okay."

"Of course; it's my job!" Kim said with fakeness that I could see right through. I hated her so much.

Kim wished us the best and gave each of us a hug. She mentioned she wasn't looking forward to that long flight back right away.

Yeah right!

I knew she was more than ready to leave. Here we were, in the middle of nowhere thousands of miles away and Kim knew at that moment what she had done. She left me stranded there as she went back into the small airport to return to the happiness of the West Coast.

From that moment on, I mentally checked out. I would never be the same again.

Karen and her acquaintance put our stuff in the trunk of the Carlons ugly blue station wagon. Then we all piled in to begin the drive to the house. Karen said we had about an hour's drive. We were in Binghamton and we needed to get to Candor, New York. A few minutes into the drive she spoke again.

"I was so excited," she told us. "I didn't even go to sleep last night!"

No one said anything. Abram was crammed up front with her and her friend, who was driving, and the four of us were crammed in the back seat.

A few minutes later, Karen turned around to look at us again.

"Sequoya, did you cut your hair?" she asked, studying me.

"*No!*" I shrieked angrily.

It was braided but it was kind of damaged. Unlike the last time in Vegas when Karen made the comment about my hair and was very friendly, this time she looked at me with a confident and smug look after I answered her. She turned back around. She now had a demeanor about herself that told me she was gearing up for whatever I had in store.

The rest of the ride was quiet with only Karen and her friend speaking occasionally. The station wagon was bumping along the road.

Karen needs to lose some weight, I thought to myself. She's the heaviest one in this car! Why is she so huge? I hope the tires don't go flat!

WELCOME TO THE VILLAGE OF CANDOR boasted proudly as we arrived in the deserted town and passed a gas station. I was looking for the people of the town, but didn't see anyone. Where was everybody? The houses were decent looking and cozy but not one person was outside.

We made a right onto a street that ascended into a hill called Mountain Avenue. A yellow triangular sign read **DEAD END** and a chill traveled through my body.

A few seconds later, I could see the barn and fields off to the left corner against the backdrop of mountains that were covered in trees. I had seen this in the photo album they sent. The houses on this street were mostly on the right side of the road, with one lone house that was closest to the barn. I could see a few cows wandering near the barn in the distance. They were inside a fence, thank God! I was so happy that the Carlon house wasn't the one near the barn.

We pulled into the dirt driveway at the blue house on Mountain Ave, in Candor, New York.

The farm looking house had a fenced in yard for the dogs to run around. I saw a garden off to the side of the fence. From the front porch, you could see the prairie mountain trees in front of you. They looked close to us, but you could tell it was a long walk along the cornfields that started a few yards away from the front yard. Right before the field was a trail that led into the woods on your right. A real hike. Vast land surrounded the house and I could see two other houses off to the left that were scattered with their own sufficient space.

Multiple cars were lined up on the front lawn like an auction. Karen told us we'd get our belongings out the trunk later. She led us up the steps and opened the outer door, then the screen door, which creaked.

When I first stepped in the house, I heard a dog bark and I shrieked, *"No, it's a dog!"*

Rae glanced at me annoyed. She was trying to cope just as much as I was, and I wasn't helping. I knew about the dogs ahead of time. I had seen them in the pictures. But that didn't make my fear of them just go away. I had always been afraid of them, especially the ones at Ron and Sandy Hues house.

Little did I know, Karen would use my fear of them to torment me.

For now, the dogs were hidden in the back part of the house. I could still hear them barking.

We crowded in the front dining and living room area.

"Surprise!" echoed a crowd of people.

That explained all the cars on the lawn. We stood there frozen.

I guessed these people were friends and acquaintances of the Carlons. Every person stared at us and smiled like they had never seen black children before. They looked so fascinated. Eyes skimming us all over, looking back and forth between all four of us.

No, the four of us didn't look the same. But we still looked alike. There were differences in height and skin tone and hair color and whatnot, but you could tell we were brothers and sisters.

Then, something caught my eye. In the sea of white faces, I saw one sole black woman! She wore an afro. A white man had his arm around her protectively. Were they together?

On the other side of the black woman, a young woman in her mid-twenties looked at Karen and said, "Hi Mom!"

"Cadee...these are your siblings!"

Siblings?

Cadee looked like a nicer and younger version of Karen. She smiled hugely at us. I felt an inkling of a genuine aura from her.

"Hey guys," she said to us.

Then she gestured toward the black woman and said, "This is my best friend, Chomma!"

"So, you will call her Auntie Chomma," Karen said proudly.

"I'm happy to meet you guys!" Auntie Chomma said, smiling. Her large afro wobbled on her head. "This is my husband Lenny." She gestured to the burly white man who had his arm around her. He nodded at us.

Auntie Chomma looked each of us in the eyes and there was a silent language we spoke.

Cake and ice cream was served. I declined the refreshments and held one hand on my head, and the other on my stomach. I was sick and dizzy.

"Do you want to take a nap in your room?" Karen asked me.

I was barely able to nod. I followed her up the creaky wood stairs. The first room was on our left, not quite at the foot of the stairs but close enough. This was interesting. The door was positioned for you to step midway onto the stairs when you exited the room. What kind of house was this?

Karen opened the door and I followed her into the pink room.

"There's a fan in your window. Its set so it blows fresh air into your room," Karen explained. "Your bed is the bottom bunk. Raeannah's is the top. I'm going to be checking on you to make sure you're okay. Is that okay?"

I didn't say anything. She closed my door quietly.

Instead of lying on the bed I walked through the cloth entrance of the empty closet and hid inside. At least the rooms were carpeted, despite the creaking wood of the stairs and main floor. I pulled the picture from my pocket that Benita had given me and I stared at it. I drowned out the noise of the company downstairs.

After a while, Karen came in the room without knocking. She knew I was in the closet because I wasn't on the bottom bunk. I quickly stuffed the picture in my pocket.

She parted the curtain and hung the ends on the top rail of the closet. She sat on the floor close to me, facing me at the entrance. I wanted to shrink away from her.

She attempted to talk to me. I wouldn't speak. She kept asking me what was wrong and if I was okay.

Finally, in a smug voice, I said, "I'm remembering my family promise."

"What's your family promise?" she asked. Her eyes were staring me down. She tried to appear as if she really cared and wanted to know for my happiness, but I knew that wasn't the real case.

I didn't say anything.

"What's the family promise?" she asked again, a little more persistent.

I still didn't answer.

Karen looked at me. She wasn't budging. Her huge presence in front of me was so annoying! Her determined expression, sitting Indian style in front of me, nosy and cold blue eyes, graying stringy unruly hair, was about to surely make me vomit. She was blocking the air from the fan.

"What's the promise?"

Then I said, "To never forget them!"

Karen stared for a minute with an unreadable expression. I stared back. I was proud of myself.

She finally left my room. I began to cry for my real family. I stood myself up and wobbled over to the bottom bunk and spread myself out. I fell into a deep sleep from my crying.

It was dark when my eyes opened. The fan was blowing a chill air in the room. I wrapped my arms around my body, trying to rub in some warmth. I stood up and rubbed my face. Remnant tears felt moist and crusty.

I listened for any noise. I could tell the company we had earlier was now gone, but there still seemed to be a commotion.

If I wasn't mistaken, was that Stan and Rae and Elijah I heard laughing as well? *Hmmphh!*

I stretched and opened the door. I could peer into the dining room and parts of the adjacent living room. If I laid on my stomach at the entrance, I could peer into all the living room. Such a weird and unique position. The girls room was literally built into the staircase. To the left of our room and beyond the foot of the stairs was a small den.

I stepped out to head downstairs. I ran smack into a toddler.

"Whoa!" I exclaimed.

She instantly said, "Hi!"

"Hi," I mumbled.

Cadee was walking up the stairs behind the little girl.

"We were coming to your room to see if you were awake," she said. "This is my daughter Francisca. We call her Cisca. Tell her how old you are Cisca."

"I'm three!" the little girl beamed. She had dark brown curly ringlets surrounding her face.

They reversed on the steps and I followed them down. I had slept the whole day away.

Downstairs, Neal was home from work. He looked at me shyly. I didn't blame him for still being at work and not staying home for our arrival. It wasn't that serious like Karen had made it, and we really didn't belong here.

Everyone seemed to be hyper and was running around. Cadee introduced me to her two-year-old son Fernando, who they called Nano.

I turned down dinner. But I still sat at the dining room table. I hadn't eaten since the brunch we had with Benita the previous day before the flight and I had barely nibbled on the snacks from the attendant. I had no appetite.

They made sure the dogs were locked in the back so that I was comfortable.

"You haven't opened your gifts yet," Karen informed me. "Everyone else has."

Gifts?

Karen set a few items in front of me where my dinner should have been. I opened the packages. One thing I do remember receiving was a black wig.

Yes, a wig! Mama, was she serious? It wasn't a regular wig either...it was very frilly like a lion's fur...and so fake.

"Can I see you try it on?" she asked me.

What?

"Okay," I said out loud, being a good sport. I placed the itchy wig over my braids. I pretended I liked it.

"How nice!" Karen exclaimed. "Are you going to wear it to school?"

I looked at Karen like she was crazy and removed the wig from my head. There was a moment of silence before everyone resumed their dinner.

It was the beginning of June. Our first couple of weeks at the Carlons went by. I ate very little and was so homesick. The right side of my tongue was torn from biting and chewing on it, out of my fear and apprehension of this new life.

The open cut on my tongue had turned yellow with a black and green sore in the middle of it. Karen shined a flashlight in my mouth as I cried from the pain.

"It's infected," she informed me.

"Can you take me to the doctor?" I asked her several times.

She brushed my question off and said I was going to be okay, and that it would heal soon enough.

The pain prevented me from eating the little bit of food that I could slip in my mouth because it was so painful. I took a small section of food or small sip of drink, and I would cradle it on the good side of my mouth and tongue and eat that way.

The Carlons piled us in the station wagon one day.

"We want you to see where your school is," Karen said proudly.

We headed down Main Street and less than two minutes later we turned right into a bend on the road, and I saw a small two-story brick building.

"That's Candor Junior-Senior High School," she said. "You guys have a while before you get there. Well Sequoya, you have two years. Our elementary runs from Kindergarten through sixth. The high school is seventh through twelfth grade."

Right across the field a little way was the one story elementary school. I had never seen all grades so near each other. Looking at both schools, I told myself that I wouldn't even make it to the elementary, let alone the high school. I felt so sick.

Why is it taking so long to wake up from this nightmare?

Near the elementary school was a wooden playground.

I didn't go out to the playground like everyone else. I stood off to the side by myself. I stayed clear of Abram. There was no way he was going to get the opportunity to punch me again for not participating. If he even attempted, I would go off so hard on him! Try me if you want too, I thought. Kim isn't here to hold me back from beating...

Speaking of Kim, how come she hadn't called to check on us?

Since it was the last month of the school year, Karen was concerned about how the Candor School District would respond to us attending the last three weeks. Summer vacation was starting and it didn't make sense.

It was the same situation we had at Benita's when we left Tiwanda's last May. I hoped we could just have an early summer.

If we were even here that long.

"But Mom," Abram wined. "It won't be fair if I still have to go to school and they get to stay home," I overheard him saying to Karen.

"I know Abram."

What in the world?

Karen made moves, and we were accepted into school for the remaining weeks of the school year.

She made a grand entrance with us on our first day. Every student and faculty stared as Karen proudly stood beside us. Some of the parents gaped at Karen, as if she had pulled a big number on all of them.

"Oh, my God, those children are so cute!" several of the teachers were commenting. I noticed when they said this, Karen didn't smile or say thank you. She looked stuck up and annoyed.

She told the principal she was our mother and that she wanted to be the one to walk us to our classes. She already possessed an authority about her that made adults, even grown men, jump to do what she required of them, even in their own space and jurisdiction.

The principal walked beside her as she escorted us to our classrooms. She hugged each of us like we were a prize.

"Have a wonderful day!" she said, crying as each of us went into our classrooms.

I was the last one to get escorted. When I walked in my fourth-grade classroom, everyone stared at me with excitement. The girls wanted to be my friend and the boys looked at me with fascination. There was only one other black girl in my class, in fact our whole grade. She was looking at me in shock. We made eye contact and had a silent understanding.

We were very popular for the last three weeks of the school year. I hadn't experienced anything like it. The teachers loved us and thought we were the most adorable kids in the school. We were so cute too, and we knew it. But we were humble. Karen didn't seem flattered by all the attention. She played it off. She acted as if she was insulted when they complimented us.

She would still act like she loved us and was so happy to be our mother. On the last week of school, my class went on a field trip to a museum four hours away in Albany, New York. Karen packed me this giant lunch. It was the biggest sandwich I had ever seen and felt. Along with the sandwich were goodies and fruit. I had the heaviest lunch out of everyone.

My tongue was still bothering me and it hadn't healed all the way. She should have known I had no appetite like that. I attempted to eat when we stopped for lunch during the trip. Careful of my tongue, I bit into the sandwich. Then I spit the contents back out because I felt something.

There was a folded piece of paper. What in the world? I opened it up and saw Karen had written a note.

I love you Sequoya. Have a nice day on your field trip. See you when you get home!

I got sick and dumped the whole lunch in the trash. One of the boys in my class was mad because he wanted it, even though he'd already scarfed his lunch down.

"All that food just went to waste," he pouted.

"Sorry," I said, my speech a little slurred because of my tongue. I was embarrassed.

"Forgiven," he said, grinning at me.

When I got home, Karen asked me how the field trip was and if I enjoyed my lunch.

"It was fun. Yes, I enjoyed my lunch. Thank you."

She looked at me expectantly. When I didn't say anything else, she frowned.

"I'm going to start dinner now," she said, turning toward the kitchen.

Dear Mama,

I was still crying every day. There wasn't a day that didn't go by that I didn't think of you. Stan, Rae, and I were asking to call Benita. We told Karen we knew her number by heart. Every time we asked to call her, she said maybe later, not right now. It began to frustrate me. Was she ever going to let us call?

Elijah was walking around saying, "I want my Mama Sandy," in a quivering, sad voice. He suddenly burst out at random times and looked around. He was looking for Sandy, the lady who cared for him for the first four years of his life.

Whenever he did this, Karen would take Elijah upstairs, spank him, and say in a very evil voice, "Sandy is not your mother! Don't you ever mention her name again!"

We heard him wailing as he received his blows.

I was gearing up for battle, quietly brewing.

I was crying in the living room one day. Karen walked in to see me holding the picture Benita had given me. She caught a glimpse of it before I could stuff it in my pocket.

"What's that picture?" she asked.

"My foster mom Benita," I said timidly. "She gave this to me."

"Can I see?"

I slowly handed it over. She stared at it.

"My foster mom is so pretty," I added.

For a second Karen's nostrils flared, like she couldn't believe I said this.

"I'm remembering what she told me."

"What did Benita tell you?" she pressed.

When I didn't answer, she asked again, being very persistent.

I looked Karen in her eye.

"She said this picture is also me."

Karen stared at me blankly.

"She said I'm going to be successful and shine and no one can ever dim my light. No matter what they do to me."

Karen was silent for a moment.

Finally, she asked, "Can I borrow this picture?"

I was still high on my confident rush so I nodded smugly.

"Thank you."

I never saw the picture again.

THIRTEEN

Karen took Rae and me to an appointment fifteen minutes away in Owego, New York. It had something to do with the car insurance on the station wagon. The boys stayed back with Neal. He drove a jeep. Karen usually parked her car in the dirt driveway where a permanent dent had been made from her parked car. Neal usually parked vertical, backing in reverse, the back of his jeep close to the dog fence. His parking spot had permanent lines as well.

We sat down in the cold waiting room. We were the only people in the place. My sister and I became bored, so we decided to pretend we were dancers. The floor reminded me of a runway. So, we took turns walking down this imaginary runway, with a twitch to our steps. We were shaking our behinds as well.

We poked our behinds out and bent all the way down to the ground, moving our hips in a grinding position, *while* walking down the runway. We were very serious as we did this.

I looked up and saw Karen peeking at us from behind a magazine she was reading. She instantly ducked behind the magazine again.

Back at home, she had a talk with us.

"You know," she said, a little angry. "I'm very appalled by the way you two dance! That was very inappropriate what you did today inside of the insurance office. I really can't believe it!" She was shaking her head like we had committed a major crime. She didn't say it nicely. She just made us feel guilty for being who we are. She made us feel like we were horrible little girls.

"From now in," she said. "You dance like this…look."

She held her hands out, clapped and stomped her feet, like people do at church.

"This is the proper way to dance," she said.

We looked at her. In my mind, I was thinking *Oh heck no! That isn't dancing! Please lady, I won first place in my cheerleading dance competition. We know how to dance, thank you very much.*

"You will lose your privileges if I ever catch you dancing in that manner again. Do you understand me?"

We nodded. From that point on, she watched us closely. We didn't dance that way in front of her. Even when we weren't dancing, we naturally made certain motions with our walk and body. We had rhythm. She would glare at us.

"What?" we asked, wondering what she was mad at now.

"I didn't say anything," she said with an attitude.

Eventually, her possessive and dominating aura, combined with her icy blue eyes, would put us to fear. Our confidence level was slowly slipping away…without us even aware of it.

We didn't realize that Karen had a trick under her sleeve as summer vacation started that year. Over that summer without us knowing, she slowly got rid of our cute clothes that Benita bought us. They were very appropriate and decent clothes. We matched and there was plenty of them, so I didn't understand where they had gone.

Our first summer at the Carlons went by alright. I hated that the screen windows in the house were torn and scratched because of Abram's large black and white housecat, Ernie.

Karen took the tattered screens out but still left the fans. The only air-conditioned part of the house was Neal and Karen's bedroom and adjacent bathroom. None of us were allowed in their room. Abram happened to wander in and out of Neal and Karen's room when he wanted cool air.

Every room in the house needed a fan in the windows. I was terrified of the bees and flies that flew into the house. I have always had a severe fear of bees.

More on that later, Mama.

Everything was going somewhat okay for the first few months. Before school started again, I was still going by my birth name, Sequoya.

Neal and Karen sat at the breakfast table one morning to share something with us. Well, Karen did. Neal was always silent. It was already established who was the boss.

I had asked Neal his age one day.

"I'm twenty-nine. I'll be thirty in November."

"How old is Mom?" Yes, surprisingly I was saying Mom and Dad, to make an effort.

"She's forty-five."

I began counting on my fingers.

Before I finished, Neal said, "She's sixteen years older than me."

"Oh," I said.

Neal seemed very comfortable letting Karen run things and be the speaker of everything.

At the breakfast table on this particular morning, Karen started off by telling us that we were a blessing from God to her and she cherished us. She began her speech.

"One day in 1994, two years after Neal and I were married, I received a word from God. Abram was a year old...a man from the church we attended came to me and said, hey Karen, I saw Abigail Mae playing in the fields! He prophesized that God would bless me with a girl named Abigail Mae..."

She looked at Rae as she said this. Rae didn't flinch.

Oh no!

Karen went on to tell a grand story about each name God had given her to name her children.

She told us about the name Isaiah Daniel, and she looked at Stanford when she said this, who silently bowed his head. I know my brother was like *'what the?'*

When she looked at Elijah, she briefly told him the story about Zechariah in the Bible, but that she liked the name Elijah too. His born name was Elijah Roydean Howard. Karen liked Elijah Zechariah Carlon much better.

My baby brother didn't flinch.

Then Karen briefly told us the story about Abraham and Sarah in the Bible.

Abram and I refused to look at each other. We didn't like each other and hated being in the same room. What was wrong with this bat crazy lady? Why on earth would she want a brother and sister to have the same names as a sacred couple in the Bible?

"But the name God has given me for you Sequoya...is SaraJane Faith Carlon."

"*No!*" I shrieked angrily. "My Mama named me Sequoya Saquantah Griffin!"

Karen pursed her lips together. She looked at Neal, who looked down at his food. Everyone else was ready to take their new names. I could not believe it!

I looked at Stan, Rae, and Elijah. They were young and had finally begun to throw in the towel and accept the Carlons as their family.

In a way, I can't blame them. I was the oldest out of them. I had more time and understanding with our biological family. I would never forget them. I would always remember the family promise. No matter what.

"I like my own name," I said.

There was silence.

Then Karen said, "We want you to have biblical names."

But I thought God gave these names to her? So, what is the real truth?

"So, did *Abram* have another name before?" I asked sarcastically. I didn't look in his direction but I knew he was mad.

"He did," Karen answered me patiently. "I'm going to tell you another story. Dad has two sisters named Tammy and Terri. He's the oldest, then there's Terri, and then Tammy is the baby sister. When they were young, Dad's father died. Dad was only nine. His mother raised all three of them by herself. Tammy became very promiscuous. That means she became sexually active at a young age. My two oldest children, Cadee and Colin, were just about grown up. But I was pregnant again...not by Dad by the way...so this is before we met..."

She looked at Neal before continuing. He didn't flinch.

"I got into a car accident..." Karen's voice was becoming dramatic, which would be her signature tone to help seal the emotion to always get anything she wanted. Tears were beginning to form in her eyes.

"And I lost my son!" she cried.

I could see everyone at the table was falling for Karen. Neal and Abram were falling all over again. Yeah it was sad, but not sad enough for me to change my name for her.

She wiped her tears and cleared her throat.

"The car accident wasn't that bad, but it did enough damage to where I lost the baby. Then Tammy became pregnant at only sixteen. The father was an older guy who skipped town as soon as she told him she was pregnant. Tammy and I bonded and we had talks throughout her entire pregnancy...and she agreed that she wouldn't be able to care for Abram like Neal and I could. She decided to do what was best for Abram's overall wellbeing. She agreed to give him to us. And that was God giving me another son...after losing mine in the accident."

She squeezed Neal's hand.

"So, Abram is really Dad's nephew?" I asked.

"He's my dad!" Abram said angrily, shooting me a dirty look.

"Yes, he is Abram, but Tammy gave birth to you. You were born Dad's nephew, but since you were a baby you have been ours. We adopted you. You are our son." Karen officiated.

"Where's Tammy now?" I asked. Should we call her Aunt Tammy? I was wondering.

"Forget that whore!" Abram shouted. He jumped from the table and sprinted up the stairs. The door to the boys room slammed.

"What was Abram's name at birth?" I asked.

"It was Patrick," Karen smiled.

My siblings were already going by their new names. Everyone was just waiting on me. One day Karen and I were in the kitchen baking, talking, and what she called "bonding."

Karen slipped and called me "Sara."

"Oh, I'm sorry. I mean Sequoya!"

She immediately corrected herself. She didn't want me to get upset. She looked very nervous. She fervently resumed her cooking.

Still to this very day, I don't know why I did, but I softened.

"You can call me Sara," I looked at her, surrendering.

Karen's face lit up so brightly. Her blue eyes were the happiest I had ever seen towards me since we'd first met.

Not too long after, Neal and Karen took us to the Owego Courthouse to get our names officially changed.

Elijah Roydean Howard was changed to Elijah Zechariah Carlon. Raeannah Tasha Griffin was changed to Abigail Mae Carlon. Stanford Cordero Griffin was changed to Isaiah Daniel Carlon. My name, Sequoya Saquantah Griffin, was changed to SaraJane Faith Carlon.

I was unaware that new copies of our birth certificates and social security cards were made. Karen and Neal were listed on our birth certificates as the parents who gave birth to us in Las Vegas, Nevada.

Dear Mama,

Later during arguments, Karen claimed we had a choice to pick any name in the world that we wanted to be called. Yeah right! That was a lie because they sat us down at the breakfast table with some bogus psychic story and Karen already had the names picked out...and **duh**, *I would have kept my real name you gave me!*

Karen always says that Abram and I try to be the dominant ones of the house and that our violent behavior shows it. Actually, I'm only rioting for my God given rights! It usually goes like this:

Abram gets treated different or better than us. So, I speak up about it, just like he spoke up about us having to go to school in June because it wasn't fair. After speaking up, Abram gets mad, demands from Neal to still have his way, and then Neal tells Karen to leave him alone about it. He doesn't want to hear Abram's mouth. Then Karen, upset that I'm not backing down either, gets into it with me, trying to subdue me into submission to just "accept the fact" that Abram is going to be treated better than us.

Sometimes, the walls in the whole house feel like they're shaking. I'm so loud and screaming and battling Karen, and Neal is so upset so he starts yelling at his beloved son to knock it off. Then Abram starts battling Neal. At that moment, everyone else is covering their ears. Then Neal and Karen get into their **own** shouting match, saying that Abram and I need to stop thinking we run the house.

Then it calms down. Stop, start again, and then repeat.

I just don't understand why we have been adopted in the first place if there's going to be differences in treatment. Anyway Mama, more on that later.

Karen and Neal took us to a church called Abide in The Vine, at the top of a hill that overlooked the green hills of Owego. The building resembled a school.

"This looks like a school," I said.

"Yes, it used to be Owego High School before they built another building somewhere else," Karen explained. "Our church service is held in the old gymnasium."

We walked into the undecorated lobby and down a long dark corridor. The only light we saw was coming from the end of the hall. Worship music was already playing.

The bleachers were stacked at the back of the room. Children had climbed to the top for their own hangout.

"Abram!" some of them exclaimed, while also looking at us with curiosity.

The rest of the gym had nice cushioned chairs placed in two separate sections. A raised-up platform was the stage, along with an overhead projector displaying the song lyrics being played. There were a few people who served as the "choir." This was new to me because I was accustomed to a big, robe wearing choir. The songs being played were also new to me. The sound was...much different.

The singers...well let's just say my young mind wasn't "open" to this kind of sound.

Everyone smiled and greeted us. The pastor and first lady had our family stand up and a microphone was handed to Karen. She grabbed it firmly.

"This is SaraJane, Isaiah, Abigail, and Elijah. They're an addition to our family. We have adopted them from Nevada."

Exclamations and claps rang all around. Once seated, I looked around and observed more. I noticed a family that all looked alike. There were two teenage daughters, and another girl who looked to be in her early twenties. She was biracial, but she still resembled the younger ones. She smiled at me and I smiled back. Then I looked around to see if anyone else of color was in attendance.

There was an elderly lady who sat alone. But on her lap sat a young biracial boy who looked to be around Stan's age. He looked over at us, his eyes widening. The elderly lady looked at us politely. Karen saw me glancing at them. She hadn't smiled at the lady like she did the other members of the Church.

There was an older Caucasian lady with long grayish white hair down her back. She reminded me of Rapunzel. In my head, I would call her "Rapunzel's mom" but not dare say it out loud. I felt kind of funny because her hair was gray. Her name was Sue. She reminded me of Karen a little bit. They could pass for sisters. She introduced herself as Karen's best friend. Or something like that.

The children were escorted to the hallway and down another corridor that led to a wing of classrooms. It was dark and cold.

"Why is it so cold?" I asked. "Why are all the lights off?"

"We haven't been here that long," one of the Sunday School teachers explained. "Soon, hopefully in the near future, the whole building will be ready. We're redecorating this whole wing that belongs to the church."

"Is the whole school the church?"

"No. Other businesses want to inquire about the other wing of hallways. But it won't take away from our wings and the gym. We're trying to get the whole building to turn it into a homeschool. A Christian school."

We entered the cold classroom. I sat at one of the tables shivering for the remainder of Sunday School. I was always cold after leaving Las Vegas. At Candor Elementary during the last month of school, I shivered during recess, even though it was June. Any slight breeze welcomed goose bumps on my body. My teacher had draped her light jacket around me. I was just familiar with the dry heat of the West Coast.

One of the Sunday School teachers was holding a video camera.

"We would like to have our new students introduce themselves," she said proudly. "Tell us your names and what God has done for you…how much do you love our Mighty God?"

When she pointed the camera at me, I was very irritated. I was also sad. I didn't want to be in this church for some reason. I didn't like to have their camera pointed at me without them asking.

I remember saying I loved a song called "Welcome into this Place," a song we had learned at Benita's church. Very soulful.

"Can you sing it for us?" she asked.

Crap.

I just wasn't in the mood. At all.

I sang about two lines, before stopping and shaking my head with an expression like *'Please, just leave me alone.'*

She finally got the hint and put the camera on someone else. When we got home later, Karen asked me if I liked Abide in the Vine.

I nodded. That wasn't entirely true, at least for the moment.

"What about the worship songs?"

"I don't know…they sound different."

"Different how?" she was now looking at me very curiously.

"They don't sound like the other churches in Vegas."

"How do the other churches sound?"

"They sound better," I said bluntly. I was too young to explain that there was no "soul sound" aura of a thriving, piano playing, drum rattling, rhythm having choir and equally excited congregation.

Karen frowned as she tried to give a little chuckle. But she was looking at me as if I had insulted her.

"Well, church is where you fellowship with Jesus. It doesn't matter who does or doesn't sound better."

Okay, she can have that one.

Abide in the Vine held their annual church picnic that summer. It was hosted at Sue's house in Owego. Sue lived on a nice property not too far from the popular Hickories Park. Her house was decent sized and she had a huge swimming pool. Fields were spread out surrounding the vast area.

Sue's children and grandchildren eagerly hosted. The picnic tables were filled with food. Sue grabbed Rae and me and showed us the inside of her house, which was a lot of low tone colors and random abstract pieces all over the walls. We stayed inside in the air conditioning chatting with her in the kitchen and playing with her long Rapunzel hair.

Karen came in after a while to hand us a bag with our bathing suits. She had told us she wanted us to be baptized. We told her that Stanford had already been baptized at Benita's church. I had looked at the cold water they placed Stan in. When he came back up from the water he was shivering so bad that Benita regretted it for a moment. She was upset the church hadn't warmed up the water.

"Well, this water is already warmed up from the heat outside," Karen said.

Elijah and Rae were too young to get baptized, according to Karen. So, she talked me into doing it.

Might as well. Water is warm, water is warm, I repeated to myself.

Church members and guests cleared the swimming pool for the baptisms to take place. Karen grabbed me by my hand and led me to the edge of the pool.

"I don't know how to swim," I reminded her.

"Don't worry. We're at the shallow end and we won't let go of you!" she reassured me.

We stepped down into the water, which was warm like she said. The pastor stood with a white sheet robe over his large protruding belly. He reminded me a little bit of Santa Clause.

I'm not sure exactly what happened, but as the three of us stood in the water, Karen suddenly looked at the pastor in earnest.

"I want to baptize my daughter," she told him.

The pastor looked at her surprised for a second before nodding his head. Karen was using her authority that made everyone halt.

Karen held me as the pastor spoke a few words.

The next thing I knew, she grabbed my shoulders. Her voice was so loud as it carried over the swimming pool area and to the picnic tables and basketball court.

"SaraJane, I baptize you by the blood of Jesus!"

I was pushed down into the water with her strong forceful hands, holding my breath, my natural ponytail billowing in the water.

Members of the church were playing volleyball and basketball. I stood with a group of girls who were a few years older than me. We weren't too far from a picnic table where Karen was setting our meal.

These girls were able to call themselves grown teenagers, but I couldn't yet for a few years. I felt like I was one of them as we talked and laughed. I noticed that Karen kept eyeing us sternly, which was uncalled for because we weren't doing anything questionable.

Karen came over to our girl group and said it was time for me to eat.

One of the girls looked at Karen, then back at me, and said, "Bye beautiful chica!"

Karen looked like she had been insulted. She scowled.

The other girls definitely saw this look she gave. They stood there glancing at each other like *'okay maybe we have done something wrong!'*

I was kind of embarrassed. This was not good. I hoped she wouldn't act like this with every friend I made. I smiled neutrally at the girls and then followed Karen to the picnic table.

"Time to eat!" she called to the others. A few church members were looking at all of us.

As we ate, the young biracial boy who was on the elderly lady's lap wandered over to our table. We had been introduced to him during Sunday School. His name was Steven. We learned that the lady who brought him to church was his grandmother.

Steven liked Stan, Rae, Elijah, and me. But from the beginning, Karen did not like Steven. For no apparent reason. I didn't know why. She especially didn't want us to be friends with him, and she was down our necks at the church. She would even check on us in the Sunday School room.

Steven was a good kid! He was a little hyper, but all kids were.

At the church picnic, Steven was trying to get us to play a ball game with him, but Karen wouldn't allow us to play. We had to remain sitting at our picnic table. Even when we were done eating! We didn't understand why Karen made us sit still for the remainder of the church picnic. We wanted to get up and play with the other kids!

Eventually, Steven just stood by the picnic table to chat with us instead. He was just a little boy who wanted to be friends with his fellow Sunday School mates.

A few minutes later, walking back out of Sue's house, Karen approached the picnic table and gave Steven the meanest look ever.

"You need to stay away from my children!" she yelled at him. "They are good kids and I will not allow you to harm them!"

What?

Steven looked at Karen so confused, then at us. We were equally confused as well.

No one said anything. We couldn't. Steven finally walked away looking embarrassed.

Every Sunday, Karen confronted us after service. She asked us if Steven had done anything unusual. He was known for being hyper and Karen didn't want him to be a bad influence for us.

What a stereotype.

We just told her that all he did was exactly what we did, which was laugh and talk with the Sunday School teachers and other children. She informed us one night that she had called his grandmother and spoken to her.

"Don't worry guys, Steven was disciplined by his grandmother tonight. He won't be a bad example for you no longer," she had said.

What the what?

What did she have against Steven? I sure wanted to know.

We were unaware that first summer that major and drastic changes would be taking place. I was still asking Karen if I could give Benita a call to catch up with her. Karen would never let me.

"It will cost us a great deal of money to call long distance to Nevada," she would say.

On other days, she mentioned that we needed to let go of anyone we knew because they most likely had forgotten about us all the way in Nevada.

This really made me seethe with anger. The way she would say this with such compassion in her face, looking me dead in the eye and telling me that my real family had moved on with their lives!

Whenever we talked about Mama and Dee and the others, Karen's eyes would narrow and she would say that she and Neal didn't want to talk about our family with us anymore. They didn't want to hear it. Every time I attempted, Karen already had a rehearsed rebuttal just waiting to shoot out of her mouth.

But she couldn't extract anything from already within me!

Karen also got to work on correcting our speech.

If we said, "Can I ask you a question?" she would roll her eyes and sigh with exasperation.

"It's not *can I ax* you a question...like you're going to chop my head off with an *ax!* Do you want to kill your mother? It's *may I ask you a question!*"

If we said, "I ain't got it," she would correct us.

"No, it's *I don't* have it."

The Carlons made sure to correct us with every sentence until we got it right.

More changes were taking place was well. Abram wasn't the only one getting better treatment and a place to have his voice heard over everyone else. Cadee, Karen's adult daughter, would drop her toddlers Cisca and Nano off during the day while she went to work. Since Cisca was three and Nano was two, they were closer in age to Elijah, who was four. Karen had the three of them play together in the living room.

I noticed that if Nano beat up on Elijah while they were playing, he was allowed too without consequence. If Elijah tried to beat on him back, he was disciplined.

One time, I stood on the far side of the living room watching the two of them play. Nano became upset over a certain toy Elijah had. So, Nano jumped on Elijah, and my baby brother couldn't get up. He started resisting, kicking and pushing, but Nano wouldn't let him get up.

Suddenly, Elijah got his strength and pushed Nano off him and then he walked away. It wasn't done hard, and Nano wasn't hurt at all. Karen stared at Elijah's backside, glaring with anger at him. She followed Elijah to the boys' room and disciplined him. We could hear him crying from the boys' room as Karen spanked him with her fat heavy hand.

They were both toddlers, and they both should have been disciplined! When I brought this up, Karen glowered at me.

"Mind your business Sara," she said, and then changed the subject.

One time, Neal and Karen were in their room. The rest of us were in the living room. As usual, just like Nano, Abram would get mad at Stanford if he beat him in a game or something. He would start a physical altercation with him. On this day, Abram was kicking and punching Stanford, claiming he was just being playful.

"I'm just playing," he said, in a fake voice and mean eyes that really said he was truly pissed off.

So, the "playful" beating started off not really hurting Stan. But after a minute, Abram began to kick and punch harder. His blows revealed his true anger towards my brother.

So, Stan kicked and punched him back. Then Abram started crying like a coward.

Neal and Karen ran out their room and started screaming at Stan.

"No one is to use any violence!" they yelled.

Despite this demand, Abram was still angry, so he began to punch Stan again, accompanied with an annoying anger cry that sounded like the wuss and coward he really was.

"Stop Abram!" Karen yelled, but did nothing to pull Abram away. Neal did nothing to stop it either.

Stan's eyes were turning angry.

"Do not touch him!" Karen warned Stan, as she watched him receive blow after blow.

I could not believe this! They didn't do anything to stop him! I could see that it was now starting to hurt my brother. I had been sitting on the couch.

Full of fury, I stood up. Before I could even step forward to defend my brother, Karen's fat self quickly snatched me up and slammed me down on the couch with triple the amount of anger Abram had, and I hadn't even done anything!

She pinned me down on the couch, holding me down tightly.

"Don't you ever put your hands on Abram! Do you hear me?" Her mouth was twisted in anger with her spit landing on my face, gripping me down and digging her nails into my arms, as if she'd been wanting to do this to me all along!

I sarcastically rolled my eyes to be defiant, which made her dig her nails even farther into my arms. The adrenaline rush I was experiencing helped to block out the pain.

When Abram was done venting on my brother, Neal lightly scolded him and took him to another room to talk to him.

Stan was so angry…and it takes a lot to get him angry. When he gets angry, his eyes squint into small beads and he becomes reserved. He was reserved to himself for the rest of that day.

I admire Stan so much, because when we lived in Las Vegas, he was kind of a bad kid, always getting in trouble. I'm very proud of him because he has come a long way. I was the angry and defiant one at the Carlons. The whole time he lived there, he had more control of himself than anyone else in the house! That's what Karen could not stand. She could always get to me, but she could never get to Stanford. He controlled himself.

Neal and Abram could never control themselves, and they were the "privileged" men of the house.

FOURTEEN

By the end of the first summer, Karen closed the daycare she ran in her house.

"It's just too much," she exclaimed. "I have the five of you, *plus* Cisca and Nano, *plus* a few more...it's just too much!"

The parents of the other children would drop them off early in the morning and Karen would already have their individual play mats on the living room floor. Karen depended on the rest of us to entertain the others all day while she retreated into her air-conditioned bedroom.

She blamed the daycare closing on Stan, Rae, Elijah, and me, saying that our addition to the house had made the parents stop bringing their kids. She made us feel guilty for having been adopted, a choice that she unfairly forced on our lives and one that I *certainly* had not wanted. I was thinking, why were we even adopted by you in the first place?

It was also time to go back to school. Rae and I begged her to please get our hair done. There wasn't any black people or beauty parlors to get our hair done right.

Karen rolled her eyes while we complained about our hair. She didn't understand the importance of it, and what it did to our psyche. Or maybe she did. When we told her about braids and "tie knots" like how we looked on our adoption photo on the website, she looked angry and told us to drop it.

"You girls should be grateful!" she said, staring at us. "You need to embrace your natural hair and be happy that God blessed you with it!"

So, we were forced to wear it afro like, an assortment of "nappy" ponytails that stood like sponges on the top of our head. We didn't know how to do our own hair and she didn't buy any moisturizing or conditioning products when we asked for them.

When we first arrived at the house, I stumbled upon a set of books. Some of the titles were labeled *How to Care for The African Girl's Hair* or *Braiding Styles for the African-American Girl*. I could tell these books were written by Caucasian people. The pictures in the books made me cringe. The African girls still had very unruly and nappy hair. Their sides, or "edges" weren't smoothed or slicked back to give that "looking really good" effect.

"I don't like any of these styles," I pouted.

I wished to God to be back at Benita's salon, or on Tamera's bed at Mama Mary's to get my hair done! Tamera was Mexican, but she did black girls hair so well that all the girls had been getting their hair done by her!

I even entertained the thought of Tiwanda Banks. No matter what had happened, our hair was laid while we were with her. It's just something that's very important for black girls, and especially for our self-esteem.

"Well, you're going to have to choose one!" Karen said. "After we visited you in Las Vegas and I tried to assist you with your hair, I knew I had to do something. That's why I purchased these books."

"Since you don't know how to do our hair, can you please take us to another city to get it done? I know there's places out there. There just *has* to be!"

Karen scoffed. She rolled her eyes and said, "I'm not spending any money for you to get your hair done. These books have more than enough styles to choose from."

We began crying. Karen shook her head like she couldn't believe it.

Ironically, she said we had to embrace our culture, but yet she stripped us from our identities and changed our birth names that were actually our culture.

A few days before school started, she showed us a new book that had beading and twisting styles on the cover. She also bought a huge case full of assorted colored beads. Some were solid colors; some were clear colored. She sat Rae and me down in the living room and told us that she had spent hours on the Internet learning how to do a brand new style.

She sounded so serious as she explained that she was going to do "individual plats." They were sectioned off strands. She was going to divide each section into two parts and then twist them together. Then she would put the beads on. She let us choose two different colors of beads we wanted.

I cried inside, aware of the fact that I was going into the fifth grade wearing little girl beads.

Wow.

Karen did Rae's hair first. Then the next day, she did mine. She sat on the couch while we sat on the floor in front of her. She concentrated hard. It took her hours to do it, even though the parts didn't come out right. No one could see our scalp lines, which meant it was still raggedy and busted looking at the roots. But we sucked it up because we had no choice.

She was very proud of her work and looked at us like she just accomplished something very major. I mean, at least she tried. Rae and I shook our heads from left to right, to make the rattling sound of the beads. To show our appreciation of her. I was mad because parts of our hair had broken off over the summer, so our beaded plats only went to our neck. So, we weren't really "rattling" much.

Dear Mama,

I wore my hair like this for most of fifth and sixth grade, sadly to say! They were a pain to take out too! One time Rae and I asked Neal to help us take them out because Karen wouldn't. He stared at us like we had asked him something in a foreign language. He said no, continuing to watch his Nascar race on television.

Karen stopped doing my hair after she spent the whole day doing it on one occasion. After doing my hair, we got into an argument over something. I angrily took out all her hard work. Then she said she would never do it again. That's the reason I stopped wearing them in sixth grade. But I did notice my hair had grown!

We started school that fall with ugly clothes and ugly hair. Our outfits were horrible and mismatched, like she had organized it all on purpose. Our pants were above our ankles and our tops were baggy shirts or sweaters. Basically, grandma sweaters. Our shoes were equally ugly. Stan and Elijah were kind of okay the first couple of years because they were boys, and little boys don't think much about that stuff until a certain age.

On the other hand, Rae and I were traumatized.

"Wait..." we asked her. "Where are our clothes that Benita gave us?"

"They must have gotten lost," she reasoned.

"But there was a lot of them!"

Karen retrieved a box from her room and opened it up. There were only two items left that I recognized from Benita, but not significant enough to make one full outfit.

"This is all you guys had in here," she said. "See?"

I was in disbelief. Nonsense! Lies all around. What angered me the most was the way she stared at us compassionately, like she really cared that we were upset.

We begged her for new clothes. She said we sounded very ungrateful and that we needed to appreciate what we were given. She said there was nothing wrong with getting clothes from the Salvation Army, which she said was her favorite place to shop.

However, Abram had very nice clothes on.

"Hey!" I said to Karen. "His clothes aren't from the Salvation Army!"

"Sara, mind your business."

"It's not fair!"

"What Dad wants to do for Abram, is their business!"

Karen restricted the rest of us from asking Neal for anything. She said if we needed or wanted anything, we had to come to her about it. If we got caught "pestering Dad" like she called it, we would lose our privileges.

Cisca and Nano were also dressed nicely, because Cadee was their mom. She was always more hip and cool to the times, as she was in her mid-twenties. One Sunday after church she asked me if I wanted to go to the mall with her.

"Mom, I want to take Sara to the Endicott Mall for lunch and to hang out," she said. "I need to bond with my sister." Cadee was making a huge effort with me.

"Fine...go ahead," Karen pouted, as if someone had wounded her.

Why did she always act like that when someone wanted to do something for us? Wow, weren't we sisters?

Cadee took me to the mall and we ate hot fudge Sundays at Friendly's. Afterwards, she walked me into the GAP store. I instantly felt unworthy as she told me to pick out a pair of jeans.

I hung my head, ashamed. Karen's image was in my mind. Her success at filling me with false guilt had already been ingrained in me without me realizing.

"Sara, pick any pair you want," Cadee prodded me.

"I'm going to get in trouble," I said nervously. "I'm not supposed to ask anybody for anything. We can't ask Dad either."

"That's nonsense!" Cadee looked puzzled. "I will buy my sister a pair of jeans. Mom will just have to deal with it!"

When I still didn't pick anything out, Cadee selected a pair of white flared jeans.

"These look nice; don't you think? Here...try them on."

I tried them on the dressing room, and wow they fit very nice! I looked at myself in the mirror. A small tiny surge of self-esteem momentarily crept to the surface.

I was nervous on the way back home but Cadee kept looking at me like I was worrying for no reason.

Of course, back at the house, Karen was upset with her.

"I already have clothes for them," she told Cadee.

I walked upstairs to the girls' room, but still eavesdropped.

"Mom, *I* wanted to take Sara out to lunch...and *I* wanted to buy her something. I can buy her what I want! It was *our* outing. I'm not hurting anyone."

"You and Colin are grown up now! These are *my* children and you will not..."

I felt sick by what I was hearing. I had yet to meet Cadee's older brother Colin, who lived in North Carolina.

Despite this incident, those white pair of jeans were one specific item that Karen never took from me.

When we started school that fall, the kids looked at us differently than when they had just a couple of months before when they were all over us. They looked at us like we were weird. The boys didn't talk to me. The girls would stare at me, and I'm positive I could see some of them laughing.

Everyone was also confused because our names were now changed. When the teachers read our names out loud, some of the students looked at each other in a conspiring manner like *'I thought their names were'*...

Then they'd change the subject if one of us was watching them.

Karen allowed us to participate in school activities that fall. We didn't know it would be our first and only time being able to do anything like this.

Reminiscing about my cheerleading league in Las Vegas, I was signed up for football cheerleading. Karen asked me if I also wanted to try soccer. I didn't care for it. But since she suggested it, I agreed. Stan and Abram were signed up for soccer as well. The three of us were the oldest in the house that could participate in the sports. After school practices and weekends when game day arrived kept us all very busy. Karen and Neal shuffled the three of us around at different locations. Even though Abram and Rae were the same age, Karen didn't allow her to participate in any sports. She also held Rae back in the first grade to repeat that whole year again, which we didn't understand why.

Soccer was really Abram's sport. He was very excellent at it. Even as early as age three. A child prodigy. Everyone knew who

Abram was. Fathers of the other children would shout "Abram!" when they saw him. They would get more excited over Abram than their own sons on the team. Even parents from opposing teams would give their respects. Everyone always said that boy could handle the soccer ball with his foot so well...and it was true. Even though we didn't get along, I would watch him and see how passionate he was about the sport. He put his all into it. He smiled a winner's smile with each goal he effortlessly scored.

That was something that Karen and Neal enjoyed raving to people about. His soccer pictures and trophies were all around the house. Age three, age four, age five, age six, etc. Some pictures were in the same years but with different leagues and divisions, as he didn't play for just the Candor School District. We all had a feeling he was going to be a professional soccer player someday.

One thing that annoyed me with the cheerleading was that it was very different from the cheerleading division I was in back in Nevada. Our uniforms had been much better and our "chants" had been hipper, considering we had lived with Mama Mary on the notorious Westside of Las Vegas.

This one wasn't really exciting to me. Our tops were regular white t-shirts and our skirts were a 1950's style blue skirts. Our chants were the "clap your hands and stomp your feet" routines and "Go team go!" patter that Karen liked. I guess it was appropriate for our age group, as we were only ten and eleven-year-olds. However, from the elementary school field, I could see across to the high school field and see that the much older cheerleaders' outfits were how the younger girls in Las Vegas were. They still couldn't hold a candle to even the youngest girls of Las Vegas when it came to the dance and chants.

The other girls thought it was a big deal that I was becoming tall and lanky for my age. The coach decided to use me as one of the stunt girls. Another girl and I were the ones to hold the other girls up, as she was overweight and I was tall. But somehow, everyone would end up leaning their weight on me, and we'd all fall. There were many laughs at game time coming from the bleachers.

Sheesh.

Things at the house were already being set into place after fall sports ended. When I say this, I'm talking about the roles were being established without us being aware. It crept up on us before we could hit the pause button to see how it came to be.

Stan, Rae, Elijah, and I were disciplined or had our privileges modified if we had any traces of an "attitude."

When Cisca and Nano wined for no reason because that's what toddlers do, Karen frantically flew to their sides and blamed us, as if there was no possible way they could be crying just to be cranky and spoiled brats.

"What did you guys do?" she would glare at us.

The heck?

Even though they were toddlers, they were now smart enough to detect that all they had to do was cry or something, and Karen would instantly suspect we had done something. So, they started to use this as an advantage, especially Cisca, who would later be responsible for certain unfair punishments that Rae and I would be subjected to.

Abram would most certainly use this to his advantage as well. Neal was still kind of cool at this time. I could tell that he was in complete denial of Karen's acts and he didn't discern just how deep her issues and her cruelty ran. I'm sure he was hoping it would pass someday.

He was about twenty-one-years-old when his thirty-seven-year-old boss at the gas station named Karen began a relationship with him. It didn't matter that she had a son and daughter close in age to him. Karen saw the vulnerability in this young broken man who had been raised in a dysfunctional family of just a mother and two sisters. They were married shortly thereafter. Not too long after that, they adopted his nephew Patrick, who became Abram. From 1992 to the year 2000, they had a seemingly blissful marriage where they gave their only child the entire world. Then came Karen's sudden desire to disrupt their bubble with four black children from across the country, headlined by a ten-year-old girl who wouldn't keep her mouth closed to the crookedness of it all, which was me.

When they came to visit us in Las Vegas, I could already see that Neal didn't want any part of this, and that's what I really liked about him, because I didn't want any part of it either. We both had that in common!

Later during repeated arguments, he never shied away from shouting, "**You** *are the one who just had to get the four* **black** *ones from Vegas..."*

That was his most favorite line to shout at Karen during their arguments. He didn't care about saying it in front of us. Then Karen threatened to leave him, a tactic she liked to use on him.

"The only reason why I said yes to the adoption was because you said you were going to divorce me if you couldn't have these kids," he would whine.

Karen would look satisfied when she saw his worry and fear. A real man would have left her ass for another woman who didn't want black children!

In the beginning, he was very cool and did a lot of fun stuff with us, before Karen wanted to sever that tie completely as well.

He pretended to be stern with us while in front of Karen. If she wasn't there, then we were laughing loudly and running around. Very carefree. On one occasion, she ended up being gone for the whole day. So, Neal took us on a ride in the station wagon so we could get out the house.

If Karen had been with us that day, we wouldn't have been allowed to leave the house with Neal. That's why we were so ecstatic that he took us out the house for a ride. Neal let us scream and laugh in the car, but told us to be careful and to put our seatbelts on. Being how kids are, we instantly took our seatbelts back off, not listening to him. We literally jumped from our seats, into the back trunk area, and back to our seats, in a hysterical laughing mania that intensified because the car was driving in motion.

He drove a little slower as we showed no signs of calming down. I know he was trying to focus on the road and he couldn't see through the back window because there were five bodies hopping and blocking the view. We were driving him crazy.

He made a left on Main Street to take us to the park near the schools instead of heading to Mountain Ave.

"Okay, you have to calm down now," he said patiently and quietly. "You have to be calm before Mom gets home...look at you guys...all out of breath."

He laughed with us for a bit. We were still rowdy and our chests heaved with exhaustion from outdoing ourselves. Unfortunately, all of us genuinely getting along with Abram ended abruptly, like it did a lot of times.

Abram and I started arguing over something I can't recall. Being violent like he always was, he hurled a toy at me with all his might, and it hit me in the face very hard.

I began punching him over and over and over until he cried. Then I stopped. Most of the time he was a wuss at everything so he would start crying. He always liked to strike someone, but couldn't handle it when they struck back.

Neal instantly started the car. He headed home with an *'I should have known'* expression on his face, as he just witnessed his beloved son take a beating.

That was enough ammunition for Neal. He was so protective over Abram, no matter what Abram did to anyone else. He worshipped his son. Neal would also have to cover up for why he'd taken us out the house in the first place. He would be forgiven easier if I was made to be the Monster.

I was in trouble when Karen got home. After she spoke to Neal and Abram, the three of them emerged from the parents' bedroom to face me as I sat solemnly and secretly gloating at the dining room table.

Karen claimed that I was intentionally trying to hurt Abram.

"He could have lost his life," she said to me, regarding me as if I had actually murdered him.

Where they serious? Yes, they most certainly were. That is the sad part. Deep down, I felt they were so mad because I had the nerve to fight back, after it was ruled in the house that none of us were to ever touch Abram, even though he got to hit us and throw things at us all the time. I know Karen was mad because she hadn't been there to slam me down and stop me from defending myself.

I was in deep trouble and lost all my "privileges" for a couple of weeks. The Carlons were too country and they exaggerated everything to the extreme! On another occasion, Abram started hitting Rae on her head with these gel pens and she kept saying, "Dad! Dad, Abram won't stop hitting me!" Neal didn't do anything. So, Rae finally beat him up as well, and Neal screamed at her with spit coming out his mouth. The Carlons said the same thing, that she could have killed him. Abram was never scolded for hitting us first.

I was sitting at the dining room table one day but I was in perfect view of the living room, which Abram was in.

Abram and I were arguing. He threw a ball at my face. The kind that kids use for kickball. He shouldn't have even had that kind of ball in the living room to begin with. I happened to be wearing a pair of these fake toy sunglasses. When he threw the ball, it whisked the glasses clear off my face. By this time, I knew not to touch Abram, and Karen was on standby in case she had to "get us" for standing up to Abram.

Yet another time, we were all eating breakfast at the table and were arguing again. Then Abram grabbed his huge glass of milk and chucked it at my face, dousing my face and afro with milk.

Before I could throw a food item back, Karen rushed her fat self over to me and grabbed ahold of both my arms and began screaming. She pulled my arms behind me over the back of my chair, pulling them down into a police cuffed position so I couldn't move.

As I screamed and wrestled to break free from her grasp, my wet afro was sagging and I sputtered to shake the milk from my face and eyes.

I was angry as everyone tried not to laugh. But I ended up laughing later about it, when Stan and Rae and Elijah crowded around me in the den upstairs. They were always happy when I was the "warrior." It was funny I admit. Not what Abram and Karen did to me, but the way the milk and my afro looked.

Whenever Abram hit us or threw objects at us, Karen and Neal would say very softly, "Abram stop...okay come on now Abram..."

But Abram was already *their* boss. I thought it had begun after the park incident in Las Vegas, but who knows how long he had ruled them! Most likely the day Karen had snatched "Patrick" from Tammy's womb.

I'm sure that one of the reasons why Abram lunged out in anger and threw stuff at us was because of the realization that he would never be able to control our mouths, no matter how much power he had in the house over us. His eyes got wild and deranged when we spoke back to him, our attitudes letting him know that he wasn't our boss. How frustrating it is, when you are King of the house but your defiant ones are not bowing down to you *at* all.

The Carlons yelled and screamed at us for little stuff, like rolling our big beautiful eyes. But if Abram used violence, they spoke to him softly. We were dealt with like we were convicts. They knew from the beginning that they, along with Abram, were the real cowards.

Again, somebody please explain to me why in the world were we adopted? I'm lost. Scratching my head.

Hello, anybody out there?

FIFTEEN

Karen and I got into our first major mother daughter blowout on the evening before Thanksgiving.

She was stressed by my anger, but at the same time very determined to keep me under her rule. I believe she just wanted to prove that she could handle me, which she would *never* be able too, no matter what she told herself and everyone else.

The shouting match was too much for her that day, and I made sure that it was! I called her every name I could think of. I said it so meanly and piercingly, all the rage on my face that a ten-year-old could muster.

"You are not my mom!" I shouted. "And you never will be! I want my name back...I hate you! Email Kim and tell her that! I want to go back to Las Vegas with my *real* family! My real name is Sequoya Griffin. *Get that right!"*

With a worried and panicky expression, Karen went to her room to make a few calls. I was still fuming when she came back out. Everyone was at the dinner table. The whole argument started because I was once again standing up for my siblings and me against something that Abram had done and wasn't held accountable for.

Abram watched me with anger. He saw I wasn't scared of these clowns that he called his parents. I could tell he wanted to throw something at me. I saw him move his head around looking for something, but nothing was in his immediate reach. Neal gave him a look like *'Not now, we have to see how far this is going to go.'*

Karen had kept us from calling Benita. At the same time, she dangled our dreams in our face, by letting us know whenever she received an email from Kim back in Las Vegas. Each time an email came, I would cry and beg to speak with Kim. Karen wouldn't let me. I knew that Kim was also emailing to be nosy...

As Karen stood in the dining room, she looked very solemn.

"I called Social Services of Tioga County...and I also called Kim in Las Vegas. She didn't answer. I emailed her," she informed everyone.

"So, can I leave now?" I asked. "I'm ready to get out of here!"

Everyone looked at me. I know Stan, Rae, and Elijah were in awe of this breakthrough I was exhibiting. I had rattled Karen to the point where she was actually looking scared of me. Or was she?

"It's the night before a holiday, so no one is at Social Services. But they have someone on call."

"What did they say?"

Karen clasped her hands together. She pursed her lips, eyes clouding over in sadness.

"Can you take me to Social Services? Please?" I prodded.

"The lady who is on call told me that if we need someone to intervene, they will meet us at Social Services...but if we possibly can, to try to work it out. Tomorrow is Thanksgiving."

"No!" I shouted. "I want to leave. Now!" I continued my rant of endless insults.

Everyone watched in silence, wondering what was going to happen next. Was I really going to go back to Las Vegas?

"Well Sara, if this is what you really want...then I have no choice but to let you go," Karen said slowly.

With that, she clasped her hands over her face and started crying. Everyone began to look sad. Not me.

Then Karen said through her tears, "If you want to pack your things...you can."

As I was walking up the stairs I stopped to lean over the banister.

"Okay Mom, I mean *okay Karen Carlon, adoptive mother!*" I hissed, to make her feel even worse over the fact that I identified with her only being an adoptive mother. Not my real mother.

I was filled with adrenaline and happiness as I packed a few things in a small bag. Las Vegas was waiting right around the corner for me. Everyone was staring as I walked downstairs with the bag.

It was like a soap opera. Very dramatic. Karen had grabbed her coat. Faces were sad. Raeannah looked the saddest, as she would be the only girl left. Her big sister was leaving. I looked at her with a 'Sorry sis, I can't do it anymore, but I will send for you' look.

Abram now had an unreadable expression. Neal was silent. Before we walked out the front door, Karen asked me if I wanted to say goodbye to everyone.

"Bye," I said, looking at everyone.

We took the station wagon. It was snowing very heavily outside. Karen drove carefully over the ice and snow. She was crying uncontrollably.

"I love you," she kept saying to me, tears down her face.

I would not budge.

When we got to the snow packed parking lot at Social Services, she parked and wiped her face with her arm, but more tears kept coming. There were no other cars in the parking lot. The building was empty. Doors and windows bleak and dark.

We waited….and waited. Karen cried the whole time.

"I just want all of us to be a family," she cried, like someone had shot her. "I tried my best. My absolute best!"

I sat in the passenger seat not caring what she had to say. I couldn't figure out why in the world she was crying, because everyone could see that things were not fair in the house. There was already a major division. There was special and different treatment for Abram, Cisca, and Nano. I brought this up to her.

Karen considered what I was saying. The next thing that came out of her mouth was used to play a mind trick on my ten-year-old psyche, even though I wasn't aware of it.

"The reason why we want Abram to feel special…is because we don't want him to feel left out. When we were preparing to adopt you guys…Dad and I were very concerned of the jealously he was showing. We didn't want him to feel left out. He was already showing signs of this before we even flew out to see you. We have had him since he was a baby. He has already had six years with us...the only child."

So that's why they gave him attention? Was that truly the real reason? Well, they sure took this special attention to the extreme! They could have treated us the same way they treated him! What about the different clothes...and the different meals? Whatever!

But I was ten at the time, and she had just told me a lie to keep me satisfied for the time being.

I finally began to feel bad as Karen's body shook from crying so hard. I mean, she was practically heaving, and I thought maybe she was the one who needed an inhaler.

Our conversation turned into us reasoning with each other. We ended up talking for a long time. She said she knew for a fact that God gave us to her, and she wasn't going to fail God. She was going to make us all a happy family.

I gave her the benefit of the doubt. She sounded so sincere. She was looking at me in such a way that kind of scared me. As if she had never seen a young girl like me before, and she wanted me to be her daughter so bad. Or else her life would be over.

We suddenly realized how late it was.

"I think the person on call didn't want to drive all the way in this snow," she said.

She started the ignition and the station wagon plowed through the thick mass of whiteness. On the drive back she looked at me with a curious expression.

"Sara...did you pray that the person wouldn't show up?" she asked, looking at me like she believed that I had the heart to actually pray for something like that.

"No," I answered truthfully.

She still looked relieved anyway. Her eyes were still very watery and she was sniffling.

Everyone was in the living room when we got back to the house. I walked in the door behind Karen. They looked shocked. Relieved at the same time. Abram didn't look mad anymore.

The next day, Karen prepared a giant Thanksgiving dinner. Cadee, Cisca, and Nano came over. Neal turned on the television to the annual Macy's Thanksgiving Day Parade that was recorded live from New York City, which was four hours away.

Cadee and I helped Karen prepare the table and bring the food out to the dining room. The table was jam packed with food. Our stomachs hurt after eating so much. Karen was very attentive to everybody. Everything was okay for the time being.

Karen and Neal kept complaining about our habit of playing with our toys and then leaving them lying around. They told us we needed to clean up after ourselves.

Whenever we left a toy on the floor, Karen snatched it up. Before long, we realized our toys were disappearing. We begged for them back.

"We threw them all away," Karen informed us.

This started many arguments and sulking. Karen told us she had warned us before, so we had no room to cry about it now.

Our first Christmas was right around the corner and the whole family got into a major argument. Then Karen told us there would be no Christmas, especially after the blowout we had about the toys she had thrown away.

Then she ended up changing her mind. She sat us down in the living room one day.

"Neal and I want you all to have a great Christmas. But there are five of you, including Cisca and Nano. So that makes seven. It's very expensive to buy everyone a lot of gifts. We will do the best we can…everyone will each get two gifts."

None of us said anything. She had laid the speech on thick. So, we nodded and accepted this fact.

"Sara, Isaiah, Abigail, and Elijah," she continued. "Neal and I completely understand that you guys have never had parents or a family to really care for you. We want you to know that we love you and care for you."

We sat quietly soaking in her words as she said this.

Wintertime on the East Coast is big because of the snow. Everyone makes hot chocolate and marsh mellows and they watch Christmas movies on television. They build gingerbread houses with lots of candy. Karen helped each of us make our own gingerbread houses to give to our teachers.

Our classmates seemed jealous that they never thought of this idea for the teachers. Back at home, everyone joined in on decorating the tree. On Christmas Eve, Karen placed everyone's two gifts underneath the tree.

There was one extra gift that she said was for the whole family. She let one of us do the honors of opening it, as an early "night before" treat.

It was the Pixar movie Toy Story 2. It instantly brought me to the memory of Benita dropping us off at the movie theaters by ourselves with a group of friends so we could see it and feel grown up without an adult.

We were all so obsessed with the whole franchise. Karen placed it in the VHS system and we watched it. Then we went to bed.

The next morning, before anyone could get out of bed and fling open our doors, we heard Karen at the foot of the stairs, loud and clear.

"Stay in your rooms. Do not open your doors until I call you!" she ordered.

Alright, then.

Rae, Cisca, and I became bored and played an imaginary game like we always did. We wondered what the boys were doing in their room.

When Karen finally called us, we tried not to act all excited as we walked down the stairs. I still remember the very moment. Seven children walking down the stairs, gazing over the banister, nostrils taking in the food, seeing what was in store as our eyes came into view of the dining and living rooms.

We were shocked to see that Karen and Neal had added many more gifts, despite the two they set out for each person the night before. In fact, the whole living room was filled with gifts, some big and some small. Honestly, the living room looked like a toy factory!

We had to eat breakfast before we could tear our gifts open. But we were just too excited! Karen had prepared these huge bowls of sugary cream of wheat that she called "hot cereal" that was accompanied with huge glasses of milk. We ate what we could. She finally gave in and let us leave the table.

We tore our gifts open. We noticed there were also a few black trash bags near the far side of the wall. After we opened our gifts, Karen told us those bags were for us as well.

When we opened them we realized they were the toys that she and Neal had snatched up when we left them lying around! They claimed they had thrown them away but they had them the whole time! I wondered where they had been hidden.

We were warned to take care of our toys from that point on.

Dear Mama,

As the next year started, the roles in the house were firmly being established. We were still attending Abide in the Vine. The church members loved us. Neal and Abram had gone to church for the first couple of months. They stopped going because they just didn't want to attend.

The rest of us felt it was unfair because church was kind of boring to us then. Karen didn't allow us to sit at the bleachers with the other children during worship. She would select our row and then tell us to remain seated. One time, I heard a lady whispering to another person from behind us. She said, "Those kids sit as still as statues."

We were upset that Abram could do anything he wanted. He got to stay at home with Neal. If Neal wasn't watching a Nascar race, he and Abram went somewhere for fun. We'd return home from church to see Neal's jeep gone. When we brought up the fact that Abram had a voice in whether he wanted to go to church or not, Karen told us to mind our own business and to worry about ourselves.

After a while I began to see that going to the church was a good thing. The people cared for us and I was learning a lot in Sunday School. I was learning more and more about God.

Within time I would be able to see that what Karen thought would irritate us would actually be for our good, and I'm not just talking about

church. I'm talking about the malicious mind games and unfairness she happily thrived upon that were just starting.
Stay tuned.

There was a brief time when we felt free before the bad things started happening. We were allowed to walk in any section of the house that we wanted. Or we could go outside to play whenever we wanted. There was a drastic change that crept up under us without us realizing it...until it was the **law** we had to follow.

Enter the "Privileged Five." This consisted of Karen, Neal, Abram, Cisca, and Nano. I'm not sure how Karen raised Cadee and Colin, but it seems that Cadee was very unaware of the severity of her mother's cruelty.

Enter the oppressed, whom I call the "The Four." This consists of Stanford, Raeannah, Elijah, and me. All we wanted was to be loved by a genuine family. We couldn't understand why we had been adopted if we weren't going to be loved. If we weren't loved, why couldn't the Carlons send us back to Nevada?

Karen was so powerful and dominant. She skillfully planted this fear into us that made us terrified of her, without having to downright beat us. At least not yet. It was a look she would give. As she gave *the look*, she would walk over and stand in our faces, looking down at us with a cold glare in her icy blue eyes that told us if we even dared challenge her, we'd be sorry.

She used verbal and emotional tactics. Fear and mind games. She had us in fear that if we ever tried to run away or tell anyone, no one would help us and they would tell us we were the problem anyway. Being children, we believed her. So, we didn't seek help in the early years.

Our fear got to the point where we wanted to be on her good side. Even if it meant we had to tattle on each other to get in her good grace. I rarely made it into Karen's grace, as I was the rebel warrior and we were always fighting. I was the one who had the fewest privileges, along with Elijah, who was the youngest. Karen never allowed him to have any fun. Her thing with Elijah was that he was the youngest out of The Four, and he didn't remember our biological family. That meant Karen could hold onto him longer than the rest of us. From the beginning, she had my four-year-old brother brainwashed against me, which would have lasting effects for years. He thought I was evil.

Karen treated him just as badly as us but she also decided that she was going to build him a separate room.

Past the girls room was a small den after the top of the stairs. In the beginning, it was a recreational room for everyone. There was an old black and white television. We played video games and watched movies. There was a bucket of toys. Then past the den was the boys room.

Elijah was unaware of what Karen was doing when she told him he was going to get his own bedroom. She hired someone to come in and put a wall in the middle of the den. A door was built into the wall.

This added room was the size of a small walk-in closet! She placed a kid sized bed in it. She kept him away from us. She told him that he would not want to get into any trouble talking to the rest of us. She especially didn't want me to "poison his mind" with supposed lies I told him about the Privileged Five. She brainwashed him to the fullest. He had no idea who the real mind poisoner was. I was telling all my siblings the truth.

When we talked to him, he would defend her. When we asked him if he remembered "Mama Sandy" he would shake his head no. He claimed that Karen was the only mother he could remember. She successfully beat the "memory" of his Mama Sandy out of his subconscious with her spankings.

Elijah was too brainwashed to realize that Karen may have made him feel like he was special...but she still didn't let him have the same privileges as Cisca, Nano, and Abram. Occasionally she let him join them in the living room or outside to play, but the rest of the time he was to be in his closet-sized room. She made him practice writing over and over. He also ended up reading. By nine-years-old, he completed the Harry Potter series that were up to date at the time. He sneaked them from school because Karen forbade him to read them.

Being so brainwashed, during the times we sneaked in to talk to him, he told on us! This would be after we sneaked in his room to talk. Karen talked to him every day with just them two by themselves, then she would find out we had talked to him.

There were occasional times where everyone got to be in the same presence of each other but we were always monitored. We never felt free anyway because Karen was down our necks. Everything we said or did, she was obsessed with witnessing it. If we were laughing and having genuine fun like kids do, that was a major problem. One of us, if not all, got in trouble for no reason! It made her sick to see all of us having fun together. During meal times, which she and Neal didn't sit with us to eat anymore, she told us to be quiet and not talk while eating. If we were done eating, we had to ask to be excused, even though she wasn't in the room. Her room was past the dining room and she left her door cracked.

"Mom, may I please be excused?" was the proper way we were instructed to say it. One by one we said it and she made sure each person said it loudly and clearly.

"Yes, you may," she answered with a proud flair in her voice. It pleased her when we said this. Her eyes would light up with happiness.

It was funny if we all finished eating at the same time. Each of us still had to say it. It was like a heightened choir, much like the baritone, tenor, alto, and finally the soprano echoing the same line.

There was a period of time when Karen pitted the boys against the girls before the permanent abuse started to take place.

Stan and Elijah were supposedly "Abram's brothers." Karen and Neal claimed that Abram always wanted siblings, especially brothers. He stopped talking to Rae and me long before he did with them. The summer of 2001 is when we first noticed the "Boys against Girls" game that Karen put into place.

She had established that Rae and I were bad and that we weren't allowed to have certain privileges the boys had. Since the girls' room was on the stairs, we used to sit by our room door and strain our ears to hear what was going on in the house.

Eventually, our room doors had to be closed at all times because we were nosy. Every Saturday when Neal wasn't working, he took the boys somewhere fun, but not the girls. Elijah could go too, but not often. This was before his complete "confinement sentence." Rae and I had to stay in our room.

We became bitter and whenever we heard the car leave and Karen shut herself in her room, we talked mess for hours about everything. When we weren't talking mess, we played with our dolls. We performed our own skits for an imaginary audience. Before being outside was forbidden, we could be outside in the backyard and fields.

One afternoon there was an incident. Rae and Cisca had the same exact Barbie, a popular collection called Torie Dolls. Rae had received hers first. When Cisca saw it, she wanted to play with it, and Rae let her. Then Cisca told Cadee she wanted one just like it. So Cadee bought her daughter one.

The three of us were playing with the dolls outside in the backyard. Cisca's Barbie broke. She never took care of them or played with them properly.

The little girl began to cry as we gaped at the Barbie's leg that was severed as Cisca tried to pull it through the dog fence.

"You broke it," Rae exclaimed.

Cisca wailed uncontrollably.

Rae and I looked at each other. Uh oh. One of the Privileged Five was crying. We knew what was next.

We followed Cisca back in the house apprehensively. Karen was in the kitchen preparing something. She turned away from the counter to face us as we stood in front of her.

"What's wrong Cisca Mae?" she asked, after briefly giving Rae and me a cold glare.

"My Barbie broke!"

"How did it break? What happened to her leg?" Karen took the Barbie from Cisca to examine it.

Cisca thought for a minute. Her eyes landed on Rae's doll, an identical version of her very own. Rae was holding her doll with a determined passion, her eight-year-old self slowly becoming aware that something unfair was about to happen…but it sounded so preposterous that maybe she was just being paranoid about it.

"What happened to your doll?"

Cisca pointed at Rae.

"Rae broke it!"

What?

"No she didn't!" I blurted out.

"I didn't break her doll!" Rae echoed.

I jumped in to explain the dog fence that Cisca tried to pull her doll through, but Karen held her fat palm up in midair.

"I'm asking Cisca what happened to her doll! Sara, mind your business!"

I was fuming. Rae didn't break it, and neither did I. Cisca knew better than to point at me.

Karen placed the broken doll on the counter.

"Cisca Mae," she said in a soothing baby tone. "What would you like done about your broken doll? I'm so sorry it has been broken."

Cisca jerked her little finger at Rae's Torie Doll.

Rae began whimpering.

"I want hers," Cisca said, like she had just chosen the best luxury car at a lot.

"Abigail, you need to give your doll to Francisca," Karen demanded to my sister.

Rae held her doll tightly as her face scrunched up from crying so hard.

As I looked at Karen, I saw she was loving this whole scene that she was in control of. A scene of taking a doll away from a little girl, to give it to another little girl, whose own mother was capable of getting her daughter another doll.

"Cisca is claiming your doll Abigail," she said very smugly. "You have to give it up."

"We didn't break her dol-" I began again.

"Sara, mind your business!" Karen's head shook. We had noticed that whenever Karen was concentrating, or studying or reading something, or yelling at us, her head would shake. But not a regular shake. It reminded us of a cat that had an item placed on its head involuntarily, so its head would do a vibrating shake. We always whispered that Karen's head was "shaking." The sight of it was annoying. She mostly did it when she was being calculating.

Rae backed away from Karen and Cisca as she held her precious doll. Karen reached forward and she and Rae had a tug of war over the doll.

"I didn't break her doll!" my sister was crying. Cisca watched.

Karen snatched the doll out of Rae's hand.

My sister threw her body on the kitchen floor and sobbed.

Karen handed the doll to Cisca, who grabbed it and smiled, not caring about my sister crying that her doll was taken unjustly over a lie.

I was so angry.

"*Witch!*" I shouted at Karen, before turning and running up the stairs to the girls' room.

"Sara, you have lost your privileges until further notice!" she called after me. "Maybe if you minded your own bus…"

Boom! The door slammed shut as I used all my strength on it. These incidents and outbursts were becoming more frequent, about once a week. Things were so unfair and I didn't hold my tongue!

SIXTEEN

Neal was only taking Abram and Stanford and Elijah on his Saturday outings. If they happened to be home during mealtime, we tried to be friendly with them. At this time, Karen's dirty work had only just begun.

Stan and Elijah would look at us with sympathy. But they also knew that if they were with Abram, they had privileges.

Karen came to the girls' room one afternoon before lunch. She had a serious expression on her face.

"Sara…Abigail," she regarded us.

We looked at her.

"I'm here on behalf of the boys." She clamped her palms together.

Huh?

"Are they back?" I asked. I already knew they were back for lunch because I heard the wooden chairs and dining room table creaking.

"Yes. They'll be eating their meals first. Then you and Abigail will eat after them."

Come again?

Rae and I looked at each other, confused. Then we looked back at Karen.

"The boys have complained that you two have horrible table manners," she informed us. "They cannot tolerate eating with you. You'll have your meals at separate times. I have no choice but to go by their wishes."

We were speechless.

I knew that all of this was coming directly from Abram. Karen added my brothers in on it too, who desperately wanted to have privileges. Abram was their ticket to the good life.

So, Karen faithfully prepared two separate meal times for the boys and the girls every day. Six different times a day. Rae and I didn't run into the boys for a few weeks, until Karen wanted to attend the New York State Fair.

The Great New York State Fair takes place every summer. After an early breakfast, Karen told everyone we'd be going to the fair and to get in the station wagon. Rae and I were shocked that we were going somewhere!

Karen and Neal were in the front. She kept turning around to observe everyone with a glare. Rae, Elijah, and I were in the middle, and Stan and Abram took the very back. They were laughing and joking around while the rest of us were silent on the three-hour drive to Syracuse.

Once we neared the fairgrounds Karen sucked in her teeth at the long lines and parking spots. We would have to walk a distance.

"Take the boys in," Karen instructed Neal. "I'll find a parking spot. Buy each of them a wristband."

Neal nodded as the boys excitedly stepped out the Wagon. Karen pecked Neal on the lips and then he eagerly guided the boys toward the lines.

After Karen found a parking spot, she instructed Rae and I to follow her and to not dare lose sight of her. If we did, we'd be in trouble. Weren't we always in trouble?

She grabbed an icebox from the trunk and we followed her into the fair. Naturally, people always stared like they usually did, to see a parent with black children.

"Your daughters are beautiful!" A lady gushed as she walked by with her family.

Karen ignored her.

"This way," she ordered us.

Karen walked right past the wristband line. Rae and I looked longingly at it.

"Sara and Abigail," she said as we walked through the large crowds and concession stands and the noise of children screaming at the top of their lungs on the rides. "You cannot eat any of the food at this fair. I have packed a lunch for you. You will not be allowed to go on any rides. You are only here by default. That means I wanted to come to the fair, but I can't leave you home alone."

She led us to a picnic bench and pulled out water bottles and peanut butter and jelly sandwiches.

We ate quietly, trying not to act out. I wanted to really flip something! Karen was also studying us to see what we'd say or do. She was waiting for me to add more "time" to our sentence.

"Sara," she said suddenly.

"Yes," I answered, trying to swallow the peanut butter.

"I'm surprised you don't have anything to say."

I shrugged.

"Don't you think this discipline is fair for what you two did?"

I nodded. Deep down I knew it wasn't. We had been in trouble for the whole summer! All because on the last week of school, we came home with stuff written in our notebooks. She had gone through them and saw that we wrote down our crushes names. We wrote about who we wanted to "flirt with" when school started again that fall. We described exactly how we'd flirt too. I had also written a song we both sang. For that, we were in major trouble.

Many girls did that! I didn't understand what the problem was. She also told us that we were one day going to be "baby mothers with multiple children."

What did *she* know?

Neal and the boys met up with us at the picnic table. They were out of breath and faces flushed from the excitement of going on the rides. They held hot dogs and popcorn and ice cream cones.

"How's lunch?" Karen asked them merrily.

They all said, "Good!" as they quickly glanced at Rae and me before looking away.

"Go on some more rides," she encouraged them. "You still have plenty of time. Meet me back here in about…three hours."

"Okie Dokie!" Neal said in his regular goofy manner. After a few minutes, he and the boys walked away.

Karen had Rae and me follow her around the fairgrounds as she stopped to look at different things. We were very sad but trying not to show it. She kept looking at us too.

"See, you could have had fun too, but it's all your fault!" she kept telling us with pursed lips and a false compassionate expression.

I recalled the morning she came home with these huge assorted Danish pastries. We had cried as she held the box open with grandeur and she smiled at the boys. Now as the summer was winding down, we were so fed up with her stupid tactics.

Why was she so mad? Most of the stuff we ever did would not be considered bad in any other family's eyes. Who grounds a child for months for writing her crushes name in a notebook? Abram could get away with a thousand more worse things than we ever considered doing! At the State Fair that day, Karen made my sister and I feel very low.

On the long ride back home she and Neal had the radio on.

The host was was speaking somberly Aaliyah's "Try Again" blared into the car.

"Unfortunately, we have to say goodbye to Aaliyah...she was tragically killed in a plane crash..."

My heart thudded inside my body and my ears burned hot. What did I just hear him say? But I couldn't speak.

I wasn't allowed to speak. Karen had forbidden us from speaking and we were now in fear. I couldn't even release my emotions for the talented singer who I had known about *long* before I was adopted by this witch lady.

Karen had no idea I already had embedded within me a culture that I would never let go of. She always had a weird expression on her face when I brought up places or people. She would give me a look as if to say *'I think you better forget what you know and what you like.'*

That night I got ready for bed in The Four's bathroom. I had to pass by the dining and living rooms to make it to the stairs. Karen and Neal were watching the evening news. There was a segment about Aaliyah.

I caught a glimpse of her sleek and shiny glowing black hair in a photo still displayed across the screen. I quickly looked away. Fear was already ingrained in my eleven-year-old subconscious mind.

Karen was looking at me before I could look even further. By now, we had to follow the "don't look rule." This meant if we passed by the living room, we were not to look at the television. The dining room table was adjacent to the living room. If we were eating, and Neal or one of the other Privileged Five was watching television, the rest of us were in trouble for turning our head to look at the screen. Even for a second. Karen was always watching.

"Goodnight Mom, goodnight Dad," I said, as we were instructed.

"Goodnight," they answered. Neal didn't really look at us much anymore during "Goodnight Time." He seemed uncomfortable by this routine.

I creaked up the stairs to the girls room and laid on the bottom bunk. I didn't bother to speak about Aaliyah to Rae, who had just moments before took her turn getting ready for bed. We all had a schedule Karen had put in place.

I fell into a stressed and disbelieving sleep.

Within time Karen took Elijah out of her good grace and that's when his sentence in his tiny separate room was set in stone.

Now it was Rae, Elijah, and me who were the "horrible" ones. Karen had brainwashed Elijah into believing that he was still special too, even though he had no privileges.

Even worse, he still defended her. He was basically saying, "Yes, I must sit in my room and stare at four walls all day…and get spanked with a fly swatter…but I love her she is the best mom in the world."

Karen spanked him with a fly swatter whenever he did something. Or she would use her heavy hand. I watched her one day as she took the dirty fly swatter and angrily slapped him with it. The look in her eyes was full of pure hate for my five-year-old brother. What was her problem? He was just a little child! She never used a fly swatter on Cisca and Nano.

The way she disciplined him was very painful to him. One of the saddest sounds in the house that still haunts me to this very day is how Elijah cried whenever he was disciplined. Even Neal, Abram, Cisca, and Nano would stop in silence and look sad.

Everyone had a fear of Karen. Deep inside, The Four wanted to rip her to shreds. But every time she saw our angry expressions, she'd shrug and do her signature vibrating head shake.

"Everyone will just see how you kids really are," she would hiss. "They will take my side. No one will believe you," she had put in our heads.

"If we're that bad, why can't you send us back to Vegas?" I would ask sarcastically, to make her mad and hate me even more.

Her face and eyes turned so dark. She never really had an answer for that. If the argument wasn't as bad, she'd mumble something like, "I promised God I would care for the four of you and I'm not going to disappoint Him."

Same old crap.

Dear Mama,

The period that Stan was still privileged with Abram was very annoying to me. You see, Stan doesn't like conflict. Even at this early stage in his life he tried to steer clear of any conflict so he would be treated alright. Or so he thought.

As his sister, I don't hold it against him anymore like I did as a child. We were children who were the personal puppets for a very disturbing lady who "got off" on her own set of games she ran in her house.

Stan had a period of time where he had all the privileges he wanted and he and Abram were the best of brothers. Even though Abram was almost a couple of years younger than Stanford, he was still the one with power.

Neal took them everywhere. Everything Abram had, Stan had, except for the good clothes. Karen *never* compromised the dress code for The Four.

During that second summer, Karen and Neal bought them a life-sized cabin! They had it placed in the backyard. It could fit a few people in it. It was their own hideout.

Only Abram, Stan, Cisca, and Nano were allowed in it. If Rae, Elijah, and I even *dared* to look at it or walked toward it while we were outside during our separate play times, Karen came outside and yelled at us. Her and Neal's room led into the laundry room, which led to a back patio door into the backyard. Karen spent a lot of time watching us from the window as if she had nothing better to do.

One afternoon everyone was allowed outside at the same time and Karen was outside too. I watched as the selected ones kept running in and out of the cabin. It looked so fun! I desperately wanted to peer inside of it to see how it was decorated. I truly wanted to see the layout.

The rest of us could stand only a few feet away from the cabin. Karen stood in the middle of the yard like a guard, eyes gleaming at the sorrow and longing we had to be near the cabin. She did that out of spite. Stan and Abram were inside of it and they occasionally stepped on their porch to look at their surroundings.

Our second summer was drawing to a close, and our roles in the house were now permanent.

Karen came up with another game shortly after school started again. She grew tired of the separate meal times. She decided that everyone would eat at the dining room table together again, minus her and Neal.

But there was a new game called "Separate Food." When we first realized this, none of us said a word. We were confused. We felt we must have done something bad in her eyes to be given a menu of separate food.

Abram, Cisca, and Nano were fed something different than The Four. At first, Stan received what they did. Or he would get a substitute. For example, Abram, Cisca, and Nano would receive a sugary, tasty cereal for breakfast, such as Captain Crunch or Froot Loops.

Stan would get Raisin Bran or plain Cheerios.

Rae, Elijah, and I would get sugarless oatmeal, with barely enough milk in it for it to be tasty. It stuck to the roof of our mouths.

I confronted Karen before school one morning.

"Why do you make different food for us?" I asked.

Her eyes lit up. She had been expecting my question any day now.

"First of all Sara, you need to mind your business. Cadee brings Cisca and Nano their own cereal. She leaves their cereal here for them."

"But what about..."

She held her palm up. She knew I wanted to know about Abram, and Stan, who was the "borderline" person on the menu.

"If I give you oatmeal, you need to be grateful! It's very healthy for you. I want you to be strong and healthy."

"But dinner is different too," I pointed out.

"Sara, drink your water and head to school," she instructed me.

I peered down at the large purple cup she already set out for me on the counter. It was next to a large pink one, which was Rae's. Every morning before school Karen made Rae and me drink water from those dirty cups she kept by the sink. There was always little stuff floating in the cups. She purposely did not clean them. I was yelled at one day for dumping the water in the sink and trying to clean the cup before refilling it.

It would take us a century to gulp the tap water down. We were timed because she would warn us that we needed to hurry up and start walking to school.

Whenever Karen was upset with Stan, he received the same food the rest of us got. When he was being her "soldier" he *occasionally* received what the privileged ones got, not something in between the three separate groups Karen had divided us into.

For lunch or dinner, the privileged ones would get foods like hamburgers, pizza, big sandwiches, or anything else good. They drank juice or soda as their drink.

The rest of us would always get soup or beans, and water. Karen purchased four different bowls for each of The Four. She called these our soup bowls. Mine was a dark purple, Rae's was red, Stan's was blue, and Elijah's was green. The privileged ones weren't assigned any bowls.

Karen told us about these different soups she wanted to feed us, such as Split-Pea soup. That soup was actually pretty good.

"Do you guys like Split-Pea soup?" she asked us, watching us eat.

We nodded our heads and smiled.

"I want you to make more Mom!" Elijah said.

Karen didn't really say anything. After that, she never made Split-Pea soup again.

Instead she would fix this broth and watery soup with very few beans in it. One time I counted about six beans total in my bowl. Everything else was just hot liquid.

She told us that she wanted all of us to be healthy. We didn't say anything to her about it. By this time, we didn't speak on what the others were eating. The sight of their stacked cheese and ham and mayonnaise sandwiches and Cheetos and juice boxes and cookies made our mouths water...but if we looked, we would also see Karen's smug expression watching. She knew that we craved what the others had and she absolutely loved it.

Everyone had their own assigned table place as well. When we first were adopted, everyone sat at the dining room table together. As time went on, The Four were the only ones at the table with a "meal schedule."

The Privileged Five ate in the adjacent living room with table stands. Neal always sat in the recliner chair with the foot rest pulled out.

Karen would slam our bowls on the table and scream, "Dinner's ready!" to the rest of us like we were animals. We'd have to pass by the privileged ones on the way to the table. Within time, they pretended they didn't notice us. Only when they wanted to get us in trouble.

As The Four sat eating solemnly, Karen proudly carried the privileged ones food out like she was a prominent waitress. She was looking at us from the corner of her eyes as we glanced up to see what the others were eating. She loved it. Her two hands sported about three to four plates as she waltzed past us in the dining room and stepped into the living room, placing their food on their table trays like they were exquisite platters.

One day after school we very shocked to see Karen with a stricken look on her face. She told us to come in the living room.

What? Us, back in the living room again? What was going on? What had we done now? She had the news on.

"Something very tragic has happened to America today," she said. "Have a seat on the floor."

We looked at the TV to see multiple images of two planes plunging into the Twin Towers at The World Trade Center, which was four hours away from where we were.

The sight of all the debris and bodies plunging from the windows to avoid the fire made my stomach very sick. What a sad unfortunate set of events. It was so very sad to see people giving up hope and dying. It was heartbreaking to see people wandering around holding up signs of their missing loved ones. Reporters were showing plenty of people in distress.

I became even more paranoid than I already was.

Since we had to leave at different times to walk to school, I would think about the sad events as I walked alone. I looked down at the ground as I clutched my backpack. Karen had started to make Rae and me wear boys clothes. Very baggy and tomboyish. We wore boys jeaned shorts that went to our shins and shirts that went below our knees. I was so humiliated at the stares and giggles every day.

But I had no choice. I was now praying that our church Abide in the Vine was serious about opening up a homeschool. Karen had even told us she wanted to homeschool us, but she was denied by the school district.

What was devilish was that she made Stan and Elijah wear girls shorts! My brothers cried in the beginning as they got ready every morning. The shorts were *above* their knees!

They learned to internally deal with it. I had even seen their friends sneak them better shorts to wear during school. Before the day was up, they returned them. Rae and I never snitched on them. We smiled inside at the deception that felt so very good!

Vrrroooooomm!

The very loud sound of an airplane soaring over Candor sounded.

No! No! No! I screamed inside.

I held my chest as it thundered against my whole entire being. Then I covered my ears and sank to the ground in distress.

The airplane. It's going to crash right here. That's why it's so loud and getting closer.

I began to cry.

No! I don't want to die!

I don't want to die.

As I held my ears, I thought I was going to vomit. But it wouldn't matter…because the plane would be crashing at any second. It was so very loud and only a few more seconds to go.

I don't know how long I was on the ground. But time must have passed. Because at first, the sound was deafening. It had gotten closer. Now it faded away and disappeared.

I opened my eyes and looked at my surroundings. I was still on Mountain Avenue and hadn't even walked down the hill yet! I was going to be late for school. Hopefully Karen wouldn't pull out the dirt driveway in the station wagon to see me still there.

I slowly stood up and held my chest as the beating slowed down. I had survived another panic attack from the sound of an airplane. Once again, it hadn't crashed like I thought.

SEVENTEEN

Dear Mama,

I'm twelve-years-old now. In one more year I'll be a teenager. That's the age Dee was when you had me. I love you and I miss you so much. I wonder how much longer it's going to take to be back with you. I will never give up. And I know you never will either. I still remember Apartment C in Carey Arms. Our family will be back together again someday. Just watch.

The time is going by slowly here. I feel like I've been waiting forever. The Carlons make us stay in our rooms all the time now. We didn't even watch the Macy's Parade for Thanksgiving or celebrate Christmas. And we don't even care about Halloween anymore. When we first moved here we cried because Karen said Halloween was out of the question and it was evil. On Halloween we have to stay home from school from now on. We aren't allowed to get costumes and candy and have fun with our classmates.

At church, they hold a family fun night on Halloween that is in God's favor. Children win prizes on memorized Scripture. But Karen won't even allow us to go to that! She got in an argument with the pastor and the Sunday School teachers. She said even though it was family oriented, it still takes place on the night of Halloween, so therefore we are still participating in "evil." It's so unfair...because we are the only kids unable to go.

Anyhow, I'm getting taller and thinner. And every now and then I get this very sharp pain in my lower stomach. It hurts very bad! I also see fuzzy stuff. I get scared because I'm unable to see and I don't want to go blind! Everything goes black with a patch of sparkly white spots. Like a bunch of stars at night. I have to lie down and drink water. The pain is so bad that I cry. But after a little while it goes away and my sight returns.

Karen says that "I think I'm all that" because I will be a woman soon. What does she mean by that? She says that's why I'm hurting and I'll be fine.

I think it's because I'm very hungry and she needs to feed me more portions of food.

The Four may have been eating healthy if you thought about it, but not really. Karen wasn't giving us enough portions to make us full and satisfied.

We were thin. The teachers and other students at school noticed us too. Some of our peers felt very sorry for us. They shared their lunches and snacks with us. Sometimes the lunch lady would scoop an extra portion of food on our trays with a sympathetic expression.

If this got back to the Carlons, Karen's control freak radar would be in distress. She went to the school to speak with the principal, Mr. Hunt. She told him that her children were to be watched and that we weren't allowed to eat anything that anyone gave us. When she popped up in the cafeteria during school hours, everyone looked very uncomfortable. The teachers looked slightly annoyed. Karen claimed that she was just concerned about her children. But how come her facial expression didn't look truly concerned for us? She didn't smile or hug us. She just observed us like an FBI agent.

When it got to be too much, she stopped popping up randomly for the time being. By the next year when I went to the Junior-Senior high school, Karen would apply for a job at the Head Start, which allowed her to walk the halls of the elementary school. My younger siblings would be in trouble about something almost every day. One time Stanford was in trouble for running in the hall with a classmate and laughing on their way back to class. The horror of running into your "mother" during a fun time with your buddy.

As I got ready for bed one evening I overheard a conversation between Karen and Neal. They both sounded very smug.

"These kids are just built skinny," Karen was saying sarcastically. "Don't people see that?"

"They're skinny because it's in their genetic makeup," Neal said, trying to sound very matter of fact.

Genetic makeup? I had never heard anything like that before.

"Exactly," Karen exclaimed.

She sounded very exasperated that we were the talk of the small town. But at the same time, why weren't we fed what the privileged ones were fed? Why was it a major problem if a friend gave us something to eat? Something was not right, and the town of Candor had noticed.

Yummy yummy yummy!
I want to eat Hot Cheetos again someday.
I have never seen them in the stores out here.
I want pancakes.
Dipped in a lake of syrup.
I want to drown in the syrup!
And I want donuts too.
The pastries with all the sugar and frosting.
Then I want a large sandwich with lots of turkey, mayonnaise, and cheese.
With some crunched Doritos in it like she does for Cisca, Abram, and Nano.
I wish I could try it.
They bite into their sandwiches with such big smiles on their faces.
They never look sorry for us.
They enjoy seeing us eat our soup.
We are lucky if we get her goulash.
Which is basically white rice with tomato sauce.
It doesn't taste very good. It has no seasoning.
I'm so hungry!
I want a huge chocolate cake.

Occasionally I wrote letters to myself of all the food I wanted to eat. Karen found one of them once. Her face looked so smug as she read it. Then she handed it back to me. She had begun going through everything in our rooms.

She searched every day to see if we had snacks from friends. Her searches for food would eventually turn into searches for our original artwork, clothes and music from friends, and razors that Rae and I would shave with later. She didn't allow Rae and me to take our purses to school that a lady at church had given us.

Karen had become very obsessed and her control freak ways made her look like a madwoman. We didn't understand why she was acting like this, as if we had betrayed her for being normal children. It didn't make any sense. Especially because Abram was the one with freedom. All he had to do was tell her off, and Neal came to his rescue. Karen would leave them alone. If the rest of us dared try the same thing, she gave us the icy blue stare and we were in major trouble. We were in fear of her.

On the weekends when there wasn't school I dreamed about food and couldn't wait until Monday! The weekend was just very sad because it was a whole two days away from school and we couldn't get extra food. Holiday breaks were even more harder. Summer vacation was hell! I didn't look forward to the end of the school year anymore. None of The Four did.

I have always been tall so my skinniness was always noticeable. Same with Stan. Karen had the nerve to call us greedy gluttons, which she was contradicting herself, because we were very thin.

The four of us ate every single spot of food she gave us and we dreamed when we could next eat again. This is very heartbreaking to reveal, but a few times there were incidents where Rae and Elijah took something out of the garbage can that was left over from the privileged ones. They ate it with no hesitation.

Rae was so hungry waiting for her next meal one day that she ate her chapstick! She ate that with no hesitation. She felt sick for a whole week after that. She told her friends at school. More whispering happened around town.

Eventually Karen started to pack us lunch. It was very sad. For a sandwich, she took a spoon and put one spot of peanut butter on the bread, and one small spot of jelly. So, when we bit into the sandwich, all we tasted was bread. She gave us a small container for our water. We used the same lunch bags day after day. She never cleaned them for us. Stan's lunch was leaking in his back pack one day. He was so embarrassed when someone pointed it out.

She told us we were crazy when we noticed these little insects in our lunches! We saw bugs. One day Rae took her sandwich apart and showed her teacher and classmates. Her teacher stared at it in horror. There were tiny black insect bugs on the bread and in the bag.

Karen was angry with Rae that night.

"The school called me today!" she spat angrily at Rae. "You made a huge scene during lunch. You were dramatic. You didn't have to do that."

"But everyone saw the bugs!" Rae protested. "And it's happened on other days too."

Karen was silent. She told us that were being dramatic. If she caught us looking through our food at the table, she was upset.

"Stop examining your food and eat!" she would scold us with a cold glare.

She made this particular soup one night, claiming that she saw children in a village on a missionary trip eating it. But as we looked through it, we were able to see that it was full of nuts, peanut butter, broth, and other unrecognizable items that we didn't even want to know what they were. When I took a bite, I almost threw up! But I didn't want to give Karen the satisfaction of seeing me in pain.

I ate it, praying to God to help me shove the food down my stomach.

What surprised me was that Abram was walking through the dining room and he stopped when he saw the pain on our faces.

"What is that?" he asked us.

"It's so nasty," Stan said.

"Let me try it," Abram said. He took a spoon from the kitchen and then he scooped some of the soup from Stan's bowl.

Upon tasting this concoction, he spits the food out on the floor!

"What the heck...this is nasty!" he said in that voice he used when he thought something was incredulous. If I didn't dislike him so much, I would have smiled at him.

Karen heard the commotion and she came from her room.

"Abram, what are you doing?" she asked.

"Mom...no...that soup is disgusting. They can't eat that! What the heck is in that?"

Karen's eyes grew wide. "Why did you try it?" she was alarmed. "I already made your dinner for you." If I wasn't mistaken, she looked worried that Abram had tried it.

"It's so nasty. I spit it on the floor. I will clean it up."

After that, we didn't see the bugs or any other strange things again. But we still "examined" our food.

Karen came up with another meal as well. She wanted to make us feel special that we got to make our own food, as Rae and I had begged her to teach us how to cook. She had laughed and looked at us like we were crazy.

"What do you need to learn to cook for?" she asked us.

"Just to know how."

"Why?"

"My friends at school said they know how."

"Sara, you need to mind your business. You don't need to learn how to cook. I feed you."

"Not enough because I'm still hungry."

"SaraJane!" Her face contorted in fury.

I stomped upstairs and slammed my door with all my might that the walls shook. I loved the way the *Boom!* noise rattled the walls. It helped to mellow my pain.

Truth was, Karen didn't know how to cook. But as a child I thought she did because I thought all adult women knew how. I had no idea that Karen was doing this as part of her demented plan to keep Rae and me stuck behind most women.

Karen gave me a purple plate, Rae a pink plate, Stan a blue plate, and Elijah a green plate one day. She placed a row of sardine crackers on each of our plates. She added our own scoops of peanut butter and jelly on our plates. Each of us had a white plastic butter knife.

"You guys get to make your own peanut butter and jelly crackers!" she said happily. "See? You take the knife, swab some peanut butter on one cracker…then swab the other one with jelly…and put them together."

She watched us do just that.

"Do you guys like this?"

We nodded, pretending to like it.

It most certainly didn't feel us up. Even though we were young, we could still sense the insulting feeling of it all. The privileged people were served different and better food, and bigger portions.

Karen seemed very satisfied with herself for the time being.

Since we had to stay in our rooms all day we began reading books. At first I didn't like reading. At least anything that didn't interest me. Social Studies was boring. My grades were suffering. The reading assignments we were given were annoying. I didn't understand what I was reading. I was just reading to read the words. My Social Studies teacher had a meeting with Karen. They suggested for me to join a cognitive reading program.

Of course, Karen jumped at it. She always wanted us to be a part of many special ed classes. Even when Rae's "special teacher" said, "Abigail you are ahead of these students I don't know why you are even here," Karen had not been pleased. She tried to keep her enrolled.

"SaraJane's Social Studies grades aren't very good," my teacher told Karen during a parent teacher conference.

"Well, if you give her a book about figure skating or gymnastics, I'm sure her reports will be perfect!" Karen had retorted.

He smiled at both of us strangely.

My favorite book at the time was Michelle Kwan's autobiography *Heart of a Champion*. I was enthralled by the story of the figure skater and the glossy color photos in the center of her book. Another favorite was the biography of Dominique Moceanu, and how she and six other gymnasts were nicknamed the Magnificent Seven. I dreamed of being a figure skater or gymnast. I checked those two books out the school library over and over.

Before we had to stay in our rooms, Rae and I begged Karen to be able to sign up for gymnastics.

"Um...no!" she had scoffed.

So instead, we used these rectangular logs that a neighbor had left outside. We lined the logs in the front yard and took turns walking on our "balance beams." Back in our room, we used the white plastic bar on the top bunk as our makeshift "uneven parallel bars." We could only swing just a little bit because our torso would hit the rest of the bars on the bunk bed. We tied string around our hands and dipped them in baby powder to serve as our "chalk" before performing. Then Karen stopped letting us use baby powder all together.

Not too long after that, Karen told Rae and me to get in the car. We didn't ask where we were going. Once we pulled up to a gym in Owego, we got real excited to see children in leotards tumbling around on mats. We also saw real balance beams and uneven parallel bars! My heart pounded with excitement as we walked inside the gym.

"Sit down in the bleachers," Karen instructed us.

Before we made it to the bleachers, we spotted Cisca! She was tumbling around on the mats with the other students. Cadee was in the bleachers watching. She looked over to see Rae and I headed her way to take a seat.

"Hey!" she exclaimed.

"Hi Cadee," we said back.

"Cisca kept telling me and Nana that she wanted to do gymnastics. So, we signed her up. Look at her!"

We nodded and watched quietly. Karen came over and greeted her daughter and sat down as well. Then she looked at the students on the mats being instructed by a skeptical teacher.

"Hey Cisca Mae!" she called to Cisca, who looked in our direction and grinned.

Then Karen and Cadee struck up a conversation. Karen was also eyeing my sister and I, but we didn't show any emotion.

For the next few weeks, every time Cisca had gymnastics practice, Karen made Rae and me go along with her to sit in the bleachers and watch. We never asked her to sign us up ever again.

The summer after my fifth-grade year, she took Rae and me to the Open Door Mission in Owego, where she also purchased our clothes. I always knew we were headed to the thrift and donation store when she slowed the car down and switched to the left lane to turn on North Ave.

"There's a lot of books here," she was saying. "There's a sale going on."

Indeed. Books galore! We had been here a few times and I noticed the books were used. On this day, customers were stuffing books into large black garbage bags.

"Two dollars for one bag! Fill them up with as many books as you can!" the clerk was calling out.

"We can take as many books as we want?" I asked Karen.

"Yes."

We took our very own trash bags. I walked over to the shelves. Without really reading the titles, I just started throwing them in my bag. I walked away from the shelf and picked up more books that were in boxes on the floor.

"Take them all!" the clerk told everyone.

Some of us had to double our bags because they were about to burst. When we were satisfied enough, Karen paid $4 for our bags and we lugged them to the car. Back at home we dumped our books on the floor and organized them by the authors' names. I recognized a series of books called The Baby-Sitters-Club that I had seen at our school library. They looked very interesting. I also saw two separate series called Sweet Valley Twins and Sweet Valley High. Looking at the covers, I could tell the twin girls were adolescents in the first series, and high schoolers in the second series. I saw a series called The Boxcar Children...and another one called the Little House Books.

Rae and I got to reading! I also made a mental note to go to our school library to check out all the missing titles from the Baby-Sitters Club. I didn't have all of them in order.

The books I was reading were way more interesting than the reading assignments at school! I felt like I knew the characters. I was angry, happy, sad, and ecstatic with everything they were going through. I was right there in the story with them. After reading, I spent a lot of time thinking what could have been. Where were they now? I cried for them.

I also found that I wasn't listening all day long for Karen to call breakfast, lunch, and dinner. When she called us to eat now, I was shocked by how fast the time had passed! Once back in my room, I read until my eyes were droopy. I couldn't wait to get up in the morning so I could finish a book I was reading. I started to finish one book a day. Rae and I traded books often. We knew the same characters so we laughed at some of the events we both read about.

We were already writing short stories. I loved the feeling of creating my own characters and their living environments.

A favorite pastime that Karen loved was to tell us that our real family had moved on and that Kim no longer emailed to check in with her. She said that Kim decided it was best to stop contact after she heard I had called Karen a fat white horse.

Karen also loved to join us at the dining room table to tell us things that upset us.

"Your biological father is in prison and you will never get to see him again," she would say.

We didn't say anything.

"You mother is on drugs."

I was getting older, so now I was getting a clearer picture of what was going on now.

I still didn't let her words hurt me Mama. I told myself you were going to get better. I couldn't wait to see you again!

Whenever I asked Karen to see our adoption papers and all other paperwork from Nevada, she shook her head like she wasn't going to tell us any prized information that we wanted to know about ourselves.

"No," she said like a warden speaking to her prisoners.

"Can I see it when I'm eighteen?" I asked.

She glared at me.

"If that's what you want Sara…then yes," she said exasperated. She could not stand my questions about my past or my persistent memories that she could never remove from my DNA. It absolutely infuriated her that she couldn't bring me into her submission.

Another time, she told us some surprising information.

"Kim told me a few months ago that your birth mom was pregnant again. I told her I'd be willing to take the child for her."

Another brother and sister? Wow!

"What did Kim say?" I asked. I was actually hoping the baby wouldn't come here. I didn't want my new sibling to be hurt and abused. I prayed that Dee would take it. Why was everyone obsessed with my Mama and her kids?

"She said your mother ended up miscarrying and losing the baby."

My heart pounded. I was sad. But I was kind of relieved despite the heartbreaking news.

Then I asked what other news had Kim told her.

"She stopped emailing me," Karen said. "Everyone moves on."

We didn't say anything. After a few minutes, she stared at us with a somber look on her face.

"You know," she said. "I didn't tell you guys this…but when we first adopted you…I wrote a note to your mother. I mailed it to Kim…so Kim could give it to her."

"What did you say?"

Karen had actual contact with you? And she never told us?!

"I wrote her saying *Thank you very much for your children.*" When she said this, she looked like she had said the most beautiful and appreciative thing that a person could say to someone whose kids she took and had their whole identities changed. She said this like she had every right and supposed good intention to say this.

How dare she.

Who did this witch think she was?!

EIGHTEEN

I pulled my pants down to use the bathroom one day. I was shocked when I saw drops of blood in my underwear. I knew what it was.

"Mom!" I called out.

Karen opened the bathroom door and peered at me.

"I got my period," I informed her.

Her eyes blinked. She looked very hurt at me.

"I need to see it," she said.

She walked over to me and looked down at my underwear as I eagerly opened them up even more.

"Congratulations," she finally muttered. She didn't look very happy. "I'll get you some pads from the store."

Then she sluggishly walked out the bathroom.

I didn't understand her reaction. I felt like I had offended her. That's how she made me feel most of the time.

She only allowed me one sanitary napkin a day. I cried to her that I wanted a new one every time I used the bathroom. She made me feel like I had a phobia of using the same one. I did, because I have always been very iffy about my hygiene!

She wouldn't budge.

"Sara, just use the same one. If you use the bathroom...don't take it off...leave it on. Change it the next day."

She left them in a dresser cabinet in the bathroom. She warned me that she would only purchase so many during a cycle so I only better use one a day. I began to take the sanitary napkins they had in the nurse's office at school.

When I got home from school one day I was met with her pale evil face and icy blue eyes.

"How many pads did you take from school?" she screamed at me. "I was taking the garbage out and it's filled with pads!"

"They have them in the nurse's office for everybody!" I defended myself.

"How many times do I have to tell you guys to stop stealing things?"

She called the school and informed them that I was a thief.

"Hello? Yes, my daughter SaraJane has been stealing pads from the nurse's office...yes, I know...I see...I'm just letting you know because my children aren't allowed to accept anything that anyone gives them...*I* provide what they need...yes, I understand. Okay thank you!"

She hung up the phone and glared at me. She didn't say anything else. After that, she stopped buying pads for me. I started getting them from the nurse's office instead, as the school had informed her that the sanitary napkins were there for any girl who needed them. That was a battle that Karen lost!

Abram's large housecat Ernie had scratched all the window screens in the house. Karen removed the remaining scrags and didn't get the screens replaced. Bees flew into our rooms through the little fans on the window sill.

Rae and I were so terrified of bees. There were these wasps with long stingers. In the beginning, Stan and Elijah would sneak in our room and kill them for us because they weren't scared of them. Their privileges were taken away when Karen found out. Everyone could hear shouts and cries throughout the day as Rae and I were in agony of being surrounded by bees in our room, which was supposed to be our sanctuary. We weren't allowed to open our door.

Karen told us that we had to get over our fear of them and kill them ourselves. We were so horrified and sick to our stomachs when a bee came flying in like it owned the place. I mean, we cried and screamed so loud and I knew the few neighbors we had on the hill could hear us! After a while, Karen wouldn't allow us to scream either. If we screamed, we were in trouble. She killed the bees for us the first few times to show us but then we were on our own.

I covered myself under my blanket in the humid heat and periodically peeked my eye out. Sometimes no bees were in sight. They had flown back out the window. I breathed a sigh of relief. At times, I'd be enjoying a book and the familiar sound of a buzz entering the window made my heart sink and I would hide again and cry. If they were still in the room when we were allowed to go to the bathroom or eat, I waited to see if they didn't fly past the door. Then I leaped through the door entrance. Rae and I procrastinated and took a long time eating and using the bathroom. Karen caught on to it and yelled at us for taking too long with everything. When I got back to the door I had to hold my breath and pray as I opened it, because what if I opened it and the bees were right at the entrance?

Karen knew we were terrified of them. She insisted that we were not to run out our room no matter what. In certain incidents, she stood on the outside of our door while we were inside. She leaned her weight against the door and held the door knob so we couldn't run out. We were trying to bust out our room, and she proudly stood on the opposite side to keep us captive and torment us. We were exhausted from screaming and crying and begging her to please open the door.

At night, I was elated that the bees weren't in sight and that's when I was able to relax and go to sleep. I also knew that morning was coming soon. Then I felt sick again.

I dreaded every spring and summer just because of the bees. Back when Karen was playing the boys against girls game in the summer of 2001, she had taken us to a church member's ranch in the Appalachian Valley. Cisca, Nano, Abram, along with Stan and Elijah, were allowed inside the air-conditioned home.

Karen told her friend that Rae and I had to remain outside for the day. She even packed us a lunch to eat outside. We had hours of time on our hands! We walked the vast property and squinted our eyes from the sun. It was so hot and sticky out. There were so many bees, grasshoppers, dragonflies, and large buzzing bumblebees. This was really the country! We spent the scary adventurous day dodging the insects and clinging to each other. We were so happy when it was time to go…but we knew our regular bees awaited us back home.

One day I cried to Karen. I explained my fear of them. I hoped she would compromise with me. She started laughing and said something very rude.

"You think all the bees in the world are just out to get you? They aren't only attracted to tall skinny black girls who are afraid of them!"

She was dying with laughter.

Karen did not permit me and Rae to shave. She told us that we needed to just be natural. She confiscated a razor I got from a friend who told me I needed to shave.

"If you shave, you could really harm yourselves. You could possibly kill yourselves," she told us.

"We would die?" we asked, becoming paranoid.

"Yes. Suppose you stole a razor from your friend at school…"

Stole?

"And you shaved while you were in your room? And then all I heard was quietness after a while? A lot of time goes by and I still don't hear you? Then I finally come upstairs…and you're dead from bleeding to death from shaving?"

Our naïve eyes went wide with surprise. Was it possible we could bleed to death from shaving? She asked us again…what if we were shaving one day and she heard silence, then came to us and found us bleeding and dying?

"But every girl at school is shaving," I stated. "They said I'm supposed to."

"Sara!"

"But they are!"

"Sara, enough! Women were made to have hairy private parts. That's why we have hair there!"

"Well, how come you shave your legs?"

She looked at me with such contempt. I would never stop challenging her.

"Because Dad asked me too," she said sarcastically. "He wants me too."

Then she gave me a look like *'Now what?'*

One hot summer day before she went to a meeting somewhere, she took a shower. I could hear the water pipes running in the house. I had asked her earlier in the day for a shower and was denied.

Before she left, I was in the kitchen doing my chore of sweeping the dining and kitchen floors.

"I'll be back later," she said to me. She knew we were psychologically scarred to the point that we wouldn't sneak out our rooms, let alone run away. Neal and the rest of the Privileged Five were her eyes for the house.

"Okay," I answered dutifully.

Then she smiled happily, looked me in the eye, and said, "I showered...I feel so fresh and clean now!"

Then she flounced out the front door.

She fed and treated her dogs better than The Four. Throughout the years, there was Sampson the German Shepard, Crackers the Dalmatian, Maggie the Golden Retriever, and Hope the Doberman Pincher, who was Karen's baby. All of them were well fed and groomed. Karen washed them in The Four's bathtub. The Privileged Five used Neal and Karen's bathroom. Abram took his craps in our bathroom though.

I have never set foot in the parents' bathroom, or walked the small hallway that leads to the laundry room and back door patio into the backyard. I always wondered what it looked like in that part of the house. Rae sneaked there before and Karen nearly had a heart attack. Rae was in so much trouble. She told us that she felt a sick and eerie feeling when she walked in there.

One day I came out the bathroom to head back upstairs. I came face to face with Maggie the Golden Retriever.

Maggie was trained to sit on the kitchen floor next to the door that led to the basement and a door to the side yard. The Four were instructed to enter and exit the house from the side door. The Privileged Five entered and exited through the front door. When I asked Karen why, she said the front door made too much noise.

"Then why doesn't everyone use the side door?"

"Sara, mind your business," was always her answer.

I knew Maggie was trained not to move. I was still a little anxious around dogs. When a couple of them died from old age, I didn't feel sorry for Karen. Yes, it was sad they died, but I had no feelings for the dogs she treated and fed better than us. The same dogs that she washed in The Four's bathtub and never cleaned. A bathtub she would eventually only let us bathe in every few months due to her claims of the high water bill.

I looked at Maggie and her tail began wagging, but she remained sitting. Taking a deep breath, I said, "Hey Maggie!"

She nearly jumped up in excitement. She didn't bark but I could tell she wanted to. The Golden Retriever had a sparkle about her eyes.

"Hey Maggie, come here!" I said.

Maggie leaped up and ran to me.

Wow. I took more deep breaths.

She nuzzled a hard and wet nose on my leg. It tickled. Cringing for a second, I squinted my eyes. I looked down and began petting her, which made her more excited.

Okay, not so bad…and Maggie likes this.

I did this daily. Then it felt normal and I wasn't afraid anymore! From that point on, I would act normal and friendly around dogs. If I was chased, it was because I was being playful with them and laughing. The memory of being chased in circles by a stray dog at Matt Kelly Elementary during recess while everyone laughed seemed like ages ago.

Karen would have to use another scare tactic on me. Hang tight Mama, I will tell you soon what she did.

We began to sneak the good food that was in the house that was just for the Privileged Five. It was a thrill for a while whenever we got away with it. We snuck the packaged cupcakes and other snacks that were in the pantry or kitchen counters. The Four's bathroom was right past the pantry. We stopped at the pantry on the way to the bathroom. Then we'd use the bathroom, hide the snacks in our clothes, and then walk back upstairs to our rooms. Or we'd just ravish it in the bathroom. Rae and I liked to sneak the fig newton cookies that Karen packed for Neal's lunch during the day. We saw they fit the size to be a "cake" for our Barbies.

We sneaked food when the house was empty, or when it was completely noisy, because there were a lot of distractions. It was hard to do it at night because Karen heard *anything* and *everything*. She awakes out of her sleep with a vengeance. She is never at true rest because of her control freak paranoid ways. The memorable stairs in that house are famous for the very loud creaks it makes. Nighttime was not a go.

Each of The Four had their own "trial" whenever we were caught. Karen called it stealing food. She said we were thieves. But how could she say it was stolen food if we were all supposed to be a family like they claimed? The fact that they said we are thieves… proves that they never loved us. Their food was supposed to be *our* food too. They surely had adopted us for the wrong reasons!

We were caught at different times. One thing The Four didn't do was snitch on each other for sneaking food. We were starving and we smiled at the thought of one of us getting something to eat even if we ourselves fell short that day from obtaining a tasty snack. Elijah and Rae were caught first. Then I was caught shortly after. Stan went under the radar for years.

Raeannah's trial is the most memorable of all. It was very heartbreaking.

Karen set out everyone's cereal one morning at the breakfast table. Abram, Cisca, and Nano had their tasty Captain Crunch. Stan had his Raisin Bran. Elijah and I had our regular sugarless oatmeal.

Rae didn't have a bowl at her place.

"Today, we are going to have Operation Abigail," Karen regarded everyone with a very serious tone and expression.

I looked at Rae. I knew she got caught sneaking food because she looked very forlorn and sad. I grew angry inside at Karen's horrendous title of "Operation Abigail."

Karen stood by the dining room table and surveyed everyone. Her eyes began to light up at the excitement of another game she was about to play. She was in her full element of authority, the nearly fifty something year old who bullied black adopted children in the small deserted town thousands of miles away where their real family couldn't find her.

"Abigail has been caught stealing food!" she informed everyone.

We were silent.

"So, if she's so hungry...I'm going to give her something she can eat!"

Karen's sinister eyes looked toward Abram's pet hamster that played in its cage just beneath the bend in the staircase.

We watched as Karen retrieved a bowl from the kitchen. Then she opened the hamster cage. The hamster squirmed around with its toys and made a noise that always irritated the crap out of me. I hated that thing, and he smelled because Abram never cleaned the cage.

My heart stopped when Karen scooped some of the hamster food in the bowl. She closed the cage and then placed the bowl in front of my baby sister.

"If you're so hungry Abigail, then you better eat the hamster food!" she boomed, with a satisfied expression.

I stopped eating.

"Sara, mind your business!" she said before I could say anything.

Rae began crying her eyes out.

All of us looked sad. Including the privileged ones. It was just so rare to see Abram look sad for us with anything.

I wanted to get up and overthrow the hamster cage. Now I was angry that the hamster even existed.

For the next four hours, practically all morning, we had to sit at the table as Karen ordered Rae to eat the hamster food. She cried and cried, and we sat watching in silence. Karen even went as far as taking a spoon, scooping it in the hamster food, and holding it up to Rae's mouth to traumatize her.

My sister's tear stained face looked so very exhausted and frightened at this ordeal. She wailed and thrashed around, using her little arms to grab ahold of Karen's fat arms, trying to keep her from getting closer with the hamster food.

"You are hungry so you have to eat it!" Karen was demanding. She was really enjoying this.

The rest of us were so angry. I was filled with enough rage that I was about to throw my bowl at Karen's head to knock her out cold. I played scenes like this in my mind over and over. Every time we argued, she always said that her side would be taken over mine. I was in fear as a young girl over this. She told me I would go to a juvenile hall for the rest of my life, and did I really want that? Didn't I want to stay and be free? I should have just went along with her juvenile hall tactic. Anything was better than this house of slavery! But I didn't want to leave my siblings with her.

When Karen grew tired of tormenting Rae with the bowl of hamster food, she dumped it in the trash and poured a bowl of Raisin Bran like Stanford had eaten. She placed it in front of my sister.

"Do you promise to never steal food again?" she asked Rae.

Rae nodded, still crying.

"Repeat that."

"I promise to never steal food again."

Karen looked at her and nodded.

"I sure hope so. Everyone else may now be excused."

Karen was a calculating and swift woman. She rarely showed remorse in what she did. She loved using us to hurt each other.

She made all of us have our own room. I will explain the breakdown soon.

She wanted to make sure that Rae didn't sneak anymore food. She began locking Rae in her room every night. She unlocked her by morning. There were times when Rae peed on her bedroom floor because she had to use the bathroom so badly. This was the time that Rae was Karen's target for a while. Rae had to eat her meals separately from everyone else as well. Karen brought her food to her room and closed her door. When Rae was done, she had to put her plate outside her door on the stairs and shut her door again. Then Karen collected her plate.

I told a friend at school everything that was going on while our class was studying in the library. All the pain and anger just came out. I wanted someone I could trust. Miranda looked very concerned.

"Just promise not to say anything," I looked at her, suddenly feeling nauseous.

"I promise SaraJane," she said with wide eyes.

"No one will help us anyway."

That's what Karen had made us believe. We were basically the only few black children that lived in that town. Anyone would look at us like we were the problem instead.

"SaraJane…this is very sad. I want to call my mom right now!"

"You promised."

She nodded and looked down at her schoolwork for the remainder of the class period. Deep down, I prayed she would say something.

Later that afternoon, I was called into the guidance counselor's office. I already knew Miranda had told. I could tell by the guidance counselor's expression that she knew the day would come when I'd be sitting in front of her talking about the Carlons. The school had already noticed signs of abuse from us.

She asked me questions. I told her everything. Her demeanor was calm and unreadable. After telling her as many details as I could, she thumbed through a packet of phone listings.

"I now have to contact Tioga County Social Services to investigate what you have told me about your situation at home," she informed me.

Karen's icy blue eyes appeared as my heart thumped.

"Don't you worry about anything," she attempted to reassure me. "They will send out a caseworker to investigate."

"When?"

"I'm calling them right now. By the time you walk home they should be arriving."

The bell rang not too long after and I waked home. I was very scared. At the same time, I was thinking to myself that maybe we were finally going to be free! I had to be brave.

When I got home I should have just went straight to my room, but I got scared again. I had a lot of doubt flood all over me. Maybe it was too good to be true.

I knocked on Karen's room door to tell on myself. It was trained psychological mind control.

"I talked to the guidance counselor at school today," I said very timidly. "She called Tioga County Social Services. She said a caseworker will be here soon to talk to you."

Karen's eyebrows flew up in surprise and disbelief. She was looking down at me like she was trying to figure out why I was telling her this, and where did she stand with me in all of this.

"Why are they coming here?" she finally asked, folding her arms and doing her regular twitching head shake.

"I told a friend at school what happens here."

She was silent for a second.

"What did you say happens here?"

I told her about locking Rae in her room. The different foods she gave us. How we couldn't use the bathroom after 7:00 pm. I went on and on, tattling on myself.

When I was done, Karen stood there looking down at me with her head shaking.

"A caseworker is on their way now."

"Why did you tell these lies?" Karen suddenly screamed at me, and I jumped back.

"My friend told…not me. Well, I told her…but she said she wasn't going to tell anyone. Not even her mom."

Karen laughed a shrill sarcastic laugh as she glared at me with cold eyes like she couldn't believe it. How dare SaraJane have the strength to finally do something like this? I was going on fourteen now.

Then suddenly and rapidly, Karen's whole demeanor changed. She softened her face and cleared her throat. She was now looking at me with a weird expression.

"When they get here, you need to tell them that your friend is starting false rumors!"

I slowly nodded my head. But I already knew what I was going to do.

Then she made me sick by saying, "Good thing you told me before they came! If I had not known and they showed up...I don't know what I would have done!"

By this time, the others were arriving back to the house as well. Abram could go anywhere he wanted and could return home when he wanted so he wasn't there.

Karen told us to sit in the living room. My siblings were looking anxious as to what had transpired now. They could tell by my expression that I had made another breakthrough but they didn't know in what way.

"You know," Karen began, in a very fake dramatic voice. "I have always cared about all of you guys. It's just you have always been so mean to me. So that's why I have treated you the way I do! If you can just start behaving...then you can have everything you want!"

Then she started crying hard and told us she was very scared of what would happen when the caseworker arrived. She told them what I had done.

"The only thing that Dad and I had in mind when we adopted you was to give you a family because you really needed one!"

At this point, I was even sicker. I was so disgusted inside. I was not buying it at all. Unfortunately, Stan and Elijah became soft on her as she sat on the couch shaking and crying. They were coming of age young boys who thought she would change her ways and be a genuine mother. Rae and I pretended to agree with Karen...but we had other plans. We swiftly made eye contact.

When the caseworker arrived, Karen grabbed her stomach and wiped tears from her eyes and opened the front door. A middle aged short woman with dark hair stepped in the house carrying a briefcase. She looked at us. I couldn't tell whose side she was on. Her expression was unreadable, just like the guidance counselors had been. Before this lady could even open her mouth to greet us, Karen began talking very fast and loud. She just kept talking about how everything was a big mistake and that her household was perfectly fine.

The woman eventually shut Karen up.

"My name is Agnes Spicer," she said in an unemotional clipped tone. "You're going to be able to talk Mrs. Carlon, but I have to speak to the children first."

Karen bit her lip and crossed her arms. Her control freak tendencies were about to burst out. I saw her take a few deep breaths.

One thing I knew about this caseworker right away was that she didn't want to deal with a case like ours. She wanted the whole situation to disappear, that we'd all just stop and act like a normal family. Every time she tried to ask The Four a question, Karen jumped in, and Agnes had to quiet her. Stan and Elijah were saying everything was fine, agreeing with Karen. But Agnes could see something in me and Rae's eyes for sure.

"Mrs. Carlon, I'm going to speak with them outside on the lawn please. Then I will speak to you again. Okay?"

The look on Karen's face was priceless! But she had no choice but to step down. She had to remain inside the house.

We walked outside. Swiftly glancing at the living room window, Agnes instructed us to follow her. We walked across the dirt driveway and though the grass towards the trail that led to the mountains. We stopped by the cornfields. I purposely didn't look in the direction of the house.

"Okay, now what is going on?" Agnes looked at each of us.

Rae and I blurted out everything. We told her everything, especially about Rae being locked in her room. Stan and Elijah were silent. They didn't confirm or deny anything.

Agnes suggested that maybe Rae and I should go to someone else's house for a night or two since we were the ones showing signs of concern. My heart thumped. Agnes didn't understand. This wasn't about going away for a night or two! We needed to leave forever! My mind was racing with a thousand thoughts as we walked back in the house.

Agnes confronted Karen with everything. Karen glanced at me real quick...but she played the role. She was crying again.

"I knew it was wrong in my heart to lock Abigail in her room!" she cried with a painful wretched sob, clutching her stomach. "It's just Abigail has very bad behavior and she needed to be separated from the others."

What bad behavior? She was almost an eleven-year-old who was starving. She did what she had to do to eat!

"Mrs. Carlon, does locking a child in their room seem appropriate? Not to mention the safety hazard! What if there was a fire?"

Karen nodded.

We knew she would let us burn if she had the opportunity.

"I will have all locks removed! On every door in the house!" Karen wailed. "I'll try to find other ways to discipline them the right way." She put on such a sob story.

Then Agnes did something that made me not trust her anymore.

"Well, SaraJane and Abigail want to go somewhere else for a couple of nights. Perhaps a friend's house," she said.

Karen looked at my sister and me for a split second. Her eyes were evil. Then she snapped back to her fake role.

"Agnes...all of this is a misunderstanding."

Then Stan saw an opportunity to avoid conflict and throw us under the bus so he could get back in her good favor.

"Mom, they just want to spend the night at their friend's house!" he said, selling us out.

Karen looked very surprised at him. She was pleased. But she pretended to look confused as she turned back to Agnes, who was becoming frustrated by the moment as she tried to defend us girls.

Karen would not shut up. My own faith inside of me was now crumbling, and I could tell Rae's was too. I was so upset. Agnes was a caseworker. The way she worded our request was very passive and not correct. *She* had made the suggestion, not us. As a caseworker, she was supposed to *demand* and *inform* Karen that due to what we told her, she would need to remove us until further notice. But every adult, no matter how poised they appeared, always became weak and passive in front of Karen. She was just that evil of a person. Her aura frosted chills if you were in the same vicinity of her.

Unfortunately, Karen grabbed control again. She pleaded to talk with the caseworker alone.

"Just for a second please!" she said. Her eyes pleaded with Agnes.

Agnes drew in her breath, surrendering. She followed Karen into her room and the door was closed behind them. I glared at Stan and Elijah. They looked away, knowing they were going to get a privilege or more portions of food. Rae and I knew we were done for.

When they stepped back into the dining room, I could see that Agnes looked very stricken. She had aged in just a few minutes of being held captive in Karen's deceptiveness.

"If you guys are going to be a family…you all need to work it out together," she said in a monotone rehearsed voice.

Wow. She had taken the easy way out because she didn't want to deal with us. She didn't want to help abused black kids get their freedom.

"And no one should tell lies to get a privilege!"

What?

"Now, this case is still open. I will still have to do a little more investigation in the future."

Karen looked worried, but at the same time very confident.

"I'll be talking to you all shortly. I have to get back to the office." She seemed anxious to get out and for her work day to end. She nodded her head at each of us. Then she left.

So, this is what caseworkers did all day? Deep down, I knew she wasn't qualified for this job. She didn't seem like the type of person that cared for children at all. She didn't even ask us if we were okay! My heart ached for someone to really listen and understand us. I would give anything to be with Michelle Graven, Clinical Psychologist back in Las Vegas!

Once Agnes' car peeled out of the dirt driveway, Karen took in deep breaths. Neal walked in the front door, looking alarmed.

"Who was that lady..." he began as he closed the front door behind him.

Karen dramatically slumped her body against the door and held her stomach yet again.

"I thought I was going to be arrested!" she cried out. Tears hit her face and of course, Neal ran to her to hold her up so she wouldn't fall.

Such dramatics and nonsense!

Stan and Elijah were immediately in Karen's good grace, and Rae and I were not. Especially me. Karen had always been weary of any support we received from the outside. She and Neal were always saying that The Four ruined the Carlon family name, that we made them look bad. Actually, the truth was for the whole town to see. Everyone knew! The Carlons needed to blame themselves.

If they were truly loving parents, any child would have been happy to call them parents! I may have rejected them when I first met them, but I was a child who was evilly forced to change her identity and to forget her family and where she came from! Karen and Neal were adults. There was no excuse in the world they could ever give for what they did. I had my own periods of time where I attempted to be a loveable daughter, but it ultimately failed.

Karen stopped locking Rae in her room. She removed every lock from all doors in the house. At this time, she began hatching a plan to turn Rae against me.

NINETEEN

Dear Mama,

I must tell you about my behavior episodes I have here at the Carlons...so you can better understand...which you probably already do. I have a temper. I throw severe temper tantrums. I am an angry child who had everything taken from her since I was little. I look angry and depressed. The times I am laughing and smiling are always short lived. From the beginning of being adopted, I showed my temper. One thing about living with the Carlons is that even though I'm scared of Karen to an extent, I'm not scared to show violent and destructive behavior. What stops me from physically hurting someone is not wanting to go to a detention center for kids...or to jail.

I think what stops Karen from physically hurting us more than her occasional slaps and smacks and heavy handed spanking is the same thing...she doesn't want her and Neal to go to jail. Every time she smacks us, she instantly backs away and says she's using self-defense. For what? We are little and she is huge and fat. One time, she grabbed me by my hair and started smacking me as I sat on my bed. I have started to beat myself up and hit myself because I don't know what else to do with my anger because I feel like a prisoner. I raise my hands to my face and start slapping myself really hard while crying. Then she says, "Here Sara, I'll do it for you!" and she starts beating me up. It hurts really bad. One time I spit all over her fat leg. She wiped it off and glared at me with her evil blue eyes.

She always manipulates and brainwashes a situation. She wants to hurt us physically though, especially me. The fact that we are so angry and we fight back in other ways makes her blood boil. Talking back and rolling our eyes makes her even angrier. But Abram gets to talk mean to her and she doesn't say or do anything…she has allowed him to run her in many ways.

The main thing I have seen what she fights for is control. Control over every aspect of everything! Her fight, along with a violent SaraJane, doesn't mix well at all! The thing with Karen and I is that she had a mission from the start. She believes that she is going to make me love her as my mom, and nothing else. She vowed to Kim that she would never have to return me, and that she could handle me. Kim told her to send me back if I was too much of a problem. Kim told her before we were adopted that I was going to be the hardest one. So, Karen told herself she was going to make me love her. She won't send me back because she doesn't want me to be happy, even though she cannot stand me at all. This is her way of torturing me.

One time during an argument I told her there was no point in her ever adopting us. I asked her what did she want from me? She looked at me and said, "I want you to love me." With a hurt look on her face. She would say the same thing to the others, "I want you guys to love me." But why don't things in this house feel lovingly? Something is terribly wrong.

I let Karen know when I first met her that she would never replace you as my Mama! The fact that she is trying to erase all memory of you and Dee and them and take my identity is so evil. She could have just accepted the fact that even though she is my adoptive mother, I still have a right to know and love my real family. She hates that! One time during a screaming match I said, "You are not my mother. Katherine is!" So, she angrily said back, "She was never your mother because she never took care of you don't you get it? She was never your mother she was never there for you!"

These arguments between us can get so intense, both of us breathing uncontrollably and wanting to physically harm each other. Sometimes, I write on a piece of paper my birth name, Sequoya. Karen says this is very disrespectful. I say, "It's my name!" Then she says, "It's no longer your name since it's been changed." I say, "Sequoya will always be my name no matter what…it's still there deep inside!" Then she stares at me with such venom in her eyes.

I have always had a combative demeanor at the Carlons. It could be funny at times to my audience. Rae laughed at me a lot. One time Karen and I had been arguing and Neal came in the girls room too.

Rae was on the top bunk and they were at our door entrance. I sat Indian Style in the middle of the floor. They had done something to really set me off. I mumbled a bunch of stuff under my breath. They stood there trying to intimidate me. I had both of my hands up, sticking out my middle finger on both hands. I raised one hand up, put it down, then raised up the other. I did this over and over, ignoring Karen and Neal lecturing me. They finally gave up as they saw my fingers weren't going to stop flipping them off. After they left Rae said it was so funny because I looked so determined. Whenever she laughed at me, she hid her face and laughed silently. She said at times during my rages, Karen and Neal would smirk too, but not so I could see them. They purposely waited until I couldn't see them. I didn't know this at first. Once I found out, it angered me even more because that showed Karen really enjoyed tormenting and provoking me.

Although I feared Karen in a way when I lived there, like I said I wasn't scared to show violent behavior. Plus, I knew she had a determination to never let me go, even though she hated me. If I acted violently, she dealt with it somehow. She had this deep fear of me being set free. She had the same fear with all of us. But I was the oldest and more rebellious. I was a true rioter. I would slam doors, throw every item in my room, trash my room until everything on the walls, window, every single surface was stripped bare! I kicked and punched holes in walls. I screamed for hours on end, screaming just to prove a point, and to get Karen and Neal angry, as payback. One thing I did that was funny to my siblings was I stomped for hours on end. These were called my "Stomping Episodes."

I would jump up and down and stomp on my room floor. My upstairs floor echoed, sending a booming sound throughout the house. I would not stop until I wore my whole entire body out. Every morning after Karen and I spent the previous night in a terrible wrestling match, I woke up so exhausted. I hated the way I had bags under my eyes and puffy eyelids from crying from anger. The rest of The Four always gave me thumbs up and big smiles when Karen couldn't see. These were the best times. I was doing it all for them!

In the early years, Karen would come in my room and try to forcefully stop my rioting. She would hold me down so I couldn't move, and even sit on me, until it hurt and I calmed down. She used my fear of dogs to scare me at first. She always kept the dogs in the dog fence or locked in her and Neal's laundry and shower room. Before I got over my fear of them, she used a tactic. During an argument in my room she sat angrily seething. Then she got up and left. A few minutes later, she came back with Crackers the Dalmatian! She had her on a leash but I was still terrified. She knew it too, because as soon as I saw them enter my room I froze. Karen held the leash and sat down next to me. My heart was pounding so loud…but I told myself don't cry and don't let Karen see me scared. They sat up there with me in silence for a while before Karen left to prepare the next meager meal.

Karen and Neal gave up on trying to halt my stomping episodes after a couple of years. They ignored it, pretending they weren't peeved, but they whispered vehemently to each other. I vented and the whole house boomed with my stomps all day. Neal could not watch his Nascar races. It drove him insane. He was in the living room and my bedroom was directly above it! Turning up the television volume didn't change anything. He was so serious about his Nascar. He often spoke fondly about his dreams to be a racecar driver. I didn't understand why he never just took off and did what he truly wanted to do. He had starry eyes whenever he spoke of it.

"She is an angry child. What is wrong with her?" Karen asked Neal during an argument they had with each other.

"Because she wants to be with her flipping family!" Neal shouted with rage. He shouted it so the evil lady could know how ridiculous she was for holding children hostage that she had never loved.

Karen was silent. She knew she was wrong. When her friends came over we heard them ask her, "Why are they always boxed in their rooms?" Karen would say, "Well, Sara is reading, Abigail is having playtime with Cisca…"

Then they said, "Exactly! Boxed in their rooms!" Karen would get silent. She knew she could have just let me go. But she didn't want to see me happy at all. It was her mission that was included in her special package of hate to see me suffer.

"You know if you had *ever* treated Cadee and Colin this way…they would disown you and never speak to you again!" Neal shouted one night.

Wow! Neal was speaking to her raw as she was silent. The thing was, Karen didn't care who told her the truth. She had no remorse about anything she ever did. Neal wasn't man enough to set us free either.

Part of his turning against us was his weakness for Karen and her threatening his emotional security. She had put in his head that *we* were the reasons she was stressing out. *We* were taking their time away from each other.

Hearing these arguments, I'm screaming *'Hello, let us go then! Forget your sinister lying about God giving us to you and you having to maintain your promise to Him!'*

There had only been that short period of time where Neal got along with everybody. When we first were adopted, both he and Karen took turns going to the boys' room at night, and then the girls' room, to tuck each of us in. He always hugged Rae and me, and we grabbed his head and kissed him on his face like daughters do. Everything was always strictly a father daughter relationship. Then Karen started acting paranoid over our kisses. She accused us of "trying to show off in front of Dad." She told us we were not to kiss him at all. So, she walked with Neal to each room to say goodnight to everyone.

Karen became jealous of our relationship with Neal. Especially since we put on our skits for him. He was the only one who attended our showcases in our room to support us! Karen never wanted to watch our skits. So, what was she upset for? I had stopped doing anything for her. Every time we wanted to sing or do something in front of her in the beginning, she glared at us and it made us uncomfortable. Then we'd just lower our eyes and stop. We suddenly felt ashamed, and we had no idea as children why we felt that way, why our confidence was being deceptively taken by a troubled adult. Why agree to watch us if you didn't look happy to see your "daughters" performing? Karen told Neal to not come to our showcases in our room after the first couple of months.

When I was eleven, I sang Neal my own personalized birthday song I wrote just for him. Everyone was at the table and smiling in awe. Neal had the biggest smile on his face. Karen instantly burst into tears and her face was red. I sang it from my heart. For days afterward, Rae and Stan were humming the tune. Those were the rare special things I did for Neal that made us bond. Neal had a relationship with all of us in the beginning. He was naïve and didn't know the severity of his wife's deep seated issues.

Karen always claimed that I thought I was "all that" because I had breasts at eleven-years-old, even though I was skinny growing up. I had no idea they came from your side of the family. I developed these large breasts. Later, I would get a breast reduction.

The first thing I noticed about Karen when I first saw her was that she didn't have any breasts. Her chest was flat and her t-shirts and dresses revealed that. We were children and didn't understand why. She became very sensitive and played victim over the smallest of things.

One morning not too long after we were adopted, she left her bathroom door open as she was getting dressed. She should have left the door closed.

Stanford came downstairs and was headed to her to ask permission for something. But he saw her with her shirt half on. Karen shrieked and slammed the door shut.

She accused my brother of spying on her when Neal got home. She put on an act of crying.

"He laughed at my chest!" she cried to Neal, who shook his head uncomfortably. That was a moment when even he knew that she was overreacting.

"I was just coming downstairs to ask if I could go outside," Stanford defended himself.

'Exactly!' I wanted to shout. *'My brother dang sure doesn't want to see or know anything that you have! Get over yourself!'*

By dinnertime, Karen joined everyone at the table to tell us that she had breast cancer years before.

"I had to get my breasts chopped off!" she cried to us. "How do you think I feel? To walk around with no breasts!"

Then she lifted her shirt at the dinner table. We saw two scar lines where her breasts had been. We all looked sad for her. Her crying had really got to us. She made Stan feel horrible for having seen her while she was getting dressed. She demanded an apology from him, even though she should have closed her door. He had no idea his "mother" was getting dressed.

"I'm sorry Mom," he said solemnly.

She nodded.

Having her breasts removed in surgery was always a big thing to her. She made me wear baggy clothes. As my breasts were noticeable, I asked for a bra, like my fellow peers at school were wearing. They were the ones who brought it to my attention that I didn't have a bra.

"Sara," she sat me down one day. "You don't need a bra."

"But I have breasts, Mom. See?"

She looked, but shook her head in denial.

"Why can't I get a bra?"

"Sara...bras are actually uncomfortable. They have wire in them that hurts you when you wear them all day. You feel much better without them. Trust me."

I didn't say anything. While in my room and in the bathroom, I grabbed ahold of the large cups. I didn't know that not being allowed to wear a bra, my already heavy breasts were starting to sag. I was naïve and I took Karen's advice. I told my friends at school that bras are unhealthy and the wire hurts. They stared at me like I was crazy. They didn't bring the subject of bras up to me ever again.

After the first few months of being adopted, Karen and Neal stopped tucking everyone in at night. We were instructed to just say goodnight on our way upstairs. Within time, no one said it to anybody.

Before I fell out with Neal, we had attempted to form a bond. I was the oldest daughter in the house. I always made something for him for his birthday or for a holiday like Father's Day. He also liked to read the short stories I wrote. One time there were family events and concerts going on at Hickories Park in Owego.

Neal watched me as I studied the performers on stage.

"I think you better get on that stage!" he said, smiling at me. It made me smile with confidence.

Another time, we were at a parade in a nearby town and we watched a squad of cheerleaders waltz by us in excitement.

"Hey," Neal said.

I looked at him.

"None of those cheerleaders have nothing on you."

I smiled hard.

"You should be out there with them. You would be better than all of them."

Moments like these gave me tiny surges of self-esteem. I had never had a father's confidence boost in my life. Jerry Banks back in Las Vegas had never told Rae and me these things. There's just something about a father's love that's much different than a mother's love when it comes to a young girl's early developmental years and her self-esteem.

Karen had become paranoid and jealous about Rae and me around Neal. Within time, a change started to happen. Karen began her dirty work. I feel the father daughter relationship with Neal and I would have been longer if I hadn't allowed Karen's sickness to spread to me. This is when I started to show signs of running from small, insignificant misunderstandings.

I made Neal a special crossword puzzle book for his birthday in 2002. I stayed up all night. I used blank sheets of paper and I carefully wrote out all the letters on each page. To close the book together, I tied it with yarn. It was very nice and I was so proud of myself.

We had a few guests over that night. His mother and stepfather were in attendance. Shockingly, Karen's son Colin was there, who was a few years older than Cadee. We had never met him before. He looked at us strangely. As if to say *'Why in the world does my mom have four black kids? Why are they so silent and have to ask permission for every movement they make?'* I could tell that even Colin looked uncomfortable for us just by how we acted...most adults did when they saw our uneasy faces.

All we knew was that he was an ex-Marine and he now lived in North Carolina. He and Karen had never gotten along. We found this out by overhearing many arguments.

On this night, I noticed that all the adults kept trying to talk to Neal. I was sitting next to him at the table and I kept trying to get his attention. I looked up at him. But he didn't turn to look down at me. He was more engaged in the adult conversation than in me. But he wasn't even talking; they were. He was a naturally shy person and was easily embarrassed by any attention. He had received everybody's cards and gifts and said thank you. I felt he was not paying attention to mine enough. My gift was hard to miss. I kept looking up at him, trying to get him to notice me. He would not look at me. I felt he was ignoring me.

What I should have realized then was that he was not in fact ignoring me, or anyone else for that matter. He just had a lot of adults in his face and they were all talking. My twelve-and-a-half-year-old mind was working overtime and I told myself he was ignoring me. I became upset. Right there at the dinner table that night is when I vowed to never speak to him again. I would ignore him like he ignored me.

From that moment on, I never went out of my way to speak to Neal again. When I had to pass him in the house, I turned my head and ignored him. I avoided him. I know that at first, he may have felt surprised. But I never looked at him long enough to see. I had pride. It was always awkward whenever we had to pass each other...we got tense and quickly walked away.

By the time I was fourteen, it had been two years since we had last spoken to each other, and we lived in the same house! We only heard about each other during arguments Karen had with us separately. He always knew what was going on with me...but he never dealt with me directly. Awkward.

Karen had noticed too. I knew she was satisfied deep down, just by the expression on her face when she studied Neal and me when we walked by each other. She looked at us very curiously and amused. During arguments, she bragged to me.

"Neal is no longer trying to be a father to you because you have rejected him. He says he feels rejected by you and that you never wanted him to be your father. So he has no desire to ever be your father."

I was confused. I felt *he* had rejected me. But the ignoring game was actually my own fault. It was Karen's fault too because she had been pitting us against each other from the beginning. She had stepped in and halted a chance of Neal having a relationship with Rae and me. All of this was strange and new to him as well. He was only twenty-nine when we were adopted! Cadee and Colin were close in age of him. Something was wrong with all of this.

My arguments with Karen had reached new heights by the time I was fourteen. Such arguments would have the whole house on alert as they overheard the near boxing matches we had in my room. She was always in my room trying to subdue me and I was her inmate who bucked against her. During one such night, I was very surprised to see Neal step in my room.

Wow.

He was tired of all this. But he was still a coward to let his wife abuse us. As he tried to tell me I was in the wrong, I lost all control.

"There's no reason for you to ever talk to me!" I shouted vehemently. "You don't even exist to me!"

This took him by surprise. His chest puffed up and his face turned red.

"I do exist because this house runs on my shoulders!"

And the money you guys get for us, I thought to myself. *Money that doesn't get spent on us at all.*

"I work hard so everyone can have things!"

What things? Oh, you mean the Privileged Five?

There was a major division in the Carlon household, and the whole town of Candor was well aware. Why were Karen and Neal always in denial of this fact when they knew what they were doing? It was so frustrating; all I could do was cry.

A person who is skilled in knowing how to separate everyone for their own sinister enjoyment specializes in divide and conquer techniques. Karen needed to get everyone alone in order to carry out her magic. She needed to work on us individually.

In the beginning, the girls had their own room and the boys had their own room. Then Elijah had his little makeshift room. After that, she had a room in the basement built for Stan and Abram. The rest of us had to sneak down there to take a look at it so we wouldn't get caught. It looked like a child friendly dungeon. We were kind of jealous of how furnished and decorated it was. Abram had requested the new room. What Abram wanted, he got.

Next, Karen had me take the boys old room. She painted the walls lavender and put a border with a softer toned color. There was already a built-in bookcase in the wall. I organized my book collection. Now the only ones on the second floor were Rae, Elijah, and me. Karen and Neal were on the ground floor, and Stan and Abram were in the basement.

Next, the Cabin was put in the backyard for Stan and Abram during the time that Stan was included in privileges that Neal gave Abram. It was another hideout and isolation for them. Like all relationships in the house, Karen *could* and *would* switch something up if she wanted to. To have us where she wanted each of us.

When Stan's time was ending, she wanted to make sure he and Abram hated each other…and anyone who was against Abram was instantly against Neal. Stan and Abram were actually close. But they still had their rivalry too. There was an incident one day. Stan went to a friend's house to spend the night. He came back telling Abram about his discovery of something. Abram became a hater when he found out that Stan's friend's sister had flashed him her boobs. So, he pulled a hater move and disgraced the guy code.

He ran to Karen and tattled on Stanford, only because he didn't get any action. Stan was promptly disciplined. Everyone in the house heard about it. But it wasn't Stan's fault that his friend's sister immediately flashed the first black kid she seen at her house! After that, Stan wasn't allowed to go to any friend's house. Karen also twisted the story and called the mother, claiming that it was probably Stanford who told her daughter to flash him.

Unbelievable! Karen loved to do that a lot. Every time something happened, she had to justify a reason for it and blame The Four, even if the other party confirmed it wasn't us. She would get in an argument and tell the other party to just take her words instead. People would look so very surprised at her. What mother would knowingly lie and get her own innocent children in trouble?

Once she wanted to sever Stan and Abram's friendship, Karen began pitting them against each other. Stan was walking up from the basement to use the bathroom one day when he heard Karen's voice in the living room. He heard Karen saying his name. He was so confused. He tiptoed to the dining room entrance and he could see Karen and Abram's silhouettes through the black screen of the big television. He listened to a one-sided conversation. What he heard wouldn't register until later.

"You know Abram, Isaiah really doesn't like you," Karen was saying in a low conspiring tone.

What in the world?

"He's using you. He hates you."

"I don't know," Abram simply said in a quiet tone.

"He's just using you so he can go along with you and Dad and do everything you guys do!"

"I don't know."

Stan was so shocked. He was very confused. How much time did this old woman have on her hands to pit two naïve boys against each other? If it concerned her that much, why not just pull them apart as part of a regular separation? Instead, she planted lies. It was not really like that at all! He just didn't like conflict. It may have looked like he was going against The Four, but he wasn't.

Shortly after Karen's game, Abram started to become cold towards Stan. Stan would be friendly but Abram was already set in his mind against him. Karen even put it in Neal's mind too, that Stan was jealous of his beloved son Abram.

Suddenly, Stan was no longer included in Neal and Abram's activities. Abram ended up "moving" into the cabin in the backyard permanently. He began hanging out with school friends. He began smoking pot with them, along with other things. If the police were called, Karen helped Abram and his friends by covering for them.

It was just so unbelievable. Every time The Four rolled our eyes or spoke back, she told us that we were going to grow up to be "street walkers and convicts." But here she was covering for Abram's convict activities! Karen was truly a born racist and she was very proud of it.

Karen now had everyone where she wanted them with each child in their own room. We left for school about ten to fifteen minutes after each other. She rotated with having one older one and one younger one take the afternoon bus home from school, because the elementary and the high school got out at different times. She wouldn't have two older ones and two younger ones walk to school or take the bus home together, because that meant we would talk to each other.

At the dining room table at home, we got in trouble for laughing and enjoying each other's company.

"Stop talking!" she scolded us. "Eat your food, ask to be excused, and then head to your rooms!"

Cisca, Nano, and Abram would be in the living room eating from their trays. Since we had to be quiet, we occasionally sneaked a glance at the cartoons.

"Nana!" Cisca and Nano would call out. "They're watching TV!"

"Stop watching TV," Abram would usually say. He used a variety of derogatory words as well. If we said anything back to him, Karen would grab us up as we tried to struggle from her grip. I would then cuss her out or spit and we'd get into a wrestling match each time.

When the privileged kids tattled on us for watching television, Karen would stomp out her room and glare at us.

"Do *not* look at the TV!" she screeched through clenched teeth.

So, we silently put our heads down as we ate. From our peripheral vision, we saw Cisca and Nano and Abram watching *us*, instead of watching the television. It was their mission to see to it that we didn't turn our heads to glance at the television.

After the first Social Services investigation, Karen became slightly nicer to the rest of The Four, except for me. She made sure that it was noticeable that Stan, Elijah, and Rae received more portions of food than me, along with other stupid things.

For example, she also fixed us peanut butter and jelly often. Or peanut butter and fluff. She purposely gave me the smashed bread at the end of a loaf each time! She watched for my reaction as well. I didn't comment. I really wanted to see how long she would do this. She did it every single time. The others noticed too.

She now gave me the job of being "helper" since I had asked her to learn to cook. She did a lot of subtle insulting things. She prepared our food at the counter. She lined our plates up in the order she placed them on the table. I had observed this when I watched her carry them out.

"This one is yours, that's Isaiah's, Abigail's, and that's Elijah's," she pointed to them. "They're all in the correct order."

"Okay."

I carried them to the table as she watched with amusement. I was only allowed to do this if she was in the kitchen watching.

If she made her gross tomato and stale rice goulash, she gave the others more scoops. My portion was always visibly smaller.

I decided to test my theory on her to see if I was correct. One night, I hovered around the counter. I saw my smaller portion on my designated place on the counter. I was really hungry this night.

My heart beating rapidly, I waited until she turned her back toward the fridge and pantry.

Very swiftly and quickly, I switched my plate with someone else's. Then I pretended to clear the counter area near the sink.

"Okay, now carry the second row of plates out first," she instructed.

I grabbed two plates and walked in the dining room. But as I did, I turned my head back around to glance in the kitchen.

Like a sneaky cat creeping across a lawn, I saw Karen *switch* the two plates in the top row back! Her back had even hunched over while doing it.

Wow! I was correct!

She knew how to make us resent each other through her divide and conquer techniques. She decided for a brief time to pretend we could choose "more portions" from the middle of the table. She gave us our regular plates. But she added lame "appetizers" like apple slices or pretzels. One morning, she made fluffy pancakes! We were in disbelief.

She placed an extra plate with two pancakes in the middle of the table. Then she stepped back in the kitchen to hover around. I could see her watching us. All of us tried to eat at a regular pace, but we were anxious to see who would get the last two pancakes. Silently, we knew only two of us would get an extra one. Two of us would not.

When two of us reached for an extra one, the other two of us didn't say anything. We pretended not to notice. It was an unspeakably sad situation.

Karen would periodically do this with us. She was experimenting. She knew that games like these would make us resent each other. That's why the boys were more likely to be her soldiers versus Rae and me. They didn't know that a woman who was supposed to be their mother could truly be so deceptively manipulative. She was also going to everyone in the house individually and telling them that I was trying to tear the entire family apart and "poison" their minds with my "lies."

When Agnes Spicer came to talk to us separately at school, I kept insisting to her the cruelty in the house. I couldn't believe my ears one afternoon when Agnes shrugged her shoulders at me.

"I have seen your siblings as well..." she said, avoiding my gaze. "They have recanted what they said earlier. They have all told me that they're being fed and they aren't hungry. And your sister isn't being locked in her room anymore."

Agnes had now sided with the family against me. She knew Karen was messed up!

But she didn't care enough. My siblings wanted to eat, so they told her a lie. They told her that because they *were* being fed more than me. They were somewhat in Karen's favor now, temporarily. Until things died down.

"Why can't I just leave then?" I asked in desperation. I couldn't understand why in the world I was being abused and tortured like this! What was my true purpose in life? Why was I even born?

Agnes gave me an unreadable glance. She ignored my plea.

"Well, this case is closing up soon," she stated. "I hope things work out. Your guidance counselor will be in contact with my office should anything further happen."

Then she smiled this fake smile and awkwardly stood up. She opened the office door to let the guidance counselor know she was done.

I cried my eyes out in the school bathroom that afternoon. I was powerless and felt I had no control. My whole life so far had been this way. There was nothing I could do. Ever. My siblings were prey to Karen's manipulation.

Why couldn't they see that just because they had more portions of food or got talked to much nicer, that *still* wasn't equal to Abram, Cisca, and Nano? Karen would never consider treating them that special. There would *always* be that difference, and Karen was still making them feel insultingly low no matter what! She promised them stuff but never came through with all of it, not even part of it! She really ripped my siblings off.

Agnes knew she was wrong, along with the whole lazy office at Tioga County Social Services. They would become weary of our case. Every time a caseworker came to investigate from that point on, a new caseworker would come. In fact, Karen had become so good with her evil ways, that the caseworkers would only be at our house for a few minutes before they were already on her side. Karen always had a way of doing it. The caseworkers ended up telling us that we should be grateful for a mother like Karen.

Well, how about they bring their children to her? The only difference was; their kids weren't black. All of this was so absurd. If we were that bad, then why couldn't they place us back in the system? All it took for them was a phone call to have us removed! Sometimes I wonder if they were all in on our initial kidnapping.

No one wanted to do the right thing. No one wanted to help the four black children on Mountain Ave in Candor, New York.

TWENTY

Karen saw the bond that Rae and me had as sisters. After the investigation, she really began her scheme. Social Services had closed the case and Karen had won. She had also guilt ridden me into writing them a letter, apologizing for starting "unnecessary lies." I don't know why I even wrote that letter for her, but she deceptively convinced me to do it. I was in a very bad place emotionally and she used my feelings of unworthiness and my vulnerability and low self-esteem to get me to write it. She read the letter before she mailed it for me. After that, she returned to giving me the same food portion amount as the others. She stopped giving me the smashed end of the bread loaf as well.

She finally had everyone where she wanted them. Slowly, she worked on Rae and me. She would give Rae small privileges, like putting the old black and white television in Rae's room that used to be in the den. Then surprisingly, she gave Rae the missing VHS movies that I loved to watch. Rae told me at the dining room table. We had to whisper so we wouldn't get yelled at for talking.

I also noticed that Karen was randomly going into Rae's room and shutting the door. She would be in there for a while. I wondered what they were talking about.

One Saturday afternoon, Karen told Rae and me to go with her. Wow, we were going somewhere besides church or school? The boys stayed back.

We sat in the backseat. I was behind the driver's seat and I saw a gift bag with wrapping paper on the passenger seat. Karen drove into Owego and turned onto a residential street. She stopped at a house. Birthday balloons were tied to the mailbox.

We saw a few girls around Rae's age on the porch.

"Hey, it's Abby!" one of the girls said to another. "Look...its Abby! Did you invite Abby?"

The birthday girl looked very surprised. Kids normally handed out birthday invitations to everyone in class, but they knew the Carlon children weren't allowed to attend anything.

"Okay Abigail, have fun today," Karen said merrily.

Rae looked very surprised as well. She had an expression on her face as if to say *'Me? Going to a friend's party?'*

"Go on," Karen prodded her. "Here, this is your gift to her."

She handed the gift bag to Rae, and Rae timidly grabbed it. She stepped out the car as if she was floating and was expecting to fall at any second. Her classmates ambushed her.

"Happy Birthday!" Karen told the birthday girl. "When is your party over?"

"It's for two hours," the girl answered.

"Thank you. I'll be back to pick up Abigail then."

Karen and I were silent on the way back home. I was thinking hard. Whenever she took one of us somewhere, she only took whoever needed to go. The only time we went somewhere was if it was mandatory. I was wondering why she took me along.

Karen would start to do little things like that. Rae seemed cautious at first...because of the trial and room locking that she had endured. Suddenly, Karen was being very nice to her. She was now back in Karen's good grace.

*Or partial good grace, because there were two different "good grace" structures in the house. The highest level was the Privileged Five. The next level down was a sort of favor she gave Stan, Rae, and Elijah...but she never allowed them to get to the top level, while **still** knowing how to make them feel like they were **somewhat** special, because her direct pure hatred was spewed at me, SaraJane. Everyone knew that the SaraJane level was the lowest in the house to be on. I proudly claimed it.*

Around this same time, Karen began to summon me into the living room in the early mornings. Right when she knew the house was quiet. She knew when Rae's wakeup and bathroom time was.

Rae's room was the closest room to the stairs leading down to the living room. Rae listened to a lot of conversations and arguments that went on in the house, like we used to do when we had shared that room.

Karen said I needed a counselor. She sat in the recliner chair and I sat on the couch. She looked at me like I was a peasant. She told me that I had to confront my evil feelings that I had for everyone in the family.

Come again?

She said that I hated Stan, Rae, and Elijah too. I opened my mouth to correct her. I told her that I hated her, Neal, Abram, Cisca, and Nano. I basically let her know that she wasn't giving the rest of The Four the same things as the Privileged Five, and she quickly rushed to shut me up.

"Sara, I'm the mother!" she said. "You need to just let go and let me be the mother. I'm their mother. You have been acting like their mother since we adopted you and its time you gave that up."

I was silent at this statement. She held a lot of resentment in her voice when she said this. This wasn't the first time this had come out of her mouth. She often accused me of being "jealous" of her, because she was now the mother, and my job was strictly to be a sibling to them. Who in the world would be jealous of Karen? Certainly not me! I acted the way I acted because they were my biological siblings, and they were born of you, Katherine Kelly! I was protecting them and revealing to them the truth, and Karen could not stand me for it. Her blood boiled every time I opened my mouth to defend The Four.

"As your mother, I have to look out for your wellbeing," she continued. "I'm going to be a counselor to you. We need your mind to be healthy again."

So early every morning, she would counsel me. But her sessions didn't feel comforting to me. They were berating and she used them to spew out her hatred and contempt for me. It was as if she was the venter, not me! She had found another outlet to pick on me, under the guise of a supposed session. It was verbal and emotional assault.

I also noticed that she would talk very loudly. I would speak very quietly, and gesture for her to speak how I was speaking.

"I can hear you…I'm right here," I said. "Can you please just be a little quieter?" It was too early for the whole house to hear her loud voice anyway.

This only further excited her. She became even more louder than me. She would bring up that she suspected I was jealous that Rae had friends at school, and that Rae was growing up and realizing that she doesn't need to hang out with me anymore, even though we were only three years apart.

I reiterated that I wasn't jealous of that at all, and I truly wasn't. I was older than Rae and we were in different grades! There was supposed to be a difference!

Karen became even more smug and louder.

"It's okay Sara…you don't have to lie! You are in denial. You are jealous that Abigail is getting closer to her friends, and she's allowed to see them outside of school, unlike you!"

This was all a bunch of crap to me. She knew she was making me mad by this. Her eyes were dancing as she watched me. At one point, I exploded in a rage. Why was she doing this? As a mother, didn't she have other responsible duties to attend to? If she truly wanted to be a counselor to me, there were a couple of things she would do different.

First, she would respect my wishes and not shout loud so the whole house could hear. Second, shouldn't everything be confidential? Why wasn't she talking to me in my room? Hadn't she mysteriously holed herself up in Rae's room weeks before she started summoning me downstairs?

After I exploded, Karen looked very satisfied.

"There it is!" she screamed at the top of her lungs. "You need to confront your feelings toward Abigail and stop being jealous!"

I would scream horrible things and stomp upstairs to my room.

"Sara, I'm not done yet!" she called after me with an amused tone. "Come back here! SaraJane, come back here!" I could detect a laughing tone in her voice. She had enjoyed this.

The slamming of my door would make her stop. Karen would be satisfied. After that, Rae would open her room door and head downstairs to the bathroom to get ready for the day, respectively waiting for this everyday morning counseling session to quickly explode.

During this time, I was not allowed to talk to Rae either! Karen began telling Rae that I was jealous of her and was a bad example for her. The same thing she did with Stan and Abram when she wanted to separate them. A few times, Karen went behind Rae's back and told me that Rae did not like me either. She said that Rae was telling her that she felt I hated her because she had privileges and I didn't.

The truth was, Karen told us we needed to not speak to each other. Whenever we had to be in each other's presence, Karen made sure my sister and I didn't speak. Every day was so awkward. Karen was a control freak and she kept an eye out. If she had to leave to go somewhere, she made sure that Rae and I weren't left in the house at the same time.

On one occasion, she took all four of us with her to run a few errands so we wouldn't be at the house alone to bond. Elijah was her "soldier" at the time.

Karen stepped out the car to go in the store. When she came back, she looked at Elijah.

She asked, "Elijah, while I was in the store, did Sara and Abigail speak to each other?"

"Yes," he promptly answered.

Karen's face flushed with anger. But she didn't say anything.

Of course, my sister and I had struck up light conversation. We were sisters and there was nothing Karen could ever do about it! She was so obsessed. Her dirty work had only worked for around four months. Rae and I could never go long without speaking.

Karen was very controlling with what The Four watched. She had long since stopped letting us watch cable. Only the privileged ones got to watch it in the living room on the big screen television, or in her bedroom. Before she gave Rae the small black and white television, it was in the den. Except the den was more like a small holding area now, because the room had been divided in half when she built Elijah's closet sized room. At first it had cable, then she removed it. We were only allowed to watch old VHS movies. She created a schedule for each of us that listed when we were individually allowed to be in that room to watch a VHS movie.

I believe this contributed to love my love of old black and white movies, and vintage movies. Among my favorites were Pollyanna, National Velvet, The Parent Trap (1960s Version), That Darn Cat, Little House on the Prairie, Old Yeller, and the list goes on! We could not watch what the privileged ones watched.

Since the den was right above the stairs, we spent time slithering on our stomachs like turtles and lowering our bodies down on the stairs far enough to peer into the living room to see what the privileged ones were watching. It was either on Cartoon Network or the Disney Channel. We used our hands to grab ahold of the stair posts to steady ourselves so we wouldn't slide down. What a sight we were!

Karen caught us. She randomly crept into the dining room without making noise and our eyes would meet with her icy blue gaze.

"What are you doing?" she would ask. But she looked amused. She knew we wanted to watch what they were watching. "Get back upstairs. Actually, turn the television off and go to your room!"

Karen thrived on our desires…but she was actually doing us a favor. You see, we weren't watching mindless programs and cartoons like Abram, Cisca, and Nano! Whatever we enjoyed, she took it away, *just* because we enjoyed it! So, the things we liked, we eventually learned to *pretend to dislike*, so we could keep them! This was all a grand game for her.

Once she found out I enjoyed the old VHS movies, I was not allowed to watch the movies anymore. I had excitedly raved about them to her. She made an excuse about the missing movies, claiming I was too old or something to watch them. Is that so? She always found a way to snatch something away whenever I was becoming accepting and settled.

We weren't allowed to listen to worldly music, or what she called secular music. She told us we'd become "streetwalkers" for listening to it. She did not want Stan and Elijah to listen to rap or anything else. She said they would become convicts and harm everyone. Abram had a collection of inappropriate music though. When we brought this fact up, we were told to mind our business again. He had a bunch of Bow Wow's earlier rap music that wasn't appropriate for kids, let alone a white boy.

This was the time I grew to love contemporary Christian artists. The only radio station we could listen to was the Family Life Network. We were so scared to even *dare* use our finger to switch the radio station! She said if Rae and I listened to secular music, we'd become pregnant by the time we were teenagers and get our hearts broken. What was so ironic was the fact that we weren't even allowed to date, let alone go anywhere! The Four went to school and came directly back home. She was watching the clock, even clocking the different times she gave each of us. Karen had a lot of time on her hands. I always wondered what she really could have done with her life with the type of calculating games she knew how to play.

Karen always made it seem like she could not buy us anything because it was a hassle for her. You could tell she was a money hungry person who didn't care about others at all. One year when school was starting again I asked her if she could get me some more school supplies. I asked for a couple of notebooks and a new binder. My binder was completely done for from the wear and tear of the previous school year. I used it for all my classes! People were snickering and making jokes about my huge torn binder.

I stood in front of her as she sat in the living room watching television. What I asked for did not cost much! It was a necessity! She was looking at me like I had asked her to send me to Africa.

"Sara, use your same notebooks and binder from last year. There's still usage in them."

Usage?

Then she turned her attention back to the television, dismissing me from her presence.

Abram was sitting on one of the couches. He pretended I wasn't there. Of course, he had not a care in the world. He was already set with his brand new school supplies.

Besides the different food she gave the Privileged Five, Karen loved to flaunt material things in front of us. When we first got adopted, we felt free to walk in any section of the house. We always got to be in the living room or outside. Next, The Four was suddenly banned from the living room and the large screen television. We were not to step foot into that living room! Karen only summoned us in the living room if she wanted to lecture us about something. We stood in front of her. If she allowed us to sit on the couches, we were counting in our heads how many seconds we were allowed. It seemed so surreal.

Karen had bought a brand new mustang. Shiny blue color. Now she had the station wagon and mustang. The Four were not privileged to ride in the mustang. Elijah was walking back home from school one afternoon. Cisca and Nano were in the yard playing with a ball. They threw it toward him, but instead it rolled on the dirt driveway and stopped near the parked mustang. So, Elijah went to get it.

Then Karen ran out the front door.

"Elijah, don't you go near my car!" she screamed at him.

"I was just getting the…"

"Get away from my car!"

She didn't even give him the opportunity to speak.

Whenever we asked Karen for a towel to bathe, she gave us a hard time about it. She began to only allow us one bath a week. At one point, she did not let us bathe for half of the school year! She claimed she did not want to waste water. But why were the privileged ones showering daily in her bathroom?

I don't know how, but God wrapped his arms around The Four and no one really noticed us at school until it really got bad. I dreaded going to school. There was a girl that Stan liked at school that sat behind him. She screamed one day that he smelled so bad and that he needed to shower. Her words were really mean as she used some derogatory words as well. How damaging for an adolescent boy who wasn't allowed to shower! When it was also reported that we were not allowed to shower, Karen was furious and had no choice but to get a shower head for us.

She also started ordering us to not flush the toilet during the day. How gross. She had adolescents using the bathroom, and girls with periods. Everyone saw each other's stuff. The last person who used the bathroom at night was instructed to flush it. However, she and Neal's toilet flushed multiple times a day.

What bills was she really talking about? Neal had a stable construction job for many years in Owego, and she picked up many side jobs. I knew she was also receiving money for us! At one point, she went on a missionary trip to Bolivia for two weeks! She returned from the trip telling us that we were very ungrateful kids who had it better than the children in Bolivia. But she never told Abram, Cisca, or Nano they were ungrateful. They acted like spoiled brats and were already disrespecting her to the max.

Karen told me that she was concerned about me because I was the oldest when we first moved to the Carlons. I would be the example for everyone. So that was her reason for saying that's why she never let me go anywhere! She said she didn't trust that I would be able to handle myself in front of my friends...and in front of boys.

What? Okay, well if she was that concerned, why didn't she tell me about boys? She never even trusted me or gave me that chance to prove to her from the very beginning. So how would she really know? The others were instantly granted a chance to prove themselves. But not me...and I was the oldest. What was she so afraid of about me? Would I start talking to people about what went on in our household? The only time I saw anyone was when I went to school or church. The rest of my days were spent confined to my bedroom.

I had one friend that I was close to in class. Her name was Sasha Haner. We liked to show off our singing skills to each other. She lived a five-minute walk from the Carlon house. Sasha either took the bus home or went somewhere else after school, but she walked to school in the morning.

She asked if I could hang out at her house sometime.

"Um...I've never been allowed to go to a friend's house before," I explained.

"You're joking!" Sasha looked at me like I had five heads.

"I never have."

"Why?"

"My mom says I'm going to do bad things with boys. What is she talking about? No boys in school even like me!"

"SaraJane, you are beautiful!"

"No, I'm not...look at my nappy afro." I was already conditioned.

I looked down at my Salvation Army clothes that I was forced to wear every day. Sometimes I wanted to boycott going to school until Karen allowed me to wear clothes from the mall just like Abram was allowed to wear. She made it very clear what our attire would be.

She gave The Four only about three outfits each. We wore them over and over. It was so bad that our classmates and teachers looked uncomfortable for us. Karen was very crafty in her scheme to humiliate and damage our self-esteem. She got off on it. There was a long flower hippy skirt that went to my ankles that I had to wear with any shirt and none of the shirts matched. For my shoes, I would have to wear sneakers! Yes, sneakers with a hippy skirt!

It hurt my heart and soul to pass by this particular English teacher every morning. Before the final homeroom bell rang, he would stand outside his classroom door to make sure everyone got to class. I wore the hippy skirt about two to three times a week. As soon as I turned the corner to head down the hallway to pass his class, his presence would make me feel very small and I cringed inside, wanting to shrink into the tile floors. I was so beyond humiliated. He and I never made eye contact. When he finally became my English teacher, we acted very awkward around each other in class. Sometimes, I would glance up and he would be staring. Then he quickly looked away. I was now a great English student, so every paper came back perfect.

Every day I prayed that none of my peers thought I chose to wear these clothes! They just *had* to know! They knew that Abram was our brother! They saw him with appropriate clothes on just like them! Certainly, they had to know what was happening. But it was an unspoken taboo subject with the Candor School District.

"SaraJane, stop that! You are gorgeous!" Sasha told me. "I'm going to have my mom call yours. She will look it up in the phone book."

I nodded skeptically. The town was so small that everyone was in the phone book. Everyone listened to their radio scanners for any little thing that happened too. Everyone knew about our brushes with Tioga County Social Services.

That evening, Karen summoned me to the living room.

"You had a friend at school tell her mother to call me?" she asked accusingly.

"Yes."

"Why?"

"So me and Sasha can hang out."

"What would you do if you hung out?"

"Sing and write songs," I said timidly.

Karen chuckled. That was a classic response she always gave.

"She lives right down the hill from us. It's very close to the house."

"I know where she lives."

She was quiet as she considered her words.

"You know I have always been concerned about you going to other people's house…"

"But why? What would I do?"

"Don't interrupt me while I'm speaking."

I clamped my mouth shut with irritation. This was usually how she got me. She would already have said no before giving me a chance. Then as I argued my reason for that chance, she would smirk and say, "See! The answer is no. Now you really can't go!"

She would use my defending my case as an excuse when her answer was already no from the jump! Reverse psychology. Even when I didn't argue, the answer was still always no!

This time, I was quiet.

"I don't want you to get distracted from your homework."

I was silent as she stared for my reaction.

"She might have boys over as well."

I was silent as she stared.

"You and Sasha may become so distracted that your behavior at school begins to become an influence over the other students."

Again, she watched for my reaction as I was silent. I wanted to roll my eyes so bad. But that's what she was looking for.

After a few minutes of silence, she cleared her throat.

"I'm not going to allow you to hang out at Sasha's house."

"Okay," I said submissively.

She didn't look impressed by my submission. She wanted me to get mad.

"Do you have anything more to say about the matter before I start dinner?"

"Yes."

"What?"

"Well, since she only lives five minutes from us...can we at least walk to school together in the morning? I don't have to go to her house."

Karen was hating my cooperating and calm demeanor. "I'll think about it," she answered with a clipped tone.

Karen spent the next couple of weeks talking to Sasha's mother on the phone about me being able to walk to school with her every morning.

At school, Sasha was becoming impatient.

"My mom doesn't get why your mom is calling her everyday just to complain about her fear of letting you walk to school with me."

I didn't say anything. I was so embarrassed.

"It's so simple! It's just a yes or no. By the way, my mom thinks your mom is crazy."

I didn't say anything.

A few days later, Sasha gave me another exasperated look.

"Hey look, just forget it. We see each other every day in school, right?" She gave me an encouraging smile.

I nodded. Karen had scared away Sasha's mom on purpose, and I hadn't even been able to prove myself and walk to school with Sasha just *once!*

I was only allowed to participate in the few skits our church held. Nothing at the school. My dream and deepest desire was to be in the school Drama Club. I was so hurt because she would not allow me to be part of it. I watched as the other students were excited at audition times and show nights. I was jealous. Every time there was a musical, the school performed it three times over a weekend. We were not allowed to attend. But during the school day before show weekend, the cast gave the school a preview during an assembly in the auditorium. I lived for those moments.

The Candor Junior-Senior High School put on your typical musicals such as Annie, Cinderella, and Peter Pan. I knew I was good and I desperately wanted to express my talents. The characters in the books I was reading had regular high school lives and they could participate in regular things that normal teenagers were allowed to do. At least I could imagine I was one of them as I read about them and I was transported into their reality temporarily.

The school placed the audition scripts in the hallway on a table for the students to take. When they were putting on the production of Cinderella, I grabbed one of the scripts and brought it home. I rehearsed it over and over and pretended I was chosen for the role of Cinderella. I remembered being eight-years-old at Mama Mary's house back in Las Vegas when the TV movie with Whitney Houston and Brandy playing Fairy Godmother and Cinderella was aired. I still knew every word to every song. My school wasn't putting on this version of course, but it triggered an emotional memory for me. That's why I grabbed the script. I knew I wasn't allowed to audition…but I wanted to pretend I was. I was my own audience in my bedroom.

Karen found the script during one of her searches. I had buried it deep in my closet so she really took me by surprise by how far she went with her obsession!

"You took something that does not belong to you!" she said, acting like I was evil for wanting to be Cinderella.

The next morning Karen dragged me into the principal's office to return the script.

"My daughter took this script from the school!" she said.

Mr. Hunt looked at the script in Karen's hands as she held it out to him. She looked like a child tattling.

"I have told my children not to take anything that doesn't belong to them! That's food, secular music, papers…"

Mr. Hunt looked very uncomfortable at this whole situation. But he was used to it with Karen. He took the script and set it on his desk.

"Okay, thank you. I will hand it back to the Drama Club instructor." He made a gesture like he had to attend to something else. He didn't make eye contact with me.

"Okay, thank you Mr. Hunt," Karen said cheerfully.

We walked out his office. She went home and I went to class.

None of the teachers cared about the things The Four did…because we did what was normal! The teachers actually wanted me to try out!

One time I was so completely humble after I asked her could I try out for cheerleading in high school. She said she would finally allow me to try out, which was a miracle she even said that. But she spent days trying to get me to crack. Each day, she either summoned me in the living room or came in my room to randomly bring up an old argument. She was desperately trying to get me to argue with her. All those days I stayed humble. She was literally trying to break me down for no reason! She brought up stuff I had done years prior!

I did not break once. On the night before tryouts she came in my room. I was already tucked in bed, full of hope.

"SaraJane," she regarded me. "I'm not going to allow you to try out for cheerleading."

At those words, I turned my face to the wall and covered my head with my covers in deep pain. She stood there for a minute in silence before leaving. She didn't even say goodnight. She just wanted to see my spirit down.

That's who Karen was. She did this a lot with Stan too, promising certain things and giving us tests. When we passed each test, she was mad and still said no. None of The Four were allowed to participate in anything at the school. We brought home papers of activities or school field trips. As we hopefully handed her the papers, she looked at them. Then right in front of us, she proudly threw them in the kitchen wastebasket and said, "No."

She would say, "No!" as soon as we handed her the next one days later, before we could even finish our sentence. After a while, she made a new rule that we were not allowed to ask her anything at all.

If we were bold enough too, she looked at us like she wanted to slap us down. She looked at us like we were trying to be funny and play a trick on her.

"Why are you asking me?" she would ask incredulously. "You know the answer is no."

The privileged ones were allowed to hand her papers. She looked at them, and instantly granted their wishes.

Karen came to my room one day. "I have been in thought," she said reflectively.

My stomach tightened with anticipation for what she was about to say next.

"I was thinking that it shouldn't be a problem to allow you to have a privilege."

Huh? I, SaraJane, was getting a privilege?

"I have decided to allow you the privilege of speaking to your friends on the phone."

I was silent. My mind flashed back to the time when I was outrageously bold enough to ask her for a phone in my room. I was obsessed with the Baby-Sitters-Club. The teenagers in the book series formed a club. They held meetings at one designated person's house who was allowed to have a phone in her room. Parents called that phone to schedule for their kids to be watched by the club members. So many adventures with the kids, and so many adventures among the girls who had different personalities and sometimes they clashed over boys and clothes and family secrets and…

"SaraJane, aren't you happy that I'm giving you a privilege?"

"Yes," I snapped back in the moment.

"I'm allowing you to use the phone in the kitchen."

Oh. There was a green phone that was attached to the kitchen wall near the pantry.

"Thank you," I said.

"Saturdays will be your phone days. I will need to know ahead of time which friend is calling."

"Okay," I nodded.

"You are allowed ten minutes only."

What?

"Okay."

Karen nodded. She was looking like she had just granted me tickets to a cruise and that I had better be grateful.

I told a few of my classmates. They looked at me very strangely as I explained the rules to them.

"Only ten minutes?" they asked.

"Yes."

"Only one day a week? She's a cow."

"This is the first time I'm allowed to do this," I explained.

"And it's *not* normal," they retorted.

Sasha was shaking her head even more. "What if we have things to do on a Saturday? You should be allowed to speak during the week too. Especially because it's only *ten minutes.*"

"I know."

That Saturday, Sasha called me. She wanted to support me. She really cared about me as a friend.

Karen hovered around like a warden as we spoke. I couldn't even speak in privacy!

For the next couple of weeks, I dialed other people, as I was only allowed one friend per week. None of them could be boys. My classmates stayed on the phone with me for those ten minutes…but they sounded very eager for the call to end. Karen stood in the kitchen doing miscellaneous things.

I couldn't get anyone on the phone after those first few times. So, I lost interest in the whole phone privilege. Back at school, my classmates and I pretended this stint never happened. Just like the time Karen had arranged for me to have a "pen pal" and write a girl my age who lived in another town. We met their family at a church function. I wrote the girl a friendly letter after Karen suggested we should write. I never received a letter back.

TWENTY-ONE

Dear Mama,

I feel so ugly and unworthy. Karen took us to a function at Hickories Park for Cadee, Cisca, and Nano. She told us we only came with her as "default." The whole day, Stan and Rae and Elijah and I felt like burdens. Karen was glaring at us and she made us stand off to the side a lot. When we got home that night I cried. Before walking up to bed, I asked to speak with her. I told her that I felt like she did not care about us. I told her that I felt like we were in their way. As I was crying real tears of hurt, Karen did not look sad at all. She told me that it wasn't true. Then she told me to go to bed. She thrives off our vulnerability and uses it to hurt us.

She started paying us to do our house chores that we have always done. Every week, Stan and I receive $2. Rae and Elijah receive 50 cents. She wants to emphasize the fact that Stan and I should feel good about our pay because we're older. Every week after church, she takes us to spend it. We buy a snack at the store. What else could we spend that meager change on? But I was smart and saved up. I noticed a skirt I liked at Family Dollar. Karen approves because it goes all the way to my ankles. It isn't too bad looking. Better then what I usually wear. It cost $12. I saved my allowance for six weeks and bought it. Now she has stopped giving us allowance. But we still have to do our chores.

My chore is sweeping the dining and kitchen floors. I refuse to scoop up her dog poop. At first it was Rae's job. When Karen is angry at Stan for something she makes them switch. On his first day of scooping the poop, they got into a big argument. I sneaked into Rae's room and we looked out her window that was above the side yard where they were standing. As she yelled at Stan, he said something back to her. Then she said, "Okay Isaiah, put the scoop down. Pick the poop up with your hands instead!" For a second he just stared at her as she glared back at him. He looked like he was frozen in time. Rae and I felt he was going to pick the poop up, and smash it into her face! After the longest time, he reached down and picked the poop up with his bare hands! Karen looked very satisfied. Then she finally allowed him to scrub his hands. Later he confirmed just what we had thought. He contemplated smashing the poop in her face, then running down Mountain Ave and running away to never ever come back. Except he didn't know where he was going to go.

Now when the whole house gets into an argument, Karen and Neal get mad when we bring up the poop incident. They tell us to leave it in the past and let it go. One time Neal got so angry that we brought it up...that his face contorted like a madman and his eyes were bulging. "Stop talking about it! We get it! You picked up dog poop, okay?" Then he dramatically and mockingly imitated my brother. "I picked up poop I picked up poop I picked up poop I picked up poop!" His face was red and he shook his body like he was having a seizure. Even though we were angry, we all started laughing because Neal always got so funny and dramatic during these intense fights.

We have become paranoid and nervous all the time. I think mine is the worst though. Stan makes this weird noise out of nervousness a lot. It's like a deep hum. It lasts for about a second. Then he does it over and over and looks around nervously. He always gets in trouble for it, which makes him do it even more. One time Elijah started doing it and Karen whooped him so bad.

Karen gets angry at me for taking my time in the bathroom. She stormed in on me while I was on the toilet! I was angry and felt violated. Why was she doing this to a teenager? She really likes to get me upset so I can explode. I asked her to leave. So instead she stayed with a smug look on her face. She wouldn't leave the bathroom until I was done. She watched as I finished and pulled my underwear and pants up. After that, she has strictly enforced my hygiene time. She already had but now it's to five minutes. I'm allowed five minutes in the morning, and five minutes at night. I'm always rushing and praying silently because it goes by so fast, and most times I run out of time. I get yelled at. She says I have problems because I can't manage to get ready in five minutes. But why is she doing this to me? A lot of mornings are very explosive for us. Sometimes she gives Stan, Rae, and Elijah more time. A couple of times I overheard her saying, "Don't worry, go ahead and take your time. Get done what you need to get done." She really hates me with a passion.

We aren't allowed to come out our rooms without asking now. We have to call, "Mom!" from our room door. She also tells us to limit our bathroom trips to two or three times a day. Once when we get ready in the morning, once during the day after lunch, then once before we go to bed. Sometimes we can't help it and we have to go. She accuses us of just wanting to be out of our rooms. She tells us to hurry it up and "high tail it back upstairs."

We aren't allowed to use the bathroom after 7:00 pm. If we have to go after that, she says to hold it in till the morning. Rae peed on her floor a couple of times. I sneaked some perfume from a friend at school and we poured it over the spot so Karen wouldn't smell it. I also sneaked a water bottle from school. On the nights where I can't hold my bladder, I pee in it. I feel so relieved.

Karen had slowly snatched my identity away from me. I was trying to find myself, the little girl Sequoya. I had such a long way to go. Karen had this way of making me feel very low. This led to my ultimate feelings of low self-esteem. When I was first adopted, I wrote my songs and sang around the house. I had made up my first serious song in my head when I was six. I wrote my first song on paper at eight. Karen always claimed that she loved my talents…but how come she always had something bad to say about them? She made me feel that I would never be good enough in life.

When I was twelve, I developed bad acne. I had good skin my whole life up until that point. Then suddenly, I had spots on my face, neck, shoulders, and back. She would not get me anything for them or take me to the doctor. I can only recall going to the doctor twice while living there. She took all of us as a group both times. She told us to scrub really good the nights before and she seemed unusually nice. When a friend from school gave me an acne wash, Karen confiscated it. On top of looking like a slave with my clothes and no bra and saggy boobs, my hair was afro like, and I was tall and lanky.

Karen knew what she was doing to my self-esteem. There was a church member at Abide in the Vine who recorded Christian music, but Karen wouldn't let me practice with him. After a while I became scared of her hearing me sing. I sang to myself in my room. It got to the point where I would whisper when I sang! I continued to write songs...but I did not practice...for fear that someone in the house would hear me.

Karen and Neal got into an argument on my thirteenth birthday. Even though we weren't speaking, he bought me a little karaoke machine that came with a recorder and microphone. Cadee bought me a few secular music CDs. Karen was upset.

Upstairs in my room after dinner, I strained to hear the argument. Neal and Cadee were stating that I was now a teenager. Karen wasn't taking this very lightly.

"Come on Mom," Cadee told her. "Lighten up. My co-workers play these songs at work and I thought SaraJane would love it!"

"That's secular music!" Karen argued. "My children are only allowed to listen to the Family Life Network."

"I got them for her because I wanted to. Let her keep them, Mom."

Karen didn't take those CDs from me. I thought it was a miracle.

I recorded myself singing on my karaoke machine. Karen walked in on me one day and heard me. Embarrassed, I stopped.

"It's not very good," she said.

I put my head down. That summer of 2003 is when I really sank into further depression due to the pain I was enduring.

I played Alicia Keys album *Songs in A Minor* over and over. Each song was pain. But they gave me a sense of hope that someday I would be free and this nightmare would end. Her song called *Troubles* was the song that got me through each day.

Dear Lord, can you take it away
This pain in my heart that follows me day by day
And at night it stalks me like the shadows on my wall

Karen and I have never got along. She always sheltered me and damaged my confidence. She was obsessed with anything I had the nerve to show interest in. Just so she could take it away or make me feel guilty for being who I was. She began monitoring the books I was bringing home. I had also started reading your typical high school romance novels. She skimmed through one of the books and saw one word she didn't like and said I would go down the wrong path. She didn't even look at the whole paragraph long enough to see it was not bad at all. The character in the book was only going for a run, so the author had said something like, "She reached down to feel her naked legs."

Karen said that I would be misguided about boys and life. She even made sure that we weren't allowed to attend health class at school. When she saw I had health class printed on my schedule, she freaked out.

"You don't need to be in health class. I will teach you everything you need to know."

She had a meeting with the school to have me removed from the class. The school informed her about the importance of being careful with sex and abstinence and making the right choices. The school board was confused that Karen was upset about this. She argued that she had a right to teach her children herself. She always wanted everything we learned to come directly from her only, nothing from the outside. The school removed me from the class.

Any mention of sex sent her in a paranoid state of her lecturing us. It was almost as if we were normal teenagers who were already out dating! The thing was, we were sheltered prisoners with no after school or phone privileges! So, what was her problem?

I remember the look on her face one day as she spoke to me. I was annoyed that I was being lectured over something I wasn't even allowed to do. I impatiently said, "Well, I don't want to have it right now so stop being down my neck about it please! You don't even let me leave the house so you should not be worried anyway. I'm sure when I get older, I will learn about making love."

The look on her face was priceless! She called it sex, but I called it making love. She scowled and turned away from me.

There was this kid in my grade who was handsome though. He was one of those popular types who didn't have a girlfriend but he drew lots of the girl's attention. For some reason, he stared at me all the time. He studied me hard. I was confused as to why because I felt I wasn't appealing. Maybe my face was still pretty to him, despite my frazzled afro and Salvation Army clothes. Every year starting in the fourth grade, I caught him staring at me. By our eighth-grade year, he finally came up to me during tech class.

"SaraJane, will you go out with me?" he asked, in a low tone. He looked kind of nervous.

I looked at him, very surprised. Was he serious? Why on earth did he want to go out with me? I was in denial that he had even asked me.

I shook my head no, even though I really wanted to say yes. I didn't want to deal with the whole ordeal of explaining to him that I was a prisoner in my own home and I couldn't date until I was eighteen.

When we had our mandatory choir concert, I recall that was one of the rare times that Karen attended. I was on the girl's side in the stands and he was on the boy's side. After the assembly, Karen struck up light conversation with me as we were walking out. She liked to tease me a lot. She would always mention something about another student.

"That girl has on a very nice outfit!" Karen would exclaim. "I like her jeans!"

She knew that she didn't allow me to wear regular clothes like them. I would just smile and nod my head.

"But oh my goodness. That young man with those handsome features and beautiful piercing brown eyes was so handsome! I kept staring at him myself!"

As she described him more, I was able to tell her his name. Then I got bold.

"He asked me out in tech class," I said, with a coy tone. I was even surprised at myself for revealing this to her!

Karen's eyes shot downward. As if I had just shot her. We were silent for the rest of the way home. I did a little victory dance inside.

She enjoyed doing things to humiliate us. I was being recognized for being an excellent student at school. She had to come to the assembly to watch me receive the award. A few days before award night, she arrived home with an outfit for me.

"I'm very proud of you," she said. "I bought you something to wear."

Wow. I was in disbelief.

She opened the bag.

Once I peered at it, I cringed inside.

"I really wanted to do something nice for you." She was using that voice again. The manipulative one that meant *'I'm making an effort by trying to be nice to you and if you don't appreciate my effort than you are a horrible person.'* She used this tone when she knew she was wrong. She would use our horror and dislike against us to cover up for the fact that she was wrong.

Inside the bag was a man's shiny orange two-piece Dashiki. Not a woman's...a man's Dashiki! No other colors on it. Just shimmery orange. My heart started beating so fast with fear. But this was a chance to get into Karen's good grace. If I "hurt" her, my life would be way worse than it already was.

I was not allowed to shower before the event. I put the suit on, with a deep feeling of sadness. I pretended to be happy. I had to beat her at her own game. As we neared the school I noticed an amusing smile spread across her face.

We stepped inside and the look on everyone's faces confirmed what Karen had done to me. People were snickering and glancing at each other. The expressions on their faces were like *'Who on earth would wear something like that? She can't be serious right now. I know she dresses horribly all the time, but just wow.'*

I blocked it out mentally. I had no other choice. Everyone clapped when each person's name was called. But when my name was called and I had to walk up front, my suit was shiny bright in the dimmed room. The whole auditorium became silent. I could feel people trying not to laugh. To make matters worse, Karen proudly clapped extra loud.

Back at home, I realized that she had wanted me to be hurt. She had a very calculating way of doing it. Whenever she wanted to embarrass us, she made the situation seem like it was all good and that she was a proud mother. At first her charade was believable. Then we were confused because people would tell us how wrong the situation was.

Stan's hair grew so fast and so curly. He truly was the Romeo that Dee always called him when we were in Nevada. One day Karen said she was going to give him a haircut. He was excited as she clipped away with the scissors. He noticed that she seemed to be doing a design. When she got done, she was proud and told him how handsome he was. She sounded genuine.

When Stan looked in the mirror, he had to pretend with Karen so she would not be "hurt" and not do anything else for him. He pretended…but his heart was beating so loud. She had taken the scissors and randomly clipped different sections of his hair off, leaving some short and some long, and some still in an afro! There were strands of hair hanging from all directions of his head! The front part was cut short, but the middle and back were still in an afro. The sides were purposely uneven. He had to go to school the next day. He wanted to crawl into hiding instead.

The Four were in shock…but could not do anything. Stan's heart pounded so loudly as he walked to school. He knew it was going to be over for him when he got there. As soon as he entered the building, everyone instantly noticed. Students were laughing and the teachers were looking at him crazy too.

"Dude, what the heck did you do?" A student asked him.

"My mom cut my hair for me," Stan explained, like it was nothing.

No one could understand it. Stan was silent that whole day. He was humiliated. His friend since third grade, Taylor, never said a word, and acted completely normal as if nothing was wrong. Taylor was the only friend of Stan's that Karen miraculously liked.

That day, Taylor didn't crack a smile like everyone else was doing. He understood.

I had theories about Karen. I intentionally tested her to see if my findings were accurate. I used her own reverse psychology on her.

The Four sat eating our meager dinner. Karen hovered around, provoking an argument with me that always led to my tantrums and stomping episodes. Usually during arguments at the table I would try to get up without asking to be excused. She would use her fat large frame to block me from getting up, blue eyes glaring with her gray hair clinging to her sweaty angry face. She would stand in front of my place at the table until I "bowed down" to her.

On this particular day I told myself to go along with everything she said. Then maybe she'd back off and leave me alone! She was telling me how horrible I was and how I was destroying everyone in the house. She said hurtful things that were not true. They were just a mirror of her own self.

I stayed strong throughout this whole interrogation. She looked very surprised to see that I wouldn't fight back with her. This really upset her.

"Sara. Speak," she said.

I continued eating.

"Speak Sara! You always have something to say, don't you?"

My siblings looked surprised as well that I didn't speak up.

"Give me an explanation! Why are you such a horrible daughter? Tell me?"

I looked at her proud drama filled face. She knew that making me speak would always result in an argument. But I decided to see what would happen if I didn't argue against her unfairness. I really had to humble myself.

"You're right," I agreed. I spoke very calmly. "I'm a horrible daughter. I'm ruining the family with my behavior. And I don't treat you good." I had never said anything like this before.

Karen's icy blue eyes flashed with anger. She slammed her two hands on the table, making everyone's plates jump. We all flinched.

"*Sara!*" she screeched with such anger. Her voice was so loud and full of rage.

There it was. My findings were correct. She started things to purposely arouse my temper tantrums because she knew I always bucked against her. She used that to always have me on punishment and confined to my room. What was her problem?

Karen always tried to monitor my friendships with the ladies at Abide in the Vine Church. They genuinely wanted to be my friend. They struck up conversation with me and Karen was nearby watching us with a stern look. Then she'd wait and talk to the same person after we were done. Or we'd get in an argument for no reason back at the house. Karen always felt I was up to something, when I wasn't. How could I be up to something? I was a prisoner.

The older biracial girl, the one who I first noticed at the church when we were adopted, walked over to our row one morning and handed me a can of hair lotion.

"This is for you and your sister," she said. "Rub this into your hair every day." She smiled at Rae and me. I clutched the can. Wow! A hair product for our dry hair! She had noticed the state of our hair and she understood.

Back at the house, Karen asked to see it. I handed it to her. She read the ingredients.

"I could make this stuff myself," she grunted. "It's all very simple."

I didn't say anything as I stood there watching her. She really looked upset. As if the friendly girl at church had crossed her.

Karen didn't give the can back to me, nor did she make the product herself.

A lot of the ladies at church were curious about me. Some of them told me that they knew we were special children. One of them stopped me after church to talk to me. She kept staring at me and telling me I was beautiful.

"Do you have a boyfriend?" she asked me.

"No!" I said with wide eyes. "I'm not allowed to date until I'm eighteen."

She laughed.

Then she said, "I want you to know that you are supposed to be alone. God is saving the best one just for you."

I smiled.

One time during worship service another member came up to me and suddenly grabbed me.

"SaraJane," she said as she hugged me. "You are blessed. Your voice will be a trumpet for the world!"

I felt really encouraged. This lady hadn't spoke to me before.

"What?" Karen came over to question her.

"I have received a word that her voice will be a trumpet for the world," she repeated. She now had tears streaming down her face.

After that, Karen came home with a small trumpet from a second hand store. But it really wasn't a trumpet. It was a miniature shell from the ocean with a mouth handle.

"Practice blowing every day," she instructed me. "So your voice can be a trumpet. It can't be a trumpet if you don't practice!"

What in the world? But I was young and naïve, so I blew in the shell that tasted very badly on my lips. It actually made me feel very sick.

Dear Mama,

I'm scared that I won't make it to Heaven. I'm always nervous because Karen says that God has told us to honor our mother and our father so that we will have long days on Earth. She says it's in the Bible. She says I don't respect her. But it's very hard to honor someone who is so mean and sets a division in the house! She says that she hopes God will have mercy on me and my days. She says, "I'm on my knees praying for this family every night and you all are disobedient!" She says she's going to make it into Heaven but that she doesn't know if we will. She has privately cried to Rae saying, "It's not going to be fair if Sara gets to make it into Heaven and I don't!"

I'm so scared. So, whenever I do something, I tattle on myself. I'm the only one who does this. Everyone else just waits until they're caught. I feel the things I do aren't bad at all. But I still feel guilty because I don't want to go to Hell. If I say a bad word at school, I come home to tell her. After I confess, she tells me that I'm very bad and I don't deserve privileges and that I never have deserved them. She looks very pleased that I tell her these things. Am I considered a good person because I'm fourteen and I tattle on myself?

One day during gym class, the gym teacher had the nurse come in to look at me. She said she was concerned because she saw something that wasn't right. The nurse took both of her hands and ran them down both sides of my torso. Then she gasped. She made me scared. She told me that part of my spine was curving out on my left side and that I had scoliosis. She told me all about it and gave me pamphlets. They called Karen and told her.

Karen told a few members at church and asked them what we should do. They told us about back braces and other options like surgery. Then Karen said I didn't need surgery, and that God will straighten up my spine for me if we just prayed. So, she brought me up to the front of the church and placed her hand on my left side and prayed.

TWENTY-TWO

I am floating in the air. No wait, I'm flying. Where am I? The Sky is a beautiful blue. The Sun is shining through the clouds as I break through. I'm descending into a place that looks and feels very familiar…

"My Quoya!" I hear.

Mama! I hear your voice! That's you calling me.

"I'm coming Mama!" I shout back. I'm flying towards the Carey Arms Apartments. I remembered where we live!

I can already see the letter C.

We live in Apartment C and I have never forgotten.

"Quoya, come on my baby."

"Wait Mama!" I scream. "I'm almost there. I'm right here!"

"I love you Quoya!" I hear you say. "I'm always here."

"I'm right here; hold on Mama…"

Then suddenly, I'm awake. No!

I was on my way back to Carey Arms and I was returning to my Mama.

Now I'm in my holding cell at Karen's house on Mountain Avenue. But this dream felt so surreal…so vivid. I really couldn't wait to grow up now! My dream was confirmation. I had to just hold on. I don't know how I had managed. It had been four years. Always pleading in my head for Mama to please hold on. One time I was playing with Rae when we used to share a room and Mama popped in my mind. I felt so powerless because I was a kid. I couldn't just leave and run to her. I whispered a prayer and told her to please hold on.

After the dream, I told everyone at breakfast.

"I think our real mom still lives in Carey Arms," I said. They just looked at me.

Karen came out her room to ask me why I was talking.

"I had a dream about my Mama. She still lives in Apartment C in Carey Arms."

Karen chuckled. "Eat your food Sara."

"When was the last time you heard from Kim?"

"Sara, I have told you many times, she stopped emailing me! I hear nothing about what's going on out there. I wish I did."

Later that same day, unbeknownst to me, Karen went into Rae's room.

"You know," she said, in a conspiring and devious tone. "Your mother doesn't even live in that building anymore."

My eleven-year-old sister looked up at Karen with a naïve expression.

"Kim still keeps in touch with me and she emails me every time she sees your mother. And guess what? I know exactly what your mother is doing right now."

As Karen had a look of victory over her face, my little sister didn't say anything. She didn't understand what was going on.

Dear Mama,

Karen has told us endless stories about her past and she cries so she can make us feel sad. But when I ask her more questions about it, she gets upset. All her stories are very short and leaves me wondering with so many questions. I have always been curious about people's history. She says that her brother molested her and that her father abused her mother. She and her siblings always played with these two girls down the street but they discovered later that their neighbors were actually their blood sisters! The girls ended up moving away. When I asked where they are, she said they won't talk to her. She says no one in her family talks to her. We have only met one of her sisters, who we call Aunt Doris. When she comes over she always asks Karen why are we always in our rooms.

Karen says that no one ever cared about her growing up. She was already taking care of everyone else before she was a teenager. As a teen, the family was preparing to go on vacation and she got into an argument with everyone. She stormed to her room to hold up the process of the departure. I don't know what for! If that was me I would have got in the car! She would not respond when they called for her. Her parents informed her that if she was not ready, then they'd leave for vacation without her. Karen waited for them to come upstairs to get her because she didn't believe them. She was shocked when she looked out her bedroom window to see the family pulling out the driveway! Her family returned a week later.

She has told us that being a single mother while raising Cadee and Colin was very hard. She stole toilet paper from public bathrooms. She says that Colin has never appreciated her. She saved all her money so she could buy Colin a leather jacket that he really wanted badly. She said he was very ungrateful towards her. When he came back to get his stuff before he went into the Marines, she called the police on him and said he was breaking and entering. He was arrested. They have had a really strained relationship and we have only met him once. He has a son now and she wants to go to North Carolina to meet him. Karen says that she hopes Colin won't "shut her out."

Karen says things about her daughter Cadee from time to time. They aren't very nice. She told us that she warned Cadee not to go to Texas carelessly. That's where Cadee was with Cisca and Nano's father. Karen sounded so happy just to tell us that Cadee was abandoned on Christmas Day and so she had to fly back to New York as a single mother.

Cadee is so nice. I know she sees her mother's cruelty now. She baby-sits us from time to time. She lets us out of our rooms and we can sit in the living room with her. But as soon as we hear the car in the driveway, we bolt back upstairs! It's our secret. One time she baby-sat us late at night and I overheard her on the phone crying to somebody. I crept to the stairs and I heard her saying, "My mom is so mean to these kids. How could she do this! It's not right!" She was telling the person how cruel her mother treats us. She was crying really hard. I went to bed crying myself just by hearing her.

Karen was frequently getting into arguments with a lot of the church members. She told us little things back at the house that really confused us.

"People are having sex with other people's husbands and wives!' she exclaimed.

"They are?" I was so confused. Everyone at church seemed so nice. I didn't understand. I was young and didn't believe that such things happened.

"Yes. Right at our church. A lot of people who go to Abide in the Vine are going to Hell!"

She seemed extra mad about something. Well, if it wasn't her doing these things, then she didn't need to be so mad, I was thinking. She kept telling us she was going to make it to Heaven.

Karen kept provoking me all the same...and she didn't mind picking a fight with me at church as well. We were bickering in our row about something. At this point, I was so through and felt like I might explode if I didn't get away from this lady. I was praying that God would just end my life right then and there during worship service!

Suddenly I felt someone touch my arm. I looked up to see Suzanne Walis, whom Rae and I called Rapunzel. The church picnic had taken place at her house.

"SaraJane, come with me," she said. "Let's go for a walk." Her eyes were so full of compassion for me.

"Sue, no! She is fine where she is!" Karen's angry face flushed with disbelief that her friend had stood up for me.

"No Karen, I think SaraJane and I need to go for a walk. We'll be back."

Without caring, Sue grabbed my hand. I stood up and walked away with her. I looked back to see my siblings' eyes wide and Karen's face in contorted fury.

Wow!

Sue had a firm grip on my hand. We walked through the empty halls of the old school that was now a church with construction work almost completed for other businesses that were moving in.

"Sit down," she said.

I sat down beside her against one of the walls and she grabbed both of my hands and looked me in my eyes.

Then the tears spilled from me. I couldn't control them. My body started to shake with my ragged sobs. The secluded hallway echoed my wails.

Suzanne began crying as well.

"SaraJane!" She held me close.

We sat there for a few minutes as I cried a pain I didn't even know I had. At that moment, I felt someone truly cared about me. I didn't care if Karen was going to come bounding down our hall at any minute. I didn't care if I would be punished even worse for this. The only thing I felt that was worse than being a prisoner was death.

"What's going on?" Sue asked me. "You can tell me."

"Karen is going to be very angry," I was shaking my head.

"I have known Karen for years," Sue explained. "What I just did was show her that she can't bully me. You have to be that way with her."

"No. That only works for Cisca, Nano, and Abram. They still get privileges and better food. Because when the rest of us try to stand up for ourselves, it's even worse and we get less food."

"What?" Sue stared at me incredulously. She didn't believe me.

Right there on the tile floor, for the next two hours as church was underway, I cried to Suzanne. I told her everything that was going on. I told her everything from the very beginning. From the time the Carlons flew to Las Vegas to meet us only *one* time before adopting us and letting Abram punch me in the face, to the first couple of good months, to the games and the division and the punishments and the abuse. Even our brush with Social Services who did *nothing* to help us.

Suzanne was listening to this horror story. She looked so very alarmed to hear this news about someone she had known for years. She asked me questions, and I answered. She revealed to me that she was always asking for Rae and me to come hang out with her at her house, but Karen always made an excuse as to why we weren't allowed.

"I'm so very sorry!" she cried and held me fiercely.

After a few minutes she looked at me and drew in her breath.

"The thing with Karen...is that she has her own rules floating in her mind about how life should work," she said.

I was confused.

"What I mean is that Karen knows what she does is wrong...but she thinks she's right. She rarely shows remorse about the things she says and does."

"So she knows she is mean!" I exclaimed. "But she makes it seem like we are the bad ones. She claims that she loves us and that we are the ones who don't love her!"

"Because she doesn't care, SaraJane."

I thought about that. Whenever we tried to make an effort and love her, she gave us a simple blank look like she didn't care. Why did she always say she wanted us to love her whenever I asked why were we adopted? What did she want from us?

"But I know I'm stuck with her until I'm eighteen," I said. "All I want is to be with my real family! My Mama, Dee, Daniel, and Keyonna. And I want my name Sequoya back."

I cried some more as Sue looked at me very sadly.

"I have an idea," she said.

I looked at her.

"Do you write in journals?"

"I have one at home. I just write my poems and songs."

"Well, how about you write to your biological siblings."

"How?"

"Easy. Write a letter to them whenever you feel like writing something. Except I know you won't be able to mail them. Write to them every day until you turn eighteen. By that time, you will have a whole book to give them!"

I smiled. But I knew Karen would confiscate that, so that was a no for me.

"And I also want you to try something else with Karen. From what you have told me, you two have always battled and neither of you will give up. And standing up for yourself has not worked. I want you to try something. This is going to be very hard. I already feel your pain. But can you not argue or challenge her? Please just try it for at least a month. I know sweetie, I know! Trust me! It's going to be hard the first few times because she will be surprised and still try to irk your nerves."

"That's exactly what she's going to do! I just know it." I was already angry that Sue was suggesting I humble myself for this lady.

"Just try it. Please. Maybe God wants to see her heart in all of this. Sometimes it's not about you...it's about the other person."

I didn't understand what she meant. But she had grabbed my hands again and looked into my eyes so pleadingly.

"Okay, I will try," I finally agreed. I knew my efforts would be futile. Suzanne had no idea what it was truly like being me.

After church, I was surprised when Karen didn't start a fight with me about my adventure with Suzanne. I was sure that she was going to pick up and continue from the fight earlier. But she didn't say anything.

What happened was...we stopped attending Abide in the Vine. I couldn't believe it! After four years, she wasn't taking us anymore! We had begrudgingly gone every Sunday as Neal and Abram stayed home. Now that I wanted to go back and see Suzanne, we no longer went.

I overheard Neal asking her about it. She said she was looking for another church that was without sin.

Yeah, sure.

Dear Mama,

I decided to take Suzanne's advice! I told myself that in order to make it in this house, I would have to pretend with her. I told myself that besides the pretending...maybe my feelings would turn real and Karen and I would become close. Then maybe she would treat us the same as Abram, Cisca, and Nano.

I knew that I could not do this without venting somehow. So, I decided to write all my feelings in my journal every day. I got along with her, but I vented in my journal. And miraculously...it was beginning to work! Wow. If I was her puppet and went along with everything she said, she was pleased. I had to change my identity to make her happy. That was the ingredient. Except deep inside I didn't feel right. That wasn't really me and I wasn't happy at all. My journal became my best friend. I wrote how I really felt. I wrote the good, the bad, and the ugly. I didn't shy away from telling how I felt about every single person in the house, including my own siblings. I was upset that they had chosen to be in her "partial favor" all the time. And by me now doing it, how could they feel right about this selling out behavior? It wasn't a good feeling at all.

Everyone in the house was so surprised by my turn around! They could not believe it was happening. Rae was always giving me a knowing look like she knew I was faking and she wanted me to know she knew. But it pleased Karen, so I continued.

Every morning, she started taking me on walks with her at the track behind the high school. We went very early before she made breakfast. We had good talks. She was talking to me like she was a friend, not a mother. It all felt very different. She said she wanted to lose weight. And she was in fact losing weight. When I confirmed this, she beamed. She also got her hair cut into a man's short style because she said the muggy summer was too much for her. She said she enjoyed exercising and becoming healthier. She looked at me with such happiness in her blue eyes and I was surprised to see that I didn't recognize them…they didn't look evil then. I was thinking to myself, "Who is this person right now and can she please be like this all of the time?" I also felt a sadness and I don't know why.

She brought home a book for me that was more advanced than what I usually read. It was my first time reading a Mary Higgins Clark novel. I quickly finished the complex story that would stay with me forever. On our next walk, I told her about what I had read. Although she didn't say anything about my excited commentary, I noticed she studied my face while I spoke and I wondered if she had already read it before. I didn't ask.

I decided to try my luck one morning. We were joking and talking about being healthy. I became bold and asked her, "So I guess this means you're still going to feed me oatmeal every day until I turn eighteen, huh?" I was smiling and meant it in light fun. Then her eyes clouded and her smile vanished. Uh oh. Before she could say anything else, I changed the subject fast. I could not afford to ruin this for myself. Back at the house, she still served three different breakfasts, lunches, and dinners with no hesitation.

Karen was very happy while I maintained my humble attitude and didn't throw any tantrums. She summoned me to the living room to tell me about a dream interpretation class she was taking online.

"I started taking this class so I would know what my dreams mean," she explained. "I had a dream I was pregnant. Which is very strange...because I'm forty-nine and past my time to give birth. I haven't been pregnant since the miscarriage from the car accident I had before we adopted Abram."

I was listening.

"I believe that being pregnant in my dream symbolizes something else. I think it's about you."

"Me?"

"Yes. You act much different now. You are not the same Sara. The old Sara has died, and the new Sara is now here. I feel the dream symbolizes a new birth...and that birth is you and I becoming stronger and loving each other."

She smiled contentedly as I nodded my head, pretending to agree.

Mountain Avenue was a hill that led into cornfields and hiking trails. The fields surrounding our house and the other scattered houses nearby made each household feel secluded to themselves. One afternoon, she took Stan, Rae, Elijah, Cisca, Nano, and me on the hiking trail. She was in very good spirits on this day. We were all getting along. We followed beside her as she led the way.

"You know what would make me happy?" she asked us. We watched as she looked around at the vast land. "I would be very happy if there were seven houses built...they don't have to be next to each other...they can be scattered with plenty of space. I want my children and grandchildren to live nearby. You can get married. And when you have children, if you ever need me to watch them, I'm not too far down the road and I will watch them for you. All you have to do is call. We'll all be near each other. Wouldn't that be great?"

While a couple of them nodded, in my head I was thinking that was the last idea I had in mind. When I turned eighteen, I was out of Candor, New York!

"Sara, why are you rolling your eyes?"

Crap. I didn't know my face had showed my thoughts.

"Well...when I turn eighteen...I don't know. I kind of want to discover the world or something."

Karen stopped in her tracks, making us all pause on the trail.

"Oh, so you can just go and be a *star* huh?" she spat out in pain, putting her hands on her hips. "You just can't wait to get far away from me, can't you? You just can't wait!"

Whoa! What in the world?

"I never said that," I said. "I just said I wanted to..."

"I know exactly what you said!"

I tried to remain calm. I was doing good with my submission game and didn't want to go back into a tantrum. I didn't know what had just happened. I had four more years to go until I was eighteen. That was an eternity.

We continued on the trail. After the air had died down, Karen spoke again. What she said surprised me.

"I'm worried that all of you will stop talking to me when you get older. And Sara, you have always showed me signs of that." She sounded very sad as she said this.

It reminded me of the times she told us that everyone always ended up not talking to her anymore. Well, why couldn't she act like a real mother then?

Karen decided to get me a gift during the long months that I was her soldier. She came in my room that summer and placed a small, striped kitten on my floor. It was very cute...but I was kind of scared to have my first pet. I was scared of its sharp claws as well. I didn't ask for a pet. I felt I wasn't a pet type person.

"I think you'll like having a cat," she explained. "She's small now...but she's going to get big pretty quickly."

I knew that was true because Abram had plenty of cats over the years. I watched the kitten observe its new surroundings. Karen left, then came back with its litter box and food.

"Her litter box is an automated device that cleans up after it detects she went to the bathroom already."

Okay. It really grossed me out that this kitten would poop right here in my small room just a few feet away from my bed.

"What will you name her?"

I looked at it. "I don't know yet."

Karen left and I sat on my bed feeling very uncomfortable. I wished I had received a different gift. Like maybe a privilege? I guess this was her way of congratulating me on my humbleness.

After a couple of days, I named my kitten Rosie. As the weeks went by she grew bigger and bigger and I wasn't afraid of her claws anymore. She purred merrily as I petted her. She also did lots of annoying things. Like suddenly jump on the window curtains, shredding the material. Her poop smelled so bad.

"She's a stink pot!" Karen complained one day when she entered my room.

I nodded.

It was a miracle one day when Karen informed us that she would be gone for a whole weekend. She said it was a missionary gathering. That meant Neal would be the only adult home. He was now a non-existent parent who dodged everything and everyone after work, except Abram. If Abram wasn't in his cabin, he and Neal disappeared somewhere. To have Karen gone would just be absurd. It felt so strange.

The miracle was...Karen was going to let Rae and me go to a friend's house! My heart was beating so fast and I was in disbelief. Wow. My first time spending the night somewhere!

"Abigail, you will go to Grandma's."

Rae smiled submissively. That was Neal's mom and his stepfather's house. Each time they saw us they were very nice to us.

"Sara, you will spend the weekend at Liz Valin's house."

I smiled. At first I thought I would be able to choose a friend from school. But I was still happy, because I was getting out the house. The Valins were a family with six children. There was a child around each of our ages. They had come to the church a couple of times. They lived in Vestal, New York, about an hour away. Their daughter Lacey Valin was two years older than me.

"The boys will stay here with Dad. I'll have one of them check on Rosie while you're gone."

"Okay," I said.

After Karen dropped me off, I brought my bag into Lacey's room. Then we went out to the patio and talked. I looked at my surroundings. I just could not believe I was out of my room on Mountain Ave! My head was snapping back and forth at the scenery and I'm sure Lacey was wondering what was wrong with me.

Lacey and I got along well. She had an older brother who said hello real fast then he left for the weekend. The younger siblings hovered around us a lot. We talked about our different high schools and we got on the computer. We listened to music. A lot of secular music that I was forbidden to hear. I let her know this, but I still listened to it all the same.

Then she asked me if I heard of a singer named Stacie Orrico.

"No."

"Well, she's a Christian singer that I think your mom will approve of. She has an album called *Genuine*." Lacey went to Stacie Orrico's website and played the music video for me.

She sounded great!

"Here, you can have this," Lacey said, after retrieving the whole album from a pile in her room.

"Thank you!" I said. I knew I'd be allowed to keep something like this. We played the songs on her stereo. The words were very comforting. The thing I really liked about her sound was that even though the words were clean and Christian, the tracks were R&B and Pop and sounded like a regular song on the radio.

Being away for the weekend also came with food! I stuffed my face with chips and cookies and bologna sandwiches and sugary tasty cereal and milk and juice and popcorn and candy...

I eventually trusted her enough and I told her about my life with the Carlons and she listened to every word with wide eyes.

"But things have been better lately," I reassured her. But Lacey wasn't convinced. She looked very disturbed.

"No SaraJane...it's not better until everyone is treated the same!" Then she lowered her voice. "To be honest...my mom has always thought your mom has been a little bit cuckoo."

I didn't say anything. That's what all my friends had been saying. Why had I been adopted by a cuckoo mother then? I had no say in the decision no matter how hard I fought against it. It was a very sad and unfair series of events that really tried and tested my faith.

"When I turn eighteen, I'm going back to Nevada and finding my Mama," I said.

"I hope you do too."

"Lacey?"

"Yes?"

"Please don't ever tell anyone I told you this."

"I promise I won't. I won't even tell my mom."

"Okay."

Dear Mama,
Something terrible happened to Karen! Not too long after that weekend, she fell and broke her hip! She went to the hospital a few times. She had to use a cane to wobble and limp around. She randomly cried out in pain. It made us sad to hear that. We have never seen her that hurt and vulnerable and feeling helpless. In a way, we all hoped that her years of cruelty was now over and she would be a new person and be nice forever.

Neal told her that she was crazy for not getting surgery done. But Karen refused surgery or any other help. She just spent a lot of time crying out in pain. During this time, her mean attitude lightened a little bit. But we still weren't privileged like Abram, Cisca, and Nano. She was still kind of cruel. We were talking to her more often though, and comforting her. We helped her walk through the house. We were very concerned. She made us feel sad by saying that she had prayed to God to take her then and there, because the pain was so unbearable and she cried all day long. But He wouldn't take her. She said she had to repent to Him for even asking and ask Him for forgiveness because she was being selfish. She said the whole family needed her and she would be abandoning all of us and her promise to Him to be our mom. To be honest, I kind of melted for her then, even though we still were not a full family.

But towards the end of her recovery when she was walking more comfortably, we got into an argument about something. She no longer needed my help to walk. She was stronger now. As I walked upstairs, she took her cane, reached up, and struck me on my legs. I scrambled up to my room.

Something very humiliating happened next! Karen was taking yet another trip. She would be gone for a whole week. But this time we would have to stay home. While we stayed home, she hired a baby-sitter.

The baby-sitter was Lacey Valin!

How could Karen do this to me? I was fourteen and Lacey was sixteen! What fourteen-year-old needed a baby-sitter? Especially since I already knew her and we had hung out as peers. Wow.

"You will like Lacey as a baby-sitter," Karen informed me. "She is a very stable teenager. I would like for you to be like her."

I did admire Lacey a lot. I also knew that she was a stable teenager because she had a good mother and father and a stable house setting! She was treated normal.

What made everything even worse was that Karen told Lacey we were not to come out of our rooms. She even went as far as preparing a whole weeks' worth of food ahead of time for us! She labeled them and placed them in the refrigerator shelves as breakfast, lunch, and dinner, and she labeled our names. She told Lacey that my job was to wash the dishes and sweep the dining and kitchen floors every evening.

So, every morning, Neal would leave for work, and Lacey would arrive at our house. Abram, Cisca, and Nano weren't around. The whole house was quiet all day as Lacey sat in the living room with the television turned low. To add insult to injury, Karen had instructed her that when it was time to eat, Lacey had to come to each of our rooms to knock on our doors to let us know it was okay to come out. We weren't allowed to open our door until we heard that knock. Each time I heard it, I cringed inside. Lacey would quickly walk back downstairs. Things were very awkward.

She followed Karen's instructions and placed our food at our designated spots. Then she went back to sit in the living room. We didn't talk to her, and she didn't talk to us. A thick uncomfortable cloud was in the air. After eating, the rest of The Four would go to their rooms first, and I would do my chores. It would only be Lacey and me on the ground floor. I hurried to do my sweeping and washing dishes. I was too humiliated to say anything to her. I know she felt it too. I wondered if she was thinking about what I told her about our household.

Then I would go back to my room and read. A short while later, Neal arrived home from work. I strained to hear. Neal grunted a quick hello. Lacey muttered a hurried greeting as well. Then she would be out the door mere seconds after his arrival. Neal would go to his room for the night, and then the same routine would repeat itself.

I knew I'd never be able to look Lacey in the face again.

A forty-three-year-old Katherine Kelly arose from a troubled sleep across the country nearly 3000 miles away.

"Dee," she called.

"What's up Mama?" A twenty-seven-year-old Deniece asked.

"They slaving my kids," Mama said angrily. "I keep seeing them in my dreams and my visions. They mistreating my kids!"

"I know they are Mama." Dee was used to Mama saying these things all the time. She had a few visions herself.

"I wish I had been strong and never got them took." Her eyes were very weary.

"I know Mama. The Lord loves you and He forgives you."

"But Sequoya...I can feel her so strongly. Dee...I feel her spirit. She's crying and begging for me..."

"That's because she's our fighter! She's gonna survive. She's the strong one that's gonna help carry Stan and them through. I know her. Watch."

"I wish we knew where in New York they are. I keep going to Benita's salon. She keep saying she don't know who adopted them."

"You know dang well that's a lie. She was the last foster mom they had before they got adopted. Kim is telling her to lie."

Mama dragged herself up and walked over to the nightstand and took a sip of her drink.

"I need to find my kids."

Dee looked at her with sadness. She knew if they could just figure out what town and the name of the adoptive family, then twenty-year-old Daniel would arrange the flights so they could visit. When the Twin Towers fell in 2001, they were all so sick with worry because they knew that the tragedy took place in New York.

Mama was becoming more urgent lately.

"Kim is so wrong with what she did! She gonna have to answer to God."

"Yes, she is," Dee agreed. She grew angry inside at the memory of running into Kim shortly after the adoption took place.

Kim had smiled smugly and said, "It's all done! It's been finished! They gone to New York!" Dee had cried as Kim enjoyed the scene of the young woman breaking down.

"Mama!" A young boy said. He crawled over to Dee.

Dee reached down and picked up her two-year-old son.

"Hey Tay man," she said softly.

She stared into Katherine's grandson's eyes. They gave her comfort. She had gone through a major depression while being pregnant. She had looked out her window as she rubbed her belly. She had seen a rainbow. In the rainbow, a quick vision had appeared. There were four faces.

Sequoya, Stanford, Raeannah, and Elijah.

Fall was underway and I was in the ninth grade. We remained the usual outcasts with our afros and Salvation Army clothes. Karen had bought me a pink sweater pants suit with purple polka dots on it. I wore it about twice a week. It was an all-time favorite joke amongst the other students each time they saw it.

Lately I was feeling more and more irritable. More so than recent years. My nerves felt like they were shot. I didn't know where it was coming from, because I had spent the last six months being submissive and bowing down to Karen. Just the mere sight or thought of her made me sick. Yes, we were getting along…but I was feeling this gravitational pull towards something…and I wasn't quite sure what it was.

Rosie the kitten was also becoming very annoying. Some mornings I awakened with scratch marks on my body. I had never asked for Rosie in the first place! But if I told Karen I didn't want her, she would say I was very ungrateful and her feelings would be hurt and then she would never ever do anything else for me. I still had four more years to go. Frustrated, I vented in my journal.

Then one day, Karen summoned me into the living room. Uh oh. It was that look again. It had been a while since I saw her true look of hate towards me.

"SaraJane," she regarded me.

"Yes, Mom."

"I have noticed that Liz Valin has been avoiding me."

Crap. Lacey told her mom!

"I have tried to call her a few times for the past few weeks. After I had Lacey baby-sit, I have not heard from them."

Maybe because your baby-sitting methods and the way you treat your kids is messed up, I thought. Any person who had been in our house and was given those instructions would be able to see this was not normal.

"When I finally got her on the phone, why does she tell me that you are a bad influence for her daughter?"

"Me?" I spat out, confused. "How am I a bad influence? Lacey is older than me. Remember you said she's more stable and mature than me?"

Karen held her palm up. "Liz also brought up the allegations you made against me," she said, eyes boring holes into me.

I was stunned.

"Liz says you are a bad influence and that she doesn't believe anything you have said."

"Then why are you mad?" I asked. If she doesn't believe me, then why was she avoiding you, I thought to myself.

"Because this is one of the reasons why I never trusted you. That's why you never went anywhere Sara!"

I didn't say anything. I had been stifled, and now persecuted, for telling the truth.

"You said I couldn't go anywhere because you didn't want me to get involved with boys."

"That too," she chuckled.

"Okay, what's my discipline then?" I didn't care anymore. My six months was up. I was done trying. No more humbleness from me. Hopefully she'd take Rosie away!

She rose from the recliner chair and began shouting at me.

"Sara! You have caused trouble for me! Lacey and her mother aren't even speaking to each other now because Lacey is defending what you're saying, and Liz is defending me! You have messed up two different households now!"

It felt so warm inside of my heart to know that Lacey was standing up for me!

"Liz was on the phone in tears over the thought that I could possibly hurt my children like that!"

Well you do, I thought. The only reason why she even talked to you today was because you finally got her on the phone and quickly manipulated her to believe your side.

"I thought you had made a whole turn around! I thought you were a good Sara! But no, the old Sara is *still* there! You have betrayed me!" Her eyes were becoming satanic.

"My name is Sequoya, you fat witch!" I exploded.

Those words promptly ended my six months of being her soldier.

"There it is!" She clapped her hands together. "I knew it was too good to be true!"

"Tell that to Abram! He calls you worse names."

"Sara, mind your business."

"I hate you! And your lazy dinners."

"Sara!"

I thundered up to my room as she screamed that I had gone behind her back.

After dinner and getting ready for bed, I tried to walk swiftly up the stairs but she called me into the living room again. Neal was also in there watching TV. He looked so very annoyed at this whole thing, but he was silent. Karen was swirling her cane in her hand.

"Sara, I just can't believe you," she was saying. "You know what, you tricked me."

"How did I trick you?" My face scrunched up.

"You have been fake to me this whole entire time. All of our walks, all of our talks, was all fake, and didn't mean anything to you."

That's when I really became angry. Sad too. I had just spent six months doing what Suzanne Walis had told me to do. For me, that was hard work! Everyone in the house had been amazed. For her to tell me that my hard work was nothing, made me seethe with rage. I had wasted my strength and valuable energy on an evil human being. I had begun to tell myself that even though things weren't good there, I would eventually turn eighteen. So, I made an effort to deal with it.

As Karen turned on me, I felt her hatred full force and worse than before, and somehow it felt more painful than all the other years. I was not in good standing with her no longer. Well, everyone knew that my good time with her had to end somehow. I tried to defend myself, but she didn't want to hear it.

"There's nothing you can say to me," she said very dramatically.

From that night on, I wrote more urgently and angrier about the whole family in my journal. I also wrote how sad I was about Karen not loving me either. One specific sentence I wrote was *Mom I know you hate me…you never even loved me.*

TWENTY-THREE

Karen was now back to getting me mad out of spite. She picked fights, and she enjoyed it. She also rushed to cover herself just in case I got help from the outside.

She took The Four to a group counseling session...inside Abide in The Vine Church! It had been a while since we were there. A set of offices had taken their wing in a section of the old school.

When we sat down with the counselor, Karen took over the entire group meeting! She was the boss. If the counselor asked a question, she jumped to speak for everybody. She could do that with my siblings, but not me.

"See!" Karen turned to the counselor, trying to get her to take her side.

"SaraJane, Mrs. Carlon, both of you, please! Everyone will get a chance to speak. Let's conduct this meeting with..."

"This is exactly how she behaves at home!" Karen spat out like a brat, folding her arms across her chest. She really looked like an obnoxious spoiled child. I wanted to hurl an object from the desk at her.

By now, everyone in both towns of Candor and Owego had noticed the spectacle of the Carlon family.

"Neal and I are very sorry we have adopted you guys!" Karen screamed one night as a family argument arose.

"Then let us go!" I screeched.

When we reminded her days later of what she said, she scrunched her face up like she had been attacked and said, "I never said that!" That was one of her favorite lines, saying she never said something when in fact she did.

Karen signed us up for counseling just to make it appear as if The Four were the problem children, when in fact we were the psychologically abused being held captive. She wanted to appear as if she was the perfect parent that was getting us "help." She wanted to turn it around on us. Where was Neal and Abram? Why weren't they at the group sessions? Hmm.

Karen purposely attended each session with us. None of us got to talk and we just went along like always. I gave up trying to speak after the first meeting. I sat quietly. I made sure to bulge my eyes out wide into space and ignore each time I was prompted to speak, to emphasize the fact that we didn't have a voice. I knew this really made Karen angry. Throughout the years while she lectured me, I always tuned her out.

"Every time I'm talking to you...you're not even here," Karen would say.

It was the truth, because I was mentally somewhere else since the very day we landed there in May 2000.

Katherine Kelly was in despair. But she was already forgiven by the Lord. In fact, on Sequoya's tenth birthday on March 26th 2000 when she had seen her children, she looked at each and every one of them more than they realized. She especially studied Sequoya, Stanford, and Raeannah. Elijah had not been there but she was still the more serene.

They attended church that morning. She had spoken in tongues and surrendered to the Lord. Then they spent that beautiful Sunday together at Dee's place. They informed everyone about the adoption...about Sequoya being unjustly punched in the face...

Daniel, Dee, and Keyonna were interrogating Sequoya about the whole ordeal of these people, because she was ten and she was already the voice.

Katherine listened. She was very hurt.

But she held a secret.

You see, she already knew what would happen.

She was their mother. She knew she hadn't been strong...but she knew who she was in the Lord. It had already been revealed to her what her children were going to go through. It hurt her soul to see what she saw.

But God had already given her a comfort that all of this must be done...and that Sequoya was going to be alright.

Katherine gazed at her children with such love, adoration, and shyness on her face. As her eyes met each of theirs throughout that day, they felt she was staring at them only because she missed them and was just happy to see them.

Yes, that was true. But she was also gazing at them so intently because she was amazed and in awe of these children...and they had no clue as to why.

Katherine was getting a full and thorough mental picture of them...and through her pain, she smiled with comfort.

We were leaving our counseling session. Karen had yet again dominated the entire meeting and it ended very tensely. On the way back to the house, Karen and I argued.

I felt like I was in a daze. I had this angry rage that was filling my veins, worse than I ever had felt before. I was normally angry a lot. But on this night, I was really tripping. I felt something wasn't right...but I didn't know for sure what it was. I took that unrecognizable feeling and used the fuel for my fury. I was so volatile and every little thing made my blood boil. My eyes even felt like they were buzzing with a shock feeling.

Back at the house, my shouting match with Karen resulted in me slamming my door repeatedly over and over and over until my ragged body collapsed on my bed and I buried my tear-streaked face into my pillow and cried for my freedom.

Katherine slumped to the ground as she gave up her struggle with the police. They were called due to her erratic behavior. When they came to question her, she tried to break free. She wasn't in her right mind and was very afraid.

A wrestling match ensued. Briefly, she was brought back to the day when a four-year-old Sequoya witnessed an officer dragging her to his police car after she successfully broke free from his grasp. She ran a few feet from him, even though her hands were already in cuffs behind her back.

She had called from the jail that night. An acquaintance of hers handed the phone to Sequoya.

"When are you coming back Mama?" Sequoya asked.

"I'll be back tomorrow baby!"

"Why did they grab you like that?"

"Because I'm Katherine." Her voice sounded strong and determined.

"Are you okay Mama?"

"Yes! And I'll see you tomorrow."

"You promise?"

"I promise baby."

True to her word, Katherine Kelly returned home the next morning and scooped Sequoya up in her arms.

But on this night in October 2004, Sequoya was not there to witness this.

The officer pulled out his taser and used it on an already erratic and scared woman. She fell to the ground. She's not arrested, but taken to a hospital where she spends the next week.

Sequoya's biological father is released from prison after ten years. He and Katherine reunite.

I was having a very troubled sleep. Any and every noise disturbed me. I felt I was fighting someone. But I was asleep. Maybe I had carried my earlier fight with Karen into a dream. I had slammed my door for a long time before falling asleep.

Then, I really was fighting! My arms and face were being scratched too and it hurt.

Next thing I knew, I bolted up, and Rosie jumped off me, digging into my skin and leaving more scratch marks. She ran and scurried to the curtains, shredding the already dissolved fabric.

I don't recall everything that happened. I just vented. I was half-asleep. I don't remember much. I blacked out.

A couple of hours later I was fully awake. But it still wasn't morning yet. I stared at Rosie's lifeless form on my floor.

Oh my God! Lord, please forgive me.

I was praying hard.

Am I going to go to Hell now?

I realized that she was dead. I had no idea I had done this, or was capable of doing this. My whole body turned hot and I was very frightened. Before thinking it through, I felt I knew what had to be done.

I walked down to Karen and Neal's door and knocked softly, feeling shock and disbelief. She opened the door and peered at me with a sleep deprived cranky face. She hadn't gotten much rest after the blowout either.

"What?" she snapped.

"I killed Rosie," I said, looking at her in fear.

"What?" her eyes flew wide open.

"I did it by accident. I don't even know what happened. I think I killed her."

Karen followed me up to my room. She peered over Rosie for a minute, then she glanced at me with an unreadable expression. Usually I could recognize all her different faces, but this time I couldn't.

She grabbed a black plastic bag from the kitchen. She put Rosie in it and stepped out the house for a few minutes. The whole time I was still in my room. I was staring at everything in my room…my bed, the bookshelf, my books, the ragged window curtain…the litter box…I felt very sick.

After an hour or so, in the early morning hours, I heard Karen summoning me to the living room. She spoke unusually soft, but her face had returned to its look of hate and contempt towards me. I was still in an unbelieving daze and I couldn't register what I had done either.

"I know you killed Rosie," she said, eyes drilling into me.

I was silent. Didn't I already tell her I did? I never denied it.

"You need to give an explanation."

"I don't know what happened…all I remember is looking down at her after. Before that…I felt scratches…"

"Oh, so because she scratched you?"

"No!" I shouted, tears forming.

"There is nothing you can say Sara," she said. "I gave you Rosie as a gift and look what happens."

"I didn't mean for it to happen."

"The damage has been done."

There was a few minutes of silence. I awkwardly ran my fingers down my arm where I had been scratched.

"Am I going to Hell?" I suddenly asked.

She looked surprised for a second.

After considering her words, she said, "Possibly. You have done many things that will send someone to Hell."

My heart started thudding in my chest. No!

At breakfast, she told everyone that Rosie had died. I did notice that she told them under different circumstances, for the moment. She told me I could stay home from school. After everyone left she asked me to wash the dishes. She seemed overly nice and phony. After I was done I headed to walk back upstairs.

She was standing right at the foot of the staircase, by the front door. She looked full of anticipation.

"Sara, put your shoes on," she said in a hurried tone.

Everyone's shoes were always left underneath the staircase. I put them on without hesitation. I was in submission and my nerves were out of sync, and at the same time, I was on edge. She did things spontaneously.

As I stood back up from putting my shoes on, I glanced out the window. In our dirt driveway was a police car.

"No!" I cried. "I don't want to go to jail!" I was legit scared. I knew I had done wrong. Karen had also called me a murderer. But a biological instinct was making me feel very scared.

"You're not going to jail," she said in an unemotional tone. "I'm just getting you some help."

I was still very terrified.

"If you want help Sara, you need to accept it. I have called around to a few people for advice on what I should do. They said you're too young to go to jail."

When she said this, I saw a fleeting look of anger on her face, like she was upset I wouldn't go to jail and she resented people telling her this.

"They told me that I need to have you do an evaluation at a hospital."

Unbeknownst to me, she also called both the elementary and the high school and told them what I had done and requested that a memo be written and sent to all the parents. She also phoned the police station more than once to ask that my incident be repeated on the police scanner. Candor was a small town and everyone was always listening to their scanner for all the mundane and simple news.

We stepped off the porch to greet the officer. Karen smiled at him and said, "I'm going to follow behind you."

"Okay, Mrs. Carlon," he nodded.

"She can really throw a temper tantrum," Karen volunteered.

"Well Ma'am, she seems calm right now. I don't need my cuffs."

"Well, just letting you know," she threw her hands in the air and twisted her mouth up as if to say *'How dare you not hand cuff her?'*

He opened the door and I slid in the backseat. Karen got in her car. She didn't look like a concerned parent. She looked full of anticipated vengeance.

The officer and I didn't speak at all as we drove into the town of Ithaca. He turned on the radio and I briefly chuckled inside because it was secular music. Was Karen aware of that?

We arrived at Cayuga Medical Center. Once checked in, I was taken into a small office for my evaluation. I broke down and admitted I wanted help. They told me they would help me. I had other plans as well.

Karen joined us in the office after my evaluation.

"I want SaraJane to have a CAT scan done on her brain," she said. She was holding papers and a pen and taking her own notes.

"Um..." the doctor bit her lip. "She's already had an evaluation."

"She needs a CAT scan as well."

Here we go. She was doing the same things she always did at our school, fighting and demanding things from the teachers.

"Mrs. Carlon, we will let you know if an order will need to be placed for such measures. But for now, we will access the evaluation."

"She killed her cat!"

"Yes, Mrs. Carlon, I understand…"

"Fine!" Karen held her palm up. She was angry. "She'll have one eventually."

I smiled inside. I loved how the doctor stood up to her.

"Mrs. Carlon, we don't know how long she will need to be here…but I recommend she go to the in-house patient program we have…"

"You don't know how long? You need her overnight?" Karen was looking incredulously at the doctor.

"Yes. We have a unit upstairs for teenagers who need evaluation. I don't know how long she will stay, as we can't predict. It all depends on the individual."

Karen's eyes flashed. In a silent language that was only between us, we both locked eyes, knowing that she was livid that I would be staying away from home! I felt so victorious in that moment. Did she really think she could control my destiny? She was the one who called them on me, so she better eat it!

Dear Mama,

Karen went home in anger and told everyone the real reason why I was in the inpatient program, like I already knew she'd do. The strange part is…I feel that if a mother truly cared about her child and wanted her to get help…she wouldn't have eagerly let her ride in the back of a police car while she followed behind to add to the fragile event. A true loving mother would've driven her daughter to the hospital herself.

I really needed time away from that house. This was the first time in years that I truly felt free. My unit was fun too! I was around other teenagers and we all had a unique story to tell. They accepted me for who I was. They had their moments of teasing me too, but we all teased each other. We felt insecure about our shortcomings in front of each other.

When the night of Halloween came, we joked that the staff should let us out of the locked unit to go trick or treating. Then one of the kids said, "SaraJane, if you killed your cat, you dang sure aint going trick or treating!" Everyone was laughing. But I didn't find that very funny at all. They had tears in their eyes from laughing so hard. I was very sensitive. Then a staff member said, "I don't know why y'all even talking about Halloween to begin with, because y'all staying on this unit until discharge." Then he gave me a kind smile.

Guess what Mama? I ordered any food that I wanted! They gave us different menus for breakfast, lunch, and dinner, and we ate on trays. The food was so good! Better than Karen's food, and better than the food at school. I could ask for a snack whenever I wanted. One time, I asked for a granola bar once an hour and the staff kept giving them to me!

A cleaning person handled our trays and menus and cleaned our rooms every morning. There was cable in the recreation room. I got to watch real cable TV like Abram, Cisca, and Nano!

I had one visit the whole three weeks while I was there. Karen came with Rae. When they arrived during visiting time I sat in the rec room and proudly used the remote and turned to a television program. The way Karen walked in...alerted me to the fact that she had prepped Rae for a "monstrosity" viewing of me and my unit. But once they stepped in, even Karen looked surprised at the high quality unit and how calm and normal all of us were. Then her eyes darkened as she saw me holding a **remote** in my hand and the fact that I was watching TV! The look on her face was priceless.

They sat down on the opposite couch and Karen was trying to speak for Rae, saying that my sister was very scared of me. But my eyes met with my sister's. She quickly rolled her eyes when Karen didn't see her. My sister genuinely smiled at me and was happy to see me away and stress free! I had made a breakthrough in the house...it was huge news for The Four.

Karen put on her false front of saying I needed to get well again, while at the same time insulting me and acting snobbish towards everyone else around us. She was not in control of this situation. So, it made her uncomfortable. Every time she saw an African-American staff member, she became even more uncomfortable.

I proudly rattled on and on about how I got my bed changed every day and how I got to have a physical done, blood drawn, and urine taken. She looked upset and asked me why they needed a urine sample. I told her that they wanted to check for a urinary tract infection. She looked even more mad. Well, how could she be mad if she never took us to the doctor and took care of us properly? It all fell on her. Yet she didn't mind arguing with a doctor over CAT scans?

A psychiatrist requested the whole family to attend a meeting with the head director of the program right before my stay at Cayuga Medical Center was up. We met in his office.

Karen, Neal, and The Four were there.

"Abram is sick and I didn't want to push him to come if he isn't feeling well," Karen said to the doctor.

Yeah, right! I saw right through her lie. She should have just admitted that Abram and I didn't get along so we didn't care about seeing or interacting with each other. In fact, he was already skipping class. Karen and Neal turned a blind eye to that.

The doctor instructed everyone to write their names down on a sheet of paper and to also write their relation to me. I felt that was very stupid, because The Four were obviously the siblings and Karen and Neal were the parents.

After reading my progress notes from my chart, he looked around the room again.

"Okay, I'm going to ask each of you if you feel comfortable to have your sister back home. Everyone is to be honest."

He went around the room. Everyone said yes with clear diction. The Four tried not to smile as they said it.

"SaraJane, your family now feels comfortable to have you back home," he said triumphantly. "Are you ready to go home?"

I looked him right in the eye and said, "No."

Everyone in the room was taken aback.

"Why is that, SaraJane?" he asked, recovering himself.

"I get treated better here than I do at home."

Neal glanced at Karen. She tried to hide her anger. She cleared her throat and played it off well in front of the doctor.

"Well, I don't want to be the bearer of bad news, but you cannot live here. I'm sure you have struck up a lot of friendships and all...but you have completed your treatment plan and I believe you're going to be fine."

I gave him a sad face. I knew my time was up, but it didn't hurt to rub it in a little bit. Who knew when the next time I would be free again? I knew I'd be on lockdown after this.

Surprisingly, when I returned to the house, Karen was unusually nice to me and she said she was there for me as I got well again.

"Your mind needs to be healthy...and I'm also looking into some medication that may help you," she said.

I also noticed that she wasn't yelling at me for taking more than five minutes to get ready for school in the bathroom.

At school, there was a weird cloud in the air. I saw it. I felt it. My classmates were talking to me...but they seemed more reserved. Like they knew something major about me. I had been absent for three weeks. They would stop their conversations when I was near them. I already knew that Karen had told people. I just didn't know to what extent. Ironically, her slave master abuse and concentration camp she ran in the house was supposed to be secret and we were in the wrong for speaking out, but in her eyes, there was nothing wrong in her alerting the whole town each time The Four had done something.

I was really peeved one afternoon during chorus practice when a kid I never interacted with walked up to me.

"Hey," he said, with beady and amused eyes. "I heard you killed your cat."

I didn't say anything to him as he awaited my response. He stood there looking stupid. He finally got the hint and sluggishly walked away.

After dinner one evening, Karen told The Four to have a seat in the living room. Huh? We stepped into the living room and sat on the couch. I was surprised when Neal and Abram entered and took the opposite couch. Karen hovered around with an unreadable expression. She looked like she was anticipating something.

The doorbell rang. She opened the door and hugged a big man with a huge round belly as he stepped in looking very serious.

I instantly recognized him as Pastor Hall from our old church Abide in the Vine! We hadn't seen him in a while. But what was he doing here?

He greeted us and we said hello back.

Suddenly, Karen went from a normal expression, to launching into a crying fit, covering her face. She shook her body with her crying. It all looked absurd! We were so confused.

"You guys," she wailed. "I have brought Pastor Hall here for your support!"

What support? Were we having another counseling session?

"There is something very important I have to tell you guys. I have been withholding this information for a few weeks…because I didn't know how to tell you…"

What was she talking about?

She looked to Pastor Hall, who waited patiently.

Very dramatically, with a Broadway musical flair, she said, "I'm sorry you guys, but your birth mother has passed away."

As those words escaped from her mouth, I glanced up at her. She began her dramatic cry again. I didn't understand what she was saying…but in that split-second I subconsciously knew. As I broke down sobbing, she flew to my side, pushing Rae out the way who was seated next to me. Before her arms encamped around my face and neck, obscuring my vision, I caught a glimpse of Abram with his head down. He was smirking.

"Don't beat yourself up about it Dee," Mr. Slank said. *"Let God handle it. He got this in the bag."*

Dee was so sad about her Mama. She looked up at Daniel and Keyonna's father.

"Your mother told me what would be fulfilled. She knew. She told me I was going to be in the church someday and I didn't believe her."

"Look at you now Dad!" Keyonna exclaimed.

355

"Yes. I love that woman Katherine!"

Daniel was quiet. He was more reflective inwardly. He was thinking deep about the last conversation he had with Katherine. Shortly before her incident, she had grabbed Daniel to herself and they went for a walk. They found a spot on a curb underneath a street light. For over six hours he and Katherine sat on that curb and talked about everything. He was listening most of the time that she talked. In a very strange way, he knew that was her way of saying goodbye to him.

They all recalled Katherine's words weeks before she passed.

"Dee, I need to get my hair and my nails done! I'm about to go. I can't be looking raggedy in my casket."

"Mama, stop!" Dee had screamed in frustration. "Stop saying you gonna die. You not gonna die!" She was so mad she wanted to slap her.

"Dee, it's going to be okay. Take me to get my hair and nails done please."

Dee managed to take Katherine to get herself spruced up, not really believing anything she had to say.

Katherine had already stopped by Benita Burke's salon on Jackson Avenue one last time, to plead with the foster mother to tell her where her children were. Benita claimed she didn't know the names of the adoptive parents, or what town in New York they lived.

Katherine went home and prayed and gave the rest to the Lord, who had already started giving her visions before her children were adopted. She was at peace now.

But Dee was in distress. She had purposely delayed the funeral. She got ahold of Kim Folson, their former caseworker. She asked Kim to notify the adoptive family. So that Sequoya, Stanford, Raeannah, and Elijah could attend their mother's funeral and say goodbye to her.

Kim said she sent an email, but that she had no say if the parents flew them out or not. When Dee called back a few days later, Kim said she hadn't heard anything back.

Then the funeral home pressured Dee to finally move forward with the funeral.

I cried so hard. I was in such disbelief. I was in a mental shock, too shocked at the time to register that the Carlons had not told us.

They had purposely waited, and the funeral already took place. I had been expecting to hear more. I needed more answers regarding my birth family. Karen had quickly wanted to move on and focus on her selfish plan to keep us captive to her. She even went as far as saying that she hoped our mother repented to the Lord! Her eyes were so cold looking as she said this.

Then after a few days had passed, Karen's words suddenly blinked on like a light bulb in my head.

"I have been withholding this information from you for a few weeks..." she had said.

Wait a minute...didn't she tell us that she never heard from Kim or spoke to her anymore? But she knew when my Mama died? She had known for weeks.

Speaking of weeks...I hadn't even been back in the house for two weeks...and before that I spent three weeks in the hospital...and when I get back, she has the nerve to bring Pastor Hall over? On top of that, Abram and Neal sat in the living room to be a "support" too?

This family was divided and always had been! Neal and Abram didn't care about my birth family and our feelings! They wore different clothes, ate different food, and walked around like they were better! We rarely saw them. Neal was a non-existent coward of a father! He didn't protect us like a real man was supposed to do. He didn't set us free.

So actually, they sat in the living room as part of Karen's big dramatic game show to reveal something to us that was very heartbreaking and painful. Something that she couldn't wait to happen.

She was evil enough to withhold the news and put on a show of fake tears and magically be happy the very next day!

This lady had let her son punch me in the face on the first meeting, then kidnapped us, changed our identities, got angry at us for remembering who we were, locked us in our rooms to confinement, denied us our natural human rights to good hygiene and health, robbed us of our youth and happiness, starved us, psychologically tormented us with mind games and divide and conquer techniques, shattered our dreams, humiliated us with her calculated tampering of our appearance, stole our artwork and lied about it, exaggerated our behavior to the town to get people on her side, but *still* wouldn't let us go due to selfish gain and her not wanting to see us happy again…

She could do all of that to us…

But not allow us to at least say goodbye to our biological mother whom she had been spying on the whole entire time?! That's the last straw. I could never forgive her for that.

Karen was the evilest human being I had ever encountered on the earth. I wondered what else could she possibly do? Was she done with her antics yet? She was getting older…at some point does it stop?

I had no clue that it was only just getting started.

TWENTY-FOUR

Dear Mama,

I always told myself that I was going to see you again. There was just no question about it. How could it not be so? Even though we were shipped out to a shack in 2000, I always felt you were going to wait for us like we were waiting for you. That was my sole purpose for surviving at the Carlons.

I just could not believe it. I was so numb.

I hated Karen. Our fights escalated even worse. I started writing **Sequoya** *on my school papers, instead of SaraJane. Rae came home with papers writing* **Raeannah,** *instead of Abigail. Karen flipped out! She said she knew the day would come when Rae would be a clone of Bad Sara.*

First of all, my baby sister has always had her own mind and if anybody doesn't know that they better recognize. She was just now emerging a little bit here and there, because she was sick of it all. The fact that she was seven-years-old when adopted and had the name change and **still** *remembered how to spell her birth name...shows that she refused to be dumbed down by all the special classes that Karen was trying to force her in. Who holds their daughter back in the first grade just because she was in the same grade as Abram?*

Karen was becoming frantic. She began spending more time in Rae's room again. She and I battled until her face was practically turning blue. Her eyes really looked like a madwoman now. She kept saying she didn't know what my problem was.

What my problem was?! I was being held captive and my Mama was gone! When I reminded her of this, she looked at me so angrily. She must have been under the impression that after you died, my love for you would automatically be transferred to her. Karen always wanted me to love her as she was my mother. But she went about it the wrong way, and her true nature was revealed. In an argument, I said, "I can't call you my mother. Can't even look at you each day and call you my mother when I can never see mine again!"

In that moment, she finally knew that she could not win with me. But she still tried though. She was so determined.

I abruptly walked out the front door during our next argument. I didn't even use the side door of the house that The Four were instructed to use. I walked right out the privileged ones front door!

Surprisingly, Karen didn't scream at me to come back. I was expecting her too. I walked out the dirt driveway and made a left on Mountain Ave. I drew in a breath of the mid November night. It was cold but there wasn't any snow on the ground. I was angry and filled with so much adrenaline that the cold didn't bother me. My "grandma style" sweater and light thrift store jacket was fair enough.

I walked down the hill. Once I got to Owego Street, I contemplated on where I'd go. If I made a left, that would lead to Main Street. But if I ignored Main Street and kept going straight, I would eventually be on the long trek to Owego. If I turned right from where I stood, that would lead to a more country side area that I wasn't prepared to explore.

I turned right anyway. I didn't run. I didn't walk fast either. I didn't know what I was doing or where I was going. I didn't care. I didn't care if Karen appeared, or if the police even showed up. I felt good! Why hadn't I just done this all along? Why hadn't Karen allowed us to go on walks when angry? Why did she keep us captive in our rooms on a daily basis? It's not like we were going anywhere in this vast country with no major highways! I had now discovered how much better the outside air and my body getting exercise truly felt.

I was brought back to the memory one summer when we all stood in the front yard with Karen. An angry Raeannah had slowly started walking down the road. Karen got into the old station wagon, which was very unnecessary, drove a few yards to where

Rae was, and dragged her in the car. Then she parked the car, got out and walked around to the other side to open the door. She grabbed Rae's tiny arm and *yanked* her little body as hard as she could, and dragged her through the dirt driveway and up the front steps and through the front door. I followed behind and watched her drag my sister up the wooden stairs into the girls' room. Whatever she did to my sister made her screams echo throughout the house and out to the yards. *All* because Karen was enraged that my sister had the strength and courage to run. After that incident, we had all been scared to run away.

But we were getting older now. The small town was really buzzing about the dysfunctional Carlon family with the four adopted and imprisoned black children, a comatose father, an already juvenile delinquent white son, and a psychotic mother who was sixteen years older than the father. Surely everyone could see something was terribly wrong, and it wasn't the four black children.

I wasn't scared of this lady anymore. I would continue to stick up for myself and never stifle myself for her ever again! I had to forgive myself for even bowing down for those six months. Ugh.

I stopped at a cemetery and randomly walked around to read some of the names of the people. After that got boring, I headed back in the other direction towards Mountain Ave, but kept going straight. I made a right on Main Street and passed the Edge of Tyme Bed and Breakfast. I stopped just after the small Laundromat and made a left. I saw some parked school buses in a lot.

One of them was an old bus that I could tell wasn't in use. Its door was permanently open! I stepped inside and wiped the dust filled seat with my jacket.

Then I just sat there. Not really thinking of much. Not even angry anymore. At least for this moment. I knew by now Karen was going crazy.

I left the school bus and continued down Main Street, walking across the little two-minute bridge, passing the post office, and then turning right to Candor Junior-Senior High School. I walked in the school and headed in the direction where all the noise was coming from.

Once I arrived at the entrance to the gym, I saw that basketball and cheerleading practice was underway. Students were on the bleachers watching and laughing and talking and enjoying their lives. Suddenly, I felt very inadequate and unworthy, like I had always felt. But now it was magnified. Karen had deprived me of a normal childhood.

I was only watching for a couple of minutes when I felt a soft tap on my shoulder. I turned to see a custodian, who was a short stout woman with a buzz cut. She roamed the halls during the day.

"Hi SaraJane," she said, somewhat cautiously.

"Hi," I said.

"What are you doing?"

"Just watching. Decided to go for a walk." Suddenly I felt like a peasant intruding on a high profile VIP event.

"That's nice."

She was looking at me very strangely. She clamped her hands together.

"SaraJane, is everything alright? I have been informed that your mother has reported you as a runaway. She knows you're here."

I rolled my eyes and angrily drew in my breath.

"Well, I hope everything works out. She's on her way. The police are already here...but don't worry sweetie you're not in trouble."

"Did you guys call them?"

"We did not. Why would we?"

"I don't know," I answered, even more annoyed now. My attitude was back full force. My peaceful walk was now ruined.

She led me out to the parking lot where I saw the officer. A second later, Karen's car came bounding into the lot like she was there to collect a missing treasure.

I rode back to the house in the back of the police car. Karen spoke to him outside for a few minutes as I proudly walked upstairs. Rae and Elijah sneaked into the den to stare at me in such awe. Stan's room was in the basement so he couldn't sneak up two different flights of stairs to see me.

Rae and Elijah quickly ran back to their rooms on their tip toes when they heard the front door opening again.

Sitting in my room, something suddenly came into mind. It reminded me of a patient I had met at Cayuga Medical Center. I wasn't proud of this thought, but it was a great idea to get what I truly wanted.

Unafraid, I opened my room door and bolted back downstairs.

"Go to you room!" Karen screeched.

Instead of going to my room, I went into a rage and began screaming at the top of my lungs calling her every name in the book. My demeanor was very violent and rebellious. I contorted my face with fury.

With no hesitation, Karen called the police again. I screamed that I wanted to leave. I was acting crazy and saying crazy things just to say them.

The same officer came back. He looked annoyed.

"I want to jump over the bridge!" I screamed.

"What did you say?" he asked, eyebrows raising.

"I want to jump over the bridge."

"Why do you want to jump over the bridge?"

"I'm going now," I said, and he blocked me.

"Just hang on a minute…I have to report this now."

"She's just saying that," Karen said bitterly. She looked so pissed!

"I understand Mrs. Carlon, but there are two main things that has to be reported…whenever someone is threatening or planning to harm themselves, or whenever someone is threatening or planning to harm another person."

Defeated, Karen rolled her eyes and sulked. "Okay, so what happens next?" she asked with a taut jawline and arms crossed.

"She needs to get evaluated."

Karen's face aged in those very few seconds after he told her this. The last time I was evaluated had taken a while. I hadn't even been back home that long, and it was now time to do it all over again.

We didn't speak as we both retrieved our coats. The officer stood by the door waiting. I got into the backseat of the police car again and we drove back to Cayuga Medical Center for my intake.

But after my intake and sitting in the waiting room for a very long time, the director came out and told Karen that the unit upstairs was full.

"But she will get placed somewhere," he said. "We've called around to other hospitals. Just hang tight."

I wondered where I was going. It was late too. I looked over at Karen. She was very irritated and stressed. Her face was even paler. She refused to look in my direction. We both knew what I was doing.

If this was going to help me get out of the Carlon house, I had to do what I had to do.

I was nearly asleep in my chair when a staff informed Karen that a car was already waiting to take me to my location. Then I heard her shriek.

"Four hours away? They couldn't find some place closer?"

"No, Mrs. Carlon."

"I can't drive four hours away at this time of night!"

"We have that taken care of, Mrs. Carlon."

Now it was my turn to see her in such a daze! She was torn and conflicted. She wanted me as her prisoner in her house. She couldn't stand that I was going to be away yet again, and this time even farther away. She hated my guts on a daily basis. Wanting someone near you but hating them at the same time had to be a crazy feeling to experience every day.

As I relaxed into the backseat of a regular car, I felt so victorious! Karen got in her car and pulled out the parking lot. I wished I could hear the conversation she was having to herself as she drove home.

I fell into a tiring sleep and didn't wake up until four hours later.

Dear Mama,

This placement was called Stony Lodge in Ossining, New York. This was a gorgeous area in Westchester County! Except the residents were confined only to the property, which included three buildings and spacious courtyards. The resident age range was toddlers to eighteen. I was wondering what happened to the toddlers and why they were there. Then I remembered being at Child Haven when I was four-years-old...and I sadly understood.

This was the first time I was around a lot of black people again! There were blacks, whites, and Hispanics. Most of the kids were from New York City and the surrounding areas. I really had to get familiar with being around my own race again. I was kind of awkward. At first, they laughed at me. But then they thought it was so unique and different how I was adopted and had my name changed. The staff on my unit said that was the very reason why I was acting up and had to be there. She said what had been done to me was cruel. She said one day I would have a story to tell.

There was this one girl from the Bronx named Lucilla who was a couple of years older than me. She always gave me advice so seriously and with a deep accent. Sometimes I laughed at how serious she was sounding and she would say, "No, this is not a game this is real life!" She had me take a notebook to each of our "sessions." She coaxed me about life and told me to write down my goals. She had already been through so much for only being sixteen and her eyes said it all. She looked sad a lot. But I know she felt good about herself because she was helping someone else. That's when she was smiling the most.

Whenever our unit had recreation outside or in the rec room, I caught myself flirting with the boys just like the other girls were. For years I had been in the farm town of Candor. The boys from the city seemed way more diverse and interesting. I still did not feel pretty at all, even though the girls had braided my hair.

The residents who were on good behavior were recruited to the other building that housed the toddlers. We volunteered for their daily group activities and were called "mentors." I was a mentor for five-year-old Precious, who eerily reminded me of myself when I was a toddler at the VOA girls' house. When she first told me that her name was Precious, I hadn't believed her. But staff said she was telling the truth. Precious loved me right away and I always helped her do her artwork and reading. Staff said they had no idea what was going with her family. Someone had randomly dropped her off and left without giving clear indication of when they'd be back. But one day, I went to the building to find that Precious had finally been discharged. I was kind of sad. I hoped wherever she went, she wasn't neglected anymore. I hoped she didn't have to experience growing up how I did, in different foster homes and child placements.

At Stony Lodge, I ate like crazy! I don't know how much weight I gained. It wasn't that much but it was enough. I hadn't been eating fully at the Carlons so any weight gained was noticeable. I learned a new meal after someone showed it to me. We loaded as much peanut butter on two slices of bread as we could. Then we took a banana and sliced it and put it on the bread and made a sandwich! It was very good, and during each mealtime we could make as many as we wanted.

Being at Stony Lodge wasn't all roses either. These kids could be ruthless! They had obviously grown up in a completely different environment. They faced challenges every single day of their lives. Daily fights resulted in staff having to pull kids off each other. I got into my first fist fight with a peer. I got whooped.

But after that, it made me much stronger. It added to my resilience and I understood what makes everyone in life be the way they are and do the things they do. I was no different from them emotionally, and I knew if I had stayed in Las Vegas and never left I would have been hip to everything much earlier.

There was a "level system" here. One, two, and three. Level one was the highest and three was the lowest. Every time you were misbehaved you lost a certain number of points and you were moved down on the level chart. Residents who were on the highest level could stay up later and have more recreation time. There was a lot of provoking going on to get people on the lowest level with them. Misery loves company. After my first couple of weeks, I learned to ignore them. I wanted to advance up. I stayed at level one for the longest despite the taunting. There was this one girl who was like 300 pounds. She was one of the main instigators. She tried to get me to crack for the longest. I wouldn't budge. I went to bed one night. I felt something very hard underneath my pillow. Confused, I sat up. Something smelled really bad too. When I raised my pillow, I nearly threw up. She had wrapped a huge, rock hard turd in a paper towel and placed it underneath my pillow! I screamed and ran out to staff and started using swear words and calling the culprit obscenities. I was moved down to level two for doing so. The culprit remained on level three where she always stayed.

Unbeknownst to me, Karen was calling nearly every day to spy on my activities. But she never called me personally. Other residents were using the phone but there was no one for me to call. When Karen heard about the poop incident, she told The Four about it with a smile of victory on her face. They noticed that she was so happy about this. They weren't entertained. They remembered their chores included picking up her dog poop and the infamous incident where she made Stan pick it up with his bare hands.

I was at Stony Lodge for a little over two months. When it was time to go, I begrudgingly said goodbye to everyone and got into Karen's car. She brought a friend along on the four-hour drive. This would be the start of something that she would do, claiming that she feared for her life. But if she feared for her life, why did she still want to be our adoptive mother? Her friends didn't live with us…so what was her point? She would eventually do this with the rest of The Four as well.

Karen didn't say hello to me when she picked me up. She didn't ask me how I had been or if I was okay. I didn't speak to her either. She and her acquaintance conversed with each other but I remained quiet in the back seat, looking out the window and thinking of my next escape.

PART THREE

Ask, and it shall be given you; seek, and ye shall find;
knock, and it shall be opened unto you:
For every one that asketh receiveth;
and he that seeketh findeth;
and to him that knocketh it shall be opened.

Matthew 7 verses 7-8

TWENTY-FIVE

The rest of The Four were happy to see me! They were laughing and saying I had gotten fat. I had stuffed my face every day. My breasts were even larger than before. Someone also gave me a bra, and I wore it proudly. I was almost fifteen-years-old and I finally had my first bra after being deprived of one! When Karen saw it, she looked surprised but ignored it as I purposely played with the strap so she could see. She didn't say anything. I won that battle, even though she would never buy me a bra herself.

It was February of 2005. Karen and I were barely civil around each other. I was still so very rebellious. During arguments, I felt powerful and full of strength. Karen and Neal claimed that I picked up behavior from the kids in the city and said that I would be a convict. They said this after witnessing my newfound confidence and demeanor. I stared them straight in the eyes and basically laughed in their faces and rolled my eyes wider and shrugged my shoulders and did sassy head jerks.

I got into an argument with Abram while using this new demeanor.

"No!" Karen screamed at me, putting her face in my face with her eyes flaring. "This...this is fighting words!"

She looked so angry. She looked like she wanted to kill me but was mad because she couldn't.

Abram had called me a derogatory name, and all I did was shrug my shoulders and say, "Okay? Do I look like I care? I don't care about none of the stuff you saying."

That was a line no one had ever said before. It was very hip and city sounding and too hot for the Carlons to handle. When I said it, even Abram's eyes shot up in surprise, and he suddenly looked like a real coward. The Carlons were such country cowardly people who I knew wouldn't be able to survive anywhere else in the world with the things they did.

I was verbally disciplined. Abram was not reprimanded for calling me a name. As usual.

Unlike my previous years at the Carlons when I had felt trapped and powerless, this time I knew I did have other options. I just wasn't sure how they would fall through. Counselors were telling Karen that maybe I just needed to go for good. She was angry when they told her this.

"I made a promise to God, and to Family Services of Nevada to take care of you guys!" she kept saying.

She believed her own phony lies. That's just how good she was at lying and being evil. She had actually made a promise to herself to collect money for us and keep us held captive and treated different from the Privileged Five.

I was really Bad Sara now, throwing temper tantrums every day. I prayed to be free someday, but I wasn't aware of how soon it would be. By May, Karen was walking around the house saying that The Four had ruined the Carlon family name.

She had her nerve! She was so mad that people were talking about us and they saw her cruelty. When we brought up what she said in an argument, of course she dramatically scrunched her face up and screeched, "I never said that!"

I was still writing in my journal. It had quite a few entries in it by now. It was my best friend. I told everything, all my feelings, all the events that had occurred, and I documented all the arguments.

I was also attending anger management classes in the counseling wing at Abide in the Vine Church. I was in a group with four other teens. The instructor wasn't a very good one. He only said a few words nervously and then the rest of the meeting was spent with the teenagers taking over and finding something to talk about. How come every person who worked in this field, such as caseworkers, guidance counselors, anger management instructors…how come they weren't qualified for the job and truly didn't care about the children? Who was hiring these people for Tioga County Social Services? What did they do all day?

One day before school, I had a big fight with Karen. I was about to walk out the side door when Karen came out her room and said something that provoked me. We got into it real heavy.

We went back and forth and I screamed so very loud and crazy on purpose. I looked towards the ceiling and screamed obnoxious noises to let her know I didn't care about anything she was saying. Stan walked out the door after walking up from the basement. I had missed my walk out time.

So, Karen decided to copy me. She screamed at the top of her lungs too with her satanic eyes looking so evil. But when she did, I challenged her even more, overpowering her effort. Rae, in her pajamas still, had walked downstairs to start getting ready for school. She stood in the dining room entrance looking at Karen and me as we screamed like two-five-year-olds.

Rae was proud of me. I was at my greatest in this moment, more than ever before. Karen was struggling to get her scream out…but it was futile because I was in power. I was now fifteen and long gone were the days where Karen's scream could make me go mute.

"Blah blah blah blah la la la la fa fa ma la la aba caca la la la la laaaaa!"

I stopped screaming only seconds after Karen ran out of breath and stopped. I ended with an extra flair and sassy head jerk. Then I turned and stormed out the side door to walk to school.

Once I was out the door, Rae looked at Karen. She stared at the back of me with such evilness that it was scary. Then, she stood there just staring at the door I had just left out of, as if she couldn't move. She had so much anger and frustration on her face. After a minute, she quietly walked to her room, with such a strange look on her face, not even acknowledging Rae's presence.

A few hours later I was surprised when I was called into the office. As I walked through the hallway, I passed Stan with his friends as they were walking to their class. We both smiled hard and waved to each other, and he gave me a message with his eyes as if to say *'Good job you really showed out this morning!'*

If only I had known at the time to really savor that moment in the hallway.

Once inside the principal's office, I saw Karen! I was slightly thrown off guard. I quickly prepared myself to battle what she had in store next.

"Hi SaraJane," Mr. Hunt regarded me. He looked very annoyed with both of us.

"Hi," I answered. I took a seat.

Karen was looking full of anticipation about something.

"SaraJane, your mother is here to inform me about some concerns she has about what's going on at home."

"I have some concerns too," I said proudly.

"Okay. Well your mother is very upset…because she says that you are sexually abusing your siblings." Then he uneasily looked towards Karen, who had her lips formed in a thin evil grip.

I looked at them both…not understanding what was going on. Sexually abused?

Before I could even register this allegation and speak, Karen began speaking rapidly and straining her face.

"Abigail and Elijah have told me some things this morning!" she said, trying to bring fake tears that were very unsuccessful. "And I'm going to talk to Isaiah today. I can't imagine how long this has been going on."

"You're lying!" I screamed. "When did they say this?"

"This morning! How could you do this Sara?"

"I just saw Isaiah just now!" I realized. "I just saw him…I'm going to…" I stood up, and Karen nearly flipped shit.

"No!" Karen jumped up, almost sending her chair flying due to her sudden jump. "You will not go near him or harm him!"

Then she looked to Mr. Hunt with urgency. Why was she so scared of me talking to my brother before she could get to him first?

"SaraJane, just hold still," he said impatiently. I saw him glance at Karen with flashing eyes.

She was an adult with fake frantic tears who was constantly in the schools with her nonsense and making the whole faculty upset. She was always asking the custodians to open our lockers for her so she could see if we "stole" anything that our friends had actually given us.

This was her latest encore, and despite what she was in the school for this time, Mr. Hunt was truly fed up. He looked so detached from the both of us and from the mention of the Carlon family. I always felt that if I had met him under different circumstances and hadn't been adopted, I would have been able to crack through his persona that the other students enjoyed. I witnessed him come out his shell when he was around civilized people. Karen had ruined that for all of us.

"She has an appointment right now," Karen said. "We're actually late and need to leave now."

"I want to talk to Isaiah," I repeated, shaking my head. I was feeling very sick. Whereas earlier I felt powerful, I was now confused and distraught.

"We have to go," she shook her head.

"How did I abuse them?" I suddenly asked. I wanted to know.

"We have to go," she said quickly. "Mr. Hunt, thank you."

He barely gave a nod. He didn't say anything else.

Karen and I walked out the school. I saw her anxiously glancing through the halls. I think she was anxious that we'd run into Stan. I told myself that I would confront everyone that night.

I was in such a daze and had no idea what had hit me, or what Karen was up to. All I knew was that I finally overpowered her that morning and *she* was the one who had to bow down. Then suddenly a few hours later, I was being accused of molesting my own siblings? How? We were confined to our rooms, and she listened to everything that happened in the house. She didn't miss a damn thing. That was the control freak nature in her. Stan's room was in the basement. How could I get to him? What about Abram, Cisca, and Nano? How come she only mentioned The Four? Why was she focusing on my siblings?

I was still very naïve and had a lot to learn about life and how evil adults operated when they didn't get their way. You see, people can be very simple and basic. Some of them who are truly evil...are very unoriginal with ideas...and the first thing they see...they copy. And at that *very* moment as she was accusing me in June of 2005...the television news and broadcast stations were all in a frenzy because the most famous celebrity in the world was currently on trial for being accused of sexual molestation.

TWENTY-SIX

We argued all the way to Owego. I asked her for more details about what my siblings had supposedly said, and she couldn't give them to me. I started screaming at her about everything, all the stuff she had ever done to me, everything I had gone through. I wanted to get out the car. I did not want to ride with her. I did not want to be in her presence.

I called her a fat white horse again.

"You're just jealous of me because I've been losing weight," she said, believing her own illusion.

I laughed out loud. Jealous? Of her?

"Please witch, I am thin! My boobs just got bigger. You actually need to lose more weight, and you are still as fat as you have ever been!"

She scowled and then we got into a blowout over our weight. I couldn't believe what I was hearing with my ears! A fifty-year-old lady was arguing with a fifteen-year-old over who was fatter!

"You're bigger than me!" she exclaimed. "I've been walking while you were a greedy glutton at Stony Lodge!"

She believed herself when she said this. That was just so hilarious to me, and it's true that I have never been as big as her, even when she was her smallest! She had severe issues that I was too young to even comprehend. I didn't know that a mother could see her daughter as competition.

We argued all the way to the counseling center at Abide in The Vine. Ironically, I never even made it into the counselor's office.

Karen and I fought in the waiting room. We were loud and disturbing people. I couldn't take looking into that devil's face anymore. Suddenly, I dashed out the waiting room.

Karen kept calling, "Sara, come back here!"

I ignored her and ran through all the hallways until I got to the kitchen near the front. I opened the door and walked in, not sure what I was doing. The door slid closed behind me.

I surveyed the area, realizing how far along this building had come. It was only a church when we attended. Now a counseling center and daycare service had been added.

I hid inside of a closet pantry. I sat there as my adrenaline was racing. I was there for quite a while. I knew I was really late for my appointment by now. I had decided that I was going to run away for good this time. I just had to get out the front doors of the building. I would have to wait until it was dark because I would easily be seen. This building was located on a hill and the long driveway that led up to the hill was pavement.

I heard Karen and a few staff from the center walking by periodically but I didn't move. They had even come inside the kitchen once! They didn't check the pantry. A little bit later, I heard them talking to a police officer at the front doors. They said they believed I had run away.

The officer wasn't convinced.

"I haven't seen anyone walking down the hill...or along the highway," he explained.

I know he figured that out because right after you get to the bottom of the hill, it immediately turns into Taylor Road. It was unsafe for pedestrians.

"Check the building again," he instructed them. "I'll help you."

My heart started pounding as they walked off. When they got back to the kitchen, I knew this was their last stop.

I opened the pantry door and just walked out to them. They all looked very surprised. They had never thought to look in the pantry!

I only came out because I realized that I'd instantly be caught walking down the hill anyway, plus I had not really thought of my plans after I ran away. What would I do? Where would I go? How would I eat? I had no money.

"You know what Sara?" Karen said. "You have wasted a whole appointment over this!"

I tried to defend myself. But the officer and staff were on her side.

So right there, I threw another fit! I started saying crazy things again, and that I wanted to return to the hospital in Ossining.

Karen was so angry. She knew it was the whole process all over again. Her face flushed in fury. She was looking like *'I'm going to get you, just you wait!'*

The officer had no choice but to report my crazy sayings. He said I would need to do an evaluation. As I sat in the back of the police car, Karen got into her car to follow us. There weren't any openings to do my intake anywhere nearby. He told her that we had to drive an hour away to a city called Elmira. I had never heard of it before. But I was ready to go anywhere!

Karen huffed and puffed the whole time in the intake room at St. Joseph's Hospital. She had to leave after a few hours. I would spend the night there. I was given a gown and blankets and put in my own room.

I was awakened the next morning to a nurse telling me that I was being sent to an intake across the street.

"There's transportation for you out front," she said.

"Okay. Can I have my clothes please?"

She came back with my clothes and shoes in a bag.

"Just put your shoes on," she said. "It's literally across the street. And you have transportation."

Alight, then.

I walked to the car with a gown and sneakers on as I held my bag of clothes. My driver was a very attractive black man who was very quiet and professional. There was a tension in the air through our silence.

One minute later, we were at the entrance to Elmira Psychiatric Center.

Unbeknownst to me, back in the Carlon house, Karen appeared much nicer to the rest of The Four. But it was still insulting, because they still weren't equal to Abram, Cisca, and Nano.

She gave them more portions of food. She added new things to their menu. She let them watch TV and allowed them to go outside. She didn't yell as much.

Then, she met with each of them individually. She went to their rooms at separate times and said she wanted to bond with them and be the mother they really needed. She said she would give them even more privileges, and some that they never had before. She printed out pictures of material things from the Internet and showed it to them, saying all of that could be theirs.

She told them they could trust her and tell her anything. She said she wanted to make a change in the house finally and that Bad Sara was a negative influence on everyone and the family had been destroyed. But that it could finally be fixed now.

Then she asked them if they could remember being touched by anyone when they were in foster care back in Las Vegas. During our first year of being adopted, all of us in fact had told her a couple of things from some of the foster homes who had other relatives come over. She never took any notes back then.

But now, as she met with Stan, Rae, and Elijah individually, she had a pen and notepad.

Dear Mama,

This unit was even better than Stony Lodge! On my first intake meeting a couple of days after I arrived, Karen came with all my clothes that I owned. It all fit into one shoulder bag. I had the staff call to tell her to bring them because I knew I'd be gone a while again. During the meeting, I was frustrated that this particular intake lady took Karen's side. They were saying how horrible I was and all of that. Karen tried to make herself cry, but lately it wasn't as believable anymore.

I wanted to explode again. But I knew I had to be calm because I didn't want to start off badly at this placement. There was a level system here as well. I remember getting so mad during this interrogation. The person was a fat middle aged lady. She wore glasses and a suit and studied my chart and nodded her head to everything Karen was saying. When I attempted to speak up for myself, she shook her head and said I was bad and that I was disrupting things back at home. She said this as if she had known me all my life. Her expression was angry as she and Karen looked at each other and agreed with each other. Wow, Karen was so good.

I was sitting directly across the table from the intake lady as Karen sat on the side. I became so enraged…that I was getting ready to jump up, reach forward, and grab that lady by her hair and drag her clear across the table for having the audacity to sit up in there and talk like she knew what was really going on! She had no idea what I had been subjected to in that household. For her to not even allow me to speak…oh boy I felt steam coming from me that I didn't know I had. I even felt my feet flexing, gearing me to jump up and do it!

For some reason…I don't know how…but God must have stopped me. I was surprised when I didn't do it. Then I started thinking. If I did that, they would call the people in to give me a shot, or tie me down in what they called "four point." That's where they tie your hands and feet down and chain you to four corners as you lay on a mat. They won't unchain you until you are completely calm and they are sure you won't do anything else. Most people fell asleep after getting a shot. After witnessing this with other patients, I vowed to myself to avoid having that done on me. If I attacked this lady, that would be extra points for Karen, who wanted to prove to everybody that I was dangerous and a convict. Things would go in her favor and that's what she wanted. I had to be calm. This really wasn't about the intake lady at all; this was about someone who had hated me since she first came across my smile on an adoption website.

So, I held my calm composure and when Karen left I started to get to know the staff and other residents. I never got in trouble and I stayed on the highest level. I never saw the intake lady again. Karen came to visit a couple of times. She brought me a lot of my books. I told her thank you. I was scared to bring up my journal or ask her for it…because I knew I had so many private entries in there and I really had vented! I was hoping she would overlook it as another book. I prayed deep down she had not found it. But at the same time, I had a gut feeling that if I asked her for it, she would deny ever seeing it. That's who she was.

When she visited those two times, she didn't look very impressed to see me on the highest level. She didn't congratulate me. She acted stuck up towards everyone. I knew she was only stopping in to see if what the staff said about my good behavior was true. I knew that despite never calling me, she was aware of my every move. On the second visit, we were in the cafeteria and the chef said, "ice cream snack!" Karen watched as everyone ran to get ice cream. She turned her head away from me and tried to act like she didn't care when I stood up to get my vanilla ice cream cone. I sat back down and ate that thing right in her face like I had never tasted anything so good. She tried to appear as if she was still conversing with me, but she wouldn't look at me. After that, she never came back to visit.

She wouldn't allow me to speak to The Four at all. This made me very angry. Staff told me they would review my case plan whenever I asked them. I became friends with two girls and we had our own clique. Then one of them was discharged. She said she lived right there in Elmira so she would come visit for sure. I had to make a request to put her on my list of people I wanted to call. But I was told it was up to Karen. They called to ask her, and she instantly said no. Instead, my friend wrote down her contact in my new journal and told me to call her whenever I got out.

At EPC, we weren't confined to just the premises. The staff frequently took us on field trips. We went to museums, lakes, the library, and the drive through movie theaters. One of the staff ladies told me that I was going to be somebody and that my name would be in lights. "I just know it," she kept saying, and it made me smile inside.

We had a classroom for school related activities after the summer was over. I had been out of school for the month of June, and now it was fall again. I was a little anxious and worried about how long I would be there because I didn't want to get held back a grade.

Then, I received some awesome news! Karen no longer wanted me back on Mountain Ave at all! Wow! I realized that I was free! This is what I had wanted all along. As I completed my case plan, I had no idea that even though I was physically free, Karen was still benefitting financially from me, and she was in no way finished with a plot to tarnish my name.

I was also unaware that she had stopped responding to Kim Folson's emails back in Las Vegas completely. Kim told your oldest daughter Deniece that major trouble had arisen. So Deniece asked Kim to have me sent back out. Then Karen severed contact with Kim. She wasn't going to allow me to go back to my real family and be happy again.

In November, I said goodbye to everyone at EPC. I was transported to a nice area in Elmira called Southport. When the car turned on the intersection of Maple Street and Laurentian Place, I was surprised at how huge this house was! It was a two-story white house accompanied with a gazebo on the property.

I was led in and I timidly stood in the entranceway. The first person I saw was an African-American woman who looked to be in her late twenties. She was my height. She had walked down the stairs to see who was arriving. When she saw me she just stared. I stared back. I was going through a lot of emotions. I didn't know what was ahead for me in this house and how my life would turn out.

Then she attempted a half smile, and I sort of waved. Little did I know, she was very amused at the sight of my old-fashioned sweater suit, shy face, bushy eyebrows, and afro. This would start our infamous and hilarious friendship!

"I'm Angela," she said. "I'll show you to your room."

She led me up the stairs and I was barely aware of the long hallway and the rooms we passed. We reached the end of the hallway and she stopped and opened the door.

I had a bed, dresser, closet, desk and nightstand. My room was much bigger than the one I had at the Carlons. I placed my shoulder bag on the bed and followed Angela throughout the house as she gave me a tour of the layout. The living room and den areas had TVs. The dining room had a long rectangular table that reminded me of the ones you see in the movies where a family of twenty sits down to eat. A staff prepared food behind a grand counter in the kitchen. The basement was a huge recreation room with full length couches, a television, and a pool table.

She showed me the gazebo and grounds. Then she led me back to the dining room table where more staff was going through my paperwork.

"Do you like it here, SaraJane?" they asked.

I nodded.

"And she has me now!" Angela said.

"Yikes!" they laughed at their co-worker. I could tell the staff here had a close camaraderie with each other.

Then something came over me.

"I want to be called by my real name," I said. I felt so newfound and powerful.

"Of course!" they obliged. They had already studied my chart.

"I think Sequoya is the true you," Angela agreed.

I smiled as I sat in my chair, adrenaline running. I had been granted my right to be called my birth name! This was a very emotional moment for me. I was respected by these adults who had my best interest at heart.

"When will the other kids be here?" I asked.

"They should start arriving back from school soon."

"I'm supposed to be in tenth grade...but I've missed a few months." I was so nervous.

"We're working on that right now. Why do you look worried? Are you okay?"

"I don't want to repeat ninth again."

"You won't. What we're going to do is place you right in the tenth where you belong. We'll see if you can jump right in and catch up. If not, we suggest tutoring. But I think you'll be just fine."

I nodded.

"Sequoya, want to help me set out the afternoon snack?" Angela raised her eyebrows with excitement.

"Sure," I tried to sound nonchalant. My mouth had already been watering at the food cooked earlier and placed in the oven for later. I was ready to get my grub on!

By that night, when I saw them pull out the food, the only thing I remember being real excited about was a plate full of curly fries. I asked for the hot sauce because the last time I had it was when I was ten. I drowned the fries and smiled as I ate them. Angela was in tears laughing. She would never let me forget this moment, and I wouldn't either.

Before I went to bed that night, Angela came in my room to say that her shift was over for the day but she'd be back so I didn't need to worry at all. She told me her work schedule and that she was going to tell her mom and her two sons about me.

"My mom does hair and she will hook you up for your first day of school. You need something done with that head," she laughed.

"Thank you," I smiled. "Does she know how to press it?"

"She knows how to do it *all*! Presses, relaxers, braids, weaves."

I was in awe!

"Yeah, so you're good here I got you!"

I smiled and looked out my window.

"What are you thinking about?" she asked.

"There's no broken screens," I said. "All of the windows here have screens in them."

"Yes…why?" she asked curiously.

"That means no bees or wasps are going to fly in."

For the first time in a long time, I felt freedom. I felt peace. I would never have to worry about Karen trying to trap me in my room with the bees and wasps that I was terribly afraid of! Wow, God can bring you comfort in so many ways.

TWENTY-SEVEN

Karen was required to attend my first major case assessment. I sat on one side of the dining room table, three staff sat clockwise to my right, and Karen sat directly across from me. She looked very full of herself when she walked in. When she looked at this place, she had that same look I had seen all those years ago when she sat in Benita Burke's extravagant living room on Brynehurst Drive the first day she met me. She didn't like to see me in a loving environment with beautiful décor and sense of peace.

Then I was shocked again.

"Neal and I don't want you back home," she said proudly.

"And I don't want to go back ever," I reiterated, equally as proud.

Staff quickly changed the subject to the focus of my case plan.

"I'm going to be sixteen soon," I said, adding fuel. "And then two more years after that...*eighteen!*"

I saw Karen restrain her emotions.

"Sequoya, that's true," Staff said. "We're going to figure out the best way to assist you in your transition that we can."

"Sequoya?" Karen asked them incredulously. "Her name is SaraJane."

I smiled and said, "They call me Sequoya because that's my name."

Staff explained to Karen that while they respected her wish as my parent to be called SaraJane, they also considered the wants and needs of the residents and if it helped to aid in the best interest of their mental health, they would do it.

Karen was speechless! She was now realizing that she couldn't control me anymore. She just got done saying she didn't want me home again, but why was she upset about my name if she didn't see me every day to use it?

A few minutes later, I was dumbfounded when Karen put on her contort face and claimed I had sexually abused my siblings.

I screamed that she was lying. She was really trying to turn my staff against me and tarnish my name with her allegations. It had been a few months since I left the house and she was still at it! I started shouting that there was no possible way, and that I had seen Stan in school right before I was called into the office.

Staff looked at Karen and me as we shouted. I even stood up and put my hands on the table to express my innocence and my fury.

Karen had scrunched her face up, put her hands to her face, and dramatically gave a graphic detail of something that sounded very familiar. It was an incident I recalled one of Benita's granddaughters doing to Rae in 1999. But instead, Karen said I had done it.

I was in disbelief. I felt sick and my body was getting hot. I was very hurt. I didn't understand. I didn't believe my siblings had even said these things that I supposedly did. No, they didn't do that stuff. I had to see them face to face so they could tell me she was lying. I didn't believe her at all. I should've opened my mouth to blurt out that maybe she should question her beloved son Abram about the year he requested to see what girls looked like and he asked Rae if he could see her.

But I was in such a deep rage that I couldn't think straight. I didn't know how far Karen was trying to go. The staff had indifferent expressions on their faces. After they calmed us both down, they continued the meeting. Karen was sitting there looking so satisfied with herself. She was the epitome of evil.

Before she left, she made it very clear that she still wanted me in her custody, because she said she still had to fulfill her promise to God to take care of me.

She really thought she was fooling these qualified staff members with that statement.

Dear Mama,

Angela took me to her mother's house to get my hair washed, conditioned, and pressed! My hair is just a little bit past my shoulders! I love it. We have to be hush hush about it, because I'm still a minor and Karen is still trying to control me. They have to ask her permission for certain things. Karen told them that I was not allowed to get my hair pressed or permed or my eyebrows done. But I still got my hair done! A staff lady took some tweezers and plucked my eyebrows for me. It hurt really bad at first but it's not so bad now.

The residents get a clothing allowance voucher. They take all of us shopping at the same time. When Karen found out, she told them to just take me to a thrift store or the local Salvation Army. They informed her that they take everyone to either the mall or Walmart and they wouldn't be using the company's gas to go out of their way to take me somewhere separate than the other kids. Karen got into an argument with the head program manager. I stood in the doorway of the office and listened to the whole thing. Then the program manager said very nicely, "Okay, Mrs. Carlon. I understand. We'll take her to a thrift store." Then she hung up the phone, looked at me, and said, "Ew. Scratch that, we're going to the mall!" I smiled so hard.

I was nervous on my first day at Southside High School. The other students were excited about a new girl and they exclaimed over my height and told me I was really pretty. I was excited to see this big melting pot of different races. I was very awkward and nerdy and shy. Although I quickly became an outcast, I felt good that my appearance was better than what it was when I lived in Candor. I started right there in the tenth grade and I didn't need a tutor at all.

I have a crush on this one boy that lives here. He is so fine. He has long hair that he pulls back into a ponytail and he has a lot of tattoos and piercings. He even has a lip ring. He is strong, tall, and bulky. He has very kind eyes. He's a year older than me. He is what they call Gothic but he doesn't look like the normal Gothic type. He is magnified and just sexy. Wow. I feel strange. I feel really tingly down there. But I'm a virgin so I wouldn't know what to do anyway. We both have to walk to school together. But in the afternoons, he walks a little behind me, because he's so busy chasing this one girl who doesn't even care about him and won't give him the time of the day. She got a new boyfriend one day and walked by my crush like it was nothing. My crush looked a little hurt. Sometimes I want to tell him that he can date me. But of course, I won't ever say that!

I went to my first counseling session in Elmira. My therapist seemed very nice so I felt comfortable talking with her and finally being heard and the chance to get a lot of emotions out. She asked me how I was doing and I told her I was happy. We were getting off to such a great start, then she totally switched gears on me.

"Now it's time to talk about the more serious things," she said.

I looked at her.

"Your adoptive mother has claimed that you have sexually abused your…"

"No, I did not," I shouted. There it was again.

She clamped her lips together as she skimmed through my files.

"She won't let me speak to them either," I said. "It's because it's a lie." I explained to her that Karen had used our past trust in her to defame me.

"Well, your siblings have in fact expressed for themselves what you have done," she said.

With a flourish, she pulled out three sheets of paper and placed them in front of me. She looked like she had just presented me a verdict. She acted just like the intake lady at EPC, who had judged me like she thought she knew me.

I looked at the papers in front of me. Each paper had their own name on top. They said Isaiah, Abigail, and Elijah. Each paper had a list of things that I had supposedly done to them. The dates on the papers had been a short time after I left. Written at the bottom of each paper was their desire for me to not come home because they were scared. Their signatures were included.

Reading each of these papers, I became nauseous. I couldn't believe it. No, they did not write this, it was all a misunderstanding.

But there it was...their own individual handwriting. That really killed me.

But as I studied them closer, I noticed something. The spacing of the lines was off, and at times the handwriting was either neat, or sloppy. As if some things had been written one day, and the rest was written later. Or maybe some of it was forged. But one thing was for certain, they had each signed their signatures at the bottom of each page.

I was looking at the papers so hard. Then my shock turned to rage!

Suddenly, the therapist reached forward and snatched the papers from me before I could rip them to shreds. She protectively placed them back in a file.

I stood up to leave.

"Where are you going?" she asked.

"Home," I said. "I'm not coming back here no more." She would have to pass those bogus papers back to where she got them.

I ignored her attempt to stop me. She followed me out and told my staff I was upset and that she hoped we'd have a better session next time. Well, she could just forget that. My mind was already made up. I now had a say in which place I wanted to receive services in.

Once in the car, I brooded. I vowed to myself to never talk to The Four ever again, because they had fallen for the trick and sold themselves out just to get an insulting version of privileges that would never be equal to Abram, Cisca, and Nano.

With an amused and calculating smile, Karen sat at the dining room table while Rae did her homework. She was now allowing Rae the privilege of being outside her room for homework time.

"This is just so sad," she said.

Rae glanced up at her.

"How sad it's going to be, when I have to go to the schools and let them know that a new sex offender will be registered." Karen was very dramatic.

Rae didn't understand what Karen was saying exactly...and why did she look happy? Shouldn't she look upset instead?

Rae continued doing her homework. Over the years, Karen had always come to Rae and said a bunch of cryptic things in front of her because she thought Rae was stupid. Rae might not have known the meaning behind it, but she remembered exactly what Karen told her.

Karen was unaware that an hour away in Elmira, there was a support team of key players who saw through all the shenanigans and were quickly handling it without my own knowledge.

Angela came in my room one afternoon a few months later and sat at my desk. She was holding a book.

"I got you this book," she said. "I think you can relate to it. It's about this guy who was abused really bad as a child."

She handed me the book and it said *A Child Called It*. The author was Dave Pelzer. The cover of the young lost looking boy was already making me sad.

"He was in foster care too...before that he was with his mother. She abused him so bad that she almost killed him."

"What?" I was in disbelief.

"Yes. His case was like the worst ever reported in the history of California."

"His own real mom?"

"Yeah...that's the sad part. The only difference for you is it's your adoptive mom."

I nodded.

Then she said something that shocked me. "Your adoptive mom is psycho! You know what she tried to do?"

"What?" I looked at her with fear.

"Okay, so remember when she tried to say you did all that stuff to your brothers and sister?"

I nodded. The memory and anger was rising again after I had pushed everything into the back of my mind to try to move on with my life.

"She tried to get you registered as a sex offender!"

My heart started to beat so fast. What? How?

"Calm down, don't worry. I know. I was real mad myself! So, we got the directors together, as well as the main one at the headquarters and we all squashed her hard body! The people who deal with that asked Karen if your brothers and sister were currently seeking therapeutic services for treatment...and she said no! And she couldn't even give them a name of a supportive person or therapist who they could contact to follow up with and go talk to them to see if they were okay."

"Exactly!" I shouted, jumping up at this victory. "Plus, I know she made them write it. She doesn't want no one to talk to them. She's mad that I have support now."

Wow! Squashed!

"Right. So, she let go of that. But then she got mad."

I smiled.

"She tried to get the board out here to get you locked up in a mental institution for the rest of your life."

"What?"

"Yes! She's outrageous. We laugh at her during our staff meetings. She sends these crazy emails about you and how we should deal with you. She knows you will turn eighteen and the time is ticking. If she can get you declared mentally deranged and put in a psych ward, then she's able to receive money for you forever. Dang Quoya! She hates you."

"But I don't understand why! All I ever wanted was to just be able to talk to my real family. If she hates me this much, why adopt me? And why not send me back?"

"Quoya, she's evil...that's why."

I just shook my head.

"And this guy Dave Pelzer, you need to read his book. His mom tried to do the same thing. When he got free from her abuse she tried to arrange stuff to get him sent to a psych ward for the rest of his life too."

I sat there dumbfounded. What would make a mother hate her child so much, even to the point of trying to control their destiny after they no longer lived with them?

Dear Mama,

I would spend the next year and a half at the Community Residence. Karen would only visit me once. She found out that I had gotten my eleventh-grade school picture taken, thanks to Angela.

I had copies made of my school picture. She came by for dinner and asked to see them. I wore box braids extensions in my hair. She didn't tell me I was beautiful, or that the pictures were nice. She just stared.

By this time, I had reflected a lot on the situation and I wasn't as mad at The Four anymore. I took out five of my school pictures and on the back of two of them I wrote Mom (for Karen), and Dad (for Neal). I wrote the names of The Four on the other ones and I also wrote that I loved and missed them. I didn't get one for Abram at all. I asked Karen could she please give my siblings their pictures.

She got mad and her face turned phony again. She put on a dramatic show and said no, that they needed more time. I'm like, are you freaking serious? She still doesn't want me to talk to my own blood siblings? Then she did something even more confusing. As I put them all back in my envelope, she asked, "Can I still have one?"

I'm like, what in the world! This lady is really obsessed with me. I gave her one, even though I shouldn't have after what she had just said and did and denied me my right to talk to my siblings! She didn't care that I didn't give her Neal's picture.

On weekends and holidays, the other children get to go on home visits. It's usually just me and one other kid who are always here no matter what. But we still have a great time. The weekends are the times where the staff does more stuff with us because it's not a lot of kids they have to take in the work van. I also do a lot of volunteering. My favorite is at this place called Arctic League. On Christmas morning, I get up very early at four AM and I help pass out Christmas presents to needy families just in time before their children wake up. This makes me so happy to see the looks on the mothers' faces when they open the door and try to be as quiet as possible as I hand them the gifts.

Angela has introduced me to her whole family. She and her mother are so hilarious! Her nephews are all around my age, but I'm very shy around them and won't speak. One of them said, "Yo Angela, that girl is crazy quiet!" That made me laugh.

Angela says I'm growing up right before her eyes. She yells at me if I use a swear word and she says she'll never stop telling me that I'm not grown. It's so funny...but it makes me feel so loved. She also jokingly says that I better not have any babies, because if I do then she will find me and kick me in my stomach. She has me in tears laughing so hard. She said God has a special man waiting for me at the appointed time.

I finally had my Scoliosis surgery in the summer of 2006 when I was sixteen. Before I did, I read this book called Deenie. Deenie is a teenager who is going on auditions to become a model when she is suddenly diagnosed with Scoliosis and must wear a back brace. I want to model too...and that story really hit an emotional nerve for me.

The doctors told me that if I didn't get the surgery, one day it would really get worse. They said I was a beautiful tall girl and I needed to do what I had to do. I remembered how Karen said God would just heal it if it's meant to happen. But the doctor told me that God also gives you surgeons to help correct spinal irregularities. They also said that no one really wears braces anymore and that my case was so severe that I needed the surgery. When they showed me my x-rays, I freaked out!

The staff got my paperwork and my insurance information together. But Karen refused to sign for it! She put us in limbo for a while before she finally gave in when they threatened to report her. Since she was the mother, she was required to take the three-hour drive to Syracuse, New York to meet us there.

*She not only had to sign a couple of papers, but she was also required to **wait** there for the entire nine hours of my operation! Just in case something happened. She didn't look at or speak to me. When I was in my gown on the stretcher as they wheeled me past her to head to the operating wing, she ignored me. She didn't even wish me luck. After the operation, I was out of it on pain medication for two days. When I finally came to, I was told that Karen never even came to at least look in on me while I was in the recovery room. As soon as she heard the surgeon was done she left.*

TWENTY-EIGHT

The Community Residence staff made a good point to me. They told me that Karen had stopped cooperating with them completely. She wouldn't call or visit me. They said she was very wrong for that. Especially because she still wanted custody of me.

I was nearing seventeen. I had long since completed my case plan. I was informed that I must move on so my spot could be filled by another teen on the long waiting list.

In the beginning of 2007, they emailed her after several attempts at calling. They informed her that if she didn't make an attempt to call and check on me, they would hotline her and get me placed into state custody. They knew that I had to be in state custody to qualify for a housing program called Independent Living that was available for former foster youth.

Karen wanted control *so* bad, so as soon as she received the email she finally called them and asked how I was doing. They told her it was time for me to move and they understood it would be better for both of us if I didn't return to her house. They told her about Independent Living. Karen told them no and asked them if I could just stay at the CR until I turned eighteen. They told her no. What for? Karen was irate over the fact that I would have my own apartment at seventeen.

Then miraculously, she told them she would allow me to see The Four! She said to just give her a few weeks. During that time, I had to meet Karen and Neal at my therapist's office. Angela came with me. The first time Karen laid eyes on Angela, she hated her for no reason. Angela said the sight of the Carlons and their aura in the waiting room was very creepy and it officially sealed the deal.

I could tell that Neal didn't want to be there. He just had to go because it was mandatory. He was looking really fed up with his life by this point. Karen had stressed him out. I recalled a shouting match one time when he screamed that she was cruel for not acknowledging the fact that he was being a gentleman for not asking her for sex for over two years. He said that maybe he should go ask the neighbor down the street. So, Karen ended up creating a system where she would allow him sex on Tuesday nights. We heard plenty of shouting matches in that house.

In the office in front of the counselor, Karen had no choice but to finally say she would allow me to see my siblings.

Then the counselor slipped up and told Karen everything was falling in place for me now, especially since I would go to Independent Living.

Karen's eyes flashed with surprise. "I thought we agreed she would stay at the CR?" She was big time mad!

She and I got into an argument. This time, I remained very calm. I spoke softly and looked her in the eyes like a grown adult, which she couldn't stand. She couldn't make me go into outbursts anymore.

She was so hype in there trying to argue with the counselor. She didn't dare say anything to Angela. She couldn't even turn her face or body to look in Angela's direction.

Karen stood up to leave and motioned for Neal to get up.

"We are not ready for you to see your siblings!" she proudly exclaimed. Then they both walked out.

Wow! She really showed her true colors right there.

I was so angry and cried all the way back home. Angela comforted me. How cruel and selfish could a person really get? She did everything she did to me in that house, then bribes my siblings into falsely accusing me of molestation mere months after my biological mother passes away whom she didn't allow me to say goodbye to, then tries to get me placed in a mental institution, then turns around and uses my siblings as leverage just because I was growing up and getting my own apartment?

Hello, can somebody please tell me why was I ever adopted?

Hello, is anybody out there?

For the next couple of months, the CR tried to get Karen to cooperate but she would not. My seventeenth birthday came and went. So, they pushed forward with my IL application.

Then suddenly, Karen called to say she would see me. I was wondering what for?

Angela and I were already in the therapist's office when Karen appeared in the doorway. It was a dramatic scene out of a movie! She put on a sad forlorn face and was holding a paper.

"You know Sara," she began, and it was eerie hearing her speak to me in that fake voice she used at the house for manipulation. "I have always tried to do what God wanted me to do…"

She lurched her body and wiped her face and scrunched up. "God wanted me to be a mother to you…but it just didn't work. And now, you have finally got what you wanted the whole time."

But didn't she say she didn't want me back home though?

She handed the paper to the counselor.

"I have now signed you over to state custody!"

Careful not to stand near Angela, she backed up. Then she did this crying wail and turned and ran out the building as fast as she could without saying anything else. I mean, I didn't even get a chance to say thank you!

"What was that?" Angela asked. She busted out laughing.

I smiled weakly, overcome with adrenaline and victory.

I was truly free!

Dear Mama,

In April of 2007 I moved into the Independent Living program. I had an upstairs apartment in a co-ed house on Horner Street. It was still within walking distance to my school. The program was designed for former foster youth to transition into the real world. My roommate was named Tessa. As soon as I told her about the Carlons, she was very amused. She was also upset that I couldn't see my siblings. She had a car so she told me to let her know so we could drive down there. I looked at her like she was crazy. She said she wasn't playing; she was serious.

I sent Karen a letter near Mother's Day, to make an attempt at being friendly. In the letter, I also told her that I was doing great in school and planned to study Black History in college. I didn't hear anything back from her. When Father's Day rolled around, I sent Neal a card.

Unbeknownst to me, she saw Neal smiling hard with appreciation of the card. She started crying and said I never loved her. She and Neal got into an argument that night.

I learned the bus routes and I got familiar with the City of Elmira. I also got my first job at the Arnot Mall. I worked at Claire's.

My back healed up quickly from my Scoliosis surgery. Now I'm very happy that I went through with it. Angela suggested that I also get a breast reduction due to the weight of my breasts hurting my back.

Shockingly, I got a breast reduction. Mama, I know. They run in our family. But the strange part is, I'm not upset with myself as some people would be at me for it later.

I met a couple of friends who lived nearby. One of them was always on her computer on this website that had her picture up. I had no idea what she was doing. She kept telling me that I needed to make one myself.

It was September of 2007, and I made myself a profile on this website called Myspace.

TWENTY-NINE

I was getting familiar with navigating Myspace. In the search button, I typed in Deniece Kelly, Daniel Kelly, and Keyonna Kelly. A lot of profiles popped up. I was studying the faces, trying to see any resemblance. The first couple of days of searching brought no perfect matches.

Then one day I just lazily typed in Deniece's name again, not really expecting anything at all. I was bored so I ended up scrolling through seven pages of results.

Near the bottom of the seventh page, I saw a picture of two women in the profile picture. My heart started pounding. Although they looked more grown up, they just had that look! The older one confidently stared into the camera with her natural green eyes. The other one leaned into her, but smiled sweetly. She looked like an older duplicate of Raeannah.

I scrolled through the pictures and saw the older one with two adorable little boys. Then I saw a man who I definitely knew for sure. He had a sure swag about himself and smiled with confidence.

I knew these people were my three older siblings! They were older now but I knew it was them. I scrolled down Deniece's profile a little bit and came across a song called "My Fam." I pressed play and a rap voice emanated out at me.

Daniel was rapping about his life and the struggles he had been through. He was rapping about studying in school. He was also talking about us…The Four! He was talking about my Mama, Katherine Kelly. One of the lines was *Came home from school then my sister broke the news had to find out that my Mama…*and then the words got so elaborate and crafty that I knew I would need to get all the lyrics down on paper to process this masterpiece.

I immediately sent Deniece a message with my phone number, and then I went home in a daze. I could not believe I had found them! I did this all on my own! I didn't need any social workers, and I most certainly didn't need Karen Carlon or Kim Folson's permission!

A couple hours later, my cell phone rang with a 702-area code.

As soon as I answered all I heard was screaming! I started screaming too! Dee and I screamed with such happiness.

When she finally caught her breath, she began crying, and then I cried too.

"Sequoya, you don't understand!" she cried. "I have been searching forever for y'all!"

"I've been searching too!"

"And I saw a lot of Sequoyas…but there wasn't nan' one that looked like my pretty sister!"

I smiled.

"Sequoya…I was about to delete my Myspace account too."

"Why?"

"Because I got depressed. I couldn't find you guys. That's why I had made one. What was the point in keeping it?"

"I'm glad you kept it up. I found you on the seventh page Dee!" I exclaimed.

"And it's been seven years since we seen y'all."

"I know."

"You know what the number seven means?"

"What?"

"It means completion. Fulfillment."

I took this in. My sister was so beautiful. Already I was being brought back to the early memories of her watching me and getting me dressed and walking me to school and doing my hair and sneaking up to my school to see me…and just being the big sister she could be to me at the time when she was also too young to fully comprehend the changes our family was going through. She had been a teenager with that huge weight on her shoulders. To know that she attempted to fight the courts to get us?

*She revealed to me that in 1994, the courts had asked your sister, our Aunt Marlene, if she would take us in for two years. By 1996, sixteen-year-old Deniece would be eighteen and custody would then be transferred to her. Marlene would receive seven hundred dollars a month for the four of us. That would be an extra income of two thousand eight hundred dollars a month for Marlene. Dee begged Marlene to take us for two years until she turned eighteen. She even pleaded saying, "Aunt Marlene, just take the money we don't need it! You don't even have to see the kids all day...just drop them off where I'm at! Please Aunt Marlene, just help us until I'm eighteen...you don't have to do anything!" Marlene said no in very vulgar terms and hung up the phone. Then you pleaded with her too. Marlene said, "Forget you **and** your kids!" and she hung up on you. She had always been angry and jealous of you growing up and it continued into adulthood. After that, Dee didn't speak to Marlene for eight years.*

Suddenly, Dee's voice changed to sadness.

"Sequoya...Mama died," she said very reluctantly.

"I know," I said.

"They told you?"

"Yes."

"Daniel is going to be mad."

"Why?" I asked.

"Because we worried about y'all all these years. He was looking so hard. He just went to prison a couple of months ago. And now we just found each other."

"What? Why?" I felt anxious.

"Some crap...I will tell you later I don't want to be upset right now. But don't worry...he won't be gone that long. And he can still call you."

"Okay."

Then she started screaming happily again and asked to speak with the others. I explained that I hadn't lived with them in over two years and that Karen had kept me from being in contact with them.

"Are you serious?" she asked. Then she told me how she asked to have me sent back out. She told me that throughout the years, Kim always seemed to run into her just to "tease" her with details about our life in New York, but she would never reveal what town we lived in.

"So why would she even tell you then?' I asked. "What was the point?"

"Yeah, they dogged us all the way out and they enjoyed doing it too. Kim didn't like Mama. But at least I got to know that y'all were still alive."

We talked and cried for hours that night. Keyonna joined us as well. We were on a three-way call. By the time I hung up, my face was puffed up from tears of sadness but also from tears of joy. My phone screen was smudged with my sweat and tears. I laid down and thanked the Lord for giving us strength to endure.

When Daniel called me from prison I was so excited. My big brother! But after our greetings and catching up, he said something that made me just a little bit upset.

"Sequoya…I was really upset with you for years."

"Why?" My heart started beating.

"Because! I specifically gave *you* the pictures we took on your birthday and wrote our phone number on them! I told you countless times that day to memorize the number. We waited and waited…we waited for y'all to call."

"Benita ripped them up!" I explained. "We were going to memorize the number the very next day!" I told him about the whole ordeal. He was quiet and became more softened.

"Yeah…" he said. "Well, we kept that same number for a while."

Daniel let me know everything that was going in with his case and I told him that I loved him and we were a family that was going to stick together. He told me he loved me too.

I was looking at Stan and Rae's profiles on Myspace as well! I only looked, I didn't send a request because I was anxious about what Karen would do. I suspected they had sneaked to make those profiles at school because I just couldn't imagine Karen ever allowing that.

I was also very sad and angry, because they were really gaunt and skinny! It was even worse than before. Stan had a huge wobbly afro and his clothes draped like a blanket over spindly legs and arms. His ankles were so tiny I was sure they couldn't support him as he stood up. I could see Rae's collarbone and her ribs through her shirt.

I thought about what to do. Then, I just couldn't take it no longer! I finally sent them both a message and told them I loved them.

During school hours, which I noticed, they messaged me back! They explained that our conversing had to be done in secret because Karen was unaware of their Myspace profiles, which I had already guessed. None of us brought up anything about what had happened yet. We were just so happy to finally reconnect again.

Everything felt like a secret mission. Just like our whole life had always felt, everyone scrambling and sneaking to see each other…their own blood! It was just crazy what we had been subjected to by our oppressors.

Dee scanned and uploaded old pictures on Myspace of everyone when we were little. She also put up the pictures from my tenth birthday, the last time we all saw each other, and the last time The Four had seen their biological mother alive. Those pictures were the duplicates of the ones Benita Burkes had ripped to shreds the very next day on March 27th, 2000.

Raeannah printed one of those pictures off the computer at school and took it home. She started sleeping with it underneath her pillow.

One day, Rae heard Karen walking up the stairs. She didn't care. She wasn't scared anymore. She wasn't going to hide anything or wait to come home to find things of hers confiscated. Karen walked in without knocking. She found Rae sitting on her bed, staring at the picture.

Surprised, she peered down at the picture. Then everything flashed before her eyes.

"Where did you get that from?" she asked incredulously. She looked like she had seen a ghost.

Rae calmly told her that she got it from the Internet, and not only were she and Stan in contact with me, but they were also reunited with our siblings after seven years.

Rae handed Karen the picture after she asked. She looked at it fully. Surprisingly, she didn't confiscate it.

The next day, Karen told Stan and Rae that they didn't have to sneak around to be on Myspace. She said they could get on it right at home. She said they could come into her bedroom to use the computer. That was the first time ever because she had never let anyone go in her room to use that old machine at all!

Karen said she wanted to see more pictures of our family and that she was happy they had reunited with them. When she saw the pictures of Deniece's two sons, she smiled.

"They are just *so* cute!" she exclaimed, obsessively staring.

When that comment slipped out of Karen's mouth, Rae felt like saying, *'Yes, cute exactly. Just like we were when you saw us online and wanted to adopt us so bad and then drastically changed our appearance. You will never have the opportunity to be in these boys presence and harm them, let alone another child!'*

Karen let Stan and Rae in her room at different times that day. She distracted them both and didn't allow them to log out of their profiles. The next day at school, they both realized that they couldn't log into their accounts. They told Karen.

She suddenly had her evil demeanor back.

"I deleted your accounts. I'm not going to allow you guys to have a Myspace. If you make new ones at school, you'll be in trouble for using the school's Internet for things that aren't school related. I've already alerted the teachers." Then she clamped her hands together and stared my siblings down.

Back in Elmira, I noticed their profiles had disappeared.

Dear Mama,
Stan and Rae started using their friend's phones at school to call Dee and Keyonna and me. That's when they revealed everything to me. Shortly

after I left in 2005, Karen bribed them and promised them many privileges. They said the way it all went down was very manipulative. Rae recalled that every time Karen asked her to repeat something that happened in foster care in Las Vegas, she asked the name of the person. After Rae told her the name of the person, Karen would say, "And Sara too right?" Then Rae would start to say, "No, I didn't say Sara, I said it was…" Then Karen would talk loudly over her and say, "Sara! Sara right?" Then she would be scribbling on her notepad.

What a huge cow she was!

They revealed that after I left, Karen gave them some freedoms and lightened up a little bit. But the different food and dress code remained the way it was. Karen didn't miss not one opportunity to mention my name. She always talked me down, she could not get enough of saying the name Sara. Her signature head shake was constant.

Just like I had known in my gut, she had been cruel with my journal that she found in my room. Every day at the breakfast table, she selected a certain entry to read out loud to them. She read that journal like it was her favorite novel, and it certainly was! She would make comments trying to figure me out. She was saying stuff like, "You know, Sara is very evil…you all should see…it's right here in front of our faces."

Rae would walk down the stairs and pass the living room and see Karen sitting back in the recliner chair with her head inside the journal like it was a treasure. Karen was also brainwashing them. She told them that I hated them as well, because the whole time I lived there I was only looking out for myself and not them, because in the end I was the one who left. She asked them, "Isn't it much peaceful now that she's gone?" But they said deep down inside, they loved and really missed my stomping episodes because I fought for them! Karen even had the nerve to make them watch a program on the History Channel about World War II. When they showed Adolf Hitler, she pointed to the screen and said, "That's Sara."

She fed off their vulnerability. She outright manipulated them and promised them everything. Although they had more privileges than they had before, she didn't come through with everything she promised. They revealed to me that Abram no longer talked to anyone except Neal and he spent most of his time in the cabin. He became very cruel to Karen. He dropped out of school.

Now that Stan and Rae had found me and the others, Karen was back to being extremely cruel and everything changed again after a couple years of freedoms. She tried holding on tightly to Elijah more than ever before. She was claiming that Stan and Rae were poisoning Elijah's mind, just like she had claimed I was the original mind poisoner. But Elijah was the youngest out of all of us and he gained his strength with a new demeanor like, "Nah, back up off me homie!"

All of them made new Myspaces again. Karen could not control it. Rae had her best friend's phone working overtime at school! More of her friends were offering their phones as well. Everyone liked me and they all thought our story was so unique.

Then, Karen did something that was very hilarious. When I lived there, we were prisoners in our rooms and couldn't come out until she said so. Now that she couldn't control anyone anymore, the rule was they had to leave early in the morning and they couldn't return until night. She packed them a crappy lunch and told them to find something to do all day.

In today's world, that's how "drop in" shelters operate. Homeless people have to get up at a certain time and leave the premises and they can't come back until night. That's how Karen truly felt about them. She was showing her true character for everyone to see.

Like other things she couldn't control, she was powerless to certain residents of the town who took notice.

THIRTY

It was a stormy and rainy afternoon when sixty-four-year-old Lynda Coswell was walking home with her dog. She thought she had ample time to walk to the post office and back before the rain started. Nevertheless, they got caught in the rain.

She scurried up Main Street and passed the Laundromat. As she was making a left, she scrunched her body up to keep warm from this downpour.

But then, she had to stop in her tracks. Something wasn't right. Ahead of her, underneath a tree, were three black children huddled together trying to keep warm and dry. It was futile because they were soaking wet. Their eyes looked so miserable.

"What the hell?" she exclaimed. "What are you guys doing?"

"Trying not to get wet."

"But you *are* wet! Why don't you head home? You could get sick like this."

"We're not allowed to go home until night."

"What? Come on, my house is right up the road."

They were very hesitant. Years of feeling insecure and unworthy and full of fear came to the surface.

"Come on!" Lynda didn't understand. "You're not going to be in trouble! Hurry!"

She asked them many questions as she fixed them hot chocolate and they dried off with her big warm bath towels. She was horrified. She wanted to run up to Mountain Ave and handle Karen herself, but their eyes went wide and pleaded with her not too. They said it would be trouble, and that in the end, Karen would have favor, because they were black, like she had bragged for years.

Lynda was so angry. She told them that instead of being outside all day, they were welcome to her home at any time. She told them they had an ally with her. They were going to handle this.

She saw their eyes light up with hope at the realization that someone was truly in their corner. She would tell them time and time again that it wasn't about them being out in the rain, even though that was very sad. When she first laid eyes on those kids, she just knew there was something very special about them.

My siblings called me from Lynda's house as well. Karen still wasn't letting me see them. It was so frustrating and ridiculous.

"Call their house," my roommate said one Sunday afternoon. Tessa was a dare devil and she loved to be entertained. She was restless and didn't like being bored or having to sit still.

"No," I said, feeling nervous.

"Then I will," she said with a mischievous smile.

I told her the number. Somehow it felt easier if she did it.

She dialed the number on our house phone and when it picked up, her eyes went wide with amusement. She clamped one hand over her mouth to stifle a giggle fit.

Tessa handed me the phone.

"Hi Dad," I said.

"Hi," Neal answered.

It was an awkward conversation. I told him I had found my family. He said he knew. He sounded genuine…like deep down he was happy for us. He told me that Karen was not there at the time. I asked to speak with The Four. He was a little hesitant.

"Well…I think we have to go through Karen first," he said, and with that he really sounded like a wimpy coward again. When would he ever claim some authority?

We both knew that Karen wasn't going to allow it. I still begged him.

"Okay, well let's see…I'm going to hold the phone out and let you yell through it."

What in the world?

He called The Four to the dining room table, and he did just that. I screamed through the phone as they excitedly screamed back. So ridiculous!

Later, they called me from a friend's phone and told me that Neal broke down and confessed to Karen like the coward he was, which they couldn't understand. They believed he was going to keep it a secret. Well, they thought wrong. Karen blew up on Neal, because in every way he was one of her mentally scarred victims as well.

Karen was on watch now. After that, Tessa and I decided to prank call. I would not do it, but she did. She blocked our number and called. Neal picked up.

Tessa deepened her voice to sound like a man's. She called Neal a derogatory name and slammed the phone down. A few minutes later, she did it again.

"Who is this?" Neal asked, in his goofy country voice.

Then he said, "I know it's you Sara!"

Tessa still made her voice like a man's.

"Shut up asking questions!" she bellowed. Then she hung up.

We both died with laughter.

A few days later, our program manager came over to talk to us. She explained the seriousness of it. She told me that the Carlons had filed a petition to get a restraining order on me and that I had to go to court.

What? I was shocked. I was also a little scared. I was angry because we had never threatened them.

"Your adoptive mother tried to have you arrested. The police said that wasn't necessary. The court papers will be mailed to our main headquarters. I'll bring them over to you when they arrive."

She left with an agitated look on her face.

But when she came back after receiving the papers, she was laughing with tears in her eyes! Why was she laughing at me possibly going to jail? I had never been in trouble before.

"Take a look at this!" she exclaimed.

I nervously unfolded the papers as Tessa crowded around us.

Petition for Order of Protection

Plaintiffs:

Karen Mae Carlon, Neal D. Carlon, Abram Carlon, Isaiah Carlon, Abigail Carlon, Elijah Carlon

Defendants:

SaraJane F. Carlon

We, the Plaintiffs, are petitioning and seeking a protective order against the above named Defendants. The Defendants called our home with threats to finish us off. Defendants has threatened to murder us through multiple conversations. Defendants repeatedly called and harassed.

1) Are the above named Defendants related to, or associated with the above named Plaintiffs? Yes. Plaintiffs adopted the Defendants in May 2000. Defendants were removed from the home in June 2005 due to threats of murder. We fear for our safety.
2) Do you suspect that the above named Defendants have a gun or any other weapons to carry out their threats? I don't know. We believe Defendants may possibly have a gun.
3) Describe in detail the natures of such threats made by the Defendants: Defendants has verbally called our home and threatened to kill us. Defendants has threatened to come to our home to kidnap Isaiah Carlon, Abigail Carlon, and Elijah Carlon to take them to Nevada. Defendants verbally told us they have hired a hit man to break our legs and kill us. We fear for our safety. We are requesting an order of protection against the above named Defendants.

We exploded in laughter! What in the world was this?
"She's psycho!" Tessa exclaimed.
"Yeah, like a seventeen-year-old really has the money to hire a hit man," I rolled my eyes. "I'm broke!"

"Let's go break her legs!"

"So they can't move! Then I'll kidnap my siblings and we hop on a plane to Las Vegas!"

The three of us were having a ball at these ridiculous and false allegations. But I was also angry. Karen was a psychotic pathological liar!

The hearing was set for January of 2008. I had six key team players with me! I didn't even know they were coming; they were just outside when I walked out to get in my program manager's car. They were some of the adults who had supported me at my placements in Elmira so far. Our clan took two different cars. I was very nervous as we took the hour drive to the Village of Owego. They told me to just relax.

We crossed the eerie familiar bridge and then turned on the very basic Temple Street where the small courthouse was located. We sat on the bench waiting to be called in.

Then Karen walked in with this old looking man. I was kind of thrown off guard. I figured he was her attorney or something. When Karen saw me on the bench tucked in between my people surrounding me, she suddenly and dramatically widened her eyes and jumped back, grabbing ahold of the old man's arms.

"I'm scared!" she screeched with a fake crying voice. The man held her arm and walked her over to the opposite side.

My heart was pounding with adrenaline and anger. She was doing way too much! One of my supporters squeezed my arm.

Our case was the only waiting case in that small village, so we were called in quickly. Both parties sat on opposite sides of the small room.

Looking at this Judge, it registered in my subconscious that he was in fact the very same person who did our name changes for us in the summer of 2000! When he glanced at the now adult me and the aging theatrical Karen, he blinked for a few seconds. He looked down at our case in front of him. All he had to see was the name Carlon. That's all anybody had to see or hear in the towns of Owego and Candor.

He called court to order. He read the petition out loud with a straight face. Then he looked at Karen.

"Where is the key witness?" he asked her.

"Well, my husband Neal didn't want to be here," Karen stammered. She looked very surprised. "He does not wish to participate...so I brought a member of my church that I co-pastor. We just opened a church in Candor."

"Isn't your husband the person that SaraJane spoke to on the phone?"

"Yes, but..."

"Then he is the key witness. He needs to be here."

"I tried to get Neal to come but he wouldn't. My friend here is representing the family and that is enough."

The Judge wasn't fazed by Karen's boldness and stupidity.

"Mrs. Carlon, without the key witness, your case will not be heard."

Right in front of everyone, he tossed the papers in the wastebasket beside his stand!

"Court is adjourned!" he said, very crisply with an unemotional head nod. He stood up and disappeared back to his chamber.

Karen grabbed the old man and they bolted out of there fast. I had no idea what had just happened. It was all under five minutes!

I was brought back to the times when The Four came home from school with papers that required her permission to participate in activities and sports and the Drama Club. Before we could say anything to her, she proudly said no and tossed them in the trash.

My supporters were smirking as they walked me out.

"Am I free?" I asked timidly.

"Honey, of course!" one of them said. "You are vindicated!"

We were passing a room to our right on the way out. Subconsciously, I turned my head to glance in the glass door as the seven of us were walking out the building. I was shocked to see Karen in there! She was with the old man. She did not see me at first. She was crying very uncontrollably.

Now, this was the first time I ever saw her cry real tears. This wasn't fake and calculated. This was a cry of anger, humiliation, and embarrassment over the fact that this whole charade had gone in my favor, and it happened right in front of her face.

When she looked up and saw me, she quickly turned her whole body around with one swift movement. It was too late because we had already made that forbidden eye contact!

Stan and Rae called from a friend's phone to tell me that Karen had spent that day crying and shouting.

"Sara thought she was *mighty queen* showing up with her army of agents!" she said.

Then she tried to get Rae to turn against me.

"Sara thought she was *so cool* with her nice clothes and hair! Abigail, that's why it's not good for you to see her…because I can't afford to get your hair done like that!"

Rae knew that was not true and was laughing inside over that statement. What about all those years ago when we begged to get our hair done? She had always had the funds to do it.

There was a black man from out of state who had visited Candor. He ran into Elijah and got real excited to see another black person. He gave Elijah a very decent edge up and made him look fly. He also gave Elijah a pair of shoes after he saw the toe parts were broken and my brother's toes were peeking through without any socks. The man also took pictures of my brother's run-down shoes. He was so angry.

When Karen saw Elijah looking very nice, she went crazy. She didn't even tell him he looked good. She got in her mustang and drove over to where the man was. When she saw he was black, she jumped back dramatically. Then she told him that he was to never cut Elijah's hair again, shoved the new shoes at him and told him her children weren't allowed to take anything from strangers. The man informed her that he was reporting her. She turned her back and got in her car and sped off.

Elijah was the one who never had good sturdy shoes. Karen went as far as giving him a pair of old sneakers that he couldn't even fit.

"These are brand new," she lied.

"They look like Abram's old shoes," he said.

"Excuse me? Elijah, these are brand new!" She was playing with him and insulting his intelligence.

He put them on and they were too small. She refused to get him another pair. Stan and Rae saw the shoes and were angry.

"Yeah, those are Abram's old shoes from when he was in sixth grade," Stan told him. "I remember."

On Saturday June 28th, the morning of my graduation, I decided I would go to Candor myself to see them. I was eighteen-years-old now! What could she do to me?

Tessa was excited to finally take the hour drive. We knew we had enough time to get there and visit and be back in Elmira before the evening ceremony. Although I was happy about graduating, it was the least of my thoughts. High School had been very challenging for me socially. I was ready to end that era and never look back. The only socializing I cared about was seeing my siblings!

Tessa and I walked into the very small Candor Public Library...and there my brother was, after not seeing him in person for three whole years!

He smiled hard and I ran to him and we embraced. I touched his massive afro that wobbled with the slightest movement of his head. We sat down at the table and I looked at his artwork. I was so proud to see his already published comics that were in two different local papers!

We recalled the last time we had seen each other, that morning in the halls before I had been called into the office.

"I'm so proud of you," I said. "I'm surprised Karen let you get published."

"She didn't," he said.

"Then how?" I was puzzled.

"This man from Ithaca who's a cartoonist saw my artwork and called some people. But I'm a minor so he had to ask Karen. She wouldn't sign. Then he told her that he was paying me a salary to draw for his own paper that he owned. She still said no. So, we pretended to agree with her…but we did it anyway. He asked me what's the worst that could happen? If she took him to court, the judge would laugh at a mother who didn't want her own son's comic in the newspapers! We have to show her that she can't bully us anymore."

"Wow."

Anger was arising in me over the things this woman did. She was always trying to stifle our creativity. One year, I read a book called *Otherwise Known as Sheila the Great* and I got inspiration to create a family newspaper like the main character. In my newspaper, I drew everyone in the house and labeled it *Carlon Family News*. Underneath each picture I wrote a funny rhyme that fit each person's personality. When I showed it to everyone during dinnertime, they were laughing and happy! Neal was smiling the most. Karen was not. She picked apart each line and said I thought I was so great and why in the world would I make a family newspaper? Neal told her that it was all in fun and that it was actually funny. Then she and Neal got into an argument.

"I asked her if I could go to this art event in Spencer. She said no, but Taylor drove me there anyway. She doesn't know I went. She thought I was outside somewhere all day."

"She doesn't know that we have so many people who support and love us!" I said. "Did she really think she could do this to us forever?"

"Exactly. And guess what sis?"

"What?"

"I won the contest at the show."

"There you go! What did you draw?"

"A big portrait of Beyoncé."

"Wow. I want to see it."

"She took it."

"What?" I almost stood up.

"Yeah. I placed it in my room. I have your old room now, by the way. It was in my room and I came back from school and it was gone. It was big too...so very hard to miss. I asked her about it and she said she never saw it."

It was the same old stuff. She was a thief who had stolen all our work over the years from our room during her frantic searches. But she called us thieves for being hungry and sneaking food?

I was even more horrified to hear that Karen pulled another humiliation stunt in the school. She had allowed Stan to participate in basketball. He had only attended two practices before she showed up mysteriously. The coach looked very annoyed to see her. She had been harassing him with phone calls.

"Isaiah is being disciplined at home right now, so I think you should leave him out of the games until I say so," she would say.

"Mrs. Carlon, we need him in the game."

"Have him sit on the bench as discipline."

"With all due respect, Mrs. Carlon, I understand you are his mother, but I'm also the coach."

A mother was really in the school trying to humiliate her son! For what?

Then one night, the coach was very upset to get a call from Karen saying she was pulling Stan off the team all together! The coach had to tell everyone in the locker room that Stan had to quit the team because of his mother. The teammates looked at the coach, then at Stan very puzzled.

These were the types of things Karen loved to do. She loved to dangle our hopes and dreams in our faces and then watch our faces fall when she broke the sudden bad news. That's the only reason why she had allowed him to sign up. She was very crafty. What was she so upset for? Was it because Abram stopped doing soccer, dropped out of school, became a delinquent, and addressed her with derogatory terms? The kid who she had spoiled and said that she wanted him to feel special because he was showing signs of jealously before we were adopted?

"We met another sister of hers a couple of years ago," Stan said.

"Another sister?" I asked. We had only met one of them before.

"Yeah. She lives in Georgia. She's wealthy."

"Oh."

"Sequoya...she's so different from Karen. She put Karen in her place."

"How?"' I was full of curiosity.

"Well, the first thing we noticed was that she was a much better looking version of Karen. I mean, she was more put together and smiled a lot. She smiled when she met us. She looked very happy with her life. From what they were talking about we could tell they hadn't seen each other in years. But Karen was trying to act perfect, like she was trying to show her sister that she was living right and doing better. But she was acting frantic."

"Wow."

"Yeah, and Karen had said something weird. So, her sister just looked at her in an encouraging way and said, *Oh Karen stop it, you are always so anxious!*"

"She knows something about Karen that we don't," I said.

"Yeah, that's what we said to each other. But after her sister went back to Georgia, Karen spent days talking crap about her sister. She even said that she feels her sister is jealous of her because she lost some weight."

"That's insane," I rolled my eyes. She had accused me of the same thing.

We talked for a little while longer. Rae and Elijah were stuck in the house on this day because they were in trouble for whatever reason.

"If you come back on the fourth of July, you'll see all of us," he said in a conspiring tone. "The whole town is out for the parade. I don't think she's going to bother us that day. She doesn't even speak to us on Holidays anymore either."

I told him I'd be back for sure and he congratulated me on my graduation. We embraced again and Tessa and I got on the road.

THIRTY-ONE

I arrived at the parade on Main Street with Tessa. The townspeople were enjoying the day and I was suddenly aware at how small and tucked away this small town had always been. At ten-years-old I just saw a huge wilderness that I wanted to escape from. Now, it was a very tiny spot on the map that the rest of the world didn't know about. Candor is much like that old creepy town in a movie that's stuck in time.

Rae ran towards me before I saw her. When I saw her running along the parade procession, it was like slow motion. I walked towards her, then we both ran smack into each other! We embraced and chatted excitedly, picking up as if no time had passed at all. Then I hugged Stan and Elijah.

The Four was reunited!

People were roaming along Main Street so we stepped back further into the grass to continue our reunion.

A few minutes later, guess who we saw? We saw Karen's daughter Cadee with her children Cisca and Nano!

Nervously, Rae and I turned our bodies around.

"She waved to us," Stan said after they had walked off.

We turned back around.

"It's not that serious. You don't have to duck or hide," Elijah said. He was angry that we had been subjected to this fear for years.

"I just don't care anymore," Stan said.

"Sequoya, you are eighteen now! You have every right to be here!" My youngest brother Elijah was really lifting me up! It made my heart warm and my confidence emerge even more.

"You're right," I agreed. "I'm eighteen. I'm free!"

Tessa pulled me to the side after the parade was over. Her eyes looked concerned and sad.

"Let's all go to the Dandy gas station. I want to buy your brothers and sister something to eat. I'm so worried. They are way too thin!"

Holding back tears, I silently nodded. We went to the Dandy and ordered sandwiches and sat at the benches to eat and enjoy each other's company.

Then lo and behold, Karen had been informed and was looking for proof that I, SaraJane, was in town!

She feverishly began circling the perimeter of the small town! Literally, you could drive around Main Street and Owego Street and wrap back around in three minutes. That's how small the village was.

We sat there eating and counted her blue mustang go around four times. Wow.

My siblings said they didn't care anymore. They knew Karen would try to discipline them, but that she was slowly giving up what she could not control. That was fate.

Dear Mama,

Karen was making comments like, "SaraJane thinks she can just show up in this town and camp out!" She was just mad I could actually do it! I was free from her!

My siblings expressed that they wanted to come visit me in Elmira and to also visit our older siblings in Nevada. Karen said no, but that she would let them speak to Deniece on the phone. She was also spying on Deniece's Myspace page, as well as mine. Deniece had written something on my Myspace wall defending me from a situation that was taking place in Elmira. Karen would print out her posts and comments and say stuff like, "You know guys, your sister speaks very vulgar and gross. Look at her language." She was trying to hate on my sister's swag. Throughout the years, she felt she was an expert about our family. "You know, people always say that Sara and Abigail look alike, but they don't at all!" When people told her that we have the same eyes and smile and that we do somewhat look alike, she would argue with the person! And after we found our older siblings, she made it a point to say who looks like who and who doesn't look like who. As if her words were the golden rule.

Before she allowed the phone call, she contacted Deniece herself and said she would mail her some pictures of the three. When Deniece opened the pictures, she abruptly put them back in the envelope. She was nauseous.

"Nah, those weren't the kids my Mama gave birth to!" she would tell us time and time again. "I couldn't even look at those pictures they made me so sick. Nappy knotted hair, busted crusty chapped lips, skinny bodies, sad faces. Nah man! She changed y'all appearance on purpose and wanted y'all to be ugly. She was jealous of y'all and that was real disrespectful to send me some pictures like that!"

There was only one phone call made to Deniece. After the three got to speak for just a couple of minutes, Karen and Rae got into a fight and a wrestling match ensued. Stan stood up to protect his sister Rae, and Neal jumped up all angry just because my brother was another male presence in the house who he felt insecure about. Male ego.

Rae turned to Neal and said, "You aint gonna do nothing because you aint got no manhood!" And with that very line, she completely emasculated Neal Carlon, who was speechless. The whole house got quiet after that statement. Because it was the truth. He didn't do the right thing.

Rae emerged as the next major rebel, and Karen said she was the clone of "Sara." Rae started acting out and in one of her rages she turned the whole dining room upside down! When I lived there, I had only trashed my room all the time and stripped my walls until everything I owned was in one center pile on my floor. But Rae graduated from her room and to the ground floor by throwing all the dining room chairs, overturning the table, and breaking a lamp! Karen tried to restrain her. She started punching my sister on the head and gave her an abrasion. She made her stay home from school for a few days after assessing the abrasion. She said, "You can stay home from school if you want."

Lynda Coswell, the lady who had taken them in from out the rain called Tioga County Social Services and launched another investigation. At the mention of the Carlon family, the county yet again didn't want to do the right thing and help my siblings. Karen still turned a couple of the lazy caseworkers on her side. One of them, who was very obese, screamed at my siblings and said they were bastards who should be grateful to have been taken in by Karen. So Rae spoke back and said she was a fat frog who ate all day and didn't want to do paperwork and no man wanted her.

They assigned a caseworker named Drew Kneller after Elijah was seen with his toes poking out of his shoes. I even went to Candor on the day he stopped by. When I met Drew, I already knew he wasn't going to do anything to help. He had soulless eyes and definitely wasn't qualified for the job. He was in his early thirties. He came to Lynda's house, saw the shoes, and said he would get back with us later. Every time we called to see what he was up to as far as the case was going, he was busy or not in the office.

Eventually, as more people in the town kept hot lining on behalf of my siblings, Tioga County Social Services did the cruelest thing. Whenever the dispatch picked up and a report was made, the dispatch person would ask, "Is this about the Carlon family?" When the caller said yes, the dispatch person hung up on them! My siblings were black, and they had a white psychotic mother with a creepy scary aura, so no one cared enough to do the right thing.

For the next year and a half, Karen would do anything to hold onto whoever she was still benefiting from financially. She became enraged when my siblings used one of my old lines, "You won't let us go because then we'll be taking money out of your pocket!"

When they said that, Karen put on her phony crying voice and said, "I don't receive a *dime* for you guys!"

The house was too hostile and tense. Rae decided to be bold. She stopped coming home at night. She tested this out for a bit. Being gone for one night, then two, three, almost a week. Then Rae would not come home for weeks at a time; she wouldn't even check in with Karen! At first she thought she'd be in trouble for being bold. But to her surprise Karen didn't say anything. In fact, Karen stopped talking to all of them completely. Rae would stay with her best friend, getting ready for school there and everything, and her friend's parents absolutely loved her. Rae would only come back every few weeks for just a night or two and then leave again.

Stan and Rae also took the bus to Elmira to visit me! I was so happy to see their boldness and courage to stand up for themselves and do what they wanted to do. We knew that never in a million years would I have been able to get away with the same thing when I was their age. I admire my siblings. I wished I hadn't been as scary and just tried it out back then. Wow, times were changing!

Karen told Stan and Rae that they had to be out of the house completely no later than December 24th, 2009, the day before Christmas. Stan was only six months away from graduating high school at Candor, and Rae was only sixteen-years-old.

Fortunately, one of our supporters, a young pastor and wife who lived on Main Street, took Stanford in and said he had a sure place in their home. They told him not to worry, and that he could stay there until he went to college. He had already been accepted into Alfred University with a big scholarship that had the town talking.

Before he left, he was going to at least say goodbye to Karen. He passed by her in the kitchen and waved as he was holding his backpack of meager clothes. He felt a strange aura in the air as she looked up at him. She didn't say anything at all. She just stared at him for the longest with an evil creepy look. So, he just walked out. He said that's when he knew she truly hated him. He had never seen that type of look in her eyes before.

The issue with Karen and Stanford is pretty much self-explanatory. Karen always wanted Abram to succeed, and for Stan to be beneath Abram. At the same time, she had provoked him for so many years to act out, but she never got him to trip out like Rae and I did. She thought that making him read the book of Isaiah in the Bible in his room over and over was supposed to make him mad. She only made him do that because she had changed his name to Isaiah. She didn't even ask him what he had read or what that book in the Bible meant. Because she didn't even know herself!

Stan was quiet and didn't let Karen bring him out of character, no matter what she did to him. She was under the impression that he was black, so he must act out. But he was the exact opposite and it drove her mad. So mad to the point where she tried to say he attacked her.

Stan had been coming out the bathroom one day when suddenly, Karen emerged from the dining room and walked up to Stan and shoved her body against him.

"Where are you going Isaiah?" she asked, provoking.

"Upstairs," he answered, and began walking past.

"No, where are you going Isaiah?" As she said this, she shoved up against him in a fighting stance. "Where are you going?"

"Stop Mom, I'm going upstairs," he said, trying to push past. He was very confused as to what was happening.

"Where are you going?" Now she was shoving her body into his skinny one and using her large frame to block him at the entrance to the pantry.

"Can you let me go upstairs please?"

"Stop pushing me Isaiah!" she suddenly screamed.

"I'm not pushing you. Not even touching you. I'm asking can I please go upstairs? Mom, please move."

He tried to walk past, but she blocked.

Then suddenly, she threw her head back, let out a loud scream, and threw her fat body against the kitchen wall and screamed, *"Neal, help!"*

Neal came running out the bedroom to see Karen dramatically rubbing herself after her supposed attack.

"Isaiah just shoved me into the wall!"

"I did not!" he screamed.

"If you ever put your hands on my wife ever again so help me God!"

Neal's eyes were satanic.

"Should we call the police?" he asked Karen, who was still the boss and made the decisions.

"No...I'm fine. I'm just really shook up. I can't believe it. He's upset because he's on discipline."

After that incident, Stan knew to steer clear away from Karen. He couldn't help to think if he wasn't the only person this had happened to. He knew that being a man, you had to be very careful and not let people provoke you or bring you out of character, and to never put yourself in a situation where you could be framed. Stan and Elijah fought their battles internally, while Rae and I were proud to balance it out and be the rebel warriors.

Rae didn't want to stay in Candor. She chose to return to Las Vegas, Nevada. Karen called Deniece and booked the flight for December 24th. She had her sister Doris come with them to the airport because she said she feared for her life.

Rae rolled her eyes and was like, *'Please, this flight is the best Christmas gift in the world right now. You should be afraid of your own self!'*

Karen refused to look at or speak to Rae while in the terminal. When her flight was called, she quickly shoved Rae a peanut butter and jelly sandwich and a banana for something to eat for her trip, and then turned away from her without saying goodbye.

Karen's sister Doris smiled at Rae and hugged her and whispered in her ear so Karen couldn't hear.

"Be safe out there, beautiful! I hope you have a much better time out there than you had here."

"Thank you," Rae said, hugging Doris back.

Then Rae walked through the jet way to begin a new life.

THIRTY-TWO

In June of 2010, Elijah and I proudly sat in the chairs on the lawn in front of Candor Junior-Senior High School in the small village to watch our brother Stanford Griffin graduate!

We already knew that Karen would not show up. Stanford also had an article written in the paper for his artwork. During the ceremony, the host, who was the school's superintendent, began talking about a lot of miscellaneous things. He was all over the place. Then he threw me off guard when he began telling a little story. He spoke of something that had taught him a lesson.

"You know...I always wanted to be a racecar driver. My wife and kids would call me while I was away...you know...asking me when I would be back. I was having a ball out there man! But when I got into the accident.... suddenly I *was* back home!"

He cleared his throat and then he sounded a little sad.

"I don't want to be a racecar driver now. Even when I was driving I wasn't happy. But being back home...and being with my wife and children...man I knew what I was supposed to do. In a way, I was still bitter because of my accident. Sometimes, it's not about the dreams you want in your life...it's about your responsibility to your children. My true happiness was being a better parent."

Just as quick as he said that little story, he was rapidly on to the next subject, leaving a lot of us in the audience puzzled. I was sitting there trying to figure out how this related to the ceremony specifically.

At the end of the ceremony, the three of us got our picture taken together. Then Stan walked off with a classmate. I conversed with his friend's mother and by the time Stan came back, he was looking sad.

"What's wrong?" I walked up to him. I noticed he was holding a card.

"Dad was here the whole time. He walked up to me and gave me this card and said he was very proud of me. He said congratulations on getting accepted at Alfred too. I haven't seen him since I left the house last year."

I looked at Stan, and then I started walking towards Main Street. I wanted to see Neal before I went back to Elmira.

"He already left," Stan said. "He was looking really worn down from everything."

I keeled over, having to steady my hands on my knees. I started crying my eyes out. I don't know why but it all just came over me. This was Neal's way of apologizing. It was meant for him to show up too, to hear that story about the man being a father instead of a racecar driver. Neal had always talked about being one. I didn't let him enjoy watching it on TV either during my stomping episodes in my room which was right above the living room.

"You're going to make me cry…just by looking at you," a nosy lady standing near us said.

We were walking back towards the ceremony and my face was scrunched up and puffy from all the emotions.

Stan, Rae, Elijah, and I forgave Neal after that. Neal was so young and naïve and only twenty-one-years-old when he first got with the much older Karen.

Currently at this time, Karen was sneaking behind Neal's back.

By the summer of 2010, Karen was allowing fourteen-year-old Elijah to stay anywhere he wanted but she still wanted custody of him. He moved in with a classmate and his family.

The issue with Karen and Elijah was that she was the only mother he could remember. He didn't remember our biological family. After being adopted, he was spanked for saying, "I want my Mama Sandy," the woman who owned the ranch on the outskirts of Las Vegas with her husband Ron. They had cared for him for the first four years of his life. Karen had beat the memory of them out of Elijah and he pushed them into his repressed memory.

At first, Elijah had always been the one to submit and take up for and defend Karen the most. But now he became strong over the fact that he was being done wrong the whole entire time.

On the night before Stan left for college, there was an incident because Elijah refused to go home to Mountain Ave. Karen called his surrogate family and demanded that they hand him over.

Even though I was in Elmira, I was very much present during this situation.

The surrogate mother had called my phone in a panic.

"Sequoya!" she said. "I love your brother like he is my own son! What this lady has done to him and the rest of you guys is not right!"

Elijah and his friend and his mother had barricaded themselves in the house. Stan was on the porch standing very determined. This was the night before he left for college and he wanted to make sure Elijah was in a safe place. He would be the only one out of The Four left in Candor.

Karen had raced over to the lady's house and stood by the porch after Elijah flat out told her he preferred to be there instead.

"Elijah!" she kept screeching, trying to sound like her voice still held power. Elijah was nervous but he was also following his heart and being very brave.

She demanded for Elijah to come out but he didn't. Instead, Stan stepped further out on the porch so Karen could acknowledge him.

At the sight of Stan, her eyes grew wide.

"You did this! You set this whole thing up!" she screamed.

He shook his head.

"Get away from me!" she screamed, jumping back from an imaginary force. My brother was on the porch and he had no intention on walking down the steps to be near her. So she needed to calm down. She was doing way too much as usual.

Before he went back into the house, he tried to reason with her, but she was now refusing to acknowledge his presence.

"Just start being the mother to Elijah that he has always wanted," he said calmly and graciously. Karen turned her head away from him.

"Elijah!" she called his name again.

Stan went back inside and closed the door. They watched from the window for a few minutes as Karen stood outside like a warden. I was still on the phone with the surrogate mother as this was happening.

"Should I call Social Services?" she asked me.

"No. They won't help."

"I know; it's just I don't know what to do!" she sounded so fiercely protective of my brother. I was warmed in my heart.

"Walk outside and ask her why does she want Elijah," I suggested. I wanted to hear what Karen had to say to that question. I knew she wouldn't be able to answer it.

She walked onto the porch.

"Send Elijah out," I heard Karen say.

"I understand that Elijah is legally yours, but I care about him. What I'm going to do is call the police, and when they get here, I will have Elijah tell them where he wants to be."

I strained my ear to the phone to hear what Karen would say. But I didn't hear anything.

"What happened?" I asked.

"Wow, she actually drove off!"

"What? Serious?"

"Yes!"

We were shocked. Wow.

After that, Stan felt comfortable leaving for college the next day. Elijah remained at this house. Karen ended up signing her parental rights over to the lady.

The full set of The Four were all finally free!

When Stan, Rae, and Elijah asked for their birth certificates and social security cards, Karen claimed she didn't have them.

Dear Mama,

In 2011, I moved back to the West Coast! There was some unfinished business I needed to check up on.

Rae and I tracked down our last foster mother Benita Burkes. She was no longer at Brynehurst Drive. She had to get rid of the big house. We sat in her new place on the Westside. She had arthritis in her hands and she couldn't do hair anymore. She had cancer too. She told us we were so grown up. We were surprised when she pulled out a framed picture of Stan, Rae, and me surrounding her. I had long braided pigtails and I stared into the camera, oblivious that my life was going to drastically change not too long after that.

Benita told us that one day we should take a drive back up to Brynehurst to see our old home and we told her that sounded nice. She said she wanted to take us to Disneyland when Stan visited that summer from college. We were all game for it, but we knew Benita wouldn't get around to doing it.

She told us that you had been looking for us up until the very end. She wasn't allowed to give you any information about our whereabouts at the time or she would be in trouble. Rae and I didn't get mad at her. We also didn't bring up the fact that she ripped our pictures up after my birthday and caused us to not be able to memorize the phone number. She didn't bring that up either. Time can really make you just forget the bygones.

But I had one specific question that I wanted her to answer.

"Remember when I ran inside the salon on Jackson Avenue and told you that I saw my Mama? You said no that wasn't her and you yelled at me to drop it..."

And before I could finish, she looked at me sheepishly and said, "Yes, that was your Mama."

Dear Mama,

In 2012, Rae and I were at the Martin Luther King parade in Downtown Las Vegas with Dee and our nephews and newborn niece. There were lots of people there and I really enjoyed it.

There was one group that went by with a lady in front. The Vee-Jay announced her name. I knew that name. I looked at the lady closely as she waltzed right on by me. I was taller than her now. The name of her church was also announced.

That Sunday, I went to her church and sat in the service. She oversaw some of the programs. She was being very attentive and loving to everybody and their kids. A type of love that she had never shown to my family.

I waited until service was over and the usual clutter of talkers had dwindled down. I saw her standing off alone looking at a pamphlet. I walked up to her.

"Hi Kim!"

She looked up at me, trying to quickly remember where she must know me from.

"Do you remember me?" I asked.

She's staring at me. I can see her subconscious trying to register who I am. She knows but isn't quite sure.

"Sequoya," I said.

She blinked and nodded.

"How you been Sequoya?" she asked.

I told her I was doing alright, and so was everyone else. When she asked how Dee was, she said it with mock irritation like, "So, um, how is Dee doing?" She had her nerve to say that! She knows what she did to taunt my sister for years.

She asked about the Carlons and I gave her the breakdown. Her eyes were no longer sweet like they had been to everyone else at the church. She now had an unemotional, hard look. When I brought up the positive things that had happened out of the whole situation, she didn't say anything at all. I told her that throughout our imprisonment, at least Stan was in college and he was the first male in our birth family to attend. I told her that Rae and I didn't lose our virginities until after we were eighteen-years-old and we weren't somebody's unmarried baby's mother. If we had all grown up in Las Vegas we may have gotten involved with the wrong people. Being at the Carlons made us "square" and reading books made us even better. She didn't agree or smile. She just stared at me with hard eyes.

"I'm writing a book," I told her.

And before I could even say anything else, she opened her mouth with a wide look in her eyes.

"Well, don't make me be the bad guy. I did nothing wrong!" she exclaimed.

Why did she even say that? Did I even say she was the bad guy? It was her guilt talking.

Kim and I exchanged numbers and we were in contact for about two days after that. Then she suddenly disconnected her number on me.

Dear Mama,

It's good to know that you reunited with my father before you left. He was locked up for ten years and you saw him just in time. I'm happy to hear that you both prayed together while you were in the hospital. He also got to see you before that too. It's a beautiful thing to hear that you both asked God for forgiveness as a mother and father who made the wrong choices and your kids had suffered for it. God surely forgives you, and we do too. I didn't get to say goodbye to you in person, but what gives me comfort is you said something very important to Deniece. You said, "When I'm gone, don't visit me at my grave...because I'm not going to be there."

We reunited with our biological father Stanford Griffin in 2010, contrary to Karen telling us that we'd never see him again. He gave us more background about a few things. I feel a closure and I'm grateful for it. He has instilled more peace and confidence in each of his children.

"You know...in a strange way, I believe that God *did* give you guys to that lady...but she didn't do the right thing...she failed that test."

"Right," I said.

He also tried to cheer me up about some of my past mistakes that I have let haunt me for years.

"Sequoya, you are not a murderer," he told me. "And I'm not just saying this because I'm yo daddy. You went through trial and error. It scarred you. You snapped, but you recovered and brought yourself back. You are a survivor..."

"I know but it's just..."

"Listen, the way that lady handled you after the fact wasn't how a real mother was supposed to do it."

"I still feel sad and guilty."

"Let it go. You have to forgive yourself."

I nodded as he reminded me that what I endured would be used to help others. Especially because I have a natural gift at singing and writing. He happened to be blessed with the gift to play the organ, and had always been chosen to play at any church or event, including at the facility.

"You really don't know yo Daddy can *play!*" he exclaimed. "And I arrange music. You gonna say *aw Dad, I didn't know you could play like that!*"

I smiled.

"Say...babygirl...I got a question," he asked.

"What?"

"Was that cat a girl or boy?"

"A girl. Why?"

"Oh. She was going to be a whore anyway."

"Dad!" I screamed, and I heard him laughing at his joke to cheer his daughter up.

THIRTY-THREE

In 2010, Karen divorced Neal abruptly and kicked him out of the house that he paid the mortgage off by himself. She remarried right away and changed her last name. Her new husband moved into the house with her.

Not too long after, Karen packed up Abram's belongings and set them outside by the road for him to discover.

Neal and Abram moved to Owego.

In 2014, Neal contacted each of us and expressed his remorse. He revealed that he was very young at the time. He also said that Karen never had to work because his job paid well and he paid all the bills and the mortgage. She chose to pick up all the odd jobs because she was money hungry. He said she was receiving over four hundred dollars a month for each of the four of us, which totaled to nearly two thousand dollars a month. He said it was her own spending money and he allowed her to open her own separate bank account just for that. That was a lot of money at the time, especially for the low cost of living in Candor with a population of 5,000 people. He said we easily could have had better clothes, food, and school supplies like the others.

Neal revealed that Karen wouldn't even speak to or acknowledge him when they ran into each other. His jeep would pass her mustang on Owego Street, the same road that connects the towns of Candor and Owego together. He would wave, she'd speed up her car and ignore him. He says he doesn't know what he did to her. He stood by her for eighteen years.

It was revealed that Karen also became a school bus driver. However, a group of parents rallied together and went to the school board and had her fired, because of her talking cruelly to their children on the bus. Many residents have had encounters with Karen and have shared commentary among each other over things they have witnessed, and some have reached out to us and told us that everyone knows we were mistreated.

There was also a major surprising twist of events. A few junkies in Candor went to Stanford and Elijah, saying that Abram and Karen owed them money and that Karen was Abram's drug supplier, and that she participated in the drugs as well. *Wow.* Stanford and Elijah told the junkies that they didn't speak to the Carlons anymore.

Shortly after Neal was connected to us on Facebook, Karen was spying and suddenly sent messages to Stan, Rae, and Elijah. She simply said, "I'm sorry for the pain and strife while you lived with me."

They said thank you. But Rae wanted more of an explanation. She waited a couple of days to get her thoughts together. Then she asked Karen why she treated us that way and she asked why she lied to us about ever receiving money from us.

Karen completely ignored the money question. Then she blamed everything on me! She tried to get my sister to turn against me by saying, "Well, I didn't know your sister had so many issues before I adopted you guys."

That wasn't going to work for Rae at all! She wasn't going to allow this lady to not take responsibility and blame a lifetime of abuse on a ten-year-old frightened girl who had memories of her birth family.

Rae ripped off on Karen, really giving her a piece of her mind. Then she told Karen that she wasn't going to reply to any more of her messages ever again.

Karen hadn't reached out to me. For a few months, I prayed to God to finally help me to let go and release the past, so I can continue to be mentally free and live the happy life God has prepared for me. In doing so, I knew I would have to be the bigger person, to show her that although she tried to destroy me during my childhood, in a very special way it made me better.

I wrote her and told her that I forgave her. I thanked her for locking me in my room to read books all the time, because it helped to nurture my talent and it gave me discipline. I told her I was doing great. She pretended to leave me on what is called "unread." But I already knew she read it. She never said anything back. So, I copied and pasted it, and I sent it to as many people on her friends list who had the same last name as her new husband. I wanted to make sure she got it for sure.

A few minutes later, my Facebook profile was reported as spam and I was required to confirm my identity. I told myself that wasn't the best way to handle the situation, and to stop doing things that only let the opponent win. I felt Karen at least owed me a sincere apology. But I realized I would never get it because she won't ever bring herself to face me because she knows all the stuff she did. The abuse, the calculated framing, everything. If she had the opportunity to do it all over again to me, I absolutely know she would! I prayed about it, and then I made a new Facebook profile and moved on to start a new life.

Both Stan and Elijah graduated from college and high school in the spring of 2014 respectively and moved back to the West Coast. Stanford graduated with a Bachelor of Fine Arts. Elijah was voted Homecoming King at Candor during his senior year. At eighteen-years-old, he was the assistant manager at a shoe store in an upscale shopping plaza in Las Vegas. Now at almost twenty-one, he's the head manager himself. People have approached him to consider being a model. He just smiles graciously and thanks them. He is a great sales person and he's so humble. I admire him.

He doesn't have to worry about his toes sticking out of his shoes anymore and not having any socks. His collection of shoes is getting so big that Rae laughed and told him to come pick up his shoes from her house. God works in very special ways. Shoes were something that Elijah was severely deprived of. Now he is in abundance.

In 2015, Rae got married and posted her wedding photos on Facebook. Shortly after, Karen sent Rae a friend request. Rae decided to accept it. But she wasn't going to say anything. Karen didn't say anything either. She didn't even tell her congratulations. She was just being nosy. After a couple of weeks of Karen "sitting" silently, Rae removed her from her friends list. Shortly after that, Karen messaged her saying, "I really was sincere in my apology to you. I should have used different methods to care for you guys. And Sequoya already wrote me."

That was her way of saying she was off the hook now. I had made it easy on her by contacting her first because we knew she would never contact me directly. She still never reached out to me herself and apologized to me.

Staying true to the promise she made to herself, Rae never responded to Karen's message.

We reconnected with Steven, the young biracial boy who we met when we first attended Abide in The Vine. Karen was always angry with him for some reason and she screamed at him when he stood by our table at the church picnic.

He said that Karen should be behind bars. To our surprise, he informed us that before our adoption, his grandmother enrolled him in the daycare Karen ran in her house. She would always put the Caucasian children together at the table to eat. Then she would put Steven off in a corner by himself and say to him, "You have to sit in the corner where bad children like you belong!" He was very young but he remembered every word she said and how she treated him differently than the other kids. When his grandmother caught on to it, she promptly removed him from Karen's care. So, for her to turn around and adopt four black children really threw him off guard and that's why he wanted to be our friend. He was concerned. Karen had something against colored children.

None of us have heard from Abram. We forgive him. He was a child and a victim to destructive parenting just like we were.

I was speaking to my therapist one day and she brought up an interesting suggestion.

"You know, I'm not sure what adoption agency you guys were listed under...but they didn't seem to care that the Carlons lived across the country and they only came to meet you once."

"We were shipped out three months later," I added.

"There's something fishy behind that."

"Exactly."

"They *had* to know she was crazy," my therapist continued. "Have you ever stopped to think that maybe she was only allowed to adopt black children because maybe they knew she was cuckoo...and so they weren't ever going to give her any white children?"

Wow. That really made me think.

I explained to her that once we all became of age, we called the Clark County Family Services in Nevada to get information about what really happened.

The funny part is, as soon as we confirmed we were Sequoya, Stanford, Raeannah, and Elijah...the person on the phone instantly said, "Hey! I remember you guys' case from back in the day!"

Hmmm, interesting. Someone still worked there and they remembered...out of thousands of cases they had.

But when we asked for more information, the person said, "Sorry, I can't speak about it because the case had been *sealed*. Good luck."

I guess they really haven't met SaraJane yet huh?

The only information I have been able to find was handed to me by a helpful staff member at the Transitional Independent Living headquarters. This is an excerpt from a social summary drawn up from the information they were given upon my first assessment.

<u>**Describe the relevant family background that may affect planning and service provision for this family.**</u>

Sequoya was in several foster homes in Las Vegas, Nevada due to parental neglect and was reportedly sexually abused. On 1/5/94, Sequoya and her siblings were taken into custody. Her mother was incarcerated for possession of a stolen vehicle and child endangerment (the home was in

utter disarray; hypodermic needles were in close proximity to the children and there was little food). On 3/24/94, the court gave custody of Sequoya and her two siblings to the State on grounds of neglect. Reunification attempts were made. In May of 1996, the children were returned to live with their mother while still in State custody, however, the children were once again removed from the home on 7/13/96 due to neglect on the part of the mother. The termination of parental rights process began and was refuted by the mother. However, termination of parental rights was granted in August of 1998 given that the mother had more than four years to comply with her Case Plan and had failed to do so (preceding information gathered from Social Summary by Division of Child and Family Services in Las Vegas, Nevada). Her biological mother, Katherine, is deceased. Her biological father, Stanford, is incarcerated. At the time of the adoption, Sequoya was renamed SaraJane. She and her siblings were adopted by the Carlons in the year 2000. SaraJane, who prefers her birth name Sequoya, was ten-years-old at the time of the adoption. Visitation with her adoptive mother is supervised. Communication is minimal. Since placement with TILP, there has been no contact between Sequoya and her family.

I did happen to find some interesting facts about our case that deals directly with the foster parents, thanks to an uncle from my mother's side, as well as a former classmate of my mother's.

In the mid-1960s, Katherine Kelly, along with her brothers Robert and William were the temporary foster children to a woman on the Las Vegas Westside named...Mary Williamson!

Yes, the same Mama Mary who was our foster mother! Back then, she was a very harsh lady in her forties whom no one wanted to mess with! By the time the mid-1990s came around and she was in her seventies, God had truly worked on her. She was the best foster mother we ever had. She knew we were Katherine's children before taking us on.

Everyone knew Katherine. By the time we arrived at our third foster home, Benita Burkes had already placed a call to her neighbor named Debbie, who happened to be the mother of Tyree and Shaquoia. Debbie went to school with Katherine for all elementary, middle school, and high school.

"Guess whose kids I got?" Benita said proudly.

"Who?" Debbie asked, alert to hear anything new.

"Katherine Kelly's."

"For real? Stop it! Katherine?"

"Yes, Katherine Kelly!"

"Wow."

My siblings and I were only children. We were unaware that certain foster parents had taken us on solely because of who our mother was.

The following information can be found and studied on certain online websites such as Wikipedia.

There is an impulse control disorder called Trichotillomania, also known as hair pulling disorder. The urge to pull your hair out can lead to balding and distress and often emotional and social impairment. My sister Deniece and I suffered from this condition as children, as our early childhood trauma triggered the disorder. We have both recovered from it.

There are many children born every year without contracting the HIV virus from the parent. Stanford, Raeannah, Elijah, and I are free of the HIV antibody, which is a miracle from God. We were tested again in the year of 1998, the year that our parents' parental rights were terminated and we were declared wards of the state. We underwent another blood test in the year of 2000, by the request of the Carlons. For more information about HIV prevention at birth, visit your local Center for Disease Control and Prevention.

For the census of the year 2000, there were 5,317 people counted in Candor, and 1, 457 families residing in the town. The racial makeup of the town was 97.25% Caucasian, 0.26% Native American, 0.19% Asian, 0.08% listed as other races, and 1.37% from two or more races. Hispanic or Latino of any race was 0.98% of the population, and 0.85% of the population was Black or African-American.

EPILOGUE

Dear Mama,

There it is! I told you that I had a lot to tell you. Are you surprised I also knew a lot about you? I think you already knew I would. Because I'm your daughter and there's no denying that. Even though you left me early, you left me with a lot of instructions.

Deniece had some papers of yours with your handwriting on it. You also wrote letters and drew pictures for each of your children. You were an awesome artist I can see! You sang really well and wrote poetry as well. My favorite one is:

> *Oh Heavenly Father up above*
> *Please protect this family that I love*
> *Keep them ever safe and sound*
> *No matter when or where they're found*
>
> *Help them to know, help them to see*
> *That I love them, let them love me*
> *Then Oh Lord help me to be the*
> *Kind of woman they expect of me*
>
> *Keep us now, keep us forever*
> *Always in love, always together,*
> *Oh Lord I give thanks to thee*
> *In giving me the family you gave me*
>
> *Amen*

You wrote a letter for me when I was six-years-old:

To my precious Sequoya,
Jesus says to ask Him, and it shall be given. Seek, and you will find Him. Knock, and He will open the door to your heart if you let Him come in. Jesus says to suffer not the little children to come to Him, for such is the Kingdom of Heaven.

Mama, I love you. You left me with a lot of truth and I pray that our story will be used for God's Will to help others from all walks of life. You stated there will be a Katherine's Place someday. I'm seeing to it. Now I'm ready to let go of the past hurt and strive forward with resilience. I'm ready to say goodbye, SaraJane.

ABOUT THE AUTHOR

Sequoya Griffin is a native of Las Vegas, Nevada. Adopted as a child, she moved to Upstate New York. She spent her childhood years reading as many books as she could get her hands on. It helped to pass the time of what she calls her spiritual confinement. Keeping within her the memories of her early life before her adoption, she knew she'd share her experiences. *Goodbye, SaraJane* is a personal and emotional accomplishment of hers that took seven years to complete. She is the founder of Key Purpose Books LLC, a book and media publishing company of God-given stories. Her passion is to continue bringing awareness to all aspects of the foster care and adoption system. Every obstacle and every victory has allotted her the opportunity of expansion. The headquarters for Key Purpose Books LLC is in Charlotte, North Carolina.

To see what's happening with Sequoya and other current and former foster youth, connect at:

 /GoodbyeSaraJane    @KeyPurposeBooks

CPSIA information can be obtained
at www.ICGtesting.com
Printed in the USA
FFOW02n2127250318
45949198-46846FF